Excerpt from lyrics of "Puttin' on the Ritz" by Irving Berlin
Copyright 1928, 1929 by Irving Berlin; Copyright renewed 1955, 1956 by Irving Berlin.
Reprinted by special permission of Irving Berlin Music Corporation.

Copyright © 1990 by James Trager

Atheneum
Macmillan Publishing Company
866 Third Avenue, New York, NY 10022
Collier Macmillan Canada, Inc.

Library of Congress Cataloging-in-Publication Data
Trager, James.
Park Avenue : street of dreams / James Trager.
p. cm.
Bibliography: p.
Includes index.
ISBN 0-689-12024-9
1. Park Avenue (New York, N.Y.)—History. 2. New York (N.Y.)
—History. I. Title.
F128.67.P3T73   1989   89–14929
974.7'1—dc20   CIP

Macmillan books are available at special discounts for bulk purchases
for sales promotions, premiums, fund-raising, or educational use.
For details, contact:

Special Sales Director
Macmillan Publishing Company
866 Third Avenue
New York, NY 10022

10 9 8 7 6 5 4 3 2 1

Designed by Jack Meserole

PRINTED IN THE UNITED STATES OF AMERICA

CONTENTS

INTRODUCTION   1

1   The Vanderbilt Legacy   5
2   How Fourth Became Park   16
3   Vanished Caravansaries   37
4   Electrification   46
5   The Great Terminal   52
6   Mansions for the Mighty   63
7   Debut of the Doorman   79
8   The Boom   90
9   The Traffic Artery   115
10   Transients and Other Guests   123
11   Coming Down to Earth   150
12   Sanctums of Privilege   154
13   Literary Park Avenue   171
14   Commercial Incursions   182
15   The Right Address   207
16   Develop or Preserve?   214
17   Save Grand Central!   219
18   The Other Park Avenue   235
19   Prestige at a Price   251
20   Afterwords   259
      ACKNOWLEDGMENTS   269
      BIBLIOGRAPHY   271
      APPENDIX Chronology   277
      INDEX   288

ILLUSTRATIONS

∎

*Unless otherwise indicated, all photographs are by Chie Nishio,
and are used with permission.*

Commodore Vanderbilt statue south of Grand Central   6
Railroad Depot at Fourth Avenue and 27th Street   9
New York & Harlem Railroad horsecar at Astor Place   22
Columbia College, Park between 49th and 50th   23
Steinway Piano factory, Park between 52nd and 53rd   24
Grand Central Depot   25
Grand Central train shed   26
North end of Grand Central   28
7th Regiment Armory   31
71st Regiment Armory   33
The avenue's Murray Hill blocks   35
Clarendon Hotel   38
Park Avenue Hotel   40
Murray Hill Hotel   41
Grand Union Hotel   43
Belmont Hotel   44
Scene after Blizzard of '88 in Grand Central yards,   47
Steam locomotives in Grand Central yards   48
Marshaling yards before electrification   49
Grand Central, 42nd Street facade   57
Concourse illuminated by natural light   58
Upper level concourse   60
Elihu Root house   65
Former Jonathan Bulkley house   68
St. Bartholomew's Church   70
"Vanderbilt Portal" of St. Bart's   71
Detail of Asia Society building   71
Former Pyne-Filley-Sloan houses   72
Former Lewis G. Morris house   75
Former Thomas A. Howell house   77
Former George F. Baker house   77
Park Avenue in the '90s before World War I   80
903 Park   85

Courtyard of the Hecksher Apartments, 277 Park   93
Penthouse gardens at 655 Park   95
Murray Hill houses and clubs in the 1920s   96
Paul Wallahora, doorman at 1125   102
Park Avenue at 67th Street in 1929   103
Apartment house construction, 1929   103
1185 Park   110
Center mall north of 86th Street, 1930   121
New York Central (now Helmsley) Building under construction   122
Grand Hyatt Hotel   128
Ritz Tower Hotel   134
Swissôtel Drake   139
Christie's at Delmonico Hotel   139
Beekman Hotel   141
Le Cirque, Mayfair Regent   142
Regency Hotel   144
Waldorf-Astoria Hotel   148
1220 Park under construction   151
Yale Club   158
Racquet & Tennis Club   159
Colony Club   163
Union League Club   163
Union Club   166
1 Park Avenue   186
New York Life Building   186
Metropolitan Life, North Building   187
2 Park Avenue   187
New York Central (later Helmsley) Building   188
Lever House   191
Seagram Building   194
Atrium of 277 Park   198
Martha's   205
700 Park   210
733 Park   212
Grand Central concourse   220
Oyster Bar   229
Amtrak sign in Grand Central   233
Homeless in Grand Central's waiting room   233
Cots for homeless in St. Bartholomew's   237
Vagrants asleep in the terminal   238
Scene at north end of Park Avenue tunnel   243
View of tracks from Johnson House apartment   244
Abandoned house in vacant lot on Park Avenue   248
La Marqueta   249
Tropical fruits at La Marqueta   250

Center mall at St. Bart's, 1922   260
Christmas caroling outside Brick Church   262
Street fair on Park Avenue South   264
Cross in lights on Helmsley Building   266

INTRODUCTION

As a bullet seeks its target, shining rails in every part of our great country are aimed at Grand Central Station, heart of the nation's greatest city. Drawn by the magnetic force of the fantastic metropolis, day and night great trains rush toward the Hudson River, sweep down its eastern bank for 140 miles, flash briefly by the long red row of tenement houses south of 125th Street, dive with a roar into the two-and-a-half-mile tunnel which burrows beneath the glitter and swank of Park Avenue, and then—EEESSSSHHHHHhhh—Grand Central Station, crossroads of a million private lives! Gigantic stage on which are played a thousand dramas daily.

This overheated introduction to a network dramatic series entertained American listeners beginning in 1937. Grand Central Terminal* was less than twenty-five years old then; "the glitter and swank of Park Avenue" were every bit as real to the radio audience as Fred Astaire's top hat.

"Puttin' On The Ritz" with its wonderfully syncopated Irving Berlin rhythms was fast becoming a classic:

> Have you seen the well-to-do
> Up and down Park Av-e-nue,
> On that fam-ous thorough-fare
> With their nos-es in the air.

"Grand Central Station" aired on Saturday mornings through the 1940s and early '50s. Few who heard it, few who sang "Puttin' On The Ritz," were aware that Park Avenue was more than "glitter and swank," that "the long red row of tenement houses" was also on Park Avenue, or that the famous thoroughfare continued south of 42nd Street. From Union Square to the river's edge at 135th Street, this six-mile-long boulevard encompassed some of the city's most posh addresses—and some of its dingiest dwellings. It still does.

And although the popular conception of a Park Avenue resident below 96th Street is a plutocrat with money to burn, most people with Park Avenue addresses are neither famous nor all that well-heeled (most could not afford to

---

* To postal authorities, Grand Central *Station,* at 45th and Lexington, is a delivery station of the U.S. Postal Service; the other Grand Central is Grand Central *Terminal.* This is word mincing. In everyday language the terminal is the station. To subway riders, who use the platforms under the terminal far more heavily than they use Times Square, Grand Central is a station.

buy their own apartments at today's prices). Obscure and ordinary citizens in unremarkable apartments do not make good copy, so this book will drop some names; they should not mislead the reader into thinking that such names are in any way representative. Most of Park Avenue has names and faces that few would recognize.

The avenue that has officially been called Park since 1888 was once Railroad Alley, poverty row. For most of the present century it has smacked of money— old, new, inherited, married into, self-made, or ill-gotten and, nowadays, *serious* money. From 59th Street to 96th, Park Avenue has a look of solid respectability. If it is home to the smug, the pompous, the fatuous, and the profligate, its residents also include the industrious, the witty, the insecure, the charitable, and the desperate (bucks never did buy bliss).

No signs are posted to warn that the avenue's oldest building of consequence, the 7th Regiment Armory, may be living on borrowed time despite its landmark status; that Lever House, which began a revolution in office construction and is also landmarked, may not last beyond the 1990s; or that even its linchpin, Grand Central Terminal, may yet—perish the thought—fall to the wreckers' ball.

Before the present terminal was built, and before the tracks under the avenue were electrified, a noisy ditch—covered over but with smoke and cinders still pouring out of the gratings in its center malls—carried railway trains up and down the avenue. Open railyards stretched between Lexington and Madison avenues north to 51st Street, and even beyond that point Park Avenue was hardly suitable for pleasant residential living. Today, with Grand Central more than seventy-five years old, the avenue extending to its north and south is a monument not to city planners but to the foresight of profit-minded railroad men and developers.

Cornelius Vanderbilt IV, a journalist whose family had more than a little to do with building the great terminal and creating the avenue that runs through it, wrote a supercilious novel published in 1930 under the title *Park Avenue*, which, he wrote, "says Good- morning to Manhattan just two corners below the Seventy-First Regimental Armory, and Good-evening, just above the massive home of Squadron A, New York's famous cavalry outfit . . . Lately the railroad that really built the city plumped the world's most imposing depot right in the center of its newest thoroughfare, capped and buttressed it with stone, ran a raised ramped driveway around, at either side of it, and stuck a tower squarely in its center, through which vehicular tunnels were built."

The two armories Vanderbilt mentioned are gone, and a dozen blocks of the avenue north of Grand Central are now almost entirely lined with office buildings where once they were strictly residential; otherwise it is little changed. From 59th Street to 96th, Park Avenue remains a hushed, insulated, and somewhat hoity-toity enclave of heiresses, achievers, political fat cats, dowagers, corporate brass, fancy physicians, strivers, power brokers, divorcées, jet setters, nannies, white-gloved (and white-faced) doormen, and perhaps a few white-collar crooks.

Theatergoers in 1946 saw Harold Rome's hit musical *Call Me Mister* and heard a snooty Park Avenue family sing the praises of now half-forgotten stores. Park Avenue's ultrasmart set is no more prone than other rich people to multiple marriages (the above-mentioned Cornelius Vanderbilt IV, who was married seven times, never did live on Park), but that was the theme of the musical comedy *Park Avenue*, a short-lived Max Gordon production that opened later that year. Brooks Atkinson panned the show; Robert Garland in Hearst's *Journal-American* concluded, "Although they are artfully covered over, Park Avenue, on stage and off, is down by the railroad tracks just the same."

Exactly so. Broadway, Central Park West, Sixth Avenue, Park Avenue South, and Lexington all have subways under them, as does Park itself from 32nd Street to Grand Central, but the subway tunnels are much deeper than Park Avenue's railroad tunnel, built thirty years before the first subway. Residents pay dearly for the prestige of their addresses even when the rumble of trains down below disturbs their tranquility. The big, airy Park Avenue penthouse is the exception. Most apartments on the avenue are nothing exceptional; they are simply close to people's jobs and have enough bedrooms to raise families. The architectural and social critic Lewis Mumford has noted their failings: no views, little air, not much light, and sometimes not even much space.

In the early 1950s a popular singer, Dorothy Shay, was billed as the "Park Avenue Hillbilly." By 1962 Broadway was ridiculing Park Avenue. Herb Gardner's play *A Thousand Clowns*, starring Jason Robards, Jr., and Sandy Dennis, had his Murray Burns' shouting up to residents of Park Avenue apartments at first light, "Rich people! I want to see you all out on the street for volleyball. Let's snap it up."

There is nothing exclusive about a Park Avenue apartment. Walled as it is by buildings on both sides, Park has far more apartments than does Fifth or East End. Nor do most have any great distinction: yellow living rooms and mulberry or Chinese red libraries may be seen in scores if not hundreds of them. Apartments on Fifth Avenue, Central Park West, Central Park South, and Riverside Drive often boast splendid views; each has buildings on just one side.

Park Avenues abound. Dallas has one. So does Baltimore, Maryland; Richmond, Virginia; Miami, Florida; Arlington and Cambridge, Massachusetts; Highland Park, Illinois; St. Louis, Missouri; Lafayette Hill, Pennsylvania; Rehoboth Beach, Delaware; Port Washington, White Plains, and Saranac Lake, New York; Greenwich and Bridgeport, Connecticut. And the *Social Register*, for whatever it is worth, has people living on all of these. It lists none on Park Avenue in Fairview, New Jersey, the home of a woman whose life ended in a hail of police bullets early on an April morning in 1988 beneath the Metro-North tracks of the Park Avenue that runs through East Harlem.* A few months earlier,

---

* Lydia Ferraro, thirty-two, of 644 Park Avenue, Fairview, was an acknowledged heroin addict with a record of three arrests on drug charges in the previous six months. New York police followed her after she ran a light, whereupon she led radio cars on a wild, thirteen-minute chase. When her

on December 29, the body of John M. Goodwillie, a retired advertising man of seventy-seven, was found a mile and a half to the south on the bloodied floor of his bedroom at 1185 Park. The apartment had belonged to his late wife and he was moving out, having taken a place in Washington, D.C.; her son-in-law, a retired Marine Corps captain of sixty-five who also lived at 1185, had allegedly beaten and strangled the elderly man to death, evidently in a dispute over some books for which Goodwillie had returned. Jonathan de Sola Mendes, the assailant, came from a prominent family.

Behind its almost seamless facade, Park Avenue can be as violent as any other part of the great city.

Fortune magazine said of it in July 1939, "Park Avenue is more a state of mind than a *must* address, since side streets are smarter, the East River district pleasanter. This beautiful street, with electrified trains whizzing through its bowels, is a spine of metropolitanism. Along it, rich and nearly rich playboys and kept ladies. Within its symbol, the whole sleek East Side. Here, too, fashionable physicians, fashionable Racquet and Union Clubs, high rents, illusion of infinity."

No illusion is its air of mystery. Even to its residents Park Avenue is full of secrets.

And admire it or not, it is like no other thoroughfare in the world. When the city commissioners drew up their 1811 grid plan, they indicated it as Fourth Avenue. Earlier it had been the Boston Post Road, although that drifted off to the east before 1869. Unlike neighboring Lexington Avenue, Fourth ran along a rocky ridge of the Manhattan schist, for years an effective obstacle to conventional development.

Manhattan Island consists largely of hard, crystalline granite. Blasting this rock is expensive even today; years ago, before dynamite, the cost of excavating for large building foundations was prohibitive. Public transportation south of 32nd Street attracted builders of shops and houses to Fourth Avenue as early as the 1830s, but since the schist there was so close to the surface it was natural for developers of larger structures to build up the city's other avenues first. Not until late in the day did they come to feast on what the railroad had prepared for them.

Park Avenue is to a great extent the creation of the railroad. More precisely, it owes its existence very largely to the efforts of one individual, Cornelius Vanderbilt, and his heirs.

1974 Chevrolet was boxed in, someone shouted that she was reaching for a gun. Too late, it turned out that she had had no gun. Her bizarre death came on Park Avenue at 124th Street.

1

The Vanderbilt Legacy

FROM THE VIADUCT at the south end of Grand Central Terminal a grimy, pigeon-spattered figure gazes silently south down lower Park Avenue. The frock-coated man is Cornelius Vanderbilt. He was seventy-five, standing in the crowd along with Mayor Oakey Hall, when this bronze statue of him was first unveiled on November 10, 1869, as part of Ernest Plassman's 150-foot-long frieze gracing the Hudson River Railroad Terminal on Hudson Street. Just six months earlier, the Union Pacific and Central Pacific had linked up at Promontory Point in Utah Territory, reducing coast-to-coast travel time from at least three months to a mere eight days. One week later, the Suez Canal would open. It was an exciting time in transportation history, a time of glory for Cornelius Vanderbilt.

Today the name Vanderbilt is memorialized in Vanderbilt Avenue, a five-block stretch running along the west side of Grand Central and on up to 47th Street (with another two blocks of pedestrian walks). Brooklyn has a Vanderbilt Avenue of its own. The old Vanderbilt Hotel has become simply 4 Park Avenue, but the framework of the Commodore Hotel, built in 1919 and named for "Commodore" Vanderbilt, is at the core of the Grand Hyatt Hotel at Grand Central.

There is also, to be sure, a Vanderbilt Hall at N.Y.U. and a Vanderbilt University in Nashville—which should not lead anyone to think that Cornelius Vanderbilt was a public-spirited philanthropist. When he covered over Fourth Avenue's railroad tracks in the early 1870s it was only because he was forced to. Still, if Park Avenue was not wholly the creation of a bighearted Medici, it was

ABOVE: *Commodore Vanderbilt looks south from Grand Central's traffic viaduct*
(1988 photo)

at the very least a by-product of Vanderbilt's activities and those of his sons and grandsons. To know Park Avenue one must know something about the people who gave it its start. Theirs is a colorful story, if not always an uplifting one. Cynics will say that vestiges of the old Vanderbilt rapacity may be found in the spirit of today's New York and its Park Avenue.

Cornelius Vanderbilt, progenitor of the family's wealth and power, was himself unlettered, uncouth, unloved, and sometimes underhanded. Descended from van Der Bilts who had come to America in 1650, he was born van Derbilt (in 1794) and used that spelling most of his life. This voracious Vanderbilt never did have any patience with book learning and how to spell. Growing up on Staten Island, chewing tobacco, cursing like a wharf rat, Cornelius thrashed any man who got in his way. At sixteen, tall and rangy, he established a ferry service between Staten Island and Manhattan, sailing passengers across the harbor to and from the Battery. He graduated to schooners, married a first cousin, and prospered in the War of 1812. Within a few years he was commonly called "Commodore," a title first bestowed facetiously.

In 1818 van Derbilt persuaded Thomas Gibbons to build a big steamboat with which young Cornelius could carry cargo between New Jersey ports and New York in defiance of a monopoly granted by New York State to the late Roberts, Fulton and Livingston. Gibbons was a former partner of Aaron Ogden, who had obtained a steam navigation license from Fulton and Livingston. Working for Gibbons, van Derbilt underbid the competition and landed his cargoes in New York. Ogden obtained a court order enjoining Gibbons from continuing in business, and so van Derbilt was forever dodging the sheriff. Gibbons retained Daniel Webster to argue his case before the Supreme Court, and on March 2, 1824, Chief Justice John Marshall ruled that Ogden's monopoly violated the commerce clause in the Constitution. It was in effect the first great antitrust decision. Cornelius van Derbilt had contributed to freeing a young nation's budding commerce from the shackles of state monopoly. He took every advantage of that freedom.

Van Derbilt went into business for himself in 1829, establishing a steamboat line on the Delaware. In the extortionate ethos of business at the time, he launched a series of price wars, undercutting established steamboat companies on the Hudson River and Atlantic coast until they agreed to pay him off. In 1847, as the Mexican War was winding down, he found himself in competition with Daniel Drew, a former upstate drover with a dubious reputation for "watering stock" by letting cattle drink their fill before being weighed for sale. Three years younger than van Derbilt, Drew would butt heads with the Commodore for the rest of his life.

Having built up a fortune ferrying goldseekers to California via Nicaragua, van Derbilt briefly had his own transatlantic line. The Commodore was one of several unscrupulous shipping merchants who profiteered in the Civil War, leasing to the federal government unseaworthy vessels for transporting troops. He then took the $20 million that he had earned by various means in half a century of shipping, and began in a small way to buy up railroad shares. Not until the spring of 1862, as Union forces were winning their first victories, did van Derbilt make his first railroad investments.

His initial prize was the New York & Harlem Railroad. The only road out of New York in any direction, it had been chartered in 1831 to run from Prince Street north along the center line of Fourth Avenue as far as Harlem. By 1834 its horsecar tracks had reached Yorkville at 84th Street. Progress was blocked between 92nd and 94th streets by the rocky promontory of Mount Prospect, but in 1837 the Harlem's engineers succeeded in blasting a 596-foot tunnel deep below Observatory Place, permitting the two-track line to reach the Harlem flats. That year the New York & Harlem bought its first steam locomotive, becoming the world's first urban steam transit line. It reached Fordham in the Bronx in 1841 and White Plains in 1844. The New York, New Haven & Hartford Railroad, founded in 1844, tried to establish its own entry into Manhattan a year later, only to have the Harlem block it from obtaining trackage rights. In 1848 the New Haven bought a perpetual right to operate on the Harlem's right-of-way inside New York City.

Manhattan was a hilly town, and the steam locomotives that moved through its center provided intracity transit through sections where the steep incline made it difficult for horses to pull wagons and carriages. In 1857 the Harlem and New Haven built depots side by side, taking up the full block between 26th and 27th streets from Fourth Avenue to Madison. More than thirty trains chugged in and out of the depots each day on a dozen tracks, and some 8,000 passengers used the service. But when two engines blew up and another burned in the crowded area below 14th Street, a great public outcry impelled the city fathers to ban locomotives within built-up sections; trains coming into the city would have to stop at 42nd Street and be pulled by horses from that point down Fourth Avenue to 27th Street. Stables for Harlem Railroad horses were built on the east side of Fourth Avenue between 32nd and 33rd streets. The practice of hauling trains by horsepower would continue from the end of 1858 until 1871 (1872 in the case of the New Haven).

Stock in the Harlem, with a par value of $100, sank in 1857 to $3 a share. It was worth only $8 in 1860 and not much more when van Derbilt began buying heavily in 1862. Rumors were spreading that the Harlem might be permitted to extend its tracks all the way down to the Battery. Given the extra income generated by intracity transportation, the road would become far more profitable, and the tax-free stock would surely rise in value. The Harlem's financial condition was otherwise not very encouraging. Its incompetent and dishonest management had issued 110,000 shares of stock to help finance their stiff competition with the Hudson River line, whose route lay much closer to the river towns and whose trains seemed to be carrying all the traffic. The Harlem paid no dividends in 1862, and van Derbilt was able to buy all the stock he wanted at $9 a share. As rumors persisted that the Harlem might be extended to the Battery, and word got out that van Derbilt was buying, the stock began to rise. Van Derbilt continued to buy. When the price reached 50, the shares that van Derbilt had bought at lower prices served as collateral to buy more. By April 1862

ABOVE: *Railroad Depot at Fourth Avenue and 27th Street* (drawing from P. T. Valentine's Manual, 1860, courtesy New-York Historical Society)

van Derbilt owned more than 55,000 shares of Harlem stock, with more than $2.5 million of his cash tied up in the line.

While he bought stock, van Derbilt was sidling up to members of the New York City Common Council and bribing them one by one to secure their votes in favor of granting the street-operating franchise that would let the Harlem run south to the Battery. Today's insider trading scandals, and those involving heavy contributions by real estate developers to New York politicians, would scarcely have raised an eyebrow in the rough-and-tumble of nineteenth-century Wall Street. The councilmen of 1862 were well paid; there was every reason to believe they would deliver their votes as promised. And they did.

On the evening of April 21, 1862, the Common Council passed an ordinance authorizing the Harlem to build a street railway all the way down Broadway to the Battery. When the news reached Wall Street the next day, Harlem stock shot up to $75 and kept rising until it reached par before backing off. With help from his old rival Daniel Drew, a member of the Harlem board, van Derbilt was elected in May to the presidency of the New York & Harlem.

But Drew, conspiring against the Commodore, suggested to the councilmen that they could all get rich if they joined him in selling Harlem stock short and then revoking permission for the street railway. (Short sellers guarantee to deliver at a set price stock they do not yet own, hoping to buy it at a much lower price before the date of delivery.) Drew's plan was to wait until Harlem stock hit 75 and then sell it short. If the Common Council revoked the street railway franchise, the price would fall. Then Drew and the double-dealing councilmen would buy, perhaps for as little as $10 a share, and deliver it to buyers who had committed themselves to pay $75. The difference, less commissions, would be clear profit. But before the councilmen could complete their short sales, Harlem stock soared. On June 25, as van Derbilt's crew was tearing up the streets pursuant to the Common Council's ordinance, it hit 110.

New York's greedy councilmen vetoed the franchise, Harlem dropped in one day from 110 to 72, and the short sellers all had quick paper profits of $38 per share. They gleefully waited for the stock to fall still lower; instead it leveled off and began rising—to 80, to 95, to 108. Van Derbilt was buying. The stock spurted to 125 and then to 150. The shorts were horrified. Drew and the Council members had guaranteed to deliver at 110 more shares than could now be purchased on the market. But, as someone (perhaps Daniel Drew) said, "He who sells what isn't his'n/ Must pay the price or go to prison." As the warrants came due and the short sellers had to produce stock or go to jail, they were obliged to buy at the Commodore's price: $180 per share.

On July 1, 1862, President Lincoln signed into law the nation's first federal income tax bill; it levied a 3 percent tax on incomes from $600 to $10,000 and a 5 percent tax on incomes above $10,000. But dividends on railroad stock were tax exempt, making stock in the Harlem and other roads all the more appealing to men like van Derbilt.

By July 4 the shorts on Wall Street were out as much as $70 on every share of Harlem stock they had pledged. Van Derbilt profited mightily; the shorts lost their shirts. More important, van Derbilt acquired control of the little New York & Harlem Railroad.

The Commodore had also been buying heavily in the stock of the nearly bankrupt Hudson River Railroad, which ran parallel to the Harlem line before branching off to follow the river up to East Albany. Daniel Drew and his confederates, out for revenge, attempted to drive down Hudson River stock. Van Derbilt, out of the city when he heard the news, gave orders to buy. Again the price rose, and van Derbilt wound up making more than $3 million and acquiring control of the Hudson line as well.

Having secured the two railroads (and, presumably, taught Daniel Drew a lesson), the Commodore made plans to put them together and end their ruinous competition. In 1864, at age seventy, he went to Albany and began buying votes. The state legislators took his money, introduced a consolidation bill, and gave the Commodore every indication that it would pass. Once again, Drew tried to derail his old adversary. The legislators were bribed to sell short and then voted down the consolidation bill. Harlem stock dropped precipitously in one day from 150 to 90. But the legislators had visions of the price falling to 50 and making them all filthy rich.

Van Derbilt raised money by mortgaging other properties and wound up owning 137,000 shares of Harlem stock—27,000 more than existed. The short sellers had to come to him for stock, and he demanded $1,000 a share. Leonard Jerome, van Derbilt's ally and sometime adviser, was asked to intercede. If they had to pay $1,000 a share, the brokerage houses that had bet against the

Commodore would be bankrupted; Wall Street would be ruined as a financial center. Jerome (whose daughter Jenny would marry Randolph Churchill, an Englishman) went to see van Derbilt, and the Commodore finally agreed to let the speculators off the hook at $285 a share. At that price the brokerage houses would survive. Van Derbilt made $25 million in paper profits; because so many of the legislators filed for bankruptcy, the actual profits were somewhat lower.

William Henry Vanderbilt, the older son who had grown up in the shadow of the Commmodore's undisguised scorn, was made chief operating officer of the Hudson River line. His father, meanwhile, was turning his attention to the New York Central, a 298-mile upstate road created in 1853 by merging ten small lines which connected Albany with Buffalo via Schenectady, Utica, Rochester, and Lockport, with a spur to Niagara Falls. Erastus Corning ran the Central as he pleased and resisted efforts by Vanderbilt (as the Commodore now called himself) to gain a seat on the board. Vanderbilt, for his part, recognized the Central as a vital link in the most direct rail route from New York City to the Great Lakes and points west. A trunk line to the Lakes under one management was a mouthwatering prospect.

When the Civil War ended, Commodore Vanderbilt began quietly buying up Central stock. A year later, still not a director of the road even though he owned $2.5 million of its shares, he met Chauncey M. Depew, a rising young Republican lawyer and politician who had just been appointed ambassador to Japan. Vanderbilt persuaded him to resign the position and become attorney for the Vanderbilt railroads—and the Commodore's chief lobbyist at Albany.

Chauncey Depew, whose name is memorialized in Depew Place on the east side of Grand Central Terminal, helped Vanderbilt pull off a maneuver early in 1867 that gained him control of the Central. By year's end, John Jacob Astor III and others whose combined holdings amounted to nearly half the Central's stock had asked Vanderbilt to become president of the railway. Vanderbilt, seventy-three years old, wearing a truss to support his hernia, now controlled the railroads extending from the nation's largest city to Albany, Buffalo, and the Great Lakes. He was bent on monopolizing rail transport between New York and Buffalo—and, eventually, Chicago.

The Commodore's wife died in August 1868 while her husband was battling Daniel Drew, Jim Fisk, and Jay Gould for control of yet another railroad, this time the Erie. Efforts by his young second wife, Frances ("Frank"), to make the old man conform to Victorian morality were unavailing. He remained a constant embarrassment to his children and more than thirty grandchildren. But even as he chased after the serving girls in his household, the randy Vanderbilt continued to press ahead with his railroad projects.

While tilting against Drew, Fisk, and Gould, the Commodore bought a four-acre city park—Hudson Square, or St. John's Park—bounded by Varick, Beach, Hudson, and Laight streets and covered it with train sidings in order to load and discharge freight on his Hudson River line. It was here, in November 1869, that the terminal's great frieze, including the statue of Vanderbilt, was unveiled while Vanderbilt himself looked on.

Passenger trains coming into the city still had to be uncoupled from their engines at 42nd Street and moved by horsepower down to the two Madison Square depots. Vanderbilt found that situation intolerable. He obtained a charter from the legislature authorizing the erection of an immense union depot at Fourth Avenue and 42nd Street and the construction of underground or viaduct tracks that would carry into the heart of the metropolis not only the trains of the Harlem and New Haven lines but also those of his Central & Hudson River Railroad. Completion of a side cut from the Hudson River line at Spuyten Duyvil, following the creek of that name to Harlem, would enable Hudson River trains to give up their Twelfth Avenue route and come down Fourth to the new 42nd Street terminal. Robert Goelet, a landowner who labored under the mistaken impression that he could bargain with the railway baron, declined Vanderbilt's offer for the site of the Grand Central depot. So Vanderbilt (or Chauncey Depew) got the state legislature to pass a bill authorizing the Central to seize the land in question at an appraised valuation established by a referee.

The charter obtained from the legislature allowed New York City to assume half the cost of the spacious subterranean way on Fourth Avenue; and when the city's aldermen accepted this provision, the "Fourth Avenue Improvement" began without delay. Starting in 1869, iron tresses sprang from the ground to support the immense roof of the depot at 42nd Street. The Grand Central depot was completed in 1871. It had a train shed inspired by but dwarfing the great iron-and-glass canopies of London's Paddington (1852), King's Cross (1852), Charing Cross (1864), and St. Pancras (1869) stations. The cast- and wrought-iron arches of "the greatest train shed in the world" (it was actually somewhat smaller than St. Pancras) spanned 200 feet, rose 100 feet high, and was 600 feet long; the ticket office and waiting rooms in front were housed under mansard roofs in a great Victorian structure that would be enlarged in 1899 (and redesigned by C. P. H. Gilbert) but not replaced until 1913, when the present Grand Central Terminal opened.

Despite the terms of the charter calling for subterranean tracks, trains of what most people called the Fourth Avenue Railroad still ran at grade level, spewing smoke and cinders, posing a constant threat. The wide marshaling yard below 49th Street stretched almost to Lexington Avenue on the east and Madison on the west, and while there were safe crossings at 42nd and 49th streets it was much quicker to cut through the great switching yard and guess which siding an incoming train was headed for. In 1871, as Christopher Gray has written, the New York Times called the tracks a "death trap" and published tales of "hairbreadth escapes." "Living on the avenue itself is an impossibility," it said. But, Wayne Andrews writes, "If the Times delivered an unduly vicious attack on the Commodore, his railroad simply discontinued advertising in the hostile organ." North of 49th Street, where visibility was good along the straight double tracks, the concern was not so much with loss of life as with the depression of real estate values. For both reasons, Vanderbilt came under mounting pressure to sink his tracks.

Agitators for covered tracks discovered that the original 1830 railroad easement along Fourth Avenue permitted the Common Council to "remove the railroad on a month's notice if the 'ordinary use' of the streets was interfered with." By the 1870s, "ordinary use" meant something quite different from what it had in the 1830s; and the possibility, however remote, that Vanderbilt might have his tracks torn up forced him to face up to the issue. In the fall of 1871 the railroad volunteered to fence off its hazardous marshaling yard, which only served to arouse further anger. Was this to be a first step toward complete expropriation by the railroad of land over which it had no easement? The railroad proposed crossing bridges north of 57th Street but only on the streets that corresponded with entrances to Central Park.

The reformers would have none of these low-budget "solutions." They met with Commodore Vanderbilt and impressed on him the need to sink his tracks. That would "cost a heap of money," said Vanderbilt, stonewalling. The railroads were suspected, with good cause, of bribery, price-fixing, conspiracies, and collusion. Newspapers, Christopher Gray has written, regularly printed rumors that the New York City coroner's office was covering up deaths of people run over by trains. PEOPLE KILLED EVERY OTHER DAY AND NOTHING HEARD OF THEM was a typical headline. Along with barbs from the press and civic organizations, Vanderbilt was haunted by the possibility that his Fourth Avenue railroad easement had expired. In any event, his combined railroad traffic had outgrown the existing track line. Vanderbilt needed four tracks and did not dare propose adding tracks in the face of so much criticism.

So, reluctantly, Vanderbilt agreed to sink the tracks—as long as there were four of them and as long as the city paid half the cost. "Reform," the *New York Times* editorialized in 1872, "did not make much headway in the last legislature. Commodore Vanderbilt did." The Central was able to purchase real estate on the future Park Avenue at giveaway prices.

Work finally began on the marshaling yard in August 1872 and, six months later, on the section above 49th Street. Great iron bridges were built over the yard, and north of 49th Street the tracks were gradually depressed until they disappeared entirely at 56th Street. Instead of the unsightly ventilating chimneys originally planned, the center islands had large fenced-in openings that would later be covered with grilles. A financial panic hit Wall Street in September 1873, forcing the exchange to close for ten days, driving many companies into bankruptcy, and putting thousands out of work. Men were eager for jobs on the Fourth Avenue railroad project, and the $6.5 million enterprise—about $75,000 per block—was practically finished by 1875. The tracks were sunk only to 96th Street, where they emerged and remained uncovered to the Harlem River and beyond.

Stock in railroad companies declined along with everything else in the Panic of 1873 and Vanderbilt was able to buy up Lake Shore & Michigan Southern shares at bargain prices. When he died on January 4, 1877, at age eighty-two, the Commodore left a fortune of more than $100 million to his widow and surviving children. He was the richest man in America, far richer than anyone had supposed. Chauncey Depew told the press that Vanderbilt had left $105 million—almost exactly what the federal government had on hand at the moment—and it was clear from the old man's will that he intended to establish a dynasty. The bulk of the Commodore's fortune went entirely to his fifty-five-year-old son William Henry Vanderbilt and *his* four sons. Grandson Cornelius Vanderbilt II, thirty-three, received in his own right $5.5 million in New York Central stock. Three other grandsons—William Kissam, twenty-eight; Frederick William, twenty-one; and fifteen-year-old George Washington—each received $2 million in stock. William Henry, who received 87 percent of the outstanding stock in the New York Central, worth $90 million, was named residuary legatee; all of the Commodore's holdings not otherwise bequeathed were left to him.

The Commodore, as Louis Auchincloss has put it, "made his money by sometimes questionable means, but compared to his competitors he was a saint. Daniel Drew, Jim Fisk, and Jay Gould looted the Erie Railroad, much as today's corporate raiders subordinate everything else to personal profit; Vanderbilt, to the contrary, laid new steel rails and built new bridges." In fact, he cut the running time between New York and Chicago from fifty hours to twenty-four.

Four months after the Commodore's death, America's economy had still not recovered from the Wall Street panic of 1873. Railroads cut wages, claiming a financial pinch, and workers rioted. The Central was less affected than its competitors. William Henry showed his gratitude by dividing $100,000 in cash "among the loyal men" of the New York Central & Hudson Railroad. Two years later he sold 250,000 of his 400,000 shares in a record-setting divestiture. J. P. Morgan headed the syndicate that disposed of most of this huge block of stock, doing it with such skill that the market was unaffected. Vanderbilt received $30 million and Morgan's group was paid a tidy $3 million in commissions. In addition, Morgan received guarantees that he or one of his men would have a seat on the Central board and that the dividend would be kept at 8 percent even if that meant cutting wages and deferring maintenance on the right of way.

Europe's railroads were being nationalized; but in America savage competition was still the order of the day and workers generally earned $350 to $500 a year. Conductors, who outranked engineers and were the best-paid of all New York Central employees, earned about $1,000 a year—easily enough to support a family in New York and a good benchmark against which to compare the income of William Henry Vanderbilt: more than $8 million a year, and this in a time with no income taxes. (The tax imposed during the Civil War had been abolished by Congress in 1872.) William Henry resigned the presidency in 1883 and made his son Cornelius Vanderbilt II chairman of the Central and the Michigan Central (his son William K. became chairman of the Lake Shore & Michigan Southern). Cornelius II suffered a stroke, whereupon Chauncey Depew became chief executive officer of the Central. It is ironic that William Henry, more public-spirited than either his father or Depew, is remembered chiefly for four words spoken on October 8, 1882, in response to a badgering question from a *Chicago Daily News* reporter. The Chicago Limited, a fast, extra-fare mail train, was being eliminated. "But," the reporter asked, "don't you run it for the benefit of the public?" "The public be damned," replied the president of the New York Central. "I am working for my stockholders.* If the public want the train, why don't they pay for it?"

But the public interest will not be ignored. Less than two months after the Commodore's death, the Supreme Court handed down a landmark decision stating that certain businesses are "affected with a public interest." The case of *Munn* v. *Illinois*, decided on March 1, 1877, concerned a state law governing grain elevators and not railroads, but it was the first legal support for any government regulation of American business. No one can deny that railroads and their terminals are affected with the public interest, and in February 1887 Congress approved the Interstate Commerce Act requiring the roads to keep their rates fair and reasonable. The Interstate Commerce Commission, established in 1888, made efforts to protect farmers from discriminatory freight rates; in time it would establish a maze of regulations under which it was sometimes difficult to operate railroads economically.

William Henry Vanderbilt did not live to see that era. He died on December 8, 1885, by which time the family's fortune had grown from $105 million to roughly $200 million. "Billy" had invested in coal mines and diversified in hundreds of other enterprises. The Central in his day earned from 16 to 20 percent on its real capital, even though at one time, during a price war, it charged only $7 for the New York to Chicago run, and the "immigrant" rate fell to one dollar. By 1893 the lines controlled by the Central comprised at least 12,000 miles of track and earned more than $60 million a year.

William Henry's daughters each inherited $50 million. Vanderbilt descendants married Bostwicks, Burdens, Millikens, Osborns, Sloanes, Webbs, and Whitneys—a few of them richer even than some Vanderbilts (although the total family fortune at the turn of the century was probably about $400 million). Few of the collateral relations ever lived on Park Avenue. In the late 1980s, according to the *Social Register*, Park had only one Vanderbilt: Mrs. William H. Vanderbilt, *née* Cummings, who kept an apartment at 1192 Park. The late husband of this latter-day Mrs. Vanderbilt had at one time been governor of Rhode Island. It was his ancestor, Commodore Vanderbilt, who with his immediate heirs set in motion the wheels of progress that began the transformation of Fourth Avenue north of 42nd Street into the Park Avenue of today.

---

* Louis Auchincloss says the stockholders were mainly Vanderbilt and his family, but surely there were many others.

2

How Fourth Became Park

MARTHA BACON was fit to be tied. Her Victorian red brick "cottage" at the northeast corner of Park and 34th Street had always been No. 1 Park Avenue. Now, in 1924, it was to become No. 7. The Board of Aldermen had voted unanimously to extend Park Avenue south to 32nd Street. Mayor John Francis ("Red Mike") Hylan had signed the resolution. Mrs. Robert Bacon, widow of a J. P. Morgan partner, would have a new address: her house would remain the same, at the bottom of Murray Hill, but it would no longer have its old cachet. What the aldermen and the mayor had done was not to be tolerated. Mrs. Bacon liked living at No. 1. She hired lawyers, gained public support, won the endorsement of the Manhattan borough president, and persuaded the aldermen to rescind their resolution. When Mayor Hylan vetoed this turnabout, Mrs. Bacon sued and won. And when the Court of Appeals early in 1928 reversed a lower court's judgment in her favor there were reports that Mrs. Bacon would carry her fight to the U.S. Supreme Court. She never did, but neither did she accept 7 Park as her address: the 1929 *Social Register* gave her place of residence simply as "northeast corner of Park Avenue and 34th Street."

During the nearly four years of political infighting over extending Park Avenue south of Murray Hill into the Rose Hill section, one alderman suggested that Fourth Avenue south of 34th Street be called Park Avenue South. It took more than thirty years to implement that idea. In the spring of 1959, by vote of the City Council, Fourth Avenue between 17th and 32nd streets became Park Avenue South; since then Fourth has existed only for the six blocks between Astor Place and Union Square. But "Fourth Avenue" is what the city fathers called the entire thoroughfare north to the Harlem River in 1811. That is how it was marked in their visionary grid plan, and to many New Yorkers it all remained Fourth Avenue for more than a century.

City Hall in 1811 was nearing completion at the northern edge of the city, and although not yet finished (its uptown side never was decorated) it provided office space for these commissioners who plotted future streets—up to 155th Street, that is. Nobody gave much thought to the possibility of anything other than farm and forest north of that point. Nor was allowance made in the Commissioners' Plan for parks or for any diagonal thoroughfares other than Broadway—the old Bloomingdale Road of colonial days.

Murray Hill and Lenox Hill were still rural. The first was named for John Murray, who had come from Scotland in 1723 to farm a piece of land lying west of Kipsborough, the Jacobus Kips farm on the East River. The Murray farm lay between the Middle Road and the Eastern Post Road (both long extinct) and roughly from the present 33rd Street to 39th. The Middle Road slashed diagonally across what is now Madison Avenue; the Eastern Post Road ran roughly parallel to Lexington Avenue and then cut diagonally east at 35th Street. Murray's son Robert built a house he called Inclenberg near what later was Fourth Avenue and 37th Street (it was renamed Belmont).

Robert Murray married a Philadelphia Quaker, Mary Lindley. She and her beautiful daughters are said to have entertained the British general William Howe at lunch after his arrival at Kip's Bay on September 15, 1776, nearly three weeks after the British victory in the Battle of Long Island. According to legend, Mrs. Murray detained the general, thus covering the disorderly retreat of Silliman's Brigade and Knox's artillery under the command of General Putnam and Aaron Burr. In 1926 the Mary Murray Chapter of the Daughters of the American Revolution raised a plaque on the wall of 16 Park Avenue, southwest corner 35th Street, to commemorate the occasion, despite its dubious historical authenticity: "This tablet marks the geographic center of the farm known in revolutionary days as Inclenberg, owned by Robert Murray whose wife Mary Lindley Murray, 1726–1782, rendered signal service in the Revolutionary War." Half a mile to the north is another tablet, placed on the wall of the Yale Club by the club and the Mary Washington Colonial Chapter of the Daughters of the American Revolution. It reads: "At the British Artillery Park near this site Nathan Hale, Capt in the US Army, Yale graduate of 1773, apprehended within enemy lines while seeking information, was executed on the morning of Sept 22, 1776. His last words were, 'I only regret that I have but one life to give to my country.' "

Robert Lenox, another Scot, had come to New York as a midshipman in 1779 during the Revolution and, after resigning from the Royal Navy, returned to New York, married, and bought—for an amount said to be less than $7,000—a tract of land just west of the Boston Post Road, later Third Avenue, in the remote village of Yorkville. His farmland, once part of the city's common lands, lay between 68th and 74th streets from Third to Fourth avenues and was subsequently extended to Fifth.

The city had no public transit in 1811. Residents walked or rode in various horse-drawn conveyances, owned or hired. Twenty years later an intracity railroad was chartered by Harlem landowners who recognized that a train connection to points downtown would enhance their property values. The horsecars of the New York & Harlem Railroad, built by coachmaker John Stephenson, began operating on November 14, 1832, between Prince Street and the Bowery and 14th Street "uptown."

When the railroad wanted to extend its line north, it was told to take Fourth Avenue. Why Fourth? Because a granite ridge along the length of that avenue discouraged construction of a proper street bordered by houses and shops. Manhattan in the 1830s and for many decades after was a rolling terrain whose outcroppings of rock (the famous Manhattan schist) kept the 1811 commissioners' plan from being much more than blue-sky imagination. Leveling the hills, blasting through streets, would take money, time, and effort.

Approval to open Fourth Avenue for anything other than rail traffic was not granted until January 28, 1833. It came in response to a petition from Samuel B. Ruggles, a young real estate developer who had seen that the city's growing population could not remain south of 14th Street. Beginning in about 1825 with very little capital, borrowing from banks and individuals, he had invested in land that most developers spurned as being too far north. Ruggles, like a few others, deplored the paucity of parks in the commissioners' plan and dedicated himself to the preservation of open spaces.

Gramercy Park owes its existence to Ruggles. On December 17, 1831, he deeded to five trustees, who would hold it as parkland, forty-two lots between Third and Fourth avenues. The property had been part of Gramercy Farm, established in the previous century by James Duane and mostly still owned in 1831 by his heirs. They had sold Ruggles twenty-two acres, less some that had become city streets, and over the course of nine months, in twenty-three transactions, he had pieced together all the land needed for what would be the park and its surrounding lots. Ruggles was now ready to proceed with construction and on February 13, 1832, obtained tax exemption for the park from the Board of Aldermen, who agreed to levy no taxes on the property so long as the land was maintained purely as an ornamental square. Ruggles had argued that granting tax exemption for the park would actually boost the city's revenues: taxes could be raised on the sixty-six lots surrounding Gramercy Park, more than offsetting the loss of revenue from the forty-two lots of the park itself. Later developers would abuse the city's power to grant tax exemption; so would shortsighted city officials intent more on meeting a current budget than on improving the conditions of urban life; but the city acted wisely in the case of Samuel Ruggles and his Gramercy Park.

Ruggles was also helping to develop a collection of vacant lots from 14th Street to 17th between Broadway and Fourth Avenue into Union Square, a 3.48-acre field indicated in the commisioners' plan as Union Place and renamed Union Square in 1832. Ruggles in 1832 leased for thirty years all the lots on Fourth Avenue from 15th Street to just north of 19th, with rights to renew for another fifty years. In his petition to the city to open Fourth Avenue north of

17th Street, he had stated the need for ready access to his property, as he would be erecting "expensive and ornamental houses there" during the summer of 1833. Not until the following year did Fifth Avenue get its first great mansion, built by the merchant Henry Brevoort at the northeast corner of 9th Street, which set a style that other rich men would follow. Samuel Ruggles had more modest households in mind. He landscaped the blockfronts on both sides of Fourth between 18th and 19th streets with ornamental gardens in front of setback two- and three-story houses. Most of the leases he sold, but in 1838–39 he built substantial four-story houses on three lots between 15th and 16th streets on the east side of Union Place. One, two doors north of 15th Street, he built for himself and lived there with his family until his death in 1881. It was demolished soon after, by which time Union Square was almost completely surrounded by commercial buildings.

It was Ruggles who petitioned the city's Street Committee in 1836 to give the name Lexington Avenue (after the first engagement of the Revolution) to the new street which "ran through his own lands" north of Gramercy Park to 42nd Street. Neither Lexington Avenue nor Madison, which opened the same year from 23rd Street north to 42nd, were in the commissioners' plan. Assuming that most of Manhattan's traffic would flow from river to river, they had laid down many more streets than avenues per mile. Stephen Garvey has written, "Had not Ruggles and others sensed this deficiency when they did, and bought up land for extra avenues when this was still possible, midtown congestion today would be even worse than it is."

By 1834 the horse-drawn cars of the New York & Harlem, each holding forty passengers, were moving up and down tracks slotted into Fourth Avenue between Union Square and 84th Street. A cut was made through Murray Hill to spare draft horses from having to pull loads up the slope. Steam engines replaced horses on the line in 1837, a station was built at 86th Street (opening the way for the development of Yorkville), and the completion of the Prospect Hill tunnel under Observatory Place permitted trains to reach Harlem.

Prospect Hill, now known as Carnegie Hill but formerly Mount Pleasant, was the highest point on the east side of Manhattan and the site of Archibald Gracie's country house. Its peak, at what later would be 94th Street, afforded sweeping views to New Jersey and Long Island Sound, a fact not lost upon the operators of the New York & Harlem Railroad. When they opened a station there they built the Mount Pleasant Hotel, hoping to attract passengers.

Miles of farmland lay to the south of Prospect Hill. When Robert Lenox wrote his will, dated April 27, 1840, he noted that the farm was worth less than it had cost him. Values had declined in the wake of the panic of 1837; along the route of the railroad they were further depressed. Said the Lenox will, "I give, devise, and bequeath to my son James Lenox my farm at the five-mile stone, purchased in part from the corporation of the City of New York, containing about thirty acres, with all its improvements, stock of horses, cattle, and farming implements, for and during the term of his life and after his death to his heirs forever. My motive for so leaving this property is a firm persuasion that it may at a distant day be the site of a village, and as it cost me much more than its present worth from circumstances known to my family, I believe and cherish the belief that it may be realized to them. At all events, I want the experiment made by keeping the property from being sold."

James Lenox ignored the language of his father's will and began selling off lots, perhaps because he could not bear the trains, whose steam engines—noisy, dirty, belching coal smoke, frightening carriage and dray horses—did nothing to enhance property values. In the pastoral reaches of Manhattan north of 42nd Street, passing trains posed a threat to livestock as well as to passengers. Christopher Gray, citing an old document, writes that in 1839 "some fifteen fine, large, handsome cows . . . strayed into the line of the railroad near 58th Street;" there was a collision, and the train was nearly wrecked. South of 42nd Street, pedestrians and horses were sometimes killed at crossings.

Landowners brought pressure and city officials ordered the tracks below 42nd Street lowered into a deep cut. The cut was covered in places, but steam and smoke still belched through ventilators in the avenue's malls, making Fourth unattractive except to the poorest shack dwellers. The Fourth Avenue Boys, a gang of thugs, lived in holes dug into the sides of the cut. Elsewhere in Murray Hill, as farmland yielded to urbanization, residents were making early efforts toward zoning; in 1847 they signed covenants enjoining themselves and their heirs and assigns from building livery stables, slaughterhouses, smiths, forges, distilleries, tanneries, museums, theaters, or circuses. There was to be no manufacturing of gunpowder, glue, vitriol, ink, or turpentine. Construction, in fact, was to be limited to brick or stone dwellings of two stories or more, the only exceptions being churches and private stables. Not until the summer of 1914 would a court rule that "dwellings" might include apartment houses.

Action was finally taken in 1857 to ban all steam locomotives south of 42nd Street. Madison Square had opened in 1845 in response to a petition by Ruggles and a few others. The Harlem built a passenger depot adjacent to the square on the southern half of the block between 26th and 27th streets along the west side of Fourth Avenue. This had once been part of the old Boston Post Road and then a section of Rose Hill Farm, a Tory property confiscated after the Revolution. The New Haven followed the Harlem's lead with a passenger depot on the northern half of the block, and these two stations side by side inaugurated the Union Station idea in the United States. Trains did not steam in and out of the depots; between 27th and 42nd streets they were pulled by teams of horses.

Below the rail depots, churches had gone up on Fourth Avenue. Grace Church (James Renwick, Jr., 1847) at 10th Street actually faced on Broadway and only backed up on Fourth. Calvary Church, also by Renwick, was built in 1846 at the northeast corner of 21st and Fourth. The Fourth Avenue Presbyterian Church, a Romanesque revival structure with twin towers that has long since been replaced, opened in 1853 at the northwest corner of Fourth and 22nd, just south of the Rose Hill section. In 1855 came All Souls' Unitarian Church, also long gone, at the southeast corner of Fourth and 20th, where the pastor, Henry W. Bellows, built up a fashionable congregation near Gramercy Park, attracting the intellectual aristocracy. William Cullen Bryant, Peter Cooper, and Park Godwin were all either members or attended Sunday services. The church was designed by the English architect Jacob Wrey Mould, who had arrived in America in 1852; it was his first American commission (he would later team up with Calvert Vaux to design the American Museum of Natural History's first Central Park West building). An Italian and Romanesque structure known irreverently as the Church of the Holy Zebra because of its alternating bands of brick and Caen stone, All Souls' was demolished soon after its congregation moved in 1929 to a new building at Lexington and 80th Street. It outlived St. Paul's Methodist Episcopal Church, put up in 1863 at the northeast corner of Fourth and 22nd; St. Paul's was demolished in 1891 when its congregation moved uptown.

Cooper Union for the Advancement of Science and Art, at 7th Street and Fourth Avenue, had opened in 1859 (Frederick A. Peterson, architect), to pioneer free education for young working-class men and women. It had gained fame on February 27, 1860, when an Illinois congressman, Abraham Lincoln, made his "right makes might" speech in its Great Hall. Peter Cooper was then sixty-nine. Born in New York, he had been apprenticed at age seventeen to a coachmaker for $25 a year and board. Twenty years later he had founded the Canton Iron Works at Baltimore where, in 1830, he had built *Tom Thumb*, the first American-made steam locomotive, and where the wrought-iron beams were designed and made for Cooper Union. Cooper visited it each morning, a white-haired, white-bearded figure with green spectacles who carried a rubber air cushion wherever he went.

Farms, factories, breweries, a few tenements, and some institutional buildings occupied Manhattan north of Murray Hill in the 1850s. Squatters slaughtered pigs and herded goats along the railroad's right-of-way, scavenging coal to heat their shanties. Land was cheap.

Columbia College, whose campus had been downtown since 1754 on a site bounded by Murray, Barclay, and Church streets and West Broadway, bought property in 1856 at 49th Street and Madison Avenue; it also bought the Deaf and Dumb Asylum on the west side of Fourth Avenue between 49th and 50th streets and converted it into academic buildings. As the *Evening Post* noted on May 11, 1857, after Columbia had moved into its new home, a beautiful lawn sloped from the college southward down to 49th Street and was ornamented by some fine old trees. The site was "on a commanding eminence affording an extensive and pleasant view. That part of the city is still quite new and the hand of improvement is visible in all directions." Columbia's old buildings were sold and demolished.

Two years later, in 1859, a German piano maker, Heinrich Engelhard Steinweg, revolutionized pianomaking by building the first piano with a single cast-metal plate. The plate was strong enough to withstand the pull of strings which Steinweg had combined with an overstrung scale that not only saved space but also produced a much fuller tone than the popular Chickering and Knabe instruments. Steinweg and his sons needed a factory to meet demand. The

ABOVE: *New York & Harlem Railroad horsecar at Astor Place with Cooper Union and* (at left) *Bible House* (drawing from P. T. Valentine's Manual, 1860. The Bettmann Archive)

east side of Fourth Avenue between 52nd and 53rd streets was available, and property values were depressed by the steam-powered trains chugging up and down Fourth at grade level. Steinweg's factory opened in 1860, he changed his name to Henry Steinway in 1864, his sons carried on the business after 1871, and the factory remained in production on Park Avenue until 1910, two blocks north of the F. & M. Schaefer brewery, which continued its activities even longer.

By 1858 horsecars were moving along Second Avenue as far north as 122nd Street and on Third as far as 86th. The Madison Avenue line, begun in the 1860s, encouraged construction of brick houses along that thoroughfare, and there was some population movement into the 40s and 50s. South of the railroad depots at 26th Street, horsecars moved along Fourth Avenue. But railway cars were getting larger, and using horses to haul them from 42nd Street down to 27th was plainly ridiculous. Vanderbilt was not put off by the fact that 42nd Street was at least forty-five minutes from City Hall by horsecar, at what was generally considered the outer edge of the "civilized" city: the Commodore needed no

ABOVE: *Columbia College once occupied the west side of Park Avenue between 49th and 50th streets* (1884 photo courtesy New-York Historical Society)

crystal ball to see that 42nd Street—cut through in 1825 and now one of the few extrawide crosstown streets, newly paved with cobblestones and blessed with a new horsecar line—would be increasingly central to a city whose population was approaching one million and pushing rapidly northward.

Two residences from this period survive, altered considerably, at 629 and 631 Park; built to house three families each, they went up between 1869 and 1870, when steam trains still roared by on the surface.

Isaac C. Buckout, the Harlem's chief engineer, was responsible for engineering design and supervised construction of the new terminal. Its architect was the English-born John B. Snook, who a few years earlier had designed a house for William H. ("Billy") Vanderbilt on Fifth Avenue at 40th Street. Grand Central was built under the general direction of Commodore Vanderbilt and his son, who was a vice-president of the Harlem. Some early literature referred to the terminal as the "Grand Union Depot," but it was generally called Grand Central Depot from the start. Its train shed was the largest enclosed space on the North American continent, covering twelve tracks and five broad platforms raised slightly above track level. Grand Central occupied a structure stretching 249 feet along 42nd Street and 698 along the newly created Vanderbilt Avenue.

ABOVE: *Steinway & Sons Piano Forte Manufactory on the east side of Park between 52nd and 53rd streets* (from *Frank Leslie's Illustrated Newspaper,* September 22, 1860)

While it served three railroads (the Harlem was leased to the New York Central & Hudson River in 1873 and operated thereafter as a division of the Central), the depot had separate waiting rooms and baggage facilities for each. The Central, Harlem, and New Haven all shared the Harlem's tracks for five miles up to Mott Haven. North of the depot's marshaling yards there were still only two Harlem tracks to accommodate the combined traffic, but expansion to four tracks was in the offing.

Placing the tracks below grade at the depot itself was not deemed practical, so the grade lowering began at 45th Street, where the tracks entered the mammoth train shed. To the north, four elevated footbridges spanned the treacherous marshaling yards that reached to 51st Street. Carriages and pedestrians could cross the tracks on bridges at 45th and 48th streets, with footbridges at the intermediate streets. Beginning at 49th Street and reaching to 56th, the tracks were in an open cut between retaining walls with additional elevated bridges.

North of the railyards, Fourth Avenue looked not unlike a Midwestern cowtown street. Tracks ran at grade level between farms, factories, breweries, and tenements. At 70th Street, the peak of Lenox Hill, row houses and other buildings ran east to the horsecar line at Second Avenue. The tracks passed through the hill via an open cut or a tunnel (there is some doubt) and a shallow cut began at 80th Street for the tracks to descend to the level of the Yorkville tunnel at 92nd Street.

ABOVE: *Grand Central Depot* (1880 photo courtesy New-York Historical Society)

The three railroads finally began lowering all the tracks in 1871. Isaac Buckout worked out the plan for sinking them and providing the railroad with a separated line, widened to four tracks all the way to the Harlem River. Engineers of the Fourth Avenue Improvement Company, formed to carry out the work, had to drill and blast the cuts and tunnels through the heart of Manhattan rock. They made no effort to exceed the minimum depression possible within a regular grade, and the ceilings of the "beam tunnels" in the low 60s and 70s still create easily discernible humps at the cross streets.

From 56th Street to 66th the engineers built a beam tunnel, consisting of two single-track side tunnels connected for ventilation purposes with a double-track center tunnel open at the top and spanned by large beams, with an undergound depot; a brick tunnel extended from 67th Street to 71st, there was another underground depot at 72nd, and another beam tunnel stretched from 72nd to 80th. An underground depot was built at 86th Street, and a brick tunnel ran from 86th to 95th, with street elevated bridges from 96th to 97th. An arched stone viaduct carried the line across the Harlem flats between 98th and 115th streets; there was an elevated station at 110th and elevated bridges across the fifteen-foot-deep cut at each cross street from 114th Street to 117th. Beyond 115th Street, trains moved through an open cut north to the Harlem River, with a below-ground station at 126th Street. The gigantic undertaking employed 2,500 men. It was virtually complete by 1875, the finishing touches coming soon after Commodore Vanderbilt's death in 1877. By then the cut was completely paved over from 51st Street to 97th. The arrangement left a continuous series of ventilation slots or vents in a fifty-six-foot-wide landscaped strip down the middle of Fourth Avenue. An iron railing surrounded both the vents and the outer borders of the boulevard strip.

By this time Fourth Avenue north of 45th Street was beginning to be called Park Avenue, although most people still knew it as Fourth. It was widened to 140 feet with a twenty-seven-foot carriageway and a fifteen-foot sidewalk on either side of its fifty-six-foot-wide center mall. For institutions north of the new train shed, and for tenants of houses and tenements along the right-of-way, the development of the rail line into a major regional carrier was hardly a cause for celebration. The tracks might be out of sight, the center mall landscaped in spots, but increased traffic on the sunken, covered-over tracks meant smoke, steam, cinders, and disturbing noise around the clock.

On still peaceful Fourth Avenue, Murray Hill property owners between 34th and 36th streets had done some landscaping and called their thoroughfare Park Avenue as early as 1860; the name was applied all the way to 42nd Street by 1867 in an effort to make the avenue seem a proper residential address. So although the name Park Avenue South would not come into use until 1959, by that time Fourth Avenue between 34th and 42nd streets had been Park Avenue for close

BELOW: *Grand Central's vast train shed* (1880 photo courtesy New-York Historical Society)

to ninety years, and the two blocks between 32nd and 34th had been Park for more than thirty (some people would persist in calling it all Fourth Avenue).

The old rail depots at Madison Square had attracted traffic to the area, leading to the construction of a number of commercial hotels from Union Square north to the 20s. That New York's first YMCA was built (in 1869) at the southwest corner of Fourth and 23rd Street suggests that this was not then high-priced real estate. Fourth Avenue was for the most part a residential strip mixing ordinary dwellings with those of retail merchants who liked to have their home and place of business under one roof. In the pre–Civil War era, well-to-do residents of Fifth, Madison, and Lexington avenues shopped for household supplies on Fourth.

Upper Fourth Avenue had little in the way of shops. Iron pedestrian bridges spanned the great marshaling yards north of Grand Central in the 40s; no wagon, carriage, or other vehicle would be able to cross until 1912. And while bare malls covered the tracks north of 56th Street, steam, smoke, and cinders continued to pour out of the vents. The *New York Times* reported that "with the completion [of the track covering], the upper portion of Fourth Avenue is more than liable to become an attractive locality for residential purposes," as was the original Park Avenue in genteel Murray Hill. Nobody took the prediction very seriously. As upper Fifth and Madison avenues became fashionable in the 1880s there was a certain amount of spillover onto Park. This gentrification was confined almost entirely to Lenox and Prospect hills, where the elevation of the ground allowed smoke from the steam engines to dissipate before it reached the mall vents. Elsewhere the trains moved within a few feet—even inches—of the surface, and the avenue was built up with middle-class row houses, tenements, flats, factories, stables, and carriage houses with apartments for coachmen. In 1874 George Ehret, a prosperous Yorkville brewer, took the highest point on Fourth Avenue for his mansion, built in 1878 on the east side of the avenue and occupying what was still an almost suburban blockfront between 93rd and 94th streets. Ehret would live in the house for nearly fifty years.

Surviving from this period is 591 Park, in recent years a modern-looking brickfaced structure that has served as New York headquarters for the Insilco conglomerate but was originally built in 1878 as a five-story tenement and later became a private dwelling for one Mary Sargent Potter, who held it until 1919. In the 1880s, families who had resided downtown began to build on upper Fifth and Madison avenues, and, in a few cases, on Fourth. Two survivors are the twin Queen Anne–style residences at 709 and 711, completed in the mid-1880s in a row of ten such houses from designs by Bassett & Jones. The first, 709, built for William H. Browning, was owned from 1885 to 1926 by Laura and Cornelia Manley and their heir; the second, 711, was owned from 1912 to 1963 by Mabel S. Cromwell. Built at the same time (from a design by James E. Ware) was 890 Park, a five-story residence for J. V. S. Woolley. It was evidently one of a group facing onto 79th Street.

But most buildings on Fourth Avenue in the 1880s were tenements erected by speculators to house the city's burgeoning population. Irish immigrants

ABOVE: *North end of Grand Central from the railroad yards opposite 46th Street* (1883 photo courtesy New-York Historical Society)

occupied the tenements, putting up with the noise and dirt because rents were low. The parish of St. Ignatius Loyola, created in 1851 and taken over by the Jesuits in 1864, celebrated mass in a neighborhood saloon until 1886, when a basement church, or undercroft, was built at the southwest corner of Fourth and 83rd Street; the large present-day church, an Italianate limestone structure between 83rd and 84th streets, was erected between 1895 and 1900 (Ditmars & Schickel, architects). The apse mosaic, by Salviati & Co. of Venice, dates to 1916. Sundays a quarter century later found about 7,000 people celebrating mass at St. Ignatius, a number that would decline to perhaps 1,200 by 1989.

On March 1, 1888, less than two weeks before the famous blizzard, the Board of Aldermen resolved that "Fourth Avenue from 43rd to 96th Street hereafter be known as Park Avenue." Two weeks later, as the city swapped stories about drifts fifteen to twenty feet high, the stretch north to the Harlem River was similarly renamed. Renaming of Manhattan avenues had begun in 1880, when former Civil War General Egbert L. Viele proposed that Eleventh Avenue north of 63rd Street be called "West End Avenue" in the hope that fancy terminology would make it as fashionable as London's West End, thus raising property values.

Both Park and West End avenues would eventually be closed to trolleys, buses, and trucks, giving them a tranquility unique among the city's main thoroughfares; both also were built up well before World War II, saving them from the fate of less-developed avenues, including Fifth, on which there arose apartment houses whose design and materials would be more at home in some of the other boroughs than in fine Manhattan residential areas.

In 1896 Fourth Avenue was officially named Park all the way up to Fordham in the Bronx. But wishful thinking does not change reality; except for slightly more than a dozen years after the opening of Grand Central Terminal in 1913, when the upper avenue had quiet, smoke-free malls more than fifty feet wide with potted trees bordering serpentine bench-lined footpaths, Park Avenue has never lived up to its name.

Attracted to the upper avenue after the "Fourth Avenue Improvement"—and even earlier—were a number of hospitals, schools, and armories. Smoke and cinders depressed property values along the avenue; the city in this mid-Victorian era of efforts to improve the world was often willing to lease sites on the avenue to charitable institutions at giveaway prices; thus the postwar period saw the construction of at least a dozen brick institutions on what was still Fourth Avenue. The Hospital for the Ruptured and Crippled rose at the southeast corner of the first Grand Central Station; Hahnemann Hospital at 67th and Park (where 655 Park stands today), a Normal School (later Hunter College) at 68th, Union Theological Seminary at 69th, Presbyterian Hospital at 70th, and German Hospital and Dispensary between 76th and 77th. German Hospital (renamed Lenox Hill during World War I) paid only $1 a year for its plot.

The Normal School, founded in 1869, changed its name in 1870 to the Normal College of the City of New York. Its president until 1906 was Thomas Hunter, who from 1871 to 1874 had two neo-Gothic brick structures erected in the block between 68th and 69th streets. Countless teachers for the city's public school system were trained at the Normal College for Women, which was renamed Hunter College in 1914, lost its original home to fire in 1936, rebuilt soon after, turned itself into a liberal arts college, joined the City University (CUNY) in 1961, and became coeducational in 1964.

Presbyterian Hospital was founded in 1868 through the efforts and donations of James Lenox, who had inherited his father's farm and was now a real estate investor and philanthropist well known for his book collection; his library stood for thirty-five years on Fifth Avenue between 70th and 71st streets, a site sold, after the library was merged with those of Astor and Tilden into the New York Public Library, to the steel baron Henry Clay Frick.

Only the 7th Regiment Armory, designed by Charles W. Clinton, survives substantially intact (a one-story addition was made at its eastern end in 1927). The 7th Regiment, formed in 1806, had served in the War of 1812 and had gained some powerful friends by its performance in the Astor Place riots of 1847. It was unified in 1860 at the newly built Tomkins Market Armory, on the east side of the Bowery between 6th and 7th streets, and played an important role at the outset of the Civil War, protecting the nation's capital when it was cut off by rebel forces in Maryland. Its members included a number of socially prominent New Yorkers, and its splendid new armory, with interiors by Lewis C. Tiffany and Stanford White, is the nation's only armory built and furnished with private funds. Filling the block bounded by 66th and 67th streets between Park and Lexington avenues, it opened with great ceremony on April 26, 1880: the regiment, whose veterans included architect Clinton, marched in, and there followed a fancy ball attended by most of the city's more affluent citizens. Youngsters enrolled in the very social Knickerbocker Greys exercised twice each week under the iron roof of the great drill hall.

Today the armory is home to the 2nd Brigade, 42nd Infantry Division, and the 1st Batallion, 107th Infantry, New York Army National Guard. It houses a tennis club and has also been used as a shelter for the homeless. Since 1955 it has been leased each January for the prestigious Winter Antiques Show, a benefit for the East Side House Settlement in the South Bronx; since 1983 it has also been the scene of Sanford L. Smith's Spring Armory Antiques Show. Both events attract thousands to this vestige of the wave of institutional building which came in the wake of the Civil War.

Union Theological Seminary, founded in May 1836, moved in December 1884 from 9 University Place to 700 Park Avenue, four interconnected buildings occupying the entire blockfront between 69th and 70th streets and surrounding a hollow square. Former New York Governor Edwin D. Morgan had offered the institution $300,000 for a new library in 1880 and agreed to sell it ten lots on the west side of the avenue. The seminary's chapel, library, and lecture hall fronted on Park Avenue; a dormitory for 160 students was in the rear. Not until late in 1910 would the institution move to a new two-block location adjacent to Columbia University's Morningside Heights campus.

Almost nobody who could afford better in the 1880s wanted to live on upper

ABOVE: *7th Regiment Armory, 1880–?* (1989 photo)

Park Avenue—not with that smoke and steam and all those cinders. Not with those locomotives making so much noise. It was enough to frighten the horses. Yet, paradoxically, Park Avenue was considered quite suitable for stables. When the men's clothier Isaac Brokaw built his mansion at 79th and Fifth in 1886, he started to erect a private stable on Park just north of 79th Street—until neighbors objected. They were paying enough rent to avoid the nuisance of stables, they said, so vehemently that Brokaw backed off and arranged to build on a mixed blockfront near 82nd Street and Madison, where 1080 Madison Avenue now stands.

Put up in 1890 and still surviving in 1989 is 821 Park, one of a row of seven six-story multiple dwellings that occupied the entire eastern blockfront between 75th and 76th streets with stores on the first two floors (a Korean delicatessen at 75th Street would be a center of controversy in the 1980s). Completed later in the 1890s and also surviving is 870 Park, originally one of five carriage houses designed by A. M. Welch. Most of the row houses and tenements erected along upper Park Avenue faced on side streets, not on the covered tracks of the avenue. A few hardy millionaires, like the brewer George Ehret, did build fine houses fronting on Park at places where the elevation placed them far above the noise and steam.

As for the lower reaches of the avenue, 1894 saw the dedication of the Church Missions House, a six-story, steel-framed structure immediately to the north of Calvary Church at the southeast corner of 22nd Street. Cornelius Vanderbilt II was among the prominent businessmen who organized a drive to obtain contributions and secure the site, which was just to the south of two other buildings for charitable institutions, United Charities and the Society for the Prevention of Cruelty to Children. The Episcopal Domestic and Foreign Missionary Society, founded in 1821, engaged as architects Robert W. Gibson and Edward J. Neville Stent; they took as their inspiration a Flemish or Belgian town hall or guildhall and gave the avenue a masterpiece.

An 1894 guide by two English brothers (J.W. and D.B. Shepp) said: "Fourth Avenue and Park Avenue, which form one continuous street, is devoted to business as far up as Thirty-third street, with a group of notably fine buildings at Twenty-third, including the Bank for Savings, the United Charities Building, the Society for the Prevention of Cruelty to Animals, the Young Men's Christian Association, and the Academy of Design. At Thirty-third street are the Park Avenue Hotel and the Seventy-first Regiment Armory."

Designed by Clinton & Russell and raised in 1891, this crenellated building housed a fashionable regiment (it was later home to the 42nd Infantry of the National Guard, the famous Rainbow Division, now at the 7th Regiment Armory). Fire damaged the premises in 1902, whereupon an addition was made: a 250-foot tower modeled on the town hall of Siena. Also by Clinton & Russell, it was finished in 1905 and remained the area's most visible landmark until the 1970s.

The Rose Hill-Murray Hill area impressed the Shepps: "At 33rd Street and Fifth avenue, the aristocratic section, the real Faubourg St. Germain of New

ABOVE: *71st Regiment Armory, 1891–1972* (photo courtesy New-York Historical Society)

York, begins. Here for several blocks the west side of the avenue is lined with the most magnificent mansions in America, rivaling in cost and splendor the palaces of European kings. Three other avenues in this part of the city almost vie with this one in wealth and fashion. One of these is Madison avenue, lying next to Fifth at the east and possessing many blocks of mansions comparable with almost any in the city. Next beyond it lies Park avenue, as this part of Fourth avenue is called." The Shepps noted that "the centre of the roadway over" Park Avenue's old railroad tunnel, which had been acquired for streetcar use, was "devoted to a charming strip of lawn, with flowers and shrubbery. This avenue is one of the favorite homes of the rich."

Quite a few prominent bankers in the 1890s had Murray Hill houses on Park near 39th Street, and so did at least one prominent lawyer. Andrew Haswell Green, sometimes called "the father of Greater New York," lived briefly at 87 Park and then, at the turn of the century, moved two doors north to No. 91, a three-story house which he shared with three nieces and a nephew.

It was Green who first proposed the amalgamation of the boroughs into Greater New York in 1868. A few years later he and his former law partner, Samuel J. Tilden (who was soon elected governor), succeeded in having the notorious William Marcy ("Boss") Tweed arrested, extradited, and tried for thefts of city money. Green became city comptroller and held the office until 1886, restoring order and honesty to New York's finances. As executor of Tilden's estate, he came up with the plan for consolidating the Tilden Foundation with the Lenox and Astor libraries to create the New York Public Library in 1895. He also played major roles in creating Central Park, shaping the public school system, and organizing the Metropolitan Museum of Art, American Museum of Natural History, and New York Zoological Society. In 1897, when he was in his late seventies, Green had the satisfaction of seeing his plan for Greater New York put into effect. Then, at eighty-three, on the afternoon of November 13, 1903, he was fatally shot on the front stoop of his house at 91 Park by a jealous suitor who had waited in ambush for his rival—a different white-bearded octogenarian—and had shot the wrong man.

Shortly after Green's murder the Robert Bacons first occupied the house at at 1 Park Avenue. Bacon, a Harvard classmate of Teddy Roosevelt who had served briefly as U.S. secretary of state before being named ambassador to France, died in 1919. His widow lived on in the house at 1 Park Avenue—and, as related above, sued the city when Park was renumbered.

A decade earlier, in 1894, the Shepps had found 42nd Street to be "one of the choicest of private residence streets [with] some fine churches and the Murray Hill and Grand Union Hotels. At 42nd Street is the Grand Central Railroad Station . . . Above 42nd Street [Park] avenue is traversed by the railroads' [right-of-way], four tracks wide, partly elevated and partly under-ground, built at a cost of several million dollars a mile. The avenue is built up with apartment houses, factories, asylums, and hospitals."

And more armories. The 7th Regiment Armory, as noted, was on Park in the 60s. In 1895 the Squadron A Armory, designed by a Rochester architect, John

ABOVE: *Houses, churches, clubs, hotels, and an armory once had Park Avenue's Murray Hill blocks pretty much to themselves* (1929 photo courtesy Municipal Archive)

A. Thomas, with corbels and crenallations to resemble a medieval castle, was completed in the block bounded by Park and Madison avenues between 94th and 95th streets.

Squadron A, organized by gentleman equestrians in 1884 as the New York Hussars or First Dragoons (the Squadron A name was adopted in 1895), was more than anything else a social club; its members played polo at the armory on Saturday nights for roughly seventy years, sometimes attracting close to 2,000 spectators. Squadron A was active as a National Guard unit until World War I, when it was mustered into service as the 105th Machine Gun Battalion. Most of the armory was torn down in the late 1960s and replaced by a public school, I.S. 29, designed with a certain whimsy by Morris Ketchum, Jr., and transformed into the much sought-after, if sometimes troubled, Hunter College elementary and high schools.* (The 71st Regiment Armory at the base of Murray Hill survived until the mid-1970s, when it was replaced by an office building and

---

* Total enrollment: 366. Tuition: free, as compared (in 1988) with $7,544 to $9,207 for kindergarten and eighth grade, respectively, at the Grace Church School, 86 Fourth Avenue, where total enrollment is 328. But out of 750 applicants for Hunter's nursery school, only thirty-two are accepted; of 750 applicants for kindergarten, only sixteen. More reflective of the city's diverse population than other Manhattan private or public schools, Hunter is 55 percent white, 25 percent black, 11 percent Asian, and 8 percent Hispanic. Some Hunter parents were driven frantic in the late 1980s by indications that school policies were developing a racial bias and that it might move to East Harlem.

high school). When the Squadron A Armory was built, Park Avenue's upper reaches were still not socially acceptable for anything but polo games. Not until 1906, when the tracks above and beneath it were electrified, would the avenue north of 42nd be considered a fit place for residences of the rich. Meanwhile, New York's upper crust preferred the lower reaches of Park and Fourth avenues. So did visitors from out of town.

3
.

Vanished Caravansaries

"IT'S A NICE PLACE TO VISIT," begins the cliché—which means it must have nice hotels. For more than a century New York's visitors have enjoyed putting up at good hotels, although "good" by past standards would hardly qualify as good today. From the 1850s to the 1880s New York's best hotels were on Fourth Avenue at Union Square and directly to the north; the first Grand Central rail depot brought them to 42nd Street, and later in the century Murray Hill became popular. The nonpareil from 1893 to 1929 was the old Waldorf on Fifth Avenue at 33rd Street, expanded in 1897 into the first Waldorf-Astoria. Not until the building of Grand Central Terminal and the development of property over the railroad tunnel would upper Park Avenue become the city's smart hotel strip. Few are left to remember the elegant hostelries that once clustered near Union Square, long the heart of the city's hotel district: the Clarendon, Everett House, New Amsterdam, Putnam House, Ashland House, Florence House, and Belvedere, all on Fourth Avenue.

When the Clarendon opened in 1848 at the southeast corner of Fourth and 18th Street, Union Square was the city's social center and the heart of its hotel district. William B. Astor financed its construction, James Renwick, Jr. designed it, and the Clarendon was initially a flop. A five-story structure of yellow brick and brownstone with ornate terra-cotta window heads and cast-iron balconies, it was, critics said, too far uptown for a hotel. They proved correct; the operation went bankrupt and was acquired by a man who enlarged it to accommodate 300 guests. An enterprising new manager turned the hotel around late in 1853 when he sent a boat down the harbor to receive Lord Ellesmere, England's representative to a New York exposition inspired by the London Great Exhibition of 1851. Lord Ellesmere and his entourage took rooms at the Clarendon, and the favorable publicity brought immediate success. The hotel's prestige and prosperity continued for thirty years. Like the Brevoort on Fifth Avenue, the Clarendon was a stopping place for English aristocrats who found its ambience much like that of a hotel in Mayfair.

While no hotel had private baths in the Clarendon's early days, most had barrooms. The Clarendon had only wine cellars, but they were extensive, and the hotel offered privacy comparable to that of a high-class club, absolutely excluding the outside public. Russia's Grand Duke Alexis made the Clarendon his headquarters when he arrived at New York in December 1871 en route to hunt bison on the Kansas prairie (an armed guard slept at his door). And it was at the Clarendon in 1888, ten years before it closed, that Ward McAllister, lapdog of Mrs. Astor (*the* Mrs. Astor, *née* Caroline Schermerhorn) and arbiter of society, was interviewed by the *Tribune* and made his famous statement to the effect that there were only four hundred people in New York society (this being the number that could fit into the ballroom of Mrs. Astor's house at 350 Fifth Avenue). Demolished in 1909, the Clarendon was replaced in 1914 by 215 Fourth Avenue, an office building.

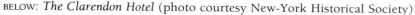

BELOW: *The Clarendon Hotel* (photo courtesy New-York Historical Society)

The Everett House, which stood until 1908 on the northwest corner of 17th Street and Fourth, fronting on Union Square, was a five-story building erected in 1853 and enlarged a few years later. The reopening was attended by the socially and politically prominent, including Edward Everett, a former secretary of state, U.S. senator, and popular orator for whom the place was named. Everett presented a portrait of himself which still hung in the hotel's reading room in June 1908, when the place finally closed to make way for 200 Fourth Avenue, an office building. A New York City guide for 1862 talked about the Everett House as being "a convenient and delightful place to stop, being not only in the aristocratic part of the city but also contiguous to the cars, omnibuses, places of amusement, etc."

The New Amsterdam stood for many years at the southeast corner of Fourth and 21st Street (later the site of 257 Park Avenue South). The Putnam House at 367 Fourth, northeast corner 26th Street, opened in 1863 and was one of the city's leading small hotels during the Civil War. It came down in 1909 to make way for a twelve-story structure. To its south was the seven-story Ashland House at the southeast corner of 24th Street. It was opened in 1868 by Horace Brockway, closed in the 1890s, sold in 1909, and replaced by 315 Fourth Avenue, an office building. The Ashland House was known for its comfortable accommodations, good food, and cleanliness. Its barroom did a large business at intermissions and after performances at the old Lyceum Theater across the street. The Florence House, which has been called the "pioneer apartment hotel," opened in the early 1870s at the northeast corner of Fourth and 18th Street. It was sold at a foreclosure sale in 1909 and razed to make way for 225 Fourth Avenue, the American Woolen Co. Building.

Better known than most of these was the Belvedere, a seven-story hostelry that opened in about 1880 at Fourth and 18th Street on property purchased from William H. Vanderbilt. Joseph Wehrle, the proprietor, had earlier managed a Belvedere Hotel at Fourth and 14th Street, the future site of the German Savings Bank (renamed the Central Savings Bank in World War I).

The Park Avenue Hotel, a year or two older than the Belvedere, was between 32nd and 33rd streets on the west side of Fourth Avenue—not Park, despite the hotel's presumptuous name. (It was, however, set back twenty feet from Fourth Avenue, so that its facade lined up with those of Park Avenue buildings that began at 34th Street.) Built with funds provided before his death in 1876 by the merchant prince A. T. Stewart, it opened in April 1878 as The Woman's Home, a residence for working women, but rates were $6 to $10 a week at a time when working girls earned only $5 to $15 a week. House rules, moreover, did not permit women to entertain gentlemen callers in the eight reception rooms, parlors, and dining rooms, and the 502 sleeping rooms were closely supervised to prevent occupants from bringing in pets, sewing machines, pianos, memorabilia, or any other expressions of individuality. Some $3 million had been lavished on the project's seven floors plus penthouse with a large interior garden. Ornate fountains graced the garden, which had at its four corners bronze candelabra made to order in Paris. But not even women who could afford the rates were about to live by Stewart's rules.

Said the comic periodical *Puck*, "The late A. T. Stewart was a man of cold disposition and frigid manners . . . Stewart and Vanderbilt are both dead, . . . but in one thing the dry-goods man has the advantage of the Commodore. His executors are men after his own heart. If the old Philistine were alive to-day, he couldn't suggest one additional item of meanness and petty tyranny in the managements of the 'Woman's Home.' " Stewart's quasi-philanthropic plan never got off the ground; in late May 1878, less than two months after the Woman's Home opened, the *Daily Tribune* announced plans for its conversion into a hotel for guests of both sexes. And so it remained for nearly half a century. The Royal Hungarian Band played in its garden courtyard on summer evenings, and it remained in style until shortly after World War I. It came down in 1927 to make way for 2 Park Avenue, an office building.

The Murray Hill Hotel, demolished in 1947 to make way for 100 Park, stood for sixty-three years on the west side of Park between 40th and 41st streets, a

BELOW: *The Park Avenue Hotel* (*Daily Graphic* drawing courtesy New-York Historical Society)

500-room hostelry with two pointed corner towers. Hugh Smith, a broker and sportsman, spent $1 million to build the square, eight-story structure of red sandstone on the site of the old Madison Avenue stage line's stables and carbarn. The Murray Hill's ornate facade, circular iron fire escapes, gilded lobbies, and plush dining rooms attracted such guests as Jay Gould, John L. Sullivan, P. T. Barnum, Presidents Cleveland and McKinley, and Mark Twain (who was there during the Blizzard of '88 and wrote home to his wife in Hartford, "Crusoing on a desert hotel"). Southern aristocrats and businessmen from New England took their families to spend the winter business season in New York's Murray Hill. Drexels and Biddles from Philadelphia reserved suites for Christmas week. The Harvard and Yale football teams stopped here, as did visiting Catholic clergymen; it was not uncommon to see devout laymen kneeling at the foot of the marble staircase to kiss the ring of a cardinal.

Public rooms of the Murray Hill had red-and-white marble floors, fifteen-foot ceilings, and an elaborate gilt decor. A portrait of William K. Vanderbilt, his side-whiskers blowing back over either shoulder as he raced his champion trotter Maud S. on Fifth Avenue, was conspicuously displayed. For many years a night's lodging with four meals cost $4. Famous for its food, the Murray Hill listed seventy-three separate items on its breakfast menu alone. It was the only hotel dining room in New York to offer half servings for those with less than robust appetites. Some of the more elderly residents came in with body servants to help them to their chairs. Dining room rules were strictly observed; smoking was not permitted until nine o'clock, when most of the ladies had retired.

BELOW: *The Murray Hill Hotel, about 1890* (photo courtesy New-York Historical Society)

Operated more like a club than a hotel, the Murray Hill had many regulars; one woman was a guest for fifty-three winters. Alf Landon made it his national headquarters when he ran for president in 1936. The 400 guest rooms retained their original furnishings—mahogany armoires and highboys, heavy marble washstands with brass legs, and the like—until 1943, when the hotel was sold for $700,000. It had changed hands only once, in 1910, to Benjamin L. M. Bates, who had bought it from the Smith estate for $1,790,500. Bates's father, a Civil War general, had owned the old Everett House on Union Square, where the younger Bates rose from assistant night clerk to manager. A bachelor, he died in December 1935, and his hotel finally closed on April 24, 1947.

Across the avenue to the northeast had stood the Grand Union, built when the first Grand Central (sometimes called the Grand Union) was new. A small hotel, the Westchester House, occupied some Fourth Avenue frontage in 1870 when an entrepreneur saw the location's potential and bought it. Within the next few years he added to the property, it was called the Grand Union as early as January 1882, and, as the *Times* said at the time of its closing, "the small hotel quickly grew to become one of the most popular and best paying houses in the city. It never changed its old character of a commercial house, and its reasonable prices, combined with the fame of its restaurant, made the name Grand Union celebrated throughout the country. In its early years it had little competition, but notwithstanding the fact that the Grand Central station vicinity has in recent years witnessed the advent of the large Murray Hill, Belmont, Manhattan [northwest corner 42nd Street and Madison, closed in 1920], and Biltmore hotels, the Grand Union has apparently never lost custom and there have been few nights in the year when it has had a vacant room."

The Grand Union had marble floors, walls, and a lavatory, but in the heydays of the 1880s and '90s few of its 350 elegant rooms had running water. Baths were on the first floor and cost fifty cents. The hotel's restaurant, one of the city's best, was a popular gathering place for politicians, and the bar was highly profitable in a time when whiskey cost fifteen cents a shot, two for a quarter. (A standing joke for years was that at the Grand Union one could tie one on for a dollar and sleep it off for a dollar, that being the minimum charge for a room.) The Grand Union closed on May 2, 1914, after the hodgepodge of old masonry structures, varying from five to seven stories, had been condemned for subway excavation. The city paid $3,577,000 for the hotel and $644,000 to demolish it in order to obtain land needed for the link between the new Lexington Avenue I.R.T. and the Fourth Avenue line of the original subway. This link would run under the corner of 42nd Street, and engineers of the Public Service Commission said it would be impossible to protect the Grand Union during the enormous excavation work beneath the foundations. (There was talk of turning the site into a World War I memorial, but its Park Avenue frontage was bought by the Pershing Square Building Corp. in 1920; its easterly portion went to the Bowery Savings Bank for an uptown office.)

The Belmont, which survived only until 1931, opened on May 6, 1906, opposite the first Grand Central on Park between 41st and 42nd streets, just

ABOVE: *The Grand Union was close to Grand Central* (1894 photo courtesy New-York Historical Society)

north of the Murray Hill and across from the Grand Union. Rising twenty-two stories (with five more floors below street level descending sixty feet into depths excavated from solid rock), the Belmont was by far the tallest building in midtown when it was put up.

B. L. M. Bates of the Murray Hill managed the new Belmont. He had persuaded the younger August Belmont, financier of the first subway, to invest in the enterprise, and in 1901 Belmont procured the 42nd Street site where a subway station was to be built. He gave Bates *carte blanche* to build a hotel that would eclipse all others (and would cost $7 million). Warren & Wetmore, designers of Grand Central Terminal, were the architects. They put a ladies' vestibule on Park Avenue and placed the main entrance, with a marble archway, on 42nd Street. W. & J. Sloane, given the contract to furnish the hotel, brought over pictures, tapestries, and furniture from Paris. Immense green velvet rugs adorned the floors of the lobby, which was resplendent with gilded walls, ornamentation, fluted pillars, wainscoting and trimmings of a reddish and mottled porphyry-colored marble from Italy. Surmounting the great monoliths were white-sculptured caryatids and atlantes, heads and busts of heroic size which supported the beams of the ceiling. Mrs. Harry Payne Whitney had modeled the figures at her studio in Newport.

Bates had a financial interest in the Belmont, as did John McEntee Bowman, who headed the Pershing Square syndicate that controlled the Murray Hill and who later would build the Biltmore and Commodore. Pictures, etchings, and rotogravures from Paris decorated the Belmont's guest rooms, each of which was near one of the hotel's high-speed elevators. For $2 a man could get "a nice little room and sleep as well as if he paid $1,000 a day for a suite of state apartments," said the publicists.

With over 1,000 guest rooms and as many employees, the Belmont quickly became one of the city's most fashionable and popular hotels. Furniture of Circassian and French walnut graced its parlor floor. Below that was the mezzanine floor overlooking the lobby, palm garden, and Rotunda restaurant (on the 41st Street corner). The main restaurant could seat 300 patrons; there were private dining rooms, as well, and five cafés and grillrooms.

By 1930 August Belmont and Co. owned the hotel; it closed in May of that year, and although it was finally torn down in 1931 the site lay idle until 1933. The world's longest beer bar, with an outdoor beer garden, opened on the site in September 1933. The Airlines Terminal building that replaced it in 1940 was itself replaced in 1982 by the Philip Morris world headquarters building at 120 Park.

The Vanderbilt Hotel, which became simply 4 Park Avenue in 1966, opened in 1912 at the southwest corner of 34th Street when Murray Hill was still the most fashionable part of the city. Alfred Gwynne Vanderbilt, a great-grandson

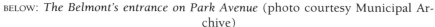

BELOW: *The Belmont's entrance on Park Avenue* (photo courtesy Municipal Archive)

of the Commodore and among the first to take up residence at the Plaza Hotel when that hostelry opened in 1907, had inherited the property from his father, Cornelius Vanderbilt II, who had moved into a new mansion at Fifth Avenue and 57th Street.

Still in his early thirties when he undertook the new hotel project at the end of 1908, Vanderbilt had inherited more than $42 million and saw the potential of a site equidistant from Penn Station and the Grand Central Terminal then nearing completion. He engaged Warren & Wetmore as architects and took a personal interest in the construction and furnishing of the twenty-one-story hotel. Windows and lanterns evocative of the work of Robert Adam and a glass sunburst marquee over the entrance suggested that the epitome of elegance lay inside, and the truth lived up to the advertising. Much of the paneling and other material was brought from Europe. In design, equipment, and decoration the Vanderbilt was considered far ahead of its time in hotel construction. Its 600 rooms with bath had eleven-foot ceilings, and it had two public dining rooms, a bar, and cocktail rooms. Fifty-four terra-cotta heads, some evidently representing a bearded Bacchus, others a mythological figure of indeterminate gender, grinned down from the roof. A fifteen-room penthouse was reserved as a town home for Vanderbilt and his family.

Vanderbilt went down with the *Lusitania* on May 7, 1915, after reportedly surrendering his life jacket to a female passenger. His widow gave up the family hotel suite, and it was taken over briefly by the newly organized Women's City Club. Soon afterward, Enrico Caruso occupied the penthouse suite. His entourage included a personal chef, Tiressa, who became the hotel's chef de cuisine after Caruso's death in 1921. The Palm Garden, Crypt bar and grill, Chinese lounge, and Della Robbia Room became popular hangouts for insurance company and garment district executives. Diamond Jim Brady, Caruso, Valentino, and other colorful personalities bent their elbows on the Crypt Room's huge mahogany bar. A male sanctuary until 3 P.M., when women were welcome for cocktails, hors d'oeuvres, and supper, the bar retained its Victorian flavor into the 1940s.

The Vanderbilt family sold the hotel to a syndicate for about $6 million cash in October 1925; less than a decade later the Vanderbilt was sold at auction for $2,416,000. Two successive hotel chains attempted to modernize it, but as the Belmont Hotel's brochure had observed in 1912, when the Vanderbilt opened, "the centre of New York has shifted many times, always moving northward with the increase in population and expansion of business." By the end of 1965, when the Vanderbilt Hotel closed its doors for conversion into three floors of stores and offices, with eighteen floors of 354 cooperative apartments, the city's business center was perhaps a mile north of 34th Street.

What had permitted this northward movement was changing technology: electric trains, running beneath the surface of Fourth and lower Park avenues, made those thoroughfares enormously convenient beginning in 1904. Two years later, upper Park Avenue as well received the benefits of electrification.

4
.

Electrification

TRAINS of the New York & Harlem Railroad began operating from the first Grand
Central Depot on October 9, 1871. Ten of its twelve tracks were stub-ended; the
two easternmost tracks extended through the station to continue south on
Fourth Avenue to the old station at 27th Street. The New Haven, because of a
dispute with the Harlem over rental charges at the new depot, used Grand
Central's two easternmost tracks and continued to operate its trains south on
Fourth Avenue by horsepower to 27th Street until November 21, 1872. (The
train sheds at Madison Square were later turned into a performing arena leased
in 1873 by P. T. Barnum and opened first as the Great Roman Hippodrome, then
as Gilmore's Garden, and finally, after William H. Vanderbilt repossessed the
place in 1879, as Madison Square Garden.)

Starting on November 14, 1871, through trains of the New York Central &
Hudson River Railroad also used Grand Central, although certain local trains
continued to run from the old Hudson River station at 30th Street and Ninth
Avenue, which remained in existence until 1931. In 1885 and 1886 the railroad
rearranged its Grand Central yards, enlarged them, and provided them with
improved interlocking switches and signals. A new annex with a seven-track,
100-foot train shed was constructed on the east side of the original depot and
was employed thereafter to receive incoming trains. At Mott Haven, five miles
north in the Bronx, a new yard was constructed in 1888 to repair, clean, and
house the Central's trains. Smoke and cinders from steam engines choked the
tunnels leading into the train shed, and accidents were frequent. After a collision
in 1891 at 85th Street, residents could hear the screams of passengers through

vents in the center mall. Several persons were crushed, scalded, or burned to death.

Why could the trains under Park Avenue not be electrified? Electric trolley cars had gone into service at Richmond, Virginia, early in 1888. Frank Sprague, a former assistant to Thomas Edison, had engineered the four-wheeled cars; lighted with incandescent bulbs, they could travel at fifteen miles per hour. Within two years some 200 American cities had electric trolley lines, but nowhere in the world was electricity used to move heavy rolling stock.

Between 1893 and 1896 the Park Avenue line, which had been placed below grade between 110th Street and the Harlem River twenty years earlier, was raised above street level on a great four-track steel viaduct more than a mile in length. A new high-level, four-track drawbridge 398 feet long was built over the Harlem River, largely to permit its conversion to a ship canal. Although the city paid half the $3 million cost, Chauncey Depew of the Central was upset. As he told a *Harper's Weekly* reporter, "It is not within reason that New York will suffer the inconvenience of having that canal cut the city in two in the middle. After a few years more it will be filled in and built over. It is a mistaken undertaking."

Depew's vision was just as cloudy when it came to electrification. The Baltimore & Ohio had electrified a four-mile tunnel in 1895, and while that was

BELOW: *Cleaning up after the Blizzard of '88* (photo courtesy New-York Historical Society)

the only place in America where electric traction was successfully applied to heavy main-line railroad equipment, it demonstrated that railroads could be electrified. Depew, however, was not about to risk money on any fool scheme to electrify the approaches to Grand Central.

Frank Sprague, who knew more about it, had greater faith in electric motive power. Early in 1899 he visited William J. Wilgus, chief engineer of the Central, and submitted a proposal for electrifying the Yonkers branch. Elevated railways in New York and Chicago were converting from steam power to electric; if they could do it, why not commuter railroads? Wilgus thought Sprague made a lot of sense. In June 1899 he completed a plan of his own for electrifying not only suburban trains but also the two outside tunnels along Park Avenue. The plan called for new tracks in a widened open cut south of 56th Street; a loop station would be built beneath Grand Central and beneath the adjacent land and streets. Replacing the old depot with a multilevel terminal would provide additional capacity without requiring any substantial enlargement of the terminal site. And, thanks to electricity, there would be no problems of smoke and gases from steam locomotives. Chauncey Depew and the other directors marveled at Wilgus' plan, adopted it enthusiastically, and then dragged their feet. To im-

BELOW: *Until 1906, steam drove locomotives through Park Avenue's tunnel into the* Grand Central marshaling yards *(1899 photo courtesy New-York Historical Society)*

plement the plan would be costly. There were other priorities, including fat dividends to stockholders. The plan would have to wait.

By 1900 more than 500 daily trains—three times the 1871 volume and then some—were operating in and out of Grand Central. The terminal was a hive of activity as trainmen struggled to keep everything moving smoothly. Inevitably, there were accidents. On January 9, 1902, the *New York Times* carried a screaming headline: 15 KILLED IN REAR-COLLISION AS TRAINS CRASH IN DARKNESS OF PARK AVENUE TUNNEL. "Fifteen passengers were killed and twoscore others severely injured as the result of a rear-end collision in the Park Avenue railroad tunnel at 56th Street yesterday morning at 8:20 o'clock. Unaccountable blunders of an engineer and unclear signals, which he said he did not see, are held to be responsible for the accident—the worst railroad disaster that ever occurred on Manhattan Island."

A commuter train from White Plains on the Harlem division had plowed into a New Haven commuter train from Danbury that was standing on an east track of an "outside tunnel." The two rear cars of the Danbury train were reserved for passengers from New Rochelle, and all of those killed (two more died within a few days) were among the unfortunate sixty who had boarded the rear car at New Rochelle. "That a train was standing on the track was indicated by several signals," the *Times* continued, "and that the engineer failed to see them is to be explained only by the circumstance that the dark passageway was at the time choked with fog, smoke, and steam."

Under the heading "The General Slaughter," the *Times* editorialized: "The killing of fifteen human beings and the maiming of many more in the Park Avenue tunnel of the New York Central Railroad yesterday awakened both the

BELOW: *Grand Central's marshaling yards before electrification* (photo courtesy New-York Historical Society)

public horror and the public indignation. That men and women should be ground to pieces in this way in the very heart of the city while going about their daily vocations passes understanding and tolerance. Upon a previous lamentable occasion of this nature ten years ago it was found that indictment was no remedy. The compelling process of legislation must now be invoked for it has long since been demonstrated that the management of this railroad will submit itself to no minor authority, and this disaster is one of which the legislature must take cognizance because the people will no longer expose themselves to the appalling perils of the conditions under which the slothful and incompetent New York Central management exercise the privileges of their franchise. The tunnel, the dreadful, smoke-filled tunnel against which all New York has long stormed and protested, is responsible for the murderous collision of yesterday . . .

"It is in these conditions of imminent peril that the New York Central managers insist upon operating their road, disregarding the public demand that they adopt remedial devices which the state of the art long since brought to practicable perfection. We think they will not much longer disregard the public demand, for the people will now speak with a voice which they have before heard and found it necessary to heed. It was after a former murderous 'accident' on their road that the New York Central managers were compelled by the law of the state to introduce the block system, already in established use upon other and better managed railroads. They must now be compelled by law to abandon the use of steam locomotives for hauling their trains through the tunnel . . . Nothing that these Central managers have done, are doing, or have promised to do will provide any safeguard whatever against a repetition of yesterday's accident. Adopting electrical traction for trains in the tunnel, leaving it un-dimmed by smoke and steam and uncontaminated by noxious gases, would be an adequate measure of relief. Nothing less will suffice, and evidently no power short of that of the whole State exercised through the Legislature will compel its adoption . . . One of its earliest enacted measures should be a law compelling the New York Central Railroad to make its horrible tunnel safe and convenient for travel."

Chauncey Depew—Senator Depew now, having been elected to the U.S. Senate in 1899—was sixty-seven. Widowed in 1893, he had been remarried less than two weeks before the tunnel accident and on January 11, 1902, arrived from Europe with his bride. "I have never come home so shocked," he told reporters. "I know the tunnel as well as I do my own library. I believe that if there is a place on earth where engineering skill, foresight, and intention to use every precaution has been taken it has been in that tunnel. The disaster is due to the disregard of one person to observe and act . . . We have tested the tunnel again and again and have found the lights—green, red, and white—perfect . . . In regard to the suggestion that the tunnel should be better lighted, we tried electric lights there once but the engineers said that they were confusing and at their unanimous request the lights were removed. Money is of no earthly value to the New York Central as compared with the safety of its passengers. There is no limit to the amount of money the road would spend to make the tunnel safe if it is not safe, but you have to come to the fact, at last, and bring the responsibility to the individual. One fellow can ruin the best system in the world. The blame must rest on one non-observing brain." The Central, nevertheless, contracted with Consolidated Edison the very next day to install electric lights in the tunnel to facilitate preparations for a change in motive power.

Only a few months earlier, in 1901, the world's first electrified railway terminal—the Gare d'Orsay—had opened in Paris. If Frenchmen could do it, why not Americans? On December 12, 1901, the president of the Pennsylvania Railroad, Alexander Cassatt, had announced that the Pennsy would build tunnels beneath the Hudson so that his trains could enter Manhattan. It went without saying that the trains would be pulled by electric locomotives.

No longer able to delay action in the face of the public outcry that followed the accident, the Central presented the 1899 Wilgus plan to the New York State Board of Railroad Commissioners and, in December, established a special Electric Traction Commission to plan the general features of the project. A prototype electric locomotive began tests in 1904, and in December 1906 the first multiple-unit suburban trains began running, followed by locomotive-hauled through trains two months later. Electric operations did not reach their planned terminals at North White Plains and Croton until 1910 and 1915, respectively. By then the New York Central had implemented a plan devised by Wilgus in 1902 for a new multilevel Grand Central Terminal.

5
.

The Great Terminal

Scientific American for January 17, 1903, showed certain features of a plan, devised the month before by William Wilgus, which included retaining the old Grand Central. The plan called for a connection between Grand Central's suburban level tracks and the new I.R.T. subway then under construction below Park Avenue. Terminal tracks would be depressed, and there would be new viaducts for the crosstown streets, which would be restored between 45th and 55th streets on girders above the tracks. Park Avenue would be extended right through the train shed, and an elevated driveway for carriages would be built within the shed for the convenience of passengers. This and various other schemes were discussed at length in the Central's boardroom. The road was under pressure from the Pennsylvania, which had announced plans to tunnel under the Hudson and bring its trains into a magnificent new station on Manhattan's West Side. If the Pennsylvania was to have what Alexander Cassatt had called a "monumental gateway to a great metropolis," how could the Central stay with its aging station? Eventually its board members decided to tear down the old train shed and headhouse, replacing them with a double-level subsurface terminal. Office quarters and revenue-producing structures would be built over the adjoining tracks.

Wilgus presented a new plan in March 1903 calling for a fifty-seven-track all-electric double-level terminal. From a single level north of 50th Street, the tracks would fan out and occupy two levels under the area between Lexington and Madison avenues. Trains would stop at 44th Street. South of 44th, extending to 41st, the terminal would need a loop. Unlike railroad stations, where trains stop to load and discharge passengers, a terminal requires a capacity to turn trains about, avoiding the time-consuming and thus costly process of reassembly. With a loop, the train is simply brought all the way around and then backed into the proper gate to take on passengers. Grand Central's lower level would have its own loop so that commuter trains could be turned round. Wilgus' 1903 plan added a few bells and whistles to his 1902 plan. An elevated north-south roadway, circumscribing the terminal structure and bridging over 42nd Street, would link upper and lower Park Avenue. North of the terminal, crossstreets and buildings would rest on steel piers above the tracks.

Preliminary estimates placed the cost at more than $43 million—perhaps $560 million in today's dollars, a staggering sum but an investment, Wilgus insisted, not an expense. He obtained approval by showing how the tremendous cost could be recovered: the Central would own Park Avenue ground and air rights above the tracks immediately north of the terminal and, by leasing them, would enjoy handsome revenues. Hotels, apartment buildings, and office towers, all supported by piers between the submerged tracks, would rise on seventeen square blocks of newly created prime Manhattan real estate. Annual rentals and other income would produce what was then considered a respectable return of more than 3 percent on the cost; operating economies and increased traffic from improved commuter service would yield further dividends. (The Central would wind up spending perhaps $180 million on the undertaking. By 1923 the improved property would be valued at about $328 million, a figure that translates into billions today.)

The Central began buying up property on Park Avenue and on June 3, 1903, presented its plans to a special committee of the city's Board of Estimate and Apportionment. Formal approval came on June 19, and construction began on July 18. By mid-August, contractors were hard at work excavating the site, knowing that the Central was engaged in a desperate race with the Pennsylvania.

For even as the New York Central was struggling to build the new terminal and its approaches, sandhogs employed by the competition were tunneling beneath the Hudson and East rivers. The city's first subway had opened in October 1904, bringing City Hall within eleven minutes of 42nd Street and Park. On October 9, 1906, while the Central was still preparing for electrification of its Park Avenue tracks, the first tunnels came together under the Hudson. They were built for commuter trains between Hoboken and Manhattan's Greenwich Village, where they veered northward under Sixth Avenue to a station at 33rd Street. Brooklyn and Manhattan were linked by a tunnel in December 1906, when the first underwater subway line was completed from Bowling Green to Joralemon Street, reducing the need for East River ferryboats. Scarcely seventy-five years after getting their first public transit, twenty-eight years after the first El, two years after the first subway, New Yorkers were demanding rapid transit without overhead clatter.

When the Pennsylvania Station opened on September 8, 1910, only the section serving the Long Island Rail Road was operative. Full service began on

November 27. Eighty-nine trains left the station that day, forty-three headed east for Long Island, forty-six west to other parts of America. The station had three levels: one for tracks and platforms, another for subway lines and for the Long Island Rail Road concourse and ticket offices, a third for the general concourse and main waiting room. All three levels were below the street; and although the pattern of walkways, exit ramps, and stairways was sometimes confusing, this was the world's first station designed to separate incoming and outgoing traffic. The exit concourse, built between the main concourse and the train platforms, ensured uninterupted movement. At the northern end below 33rd Street, a separate waiting room with ticket offices and other facilities spared Long Island commuters unneccesary encounters with long-distance travelers.

Long-distance passengers emerged onto platforms from which great steel girders rose to support vaulting glass roofs. The passenger concourse had a coffered ceiling 150 feet high with skylights to bathe it in natural light. A lunchroom and formal dining room flanked the grand staircase. There were separate men's and ladies' waiting rooms and a changing room where a traveler could rent a small chamber with toilet facilities enclosed by glass partitions and supplied with soap, towels, and a silver-handled whiskbroom. A man could change into formal wear for dinner or theater, check his bag, and emerge feeling like a gentleman.

Outside, eighty-four Doric columns, thirty-five feet high, supported the building's classic architrave. A glorious granite and travertine edifice, Penn Station was designed by McKim, Mead & White along the lines of the tepidarium, or warm room, in ancient Rome's Baths of Caracalla. Alexander Cassatt (brother of the impressionist painter Mary Cassatt) did not live to see the great station inaugurated, but it was he who had been persuaded of the railroad's obligation to give New York a monumental gateway instead of using its air rights to erect a hotel.

When work began on Penn Station in 1906, Daniel H. Burnham, the Chicago architect responsible for New York's Flatiron Building (1902), was completing Union Station at Washington, D.C., having modeled it on the Baths of Diocletian and the Arch of Constantine. Classical splendor was in vogue, and the new Grand Central could not afford to be merely utilitarian. But as preparations got underway, engineering took initial priority over architecture. Burnham had drawn up plans that would carry out Wilgus' ideas. So had McKim, Mead & White (Stanford White's plan called for a 700-foot office tower with a 300-foot jet of steam issuing from the top, illuminated at night by red lights to serve as a beacon to mariners; the plan was modified only slightly for the thirty-five-story Municipal Building at Centre Street). When the New York Central announced the winner of its competition, however, the small St. Paul firm of Reed & Stem was awarded the prized contract. The Central had stipulated that Park Avenue traffic must flow freely through the property. Where other architects' designs had called for street-level tunnels punched through the terminal, Reed & Stem devised an "elevated circumferential plaza" that took traffic by ramp around the building's periphery. The system of interior ramps, obviating any need to climb stairs, was also Charles Reed's idea. And he wanted a skylight roof high above the main arrival room.

As John Tauranac has so nicely put it, "He wanted them to know that they had indeed arrived when they got to Grand Central. That they were somewhere. He had gotten there by being Wilgus's brother-in-law." May Reed, Charles's sister, had married Wilgus in 1892. But if Wilgus had an architect in the family, so did William K. Vanderbilt—grandson of the Commodore and chairman of the board of the New York Central & Hudson River Railroad. Whitney Warren, senior partner of Warren & Whitmore, was his cousin and also a close friend. Born in 1864, he had trained in France from 1885 to 1894, worked for a few years for McKim, Mead & White, and in 1898 formed a partnership with Charles D. Wetmore, a lawyer who had engaged him to design a country house. Warren & Wetmore was best known for the fanciful New York Yacht Club building completed in West 44th Street in 1899. The firm had gone on to design elegant townhouses.

So Warren & Wetmore was charged with the responsibility of design, while Reed & Stem was left with the formidable engineering problems. Traffic at the station had grown to more than 1,000 train and switching movements per day. The Central purchased additional land and secured underground rights from the city in order to widen the suburban station under Vanderbilt Avenue and Depew Place. The site was eventually increased from twenty-three to almost forty-eight acres, and construction required blasting a two-level terminal gallery out of Manhattan's granite. The old station had to be demolished and a new structure erected in its place without interrupting regular train operations.

The excavation was anywhere from twenty-three to forty-six feet deep, as much as two blocks wide, and a half mile long. Nearly two million cubic yards of rock and more than a million cubic yards of earth had to be dug or blasted from the site. The excavation between 42nd and 50th streets extended from Lexington Avenue all or most of the way to Madison. The terminal approaches occupied an excavation under Park Avenue between 50th and 57th streets. Day after day, year after year, 400 carloads of rock and earth had to be carried from the site every day.

From four at 57th Street, the tracks would fan out to ten at 55th Street, more than two dozen by 49th. A gradually sloping ramp would carry suburban trains down to the lower level. In all, the terminal would accommodate more than 1,100 cars, over three times as many as the old Grand Central Station. Loops at the inner end of both levels would permit inbound trains to turn and clear the terminal quickly after discharging passengers. Terminal yards on both levels would extend north to 50th Street, more than 2,000 feet from 42nd Street, while ten approach tracks would fan out from the four tracks of the Park Avenue tunnel at 57th Street.

Where Penn Station and its approaches occupied twenty-five acres, Grand Central and its yards would take up seventy. Instead of sixteen miles of track it would have 33.7, including those in its yards. Instead of eleven platforms, as at Penn Station, it would have forty-eight—thirty-one on the upper level, seventeen on the lower, and 123 tracks—sixty-six on the upper level, fifty-seven on the lower. London's Waterloo Station, the Hauptbahnhoff at Dresden, the Gare St. Lazare in Paris—nothing in the world came close.

Warren discarded some of Reed's ideas, including the elevated driveway and Park Avenue Court of Honor. Instead of Reed's system of interior ramps, Warren wanted stairways. But in 1909 the plans were again substantially revised—by some accounts, at the insistence of the New Haven Railroad, whose agreement with the Harlem gave it a strong voice in matters concerning the terminal. All the basic features of the original Reed design, including interior ramps and circumferential driveway, were restored. Provision was made for the addition at a later date of office buildings at the four corners (each corner of the terminal has a bank of four elevators for a structure that was never erected) and for a Park Avenue Court of Honor.

In 1911 the Central (whose officers must have recalled the fatal accident of 1902) claimed it needed natural light to illuminate the yards north of the terminal; it was not going to cover the medians along Park Avenue below 50th Street. Local property owners pointed out that the yards below the projected buildings would be in darkness anyway. The Central then concluded that natural light was expendable. Property values on the periphery of the development were rising at a rate of 25 percent a year; the Central decided that its own property would be enhanced even more if the money was spent to cover the medians and create an unbroken promenade.

Charles Reed died in 1911 and Whitney Warren tried, without much success, to have the plans for the terminal changed yet again. (Reed's original plan had called for a tall office building above the terminal. After his death, Warren & Wetmore was awarded an exclusive contract for completing the work. Allen Stem, the surviving partner, sued over distribution of the fee and was awarded $400,000 in a 1921 settlement.)

Warren's design for the terminal has been called Beaux Arts eclectic. He employed Stony Creek granite from Connecticut and Bedford limestone from Indiana for the exterior, setting off the principal facade, on 42nd Street, with three great arched windows, each thirty-three feet wide and nearly sixty feet high. Much of the city still lay to the south of 42nd Street, so it was natural enough that Warren's grandiose facade should face south. He conceived it as a triumphal arch, crowned by a sculptural group. Jules-Alexis Coutan was engaged to sculpt three mythological Roman deities in Bedford limestone. The group is sixty feet wide, stands fifty feet high, and weighs 1,500 tons. The figures are flanked by Doric columns, and their significance was explained by Whitney Warren: "The architectural composition consists of three great portals crowned by a sculptural group, the whole to stand as a monument to the glory of commerce as typified by Mercury, supported by moral and mental energy—Hercules and Minerva—all to attest that this great enterprise has grown and exists not merely from the wealth expended, nor by the revenue derived, but by the brain and brawn concentrated upon its development for nearly a century." Surmounting the statuary group is a huge clock, thirteen feet in diameter; the

VI at the bottom, inverted to the eye of the man in the street, opens like a window.

William Wilgus was no longer with the Central when the great terminal for which he had pushed so hard finally opened. He had resigned in 1907 after a dispute with a vice-president of the road over responsibility for an accident. At midnight on Saturday, February 1, 1913, Grand Central's doors were thrown open to the public. A waiting crowd of about 3,000 rushed in, and sightseers jammed the building all day Sunday. Entering the terminal at 42nd Street and Park, they passed under the clock, descended a ramp into a three-story waiting room about 3.5 feet below street level, descended another ramp, and emerged into the great concourse, about eight feet below street level, with a barrel-vaulted ceiling 125 feet overhead. The enormous room now has fourteen entrances. Dull would he be of soul, Wordsworth would have said, who did not thrill at being within so magnificent a space.

Grand Central's main concourse is 470 feet long and 160 feet wide. It is illuminated by daylight flooding in through three gigantic windows at each end, facing Depew Place and Vanderbilt Avenue, and through five graceful clerestory lunettes set in the curve of the vaulted ceiling on each side. The soft, natural light gives the passenger concourse a quiet dignity, and nothing is permitted to interrupt that light. Catwalks between the inner and outer glass of each window are of smoked glass, lighted by fifty-watt bulbs, contributing to the subtle, soothing effect.

BELOW: *Grand Central's sculptured gods above 42nd Street* (1988 photo)

ABOVE: *Natural light illuminates the concourse* (1988 photo)

Illumination at night is from huge bronze chandeliers and from indirect lighting fixtures around the base of the vaulted ceiling. Twenty feet above the concourse floor, which is paved with Tennessee marble, a thirty-foot-wide balcony extends along three walls (excepting the south one). Walls are covered by a replica of the warm, buff-colored Caen stone with wainscots and trimmings of cocoa-colored Botticino marble. A circular information booth surmounted by a four-faced golden clock is set down in the center of the concourse at what once was the exact center of the intersection of Park Avenue and 43rd Street. Hecla Iron and Bronze Works furnished the bronze screens, bronze-and-iron window frames and railings, and iron elevator fronts, marquees, and train gates. Like Rome's Spanish Steps, the grand staircase diverges between the Vanderbilt Avenue and main concourse levels, comes together again, and then diverges once more as it descends to the suburban passenger concourse. This grand staircase from the west balcony has also been compared with that of the Paris Opéra completed in 1875.

Looking up twelve stories to Grand Central's concourse ceiling, one sees such symbols of travel as wheels, anchors, ropes, and wings—although nobody in 1913 dreamed that wings would one day supplant railroad tracks for long-distance travel. The "carvings" above the lunette windows are actually of terra-cotta, stamped out of molds. Although Reed & Stem's design called for a skylight roof over the concourse, Warren threw out that idea and commissioned a French society artist, Paul Helleu, to create a painting for the ceiling. The great astronomical mural, painted in gold on cerulean blue tempera, followed Helleu's design of the Mediterranean winter sky. It includes some 2,500 stars, of which the sixty largest mark constellations illuminated from behind with ten-watt bulbs in an adjustable lighting system that gives them the correct celestial magnitude. Confusing to amateur astronomers, the section of the zodiac depicted by the mural is backward. This was noticed after the terminal opened, and flustered officials were obliged to explain that Helleu had followed a medieval manuscript on which the heavens were depicted as they would be seen from outside the celestial sphere.

In the terminal's first half-century its lower level was strictly for commuters. This suburban level opened in October 1912, four months before the rest of the terminal. The separate concourse for the lower level was placed immediately below its upper-level counterpart and, except for its low ceiling, was just as large. Its ticket offices, baggage, and parcel rooms, and information booth were installed in locations corresponding to those on the upper level. Directly beneath the main waiting room, between the upper and lower level, was the Oyster Bar. Its cream-colored, grotto-like terra-cotta tiled vaults, and those in the corridors outside, were installed by the Spanish architect Rafael Guastavino, whose method of construction, combining concrete and masonry, had been used since the 1890s for public buildings such as Carnegie Hall.

The terminal's waiting rooms were said to be able to accommodate 5,000 persons. At either end of the main waiting room off 42nd Street were separate men's and women's waiting rooms and lavatories. The women's waiting room at the east end, finished in quartered oak, included such amenities as a hairdressing salon. A barbershop, shoeshine stand, baths, and private dressing rooms were situated near the men's smoking room.

Since incoming trains discharge passengers all at once, whereas outgoing trains must be parked while passengers board with their luggage, only five or six tracks were needed for incoming passengers from distant points, as compared with some forty tracks for outgoing passengers. Incoming passengers used to arrive at a point near Vanderbilt Avenue and 44th Street through gates that led into the "kissing gallery," so called because passengers were greeted in this room by friends and loved ones. From here, a corridor extended up to Madison Avenue and 46th Street. One could, in fact, walk underground from 46th and Madison to 40th and Third, a distance of over half a mile. Off the "kissing gallery" was an entrance to the original four-track I.R.T. subway line, which went along 42nd Street en route from City Hall, up Fourth and lower Park avenues, to the upper West Side. At the lowest level was the Manhattan end of the Steinway tunnels, a trolley line under the East River to Queens that finally opened in 1915 as part of the I.R.T. Close at hand to the "kissing gallery" is a ramp leading up to the street, and a taxi stand. Everything was designed for the convenience of passengers. When people left New York at Grand Central, they had only to walk a block and a half from 42nd Street to reach their train gate. Arriving, they could

ABOVE: *Commuters now use the upper level, once reserved for long-distance travelers*
(1988 photo)

have a redcap carry their bags a few yards to a taxi or hotel—by 1914 the Biltmore was right upstairs—without climbing stairs.

Private dressing rooms were available so that suburbanites could change into evening dress, and beginning in 1923 one exurbanite couple, Mr. and Mrs. John W. Campbell, who lived in the outermost edges of Westchester, maintained a luxurious duplex apartment off the terminal's west balcony. Campbell was a jade collector who operated a credit-rating service that later became part of Dun & Bradstreet. His elegantly furnished drawing room with its two-story cathedral ceiling, walnut paneling, oak floors, leaded glass windows, and vast fireplace doubled for years as an office during the day; his wife could take the train into town to entertain friends there. (In recent times the bedroom has served as an office for the terminal's police superintendent, and the wine cellar has been used as a holding pen for five to ten suspects per day.) Outside the police headquarters is the marble-walled lobby of 15 Vanderbilt Avenue, graced with a bronze staircase. The lobby, one of the phantom four at the terminal's corners, today serves tennis players and police officers. Two tennis courts upstairs occupy a thirty-foot-high attic running the length of the terminal's south side, space originally intended for a ballroom (it was used in the 1950s for CBS television studios). The courts may be rented by anyone with the wherewithal—the hourly charge in the late 1980s was $75—although corporate users tend to reserve the choice weekday hours.

Above the main waiting room, open to the north light (there was nothing yet to obstruct it), Grand Central had an art gallery (the Grand Central Galleries moved out in 1953 and later took space in West 57th Street, keeping the old name). With its photographic studio, clubrooms, meeting rooms, a theater, and an emergency hospital with a physician in attendance, the terminal was intended to be the linchpin for a monumental complex of office buildings, hotels, and apartment houses of similar style, all to be built above the tracks of the New York Central Railroad.

By 1920 Grand Central's annual passenger traffic reached more than 37 million, up from little more than 20 million in 1910. No one could have realized in April 1917 that the newly opened Connecting Railroad, linking Penn Station with New England, would mean the eventual demise of Grand Central as a long-distance rail terminal. But even as that function faded, Grand Central would grow in importance as a commuter terminal, pedestrian shortcut, meeting place, and convenience center in what was rapidly becoming the very heart of New York. Its underground walkway system would come to serve twenty-one different buildings. Without ever emerging above ground, one could reach buildings as far south as 41st Street, as far north as 46th, and along three blocks of 42nd Street from Third Avenue to Madison.

Most of these buildings were heated by the New York Steam Company, a Con Edison subsidiary whose customers were spared from having to maintain their own heating plants. There was no space under Park Avenue buildings in the 40s and 50s for furnaces, boilers, and fuel storage, but thanks to New York Steam they could dispense with such facilities and still have heat and hot water.

Within about fifteen years of Grand Central's opening, an array of prestigious buildings had sprung up on railroad-owned property—the Commodore, Barclay, Biltmore, Chatham, and Park Lane hotels, eleven office buildings, ten apartment houses, and a private club. If none quite matched the grandiose vision of Warren & Wetmore, they were nevertheless beginning to give Park Avenue a glow of luxury. The economic theory of William Wilgus had become economic reality.

Reed & Stem's original drawings called for a twenty-story tower on the 42nd Street side. To the north, cornice lines on Park Avenue were to be restricted to the height of the terminal, with tall buildings rising from setbacks. And for a few years, the roof of the tunnel north to 57th was a pedestrian mall, with no vehicular traffic whatever. A narrow lane for motorcars laid down on either side of the avenue, would not be widened until 1927, when Grand Central's terminal loop tracks would finally be completed on both levels. The elevated roadways that carry Park Avenue traffic around the terminal building would not be entirely finished until 1929. By that time the avenue's roadways would have been widened for most of its length, and traffic would already be thick with Rolls-Royces, Duesenbergs, Packards, Hispano-Suizas, and Pierce-Arrows.

6
.

Mansions for the Mighty

NEW YORKERS of means lived almost without exception in private houses until well after the turn of the century. Why does Fifth Avenue now have so many more big, ugly, modern apartment houses than Park Avenue? Because Fifth Avenue still had so many mansions after World War II. When altered circumstances—smaller families, higher taxes, costly servants—made such palaces no longer viable, they were pulled down. Beautifully crafted apartment buildings of lavish dimensions had replaced mansions on the avenue; after the war such construction was no longer affordable. At the zenith of Fifth Avenue's fashionability, Park Avenue was just emerging from its ignoble past as a noisy, malodorous location; it was still déclassé. Park Avenue houses came down much earlier than did most of those on Fifth, so they were replaced for the most part when building standards were still high. There are, to be sure, some jarring anachronisms in the residential blocks, but few of them replaced fine private residences. However bland these blocks may appear, their generally homogeneous look of solidity and security dates mostly to the second and third decades of the twentieth century.

Although Park Avenue has little to match the most glorious Fifth Avenue relics (none of them any longer private residences), it once had many splendid private dwellings and still has some quite respectable survivors. The oldest of the best is 23 Park, northeast corner 35th Street, a stately brick and terra-cotta Italian Renaissance mansion designed by Stanford White and finished in 1898 for James Hampden Robb, a retired banker and cotton trader who had served briefly as state senator, president of the Park Board, and president of the Union

Club but had declined an appointment as assistant secretary of state in the Cleveland administration in 1887. This is the only true Stanford White house on Park Avenue and one of the few anywhere. When the Advertising Club, which occupied the premises from 1923 to 1977, took over the place, a local minister made a speech to the members, saying, "Save as much of White as possible. He had a wonderful sense of proportion. There is something about a house where he had a free hand that gives you a special feeling of comfort. That's why I say . . . that I would rather have a Stanford White house than a painting by Rembrandt." Alas, the house was divided into a fifteen-unit cooperative in the late 1970s, and although the apartments have fifteen- and even eighteen-foot ceilings (a two-bedroom duplex was advertised in 1988 at more than $600,000), a certain amount of White was no doubt lost.

Robb, the Robert Bacons, and other residents of Fourth and lower Park avenues endured the building of the city's first subway between 1900 and 1904. (Not until 1918 would upper East Siders get their Lexington Avenue subway.) The subway ran through tunnels deeper than the trenches dug on the upper part of the avenue by Commodore Vanderbilt's engineers and made the area south of Grand Central conveniently accessible to upper Broadway. Within less than a mile and a half there were two express stations—one at 14th and one at 42nd—and four local stations—at 18th, 23rd, 28th, and 33rd streets. The rush to build on upper Broadway sparked by the subway had no immediate counterpart in the 20s and 30s. In the spring of 1906, Fourth Avenue and Park below 42nd Street were substantially the same as they had been twenty years earlier. Not until six months later did Fourth Avenue finally begin to blossom, and what went up were not private houses but commercial structures and apartment buildings. While some apartment houses were going up in the Murray Hill area and a few north of Grand Central, rich East Siders still preferred private houses. The new ones were of brick and limestone (brownstone had passed out of favor), and quite a few were on Park Avenue.

Electrification of the tracks below encouraged construction of town houses on upper Park. Within months of the legislation requiring electrification, U.S. Secretary of War (Secretary of State after 1905) Elihu Root filed plans to build a house on Park at 71st Street. The real building boom began in the months before September 30, 1906, when an electric locomotive pulled the first train out of the old Grand Central Station. In the next six years more than a dozen big houses went up in the area between Lenox Hill and what was now being called Carnegie Hill after the big mansion at Fifth Avenue and 91st Street.

The *Real Estate Record* editorialized on the subject in its June 30, 1906, issue: "Many fine private houses are now being built on the upper East Side from Madison to Third between 60th and 73rd, now fast emerging into what may be called an aristocratic residential section. The growth and development of the district in question was undoubtedly aided by Secretary of State Root's purchase a few years ago of the old flats at the southeast corner of Park Avenue and 71st Street. On the site of these flats he built a handsome house, and the result has been to improve the character and tone of the neighborhood. Others have now followed Secretary Root's example and doubtless in a few years the transformation that has taken place will be little short of startling to those who are familiar with the surroundings a decade ago. There will be tearing down, improvements, building, and rebuilding all over this section during the summer and autumn. It is being done exclusively by private individuals who wish to make their homes here and join the colony of prominent persons who live in the immediate vicinity. These include some of New York's wealthiest and most eminent citizens, which fact alone will make the section a fashionable and restricted quarter for many years to come."

Carrère & Hastings designed the Elihu Root house, completed in 1905, in a chaste English Regency style. Secretary Root leased his house soon after its completion to Paul Morton, then president of Equitable Life. Sold in 1909, it changed hands a few times before 1970, when it was replaced by 733 Park. Especially favored as a site for mansions was Lenox Hill, and 70th Street ran along its crest. In 1907, 100 East 70th Street, designed by Delano & Aldrich for the young banker Robert S. Brewster and his wife, Mabel (*née* Tremain), was finished. Brewster, who became president of the Metropolitan Opera, died in the house on Christmas Eve, 1939 (715 Park replaced it in 1949).

The southwest corner of 70th and Park was part of the grounds of the Union

BELOW: *Elihu Root's 1905 house by Carrère & Hastings inspired others to build Park Avenue mansions* (photo courtesy Museum of the City of New York)

Theological Seminary; that institution moved in 1908 to Morningside Heights and in 1910 sold its property to George Blumenthal, Susan Vanderpoel Clark, Arthur Curtis James, Anna Louise Poor, and Elisha Walker. Blumenthal was a German-born investment banker. When he became senior partner of Lazard Frères in 1904, he lived, Christopher Gray has written, "in an exquisite French Renaissance townhouse in West 53rd Street." (The house served in later years as the bookstore of the Museum of Modern Art until it was replaced by the Museum Tower.) "Congestion in midtown," Gray says, "impelled [Blumenthal] to build in East 70th Street only ten years after finishing the 53rd Street house. Trowbridge & Livingston produced a very severe Italian renaissance mansion." Finished in 1911, Blumenthal's house was the city's first private residence with its own swimming pool.

Blumenthal was president of the Metropolitan Museum of Art at the time of his death in 1941. Ten years earlier, he and the other original purchasers of the seminary grounds had registered an agreement that only one-family residences could occupy the blockfront until after February 1, 1936; a supplemental agreement made the restriction subject to the exception that any party might transfer any parcel to the Met for museum purposes. Blumenthal had an impressive collection of Renaissance enamels and canvases that included more than one El Greco. It had been his intention to leave the museum enough money to operate his home as a branch of the museum, but realizing that no one could anticipate how much would be required to maintain such a bequest, he made a final will leaving his house to the discretion of the museum trustees. They adopted most of the art and salvaged the patio with its huge fountain. The forty-four-foot-high Spanish patio may still be seen near the main stairway of the Metropolitan, where it was installed in 1964. Except for this souvenir, the house has vanished without a trace (it was replaced by 710 Park in 1948), as have most of the avenue's private residences.

The other great house in the block, completed in 1914, was that of Arthur Curtiss James at the northwest corner of 69th Street and Park. James was the forty-seven-year-old railroad magnate whose grandfather, Daniel James, had established the family fortune with mining ventures in the southwest. D. Willis James, Daniel's son, had financed the railroad ventures of James J. Hill, builder of the Great Northern and Canadian Pacific. Enhancing his patrimony, Arthur Curtiss James created a network of rails that extended from Chicago to California and accounted for nearly 15 percent of all the track in the United States. His house, designed by Allen & Collens and covered in Knoxville gray marble, was James's home until his death in 1941. It was replaced by 700 Park in 1959.

Quite a few Park Avenue houses went up in the years before World War I. A private residence designed by Hunt & Hunt for Amos R. E. Pinchot was finished in 1910 at the northeast corner of 85th Street. Pinchot, a lawyer, was the brother of Gifford, the conservationist who superintended the 119,000 acres of forest that surrounded Biltmore House, designed by Richard Morris Hunt for William Henry Vanderbilt's youngest son, George Washington, and completed in 1896. Gifford headed the U.S. Forest Service but was fired by President Taft after joining others in charging the Secretary of the Interior, Richard A. Ballinger, with conflict of interest—a cause celèbre in 1910. The Pinchot house was later occupied under lease by Mrs. Alfred Gwynne Vanderbilt, Vincent Astor, and Joseph C. Baldwin before being purchased by Edward R. Stettinius, a J. P. Morgan partner, who occupied it until his death in the late 1920s. It was replaced in 1930 by 1021 Park.

Oakleigh Thorne's house, at the northeast corner of 73rd Street, was finished in 1911. Four years earlier, and six years before the Sixteenth Amendment made a federal income tax constitutional, Thorne, a Quaker, had purchased the Commerce Clearing House, which would explain Internal Revenue Service language and would make him and his heirs among the nation's top fifty taxpayers. Originally designed by Albert Joseph Bodker in an Italian manner with tile roof, Thorne's house was scaled down and given a French style to complement some rooms and furniture acquired by Mrs. Thorne. It was replaced in 1940 by 785 Park.

A Modern Renaissance house was completed in 1911 at 600 Park, northwest corner 64th Street, for Jonathan Bulkley of Bulkley Dunton & Co., a papermaking firm founded by Bulkley's father in 1833. James Gamble Rogers designed the palatial white house, which replaced a row house and a small apartment house dating to 1879; Rogers made it seem misleadingly modest in size, as if to look askance at the pretentiousness of the Beaux Arts style then in vogue. The Swedish government acquired 600 Park in 1947 as a residence for its consul general, but there is rarely even a Swedish flag to suggest what this splendid structure might be.

Murray Hill was more appealing in 1909 to the socialite Adelaide L. Townsend Douglas, whose husband William Proctor Douglas was vice-commodore of the New York Yacht Club. She engaged Horace Trumbauer to design 57 Park, a Louis XVI-style house that is now home to the Guatemalan Permanent Mission to the United Nations. It was finished in 1911, the year after Mrs. Douglas obtained a divorce.

As mansions transformed certain blocks to the north, open railyards still dominated the avenue immediately above Grand Central. Then, on April 2, 1912, the *New York Times* carried a small front-page item: PARK AVENUE BARRIER DOWN. FIRST VEHICLES IN 40 YEARS CROSS AT 51ST STREET. As the following chapter will show, luxury apartment houses went up side by side with the single-family houses for the rich that rose on upper Park Avenue before World War I. New houses of worship were also erected. There had been churches on the avenue since at least the 1870s. The first to be finished in the twentieth century was South Reformed Church (later called the Park Avenue Christian Church), completed in 1911 one block north of St. Ignatius Loyola on the southwest corner of 85th Street. Cram, Goodhue & Ferguson of Boston were the architects, and soon afterward Bertram Grosvenor Goodhue designed St. Bartholomew's Episcopal Church for the easterly blockfront between 51st and 52nd streets. The avenue had no church for more than a mile north of 42nd Street until St. Bartholomew's opened for services in October 1918. This was the city's third

ABOVE: *Former Jonathan Bulkley house at 600 Park* (1989 photo)

St. Bart's; the second, designed by James Renwick, Jr., had opened in 1872 on Madison Avenue at 44th Street, where William Henry Vanderbilt had offered property at a concessionary price. Along with Vanderbilts, the congregation at that time included William D. Sloane (who was married to William Henry Vanderbilt's daughter Emily), Henry Clay Frick, and Charles W. Harkness. Cornelius Vanderbilt II, who, together with Chauncey Depew, effectively ran the New York Central after the death of William Henry, was a major contributor to St. Bart's; and when he died suddenly at age fifty-five in 1899 his widow, Alice, gave the church an ornamental porch as a memorial. Stanford White designed it, and the seated figure of Christ above its main portal was sculpted by Daniel Chester French. The land beneath the church, however, was soft clay rather than good Manhattan schist, and by 1914 St. Bart's was sinking; it would have to be replaced. Completion of Grand Central Terminal a block to the east had boosted land values in the area, so the church was able to obtain a handsome price. With the money it purchased the Park Avenue blockfront site of the F. and M. Schaefer brewery and seven old dwellings. The presence of the brewery had discouraged development of the neighborhood; its replacement with a church and rectory was regarded as a boon to real estate interests. (Aromas from Jacob Ruppert's brewery, built in 1915 to the east of Third Avenue at 92nd Street, would drift over upper Park Avenue for more than half a century. No such pollution would annoy noses to the south.) Schaefer built a new brewery in Brooklyn, and St. Bart's engaged Goodhue* to design a third church edifice. Well known for the Gothic design of St. Thomas Episcopal Church on the northwest corner of Fifth Avenue and 53rd Street, Goodhue was now moving into his Byzantine period. As Brent C. Brolin has written, he submitted a neo-Byzantine design for the main body of the church and three proposals: "One . . . included an income-producing apartment building next to the church. Another . . . used only the front half of the site, so the two lots on the side streets could be sold off. A third plan, the one that carried the day, used the entire site for the church and its architectural accoutrements."

Mrs. Vanderbilt paid to have her husband's memorial, with the triple portal designed by Stanford White, moved to the site of the new St. Bart's. Still legible on its bronze doors is the legend, "TO THE GLORY OF GOD, AND IN LOVING MEMORY OF CORNELIUS VANDERBILT." Completion was delayed until several varieties of marble could arrive from Europe after the war. The new church was dedicated in 1923; Goodhue died in 1924; his community house, terrace, and garden were finished in 1927; and the dome over his sanctuary was finally installed in 1930, by which time Park Avenue was well built-up with apartment buildings. Fifty years later the church and its community house would be sitting on land surrounded by commercial skyscapers instead of residential buildings, and its rector, vestry, and parishioners would be locked in combat over the future of this valuable site.

Reginald de Koven, a popular composer best known for his 1890 light opera

---

*Goodhue's own house, a brownstone renovation completed in 1909 with gothicizing elements of brick and limestone, was just off Park Avenue at 106 East 74th Street.

St. Bartholomew's Church (1989 photo)

Robin Hood and his song "Oh, Promise Me," engaged John Russell Pope to design a sixty-foot house for him just north of the Amos Pinchot house on the east side of Park between 85th and 86th streets. Pinchot had bought the property to protect his own house from commercial encroachment and had resold it to de Koven. Finished in 1913, de Koven's Elizabethan-style mansion contained a "Great Hall" with a double-story stone mantel; a plaster ceiling which replicated that of the Reindeer Inn at Banbury, England; and a carved oak screen and minstrel gallery modeled on one in the Great Hall at Hatfield House; two large bay windows overlook Park Avenue. The house has long since been converted into apartments.

At the northeast corner of 70th Street (723 Park), just south of the Elihu Root house (by then the Carll Tucker house), Gerrish Milliken in 1916 bought three brownstones built in the early 1880s, when the avenue north of 42nd Street was still Fourth and residents had to endure the noise and fumes of passing trains (although here on Lenox Hill they passed somewhat farther below the surface). The houses had been designed by John G. Prague. Milliken (who would become head of the textile house Deering Milliken in 1920 upon the death of his father, Seth Milliken) put the three together to create a single, large, rambling house that would survive until the late 1970s. Milliken & Co. would by that time be the world's largest privately owned textile firm; Gerrish Milliken II and his brother Roger would be among America's fifty richest men. The Milliken house was replaced by the Asia Society building. The Society occupies an eight-story pink granite structure by Edward Larrabee Barnes containing an auditorium, two galleries, a reference library, and offices. John D. Rockefeller III founded the Society in 1956 to educate America about Asia's countries and cultures, and he gave about one quarter of the $21 million or so that the new building cost. His widow officiated at the groundbreaking ceremonies in 1979, and it opened to the public in October 1981.

Shorter-lived than the Milliken house was one at the northeast corner of Park and 69th Street, a double house designed by McKim, Mead & White for Geraldyn Redmond and the Countess de Laugier Villars and completed in 1915 (it was replaced by the Union Club in the early 1930s). And in 1917 what Robert A. M. Stern has called "one of the last large corner houses constructed in Manhattan" was completed at the northwest corner of Park and 79th Street for John Sherman Hoyt. Its architect was I. N. Phelps Stokes, and its style combined Tudor with what Stern calls "contemporary college Gothic." This house, later occupied by the aerial photography pioneer Sherman M. Fairchild, stood until the early 1970s, when it was replaced by 900 Park. By then most of its contemporaries were long gone.

Spurring construction of impressive mansions in the first decades of the

LEFT: *Stanford White's "Vanderbilt Portal" links St. Bart's to the avenue* (1989 photo)   RIGHT: *Detail of Asia Society building* (1989 photo)

century was the perception that Park Avenue was becoming a desirable residential area, convenient to transportation yet quiet, and—most important—still affordable. Most of the private houses have long since been replaced by apartment buildings. 750 Park, southwest corner 72nd Street, replaced Frank B. Wiborg's house at 756 Park, acquired early in 1925 from the stockbroker Hamilton Fish Benjamin. Wiborg had joined with Levi Addison Ault of Cincinnati in the 1880s to form Ault & Wiborg, which soon was the world's largest maker of printing inks. Wiborg sold out to Ault in 1909 and moved east. He still owned the Park Avenue house at the time of his death in 1935.

Still standing are the Percy R. Pyne house at 680 Park (1911), the Lewis G. Morris House at the southeast corner of Park and 85th Street (1914), the Henry P. Davison house at 690 Park (1917), the George F. Baker house (originally the Francis F. Palmer house) at the northwest corner of 93rd Street (1918, enlarged in 1928), the William D. Sloane house at 686 Park (1918), the Harold I. Pratt house at the southwest corner of Park and 68th Street (1920), the Thomas A. Howell house (later the Ray Blakeman house) at 603 Park (1920), and the Oliver D. Filley house at 684 Park (1926). Most of these now have other names, most have other functions; all were originally private homes for the very rich.

Percy Rivington Pyne II, for whom McKim, Mead & White built the handsome red brick house at the northwest corner of Park and 68th Street, was a

BELOW: *Former Pyne-Filley-Sloane houses* (1989 photo)

banker who would no doubt have been astonished to find his elegant mansion occupied by Chinese diplomats and then by the Soviet mission to the United Nations. The house was sold by the Taiwan government in 1947 to the Soviet consul general; and it was here, on the afternoon of September 21, 1962, that Premier Nikita Khrushchev stepped out onto the second-floor balcony to hold two impromptu press conferences.

Three other Federal- and Georgian-style mansions extend north from the old Pyne house, filling the blockfront to 69th Street. Oliver D. Filley, whose house at 684 Park occupied property that had been Pyne's garden, was the banker's son-in-law. Mrs. Mary Pyne Filley sold the house in 1944 to the Institute of Public Administration. William Douglas Sloane headed the carpet and furniture retailing concern W. & J. Sloane, founded in 1843. He died in 1915, three years before completion of the house at 686 Park. His widow, the former Emily Thorn Vanderbilt, who spent much of the year at her Berkshire estate, Elm Court, had some of the interior detailing for the Park Avenue house taken from Belton House, Grantham, England, designed by Christopher Wren. Frances Crocker Sloane sold 686 Park in 1941 to Thomas E. Murray and his wife, Marie. Murray, a prominent engineer, was the son and namesake of the famous Brooklyn inventor. In 1959 his house became the headquarters of the Italian Cultural Institute.

Henry Pomeroy Davison, whose six-story neo-Federal residence of brick and stone at 690 Park completed the quartet, was another banker. Elected a vice-president of First National Bank in 1902, he helped found Bankers Trust in 1907, served as its first president, became a partner of J. P. Morgan in 1909, and in 1917 (the year that his house was completed) was directing Red Cross relief work, sending 125 tons of food, clothing and medical supplies to twenty-five countries. The International Red Cross was Davison's brainchild. Davison bought his property from Arthur Curtiss James, who had acquired it to protect his own palatial mansion on the northwest corner. Designed by Walker & Gillette, 690 replaced three row houses in 69th Street and one on Park Avenue. It had ten master bedrooms, nine baths, sixteen servants' rooms, a large library, living, dining, and reception rooms, two elevators, and an attached garage. After Davison's death in 1923 the house was leased by Marshall Field. Davison's widow sold it in 1925 to a General Electric vice-president. Together with its neighbor, 52 East 69th Street, 690 Park was purchased by the Italian government in the summer of 1955 for a consulate.

The *New York Times* reported at the beginning of 1965 that some of the mansions in the architecturally unified blockfront from 68th Street to 69th, the so-called Pyne-Davison row, had been saved from the wrecker's ball by an unidentified buyer who had purchased them for $2 million in hopes of reselling them for institutions or consulates. A week later the buyer was identified as the Marquesa de Cuevas, *née* Margaret Strong, a granddaughter of John D. Rockefeller, who had married a Spanish grandee. She donated the Pyne house to the Center for Inter-American relations and offered the other houses for sale on condition that they all be preserved.

The Harold I. Pratt house, an English Renaissance limestone palace at 58 East 68th Street designed by Delano & Aldrich, was built for the youngest son of the Brooklyn kerosene magnate and Standard Oil stockholder Charles Pratt (whose three other sons all built houses on Brooklyn's Clinton Avenue across from their father's place); the building later became the headquarters of the Council on Foreign Relations.

Lewis Gouverneur Morris, whose neo-Federal house was completed in 1914 at the southeast corner of Park and 85th Street, was a descendant of Gouverneur Morris of Morrisania, who helped draft the Articles of Confederation; of the first governor of New Jersey; and of a signer of the Declaration of Independence, both named Lewis Morris. Lewis Gouverneur Morris was in the Harvard class of 1906, a member of the New York Stock Exchange, and a partner in the brokerage firm of Morris & Pope, organized in 1915. The firm failed in 1917 and Morris, in consequence, went to jail in 1921. When he died in 1967 at age eighty-five, his obituary in the *Times* noted that he had been "confined in $22,000 bond in White Plains from June 18, 1921, to October 5, 1921." He was "discharged as an almost insolvent debtor after petitioning the court that his only assets were clothing and other personal effects, $30 in cash, and two tennis racquets." Morris' first wife, the former Natalie Lawlor Bailey, died in 1935; he married Princess de Braganca, the former Miss Anita Stewart, in 1946, and his death occurred at Malbon, his Newport, Rhode Island, estate. The *Times* obit noted that he also maintained a residence at "1510" (it meant 1015) Park Avenue and had been a trustee of the Museum of the City of New York.

Amos Pinchot had sold Morris a lot 25' 6" x 82' with an old five-story flat on it. Morris ordered the flat razed and replaced it with a house into which the family moved from 77 Madison Avenue. Ernest Flagg, the architect for 1015, is best known for his forty-seven-story Singer Tower of 1908 at 149 Broadway, briefly the tallest building in the world and, sixty-two years later, the tallest building ever demolished. Flagg also designed the Scribner Building with the handsome bookstore that opened on Fifth Avenue in 1913 and closed, regrettably, in early 1989. Flagg's gabled brick Morris house with its five hip-roofed dormer windows has a garage in its eastern wing; the cupola on the roof covers the elevator tower. Morris' daughters sold the house in 1967 to the New World Foundation, established in 1954 to carry out the testamentary wishes of the reaper heiress Anita McCormick Blaine. The foundation is "dedicated to revitalizing the institutions of community and public life grown increasingly fragile in the face of massive loss of federal dollars and inadequate private funds." It makes grants totalling about $1.5 million per year to scores of nonprofit organizations.

New York's construction trade was booming when the Morris house went up in 1914; it was in a slump when the Pratt house was completed in 1920. The price of structural steel had reached its highest point in the century in 1916, common brick had doubled in price between 1914 and 1918, virtually all construction had ceased when America entered the war in April 1917, and the

ABOVE: *Former Lewis G. Morris house* (1989 photo)

postwar recession had discouraged any revival of activity. For people like Harold Pratt, of course, cost was not a major consideration.

Also dating to 1920 is 603 Park, designed by Lund & Gayler (Walter Lund, Julius F. Gayler) for the sugar wholesaler Thomas A. Howell and his wife, Emilia. The five-story neo-Georgian (neo-Federal, says Christopher Gray) red brick townhouse cost the Howells $65,000. It replaced 101 East 64th Street, a rowhouse built in the early 1880s. Only twenty feet deep, 603 extends 100 feet along Park Avenue. Interior rooms cluster round a skylit stone staircase, and the original furnishings included silver and gold landscape murals painted by Allyn Cox. The Howells sold 603 in 1923 to James W. Ellsworth, a retired coal mining magnate, who died of pneumonia in 1925; his son Lincoln was stranded at the time on the Arctic icecap with Roald Amundsen. Dr. James B. Murphy, who later headed cancer research at Rockefeller Institute (now Rockefeller University) leased the house in 1927 from Lincoln Ellsworth. *American Architecture of Today*, published in 1928, called 603 Park a "friendly pleasant building . . . a most interesting adaptation of the American Colonial to a long, thin site." Dr. Murphy died in 1950 and his widow married Ray S. Blakeman. Mrs. Blakeman lived there until her death in 1987; the house was still a private residence in the spring of 1989, when it was offered for sale at $20 million. By that time the only other Park Avenue houses privately occupied were 711 and 1145. There was some question whether 603 would remain private or be taken for a consulate or foundation.

Other houses completed in 1920 include 604 and 608 Park on the west side of the avenue. The first, a six-story neo-Georgian residence designed by Edson Gage for Henry Hollister Pease, replaced two narrow row houses. The house was converted to a multiple dwelling in 1943 and acquired in 1946 by the Swedish consul general and the Kingdom of Sweden. In 1947, when it bought the old Bulkley house at 600 Park, the Swedish government added to its holdings 608 Park, a four-story neo-Federal house designed by Joel D. Barber for Clara D. Bowron, who had purchased the property in 1912 and whose estate had sold the house in 1944.

Most imposing of the old Park Avenue residences still extant is at the northwest corner of 93rd Street: the former George F. Baker, Jr., house, which was donated in 1958 to the Synod of Bishops of the Russian Orthodox Church outside Russia. Its bilingual private school, St. Sergius, was started in 1959; it has enrollment of about forty and teaches the language and culture of pre-Revolutionary Russia. The squarish corner section, designed by Delano & Aldrich for Francis F. Palmer, dates to 1918. George Baker, its second owner, was president of First National Bank. That institution possessed no branches, maintained no deposits with other banks, and had no interests abroad, but enjoyed close ties to the House of Morgan. Baker and James Stillman, president of National City Bank, had helped J. P. Morgan when he acted to avert disaster in the financial panic of November 1907. Baker acquired 1188 to 1190 Park from the L. F. Von Ohlsen estate in 1927 and had Delano & Aldrich design an L-shaped ballroom wing that began on Park, north of the original house, wrapped around it, and ended at 93rd Street, creating a large open courtyard and ceremonial entrance. In 1931 Baker had 67 East 93rd Street built for his father. The younger Baker was a director of the New York Central; beneath his huge Federal Revival and Georgian-style house at 75 East 93rd Street was a special siding for his private railway car.

By 1965, when a "French Provincial" town house was built for the banker Paul Mellon in East 70th Street between Park and Lexington avenues (perhaps the last private house built in Manhattan), Manhattanites living in single-family houses were few and far between. In the mid-1970s Hartz Mountain chief Leonard N. Stern, not yet a billionaire, bought a former carriage house at 870A Park, just south of 78th Street, and had a modern facade designed for him (Robert A. M. Stern and John Hagmann), but that was the last gasp. Where tenements and boardinghouses had once sheltered the vast majority of New Yorkers, all but a few now lived in apartment buildings. Even the very rich now occupied apartments rather than private mansions.

The city's first luxury apartment house had been the Dakota (1884) on Central Park West at 72nd Street. Impressive in its own way but far less grand was the Yosemite, a cooperative (the Dakota was a rental building) designed by McKim, Mead & White that opened in 1891 at 550 Park and was replaced in

LEFT: *For sale: former Thomas A. Howell house, offered in 1989 at $20 million* (1989 photo)   RIGHT: *Former George F. Baker house* (1989 photo)

the 1920s. Before World War I most of the city's best apartments were still on the upper West Side; by the 1960s, when Paul Mellon built his house, West Side apartments were generally considered less desirable than those on Park Avenue, which had had no true luxury apartment house at all before 1910 but which now had few rivals.

7

Debut of the Doorman

IT WAS UNREALISTIC, of course, to think that an avenue lined with tenements, row houses, institutions, and factories would somehow become a boulevard of private mansions. As early as the spring of 1906 the *Real Estate Record* noted that "the development of Park Avenue above Fifty-ninth street will bear watching during the next few years. When the New York Central announced that it was going to run electric instead of steam cars through the tunnel, it was generally supposed that the avenue would become available as a site for expensive residences and certain lots were bought and one or two houses were built on that assumption.

"But the tendency to use the avenue this way has not gained any headway; and recently there have been indications of another tendency in an opposite direction. Two sites between Sixtieth and Eightieth streets have been bought, which will be improved by large fireproof apartment houses; and it looks as if any property on Park avenue in the residential section which is available for reimprovement would be used in this manner. The avenue can never become a handsome thoroughfare devoted to private residences, because so many of the corners are already improved with apartment houses, which are too expensive to be thrown into the scrap heap, and then the East Side really needs a thoroughfare in which apartment houses of the largest size can be erected. Madison Avenue is not well adapted to the purpose because the lots are shallow, the corners are strongly held. Lexington Avenue will doubtless be lined with many such buildings; but it is not wide enough to permit the erection of apartment houses of the largest size. Park Avenue will be quieter than either

79

Lexington or Madison avenue, and it is so wide that a twenty-story building could be erected, if desired. Such buildings are needed, because of the large and increasing numbers of people who want to live in that part of the city. These people may prefer private houses; but in the course of time all but the very wealthy will be forced to put up with apartments. The area in which such people care to live is very much restricted, and there seems at present to be no chance of making it larger."

A year earlier, in 1905, a ten-story apartment hotel, the Clarendon, had gone up at the northwest corner of Park and 58th Street. It would be torn down in 1928 to make way for 480 Park, but another 1905 apartment house, the Van Cortlandt, remains at 1240 Park, northwest corner 96th Street. Designed by George F. Pelham, the six-story brick-and-limestone building, with four polished granite columns at its entrance, originally had suites of seven, eight, and nine rooms that rented for between $84 and $117 per month. Another survivor of this era, vacant through most of the 1980s, is 813 Park, between 74th and 75th streets. Originally a five-story Romanesque revival structure by Neville & Bagge, it was one of four tenements, each intended for nine families with a street-level store. Additional floors were added later.

The first tall apartment house to go up on Park Avenue was 863 Park, northeast corner 77th Street; designed in neo-Renaissance style by Pollard & Steinam, it was finished in 1907 with large duplexes facing on the avenue, simplexes on the street side, and a symmetry of fenestration even when that

BELOW: *Before World War I, tenements and five- and six-story apartment houses lined Park Avenue in the 90s* (1910 photo courtesy New-York Historical Society)

required blind windows. The largest apartments are ten-room duplexes. 540 Park, northwest corner 61st Street, dates to 1909 and has been called "the first of the high-class apartments to be built on Park Avenue." William A. Boring was its architect, and it was so successful that by 1917 most of the desirable corners along the avenue had been taken by apartment houses, if only small ones. Boring's building was itself replaced in the early 1960s by the Regency Hotel, but his work survives in 521 Park, completed in 1911 at the northeast corner of 60th Street. 520 Park, another Boring house of the period, was replaced in 1932 by Christ Church. Boring became head of Columbia University's School of Architecture.

Another survivor from 1909 is 925 Park, northeast corner 80th Street. A palazzo designed by Delano & Aldrich, it originally had twenty-one duplex apartments plus a few triplex and simplex units. The triplexes were on the three lower floors, which are sheathed in Indiana limestone rather than the brick and terra-cotta that cover the rest of the building. Apartments today range from five rooms, two baths, to ten rooms, four baths. 929 Park, midblock between 80th and 81st streets, was also finished in 1909. Pickering & Walker were the original architects; another architect, Arthur Weiser, remodeled the structure in 1935, turning large flats into small ones of three to four-and-a-half rooms.

When it was announced in 1909 that apartment houses would be built at 829 and 925 Park, the *Real Estate Record* noted that "the really modern fashionable boulevard is by the very nature of things compelled to exemplify the new as well as the old standards of living, and on Park avenue at the present moment may be seen under construction, simultaneously, both co-operative and individual houses of the highest type in their respective classes."

515 Park, southeast corner 60th Street, is a 1910 building by Ernest Greene, built as a cooperative with eighteen apartments of eleven rooms, four baths each. In 1957 it had twenty-four apartments and professional offices (rents averaged $250 per month) and was acquired by the Jewish Agency, an umbrella organization which helps newcomers settle in Israel. The agency, which occupied two brownstones in East 66th Street, asked the state rent commission to evict tenants of 515 Park who had not found other quarters. Sixteen tenants tried to block the action; the Syrian Consulate and the Syrian Mission to the United Nations went to court to delay their eviction. Not until January 1960 did the Jewish Agency take over. It added a new entrance, a lobby, and a 150-seat auditorium. The building also houses headquarters of the World Zionist Organization, the Weizmann Institute, and similar groups.

563 Park, northeast corner 62nd Street, another 1910 building, replaced five row houses that had faced onto 62nd Street. Designed by Walter B. Chambers, it has been called "the first luxury apartment house" on upper Park Avenue. Its architect made it look as if all its cooperative apartments were duplexes; actually, those facing the avenue really are, those in the rear are not. A typical large apartment had on its first floor a drawing room measuring 26' x 18' 6", a dining room 25' x 16', a private hall, a servants' dining room, butler's pantry, and kitchen; its second floor had four bedrooms ranging in size from 18' x 16' to 14'

x 9′, three baths, and two servants' rooms with sink. This was just one of several cooperative duplex apartment houses built on Park Avenue in an effort to attract more affluent tenants. Recent tenants have included Burton Tremaine and his wife, the former Emily Hall, who in forty years amassed a formidable collection of art, especially of abstract expressionist and pop art; and Carl A. ("Andy") Capasso, a building contractor who began a three-year prison term for tax evasion in the late 1980s. His friendship with the city's cultural affairs commissioner, Bess Myerson, led to a nasty divorce from his wife, Nancy, and a federal indictment of Ms. Myerson for obstruction of justice on charges that she tried to have Judge Hortense Gabel reduce her lover's alimony. She was acquitted.

Not all that lavish to begin with were five other apartment houses erected at about the same time. 535 Park, northeast corner 61st Street, is by Herbert Lucas; recent tenants have included former Securities Exchange Commissioner John S. Shad, who in 1989 became chairman of Drexel Burnham Lambert. 823 Park, midblock between 75th and 76th streets, is a neoclassical building by Pickering & Walker, as is 829 Park, southeast corner 76th Street. They replaced six of the seven Terrace apartment houses that had extended along Park between 75th and 76th streets. 830 Park, southwest corner 76th Street, is a neo-Georgian house by George and Edward Blum with two sections surrounding a central court. It replaced two row houses and a livery stable that had faced onto 76th Street. 840 Park, northwest corner 76th Street, is neo-Italian in style, also by George and Edward Blum, built on a previously undeveloped site. It was designed to accommodate eighteen families.

Over on Fifth Avenue, the phalanx of private dwellings north of 59th Street was not interrupted until 1912, when the grand luxe 998 Fifth was finished with one rental apartment per floor. Designed by McKim, Mead & White, it gained social acceptance for apartment living when Douglas L. Elliman, a young real estate broker, persuaded Senator Root to take a floor. Not for some years did 998 share its Central Park view with anything but private mansions. Park Avenue, on the other hand, was being built up with apartment houses.

635 Park, northeast corner 65th Street, is a 1912 apartment house designed by J. E. R. Carpenter. This neo-Renaissance building replaced a plebeian multi-family house, the Adelaide, built in 1887 just south of the 7th Regiment Armory, to designs of Henry Janeway Hardenbergh, famous for his Dakota apartments and (later) Plaza Hotel. Carpenter's building originally had just one apartment of thirteen rooms and four baths to a floor, each apartment being divided into discrete public, private, and service areas. Living rooms were 30′6″ x 18′6″, dining rooms 27′ x 18′6″, circular foyers 13′6″ in diameter; off each foyer was a salon measuring 18′6″ x 13′6″. Apartments had four bedrooms each (two measured 20′6″ x 14′6″ each and two slightly smaller), four servants' rooms, a servants' hall, and kitchen. Recent tenants have included former retail executive (Lord & Taylor, Tiffany) Walter Hoving.

875 Park, southeast corner 78th Street, was designed by George and Edward Blum and completed in 1912. Neoclassical in style, it replaced two small apartment houses, known as the Warrenton, and five tenements.

960 Park, northwest corner 82nd Street, is a 1912 building designed by J. E. R. Carpenter (with D. Everett Waid) for Bing & Bing, the real estate management firm founded in 1905 by Leo S. and Alexander M. Bing. Originally planned to resemble an Italian palazzo, it was to contain fifty-four cooperative apartments of nine to thirteen rooms each, with eighteen duplexes and thirty-three triplexes. Major entertaining rooms were to be arranged en suite around an entrance hall, and bedrooms laid out with no long halls. The prospectus called for sale prices of between $24,000 and $52,000, average maintenance charges from $245 to $420 per month. Mention was made of the Lexington Avenue subway, then under construction, which would add to the convenience of the location. As completed, the building occupied half as many lots with a more conventional thirteen-story apartment house, and although designed to have two apartments per floor, most were later cut in half.

970 Park, just to the north (southwest corner 83rd Street), went up at the same time. It was designed by Schwartz & Gross, also for Bing & Bing. Apartments ranged from eight to ten rooms, three baths, with three to four master bedrooms and two servants' rooms. One of the last Park Avenue houses to go co-op (it did not convert until June 1988), its recent tenants have included the theatrical producer David Merrick, who put two smaller apartments together into a duplex, and Marvin Hamlisch, the composer. Opposite is 969 Park, a 1912 building by Pickering & Walker with a forbidding flight of stairs in the lobby. Emery Roth, brought in to remodel it in 1941, divided the large apartments into flats of three to six rooms, although the penthouse still has seven, with four baths. Even in 1912, though, 969 was not the most posh of Park Avenue buildings.

More opulent by far was the Montana at 375 Park, designed by Rouse & Goldstone and completed in 1913 on the site of the old Steinway Piano Factory, filling the blockfront between 52nd and 53rd streets. At street level was the marvelous Restaurant Voisin; a children's playground occupied the roof. Thomas H. Steinway leased an apartment of ten rooms, three baths. Other tenants included the Charles Scribners. The house came down in 1956 to make way for the Seagram Building.

A few months after the first tenants moved into 998 Fifth, Bing & Bing opened 903 Park, northeast corner 79th Street, whose seventeen floors made it the city's tallest apartment house. Height restrictions were imposed soon afterward, and it would be a decade and a half before Park Avenue above 59th Street had any other structure of more than fifteen floors. 903 has been called the "first truly upper-class apartment" on the avenue. Designed by Warren & Wetmore with Robert T. Lyons, it had one apartment—up to eighteen rooms—per floor. All bedrooms had southern exposure, and most of the 20' x 40' living rooms overlooked Central Park. Dr. W. Seward Webb and his wife, the former Eliza (Lila) Vanderbilt, a daughter of William Henry Vanderbilt, paid a whopping $1,250 per month to lease a duplex of twenty-four rooms and seven baths comprising the entire eleventh floor and part of the twelfth. The Webbs had recently sold their mansion at 680 Fifth, a wedding gift from Mrs. Webb's father in 1883 (John D. Rockefeller, whose house in 54th Street abutted theirs, bought it to keep anyone from replacing it with a store or office building). Carll Tucker, treasurer of the Maxwell Motor Company, leased the penthouse at 903 Park. Tenants in the 1920s included Vincent Astor and Mrs. Hugh D. Auchincloss.* Today the largest apartment is seventeen rooms, five baths; there are also three- and five-room suites.

Other apartment buildings of the 1912–15 era include 525, 555, 565, 640, 755, 850, 930, 941, and 955 Park.

525 Park, southeast corner 61st Street, was designed by Schwartz & Gross and finished in 1915. Its top floor had just one apartment of twenty rooms, six baths. Lower floors each had two apartments, one of twelve rooms and four baths, one of nine rooms and three baths. Recent tenants have included the architect John C. Warnecke.

555 Park, southeast corner 62nd Street, by George and Edward Blum, replaced eight row houses that had faced onto 62nd Street. Recent tenants have included Paine Webber's chief Donald B. Marron, Jr. and his wife, Jennifer; former Shearman & Sterling law partner Thomas P. Ford; music publisher Rudolph Schirmer; and television journalist Barbara Walters, who put her ten-room co-op on the market in 1988 for $3 million.

565 Park, between 62nd and 63rd streets, was designed by Robert T. Lyons for Bing & Bing; completed in 1915, it replaced two small apartment houses called the Lonsdale.

640 Park, northwest corner 66th Street, is another J. E. R. Carpenter design; built by S. Fullerton Weaver, it replaced six row houses and had one apartment per floor. It still does, and while most have twelve rooms some have as many as eighteen with six baths, four to five master bedrooms, cedar closets, four woodburning fireplaces, an individual laundry, and seven servants' rooms.

755 Park, southeast corner 72nd Street, went up on a site formerly occupied by the Freundschaft (Friendship) Club, whose 1889 clubhouse had been designed by McKim, Mead & White. Rouse & Goldstone's plans for 755 Park called for thirty-eight suites. All were occupied by early 1915, with tenants paying rents of $275 to $450 per month. Recent co-op owners have included Congressman S. William ("Bill") Green and his wife, Pat.

850 Park, southwest corner 77th Street, is also by Rouse & Goldstone. It replaced four row houses built from 1882 to 1884, three 1893-vintage stables that had faced onto 77th Street, and two vacant lots on Park. 850 was a cooperative.

930 Park, southwest corner 81st Street, and 941 Park, northeast corner 81st

---

* She was the former Emma D. Jennings, whose father, Oliver B., helped John D. Rockefeller found the Standard Oil Company. "Auchinclosses," writes Stephen Birmingham somewhat acidly, "have married Colgates, Rockefellers, Sloanes, Winthrops, Saltonstalls, Frelinghuysens, van Rensselaers, Cuttings, du Ponts, Grosvenors, Tiffanys, Burdens, Ingrahams, Vanderbilts, Adamses, and Burrs—to list just a few of their connections—and have become what is called the best-connected family in New York . . . And yet, with the exception of the novelist Louis Auchincloss, there has never been a true Auchincloss of distinction."

ABOVE: *903 Park rose seventeen stories above the avenue in 1912 (895, at right, came much later)* (1989 photo)

Street, are both 1915 buildings by Schwartz & Gross. Recent tenants have included the lawyer Ralph C. Colin, Grey Advertising's founder Arthur C. Fatt, the physician-writer Lee Salk, and the late investment banker Donald S. Stralem.

955 Park, near the southeast corner of 82nd Street (a five-story building still occupies the corner), is a 1914 building by Robert T. Lyons.

Nearly two miles to the south, vacant lots lined the avenue for blocks immediately to the north of the new Grand Central Terminal. The New York Central still held out hope that a new house for the Metropolitan Opera and a fine arts museum would be built on these blocks. But money for such projects was not available, and by 1915 more luxury apartment houses were going up north of 50th Street. Late that year the Central leased the eastern blockfront between 46th and 47th to a developer who was erecting an apartment house on the west side of the avenue between 50th and 51st streets and intended to put up another one across the avenue. This plan was aborted in favor of a commercial structure built in 1922.

Toward the end of 1915 Bing & Bing commissioned Emery Roth to design three luxury apartment houses, one of them on West End Avenue close to where the Hungarian-born architect had done most of his work. The other two buildings were 570 and 1000 Park. Both have center courtyards at least thirty feet square.

570 Park, southwest corner 63rd Street, replaced eight row houses. According to Roth's grandson and biographer Steve Ruttenbaum, it showed a "delicate and refined classicism unlike anything else he had produced previously." A neo-Renaissance building with English influences, it had a white marble base, setting a tone which was "carried all the way up to its high facades of exquisitely molded white terra cotta ornament."

1000 Park, northwest corner 84th Street, is a "massive brown brick box," Ruttenbaum wrote. Roth applied "terra cotta ornament executed in a neo-Gothic style. Flanking the main entrance on Park Avenue are two Gothic figures, one a medieval warrior and the other a builder, replete with Masonic symbolism. Legend has it that Roth modeled his two figures after his clients, Leo and Alexander Bing. Additional terra cotta figures executed in a grotesque manner depict the builders of Greek temples and medieval cathedrals."

Bing & Bing in 1915 was in the process of renting its new buildings at 993 Park, southeast corner 84th Street, and 1155 Park, southeast corner 92nd Street, both by Robert T. Lyons. 993 had apartments mostly of eight to ten rooms, three baths; 1155 had some as large as twelve rooms, four baths. Living rooms at 1155 can be 25' x 20', dining rooms 24' x 14'9", bedrooms 20' x 13'. There is an inner courtyard measuring 34' x 32'. Two apartments at 1155 were put together for a tenant who wanted eighteen rooms, six baths.

So many Park Avenue apartment houses had gone up or were under construction in the 70s and 80s that a letter to the editor of the *Real Estate Record* in May 1915 complained about the absence of street signs. "On account of the large number of new buildings which have been erected in this section in the last two years, the thoroughfare has taken on an entirely different aspect and old landmarks have disappeared or are hard to find." More troubling to developers was the possibility that their new buildings might lose their light as the avenue filled up with other tall apartment houses. Many private dwellings were built before and after World War I, some with the encouragement of real estate firms that wanted protection for their apartment houses. Bing & Bing, for example, acquired two three-story houses at 109 and 111 East 91st Street to protect its investment at 1155 Park. The property was resold with restrictions, the two houses were razed, and a thirty-foot house designed by S. Edson Gage was put up for I. Townsend Burden.

470 Park, southwest corner 58th Street, is a 1916 building by Schwartz & Gross. Recent tenants have included the former Alfred A. Knopf editor William A. Koshland. 630 Park, southwest corner 66th Street, also dates from 1916. Designed by J. E. R. Carpenter, with apartments as large as seventeen rooms, six baths, with five master bedrooms and eight servants' rooms, it replaced five row houses that had faced onto the street. Recent tenants have included the publisher Theodore Newhouse.

876 Park, near the southwest corner 78th Street, was completed soon afterward. A narrow apartment house by Rouse & Goldstone, it replaced a large livery stable.

Sherman McCoy, in Tom Wolfe's 1987 novel *The Bonfire of the Vanities*, lived in a fictional building at "816 Park Avenue" which he regarded as "one of the great ones built just before the first World War! Back then it was still not entirely proper for a good family to live in an apartment (instead of a house). So the apartments were built like mansions, with eleven-, twelve-, thirteen-foot ceilings, vast entry galleries, staircases, servants' wings, herringbone-parquet floors, interior walls a foot thick, exterior walls as thick as a fort's, and fireplaces, fireplaces, fireplaces, even though the buildings were all built with central heating. A mansion!—except that you arrived at the front door via an elevator (opening upon your own private vestibule) instead of the street."

When those buildings went up it was still acceptable, as in the nineteenth century, for middle-class New Yorkers to live in boardinghouses. Classified advertisements for boardinghouse rooms and furnished apartments far outnumbered those for unfurnished flats, and except for Fifth Avenue the upper West Side, especially Riverside Drive, was still far more fashionable than the corresponding section across the park. Demand was growing, however, for upper East Side apartments. Building costs were high in the war years, and materials such as steel were hard to obtain. Some developers bided their time, waiting for a more propitious moment, while others forged ahead.

417 Park, southeast corner 55th Street, has its entrance just off Park. Built in 1917, it is the last survivor of at least thirteen luxury apartment houses, most of them built before World War I, that once lined Park between 47th and 57th streets. Bing & Bing put up this limestone-faced building and purchased the property just to its south, occupied by a two-story garage at the time, in order to prevent anyone from blocking essential windows with another tall building (407 Park remains as a low structure) and thus ruining its investment. Emery

Roth designed an elaborate overhanging roof cornice of copper, now green with age. He gave the building two elevators so that the apartments to the east would share one and those to the west another. With few exceptions, each apartment has an elevator foyer to itself, and each has woodburning fireplaces. The building's twenty-eight units include four penthouses, two of them duplexes of three and seven rooms, respectively. The simplexes range from six to ten rooms, although one has only four and one five. *Social Register* families such as the Charles A. Blackwells, Peter H. B. Frelinghuysens, and some Havemeyers have lived here.

417 Park went co-op in 1947, one of the first apartment houses to do so after World War II. Twenty years later it was home to Ivan Patcevich, publisher of *Vogue* magazine. More recent tenants have included the clergyman Dr. Ralph Peterson; wire service editor Frederick M. Winship; a well-known motion picture director and his French actress wife who had purchased the Patcevich apartment; Mrs. Washington Dodge, whose late husband had as a child survived the 1912 sinking of the *Titanic*; J. Edward Lumbard, a former chief justice of the U.S. Circuit Court of Appeals; and Baroness Terry von Pantz, who had married the owner of the Schlossmittersill near Salzburg, after the death of her first husband, David H. McConnell, founder of Avon Products.

550 Park, southwest corner 62nd Street, is a 1917 building that replaced the Yosemite, an 1891 apartment house of seven stories by McKim, Mead & White which had, in turn, replaced Holbrook Hall, an apartment house partially destroyed by fire shortly after it was acquired in an 1888 foreclosure by New York Life. A syndicate headed by John H. Carpenter bought the property from the insurance company for $600,000 in the spring of 1916 and engaged J. E. R. Carpenter to design a seventeen-story apartment building. Recent tenants have included the lawyer Martin Lipton, the investment banker William R. Salomon, socialite Mrs. T. R. Vreeland, and Peter O. Price, an executive who has run Carey Cadillac, served for a year as publisher for Peter Kalikow's *New York Post*, and headed the Park Avenue Association. Price's wife, Judith, publishes *Avenue*, a slick magazine that now focuses more on business and fashion than on giddy social goings on among the rich and famous.

Another 1917 building is 815 Park, southeast corner 75th Street (Rouse & Goldstone). The *Real Estate Record* in 1917 was calling the changes on Park Avenue north of 42nd Street "one of the most remarkable sectional developments in the city in the past fifteen years." Yet much of Park Avenue, even in the growingly fashionable 50s, 60s, and 70s, was still lined with tenements, row houses, garages, and institutional buildings.

South of 59th Street the avenue was solidly built up with apartment houses; 410 Park, designed by Julius Harder, was one of about fifteen luxury flats that came down in the 1950s and '60s to make room for office buildings. A typical floor at 410 included two apartments of eleven and thirteen rooms each. Upper floors each contained a single apartment of eighteen rooms and eight baths, with a seventy-seven-foot sweep from library to living room. The foyer of the eighteen-roomer was 23'6" x 12'6"; its living room measured 32' x 20'6", its dining room 32'6" x 20'6", its library 20'6" x 13', and its largest bedroom 20' x 19'6". There were six other bedrooms, six servants' rooms, a kitchen, servants' hall, and pantry. At 420 Park a prominent New Yorker reportedly rented the entire tenth floor and half of the eleventh—three apartments with a total of forty-four rooms and thirteen baths.

The Marguery, an apartment house and hotel designed by Warren & Wetmore, was nearing completion at 270 Park above Grand Central's trainyards as World War I ended. Built around a giant garden courtyard, the complex occupied a newly created full-block plot that precluded the need for assembling parcels of land. And it set the pattern for postwar development of the avenue below 59th Street which, like the rest of the city, would now have to conform to principles laid down in the 1916 zoning resolution, the first such law in America.

8

·

The Boom

NEW YORK CITY adopted its 1916 zoning resolution to block construction of buildings that would plunge neighboring streets into shadow. The new law would not only protect each citizen's right to adequate amounts of air and light. It would also protect land values by means of strict controls on urban development and land use; shield real estate interests by securing orderly and stable development of urban land; and promote speculative development all over the city—even on Park Avenue—by encouraging real estate values to rise to new heights. Real estate moguls used the 1916 resolution to safeguard existing investments and increase their huge profits.

Nearly a decade elapsed before the law's effects became apparent. America's entry into World War I halted most construction activity; the ensuing economic depression brought state rent laws, threatened rent strikes, tight money, inflation, labor unrest, higher prices for building materials, and shortages of such essential items as bricks and Portland cement, all of which discouraged the start of new projects. The builder George Backer admitted in the fall of 1920 that he had paid $25,000 to representatives of a powerful labor leader to end a disturbance that had halted work on one of his contracts. (He had first claimed that he had lost the money at the racetrack; a perjury trial ended in a hung jury.)

Perhaps the first postwar building to be completed on Park Avenue was 1049 Park, near the southeast corner of 87th Street (William Bottomley, 1919). 950 Park, southwest corner 82nd Street, went up in 1921. J. E. R. Carpenter designed it with A-line apartments of eight rooms, three baths, B-line apartments of twelve rooms, four baths. 300 Park, a seventeen-story cooperative by Warren &

Wetmore, was built over the New York Central tracks in 1922. Louis Sherry leased the ground floor, installing a restaurant that survived, as did the building, for nearly forty years. 485 Park, northeast corner 58th Street, opened as a co-op in the fall of 1922, replacing some garages. Also finished in 1922 was the relocated Fifth Avenue Baptist Church at 593 Park Avenue, southeast corner 64th Street. Designed by Henry C. Pelton in association with Allen & Collens, it replaced five row houses that had faced onto 64th Street. John D. Rockefeller, Jr., whose family matched all contributions toward the cost of building the church, held Bible classes in a special room in its basement. (Six years after it was built, the building was taken over by the Central Presbyterian Church; the Fifth Avenue congregation met for a year at the new Temple Emmanu-El and then moved to the new Riverside Church between 120th and 122nd streets, completed in 1930 and also financed in large part by the Rockefellers.)

Choice Park Avenue property was too costly for most developers; prices were lower north of 86th Street, and 1922 saw work begin on 1045 Park, northeast corner 86th Street (Schwartz & Gross); 1050 Park, southwest corner 87th Street (J. E. R. Carpenter); 1060 Park, northwest corner 87th Street (J. E. R. Carpenter); 1075 Park, southeast corner 88th Street (George and Edward Blum); and 1105 Park, northeast corner 89th Street (Rosario Candela). By 1923 the economy was picking up speed, and Park Avenue—along with the rest of the city—was enjoying an unprecedented frenzy of real estate speculation and skyscraper construction. By 1923 passenger elevators had been in use for seventy years,* steel skeleton construction half as long. Only now did engineers begin to use this technology on a large scale for residential buildings. In 1924 the tallest residential building proposed in Manhattan was twenty-eight stories; within four years a fifty-five-story tower would be in the planning stage. Landowners were discovering new ways to exploit their property holdings for increased profits.

When a real estate advertisement today says "prewar building," it generally means a structure built before World War II. Apartments in such buildings are almost always more desirable than newer ones, but those in buildings put up before World War I were, by and large, even larger than those built in the 1920s. Pre-World War I apartments in new residential buildings averaged 4.19 rooms, there were no one-room apartments, and two- to three-room units accounted for only about a third of the total. Ten years later the average number of rooms per apartment in new buildings had dropped to 3.37, and the number of small apartments—three rooms or less—had more than doubled. (A room generally was defined as any enclosed space of seventy square feet or more with a window to the outside. Bathrooms, kitchenettes, pantries, halls, foyers, dressing rooms, and dining alcoves were not counted.) Even on Park Avenue, apartments were getting smaller, although some built in the great boom of the 1920s were—and in many cases remain—a match for anything that had come before.

580 Park, occupying the entire western blockfront between 63rd and 64th

---

* The first passenger elevator was actually installed at Versailles by Louis XV. What the Yonkers, N.Y., mechanic Elisha Graves Otis pioneered was the safety elevator.

streets, was completed in 1923. J. E. R. Carpenter gave it a four-story colonnaded base of variegated limestone with separate entrances for doctors' offices on either side of the monumental doorway, which led to a large hall furnished in Italian Renaissance style. A co-op with fifty-two apartments, 580 was built with two eight-room and two nine-room apartments per floor. Each apartment had a separate laundry-and-storage room in the basement, and there were thirty extra servants' rooms in the penthouse. Recent tenants have included baseball team owner (and onetime publisher) Nelson Doubleday and Corning Glass heir Amory Houghton, Jr.

620 Park, northwest corner 65th Street, is another J. E. R. Carpenter building finished in 1924.

Costliest of all 1924 projects was the Hecksher Apartments at 277 Park. Occupying a full block, they surrounded a large grassy drive-in courtyard ("an acre of garden," said one advertisement; "a garden nearly half the size of Gramercy Park," said another) echoing that of the Marguery across the avenue. August Hecksher, a German-born coal magnate and real estate developer, was a major property owner in the area who in late July 1923 paid $10 million to acquire the twelve-story Grand Central Palace and its new twenty-story annex, the Park-Lexington Building. His son G. Maurice Hecksher obtained the east side of the avenue between 47th and 48th streets and engaged McKim, Mead & White to design a building which, with its land, also cost another $10 million. It included the Crillon Restaurant, with an entrance in 48th Street west of Lexington Avenue—a carnival of modernistic Russian decor with lavish amounts of red lacquer; the service was impeccable, and the cuisine rivaled that at the Marguery (famed for its sole Marguery). The 315 apartments ranged in size from two to seven rooms. Small attic rooms, originally for servants, were later rented to students.

510 Park, southwest corner 60th Street, was built by Starrett Brothers to designs by F. H. Dewey & Co. with cooperative apartments of nine to thirteen rooms. Living rooms measured 34'x 19', dining rooms 22'9" x 18'10", library/bedrooms 18'4" x 13'6", other bedrooms as large as 22'3" x 16'. For years this building had a Chase Manhattan Bank branch with marvelous antique tellers' cages; it closed early in 1989 (even banks balk at outrageous rent increases). Recent tenants have included the real estate operator Edward H. Benenson.

Just up the avenue, at the northeast corner of 63rd Street, 1924 saw the completion of the Third Church of Christ, Scientist (Delano & Aldrich). The congregation had been in the former Harlem Presbyterian Church in 125th Street near Madison Avenue. Its new church replaced two garages, formerly stables.

655 Park, occupying the eastern blockfront between 67th and 68th streets where Hahnemann Hospital had stood, was designed by J. E. R. Carpenter and Mott B. Schmidt; its low Park Avenue frontage would be broken by the opening of its interior court, which was planted with flowers and shrubbery. Trees and gardens were to be planted atop the eighth-floor setback (originally intended to be a seventh-floor setback; the rest of the building was to be only ten stories high

ABOVE: *Courtyard of the old Hecksher Apartments at 277 Park* (photo courtesy New-York Historical Society)

but this was increased to eleven). A co-op from the outset, the building had two duplex maisonettes. The one at the south end, 651 Park, was purchased in 1925 by William K. Vanderbilt, Jr. Off 651's private street entrance is a large reception hall; the ground floor also has three servants' rooms and a bath. Upstairs are a living room, dining room, kitchen, and two large bedrooms. In recent years this maisonette has belonged to C. Ruxton Love. Other recent tenants at 655 have included Carman H. Messmore, the legendary art dealer (M. Knoedler & Co.); and former congressman Hamilton Fish, who turned 100 on December 7, 1988. Descended from a historic family, Fish was an isolationist until December 7, 1941; he inherited half the apartment at 655 from his White Russian second wife, Marie, who died in the mid-1970s. She left it in equal shares to her sister Olga and to Fish, who occupied part of the apartment with his fourth wife while Olga and her boyfriend used the other part.

760 Park, northwest corner 72nd Street, also dates to 1924. Designed by Rouse & Goldstone and built by Starrett Brothers, it replaced three row houses that had faced onto 72nd Street. The living room in one suite measured 36'9" x 19', the dining room 19'3" x 17'11". A circular staircase led from the foyer to the second floor, which had five bedrooms, one of them 19' x 16'5". There were four baths upstairs, one downstairs. Each suite had three servants' rooms and a servants' hall off the kitchen and pantry.

898 Park, southwest corner 79th Street, is another 1924 building, finished at year's end. Henry Mandel, the developer, commissioned John Sloan and Adolph E. Nast, architects, to design a luxury house for a plot only 75' x 41' flanked by brownstones. They came up with a straight tower without setback and decorated its golden brickwork with grotesque heads and figures. Entrance doors were of elaborate wrought iron (later replaced with aluminum), and there were originally just seven apartments—two thirteen-room duplexes, each having more than 5,000 square feet and occupying two full floors, plus a simplex on the second floor and a doctor's suite at street level. The thirty-six-foot living rooms, Andrew Alpern tells us, had windows on three sides. An elliptical stairway from the foyer led up to five bedrooms and four baths. Ceilings are 10'9"; beams, columns, and radiators are concealed. Living rooms and master bedrooms had fireplaces, and each duplex had five servants' rooms on its lower floor. There were extra servants' rooms on the ground floor and the roof, and individual laundry rooms in the basement, which had no heating plant. Steam was piped in from the New York Steam Company. (When another architect, Simon Zelnik, converted the vast duplexes into simplex apartments in the 1940s, he left the fifth and sixth floor and fourteenth and penthouse suites intact.)

910 Park, southwest corner 80th Street, is a 1924 building by Schwartz & Gross.

1009 Park, midblock between 84th and 85th streets, is a Bing & Bing building of 1924 vintage. Emery Roth and Mott B. Schmidt designed it to have one apartment per floor, each with thirteen rooms, four baths. There were also nine-, eleven-, and sixteen-room maisonettes with as many as six baths. On some floors the flats have since been broken up into five- and six-room units.

ABOVE: *View from Hunter College looking down on penthouse gardens at 655 Park and down the avenue* (1988 photo)

Property above 86th Street was less costly, and developers put up a number of large apartment houses—mostly rental buildings, although 1045 and 1105 were co-ops—in the upper 80s and lower 90s. 1045, 1050, 1060, 1075, 1105, and 1133 Park, southeast corner 91st Street were all finished by 1924. 1060 originally had an on-premise restaurant, the Maison de Lion, and offered housekeeping apartments ranging from three rooms and bath at $141 per month to six rooms and bath at $284 to $317. Harris H. Uris, the Latvian immigrant who built 1133, bought two old four-story brick apartment houses on the site and replaced them with a structure designed by Nathan Korn to have thirty-one seven- and eight-room apartments. None of these houses has suites of the vast proportions found in buildings by some of the same architects farther south.

Buildings completed in 1925 include 15–17, 16, 71, 77, 791, 800, 860, 935, 1111, and 1160 Park.

15–17 Park, southeast corner 35th Street, replaced two stone dwellings. Fred F. French Co., whose chief architect was H. Douglas Ives, designed it for "simplified housekeeping" in the Murray Hill area then considered, in the words of the *Real Estate Record*, at the heart of the "college club and fraternity zone."

16 Park, southwest corner 35th Street, is another 1925 Fred F. French building on "socially correct" Murray Hill. Its rental apartments had three to four rooms.

71 Park, midblock between 38th and 39th streets and distinguished by its

BELOW: *In the Murray Hill section, many private houses and clubs still stood in the 1920s; apartments here were smaller* (photo courtesy Municipal Archive)

tall chimneys, was a rental building designed by Walker & Gillette with 112 apartments of two to six rooms each.

The Griffon at 77 Park, southeast corner 39th Street, by Margon & Glaser, had suites ranging in size from two rooms, one bath, to six rooms, four baths. There was a restaurant downstairs and a building staff of housekeepers, chambermaids, butlers, and valets for tenants who did not employ their own. It was here in the 1930s that Mae (Mrs. Abraham Z.) Schiebel, alias Billy Schiebel, alias Mary Briggs, ran her "parlor house" or, as the police called it, "disorderly" house. Seized in a vice-squad raid on her elaborately furnished apartment early in 1936, Schiebel was said to have had a $100,000-a-year operation which had been responsible for one customer's suicide. Names of customers found in her records included the owner of a major league baseball team, a bank president, and some major business executives. Thomas E. Dewey, serving as special prosecutor, investigated the case and accused the madam of having violated the Mann Act by transporting one "Boots" Carter from Pittsburgh to New York in September 1934 for immoral purposes. Schiebel was sentenced to four years in prison and fined $5,000. (A trashy 1955 Harold Robbins novel, 79 *Park Avenue*, was probably inspired by the case.) Nor is 77 Park the only Park Avenue building to have housed places of prostitution. Today the Griffon is a respectable condominium in which a one-bedroom apartment may sell for more than $300,000.

791 Park, southeast corner 74th Street, replaced eight row houses facing onto 74th Street and a tenement on Park Avenue; George and Edward Blum were the architects. Ivar Kreuger, the Swedish match king, took the penthouse in 1927.

800 Park, northwest corner 74th Street, replaced a row house in 74th Street and a row house and tenement on Park Avenue; Electus D. Litchfield and Pliny Rogers were the architects. Stewart Mott, the General Motors heir and philanthropist, planted vegetables in the penthouse garden in the 1980s but left after reportedly arguing with his neighbors.

860 Park, northwest corner 77th Street, replaced a tenement and a stable; York & Sawyer were the architects, and apartments included some of twelve rooms, five baths, which occupied entire floors. One such flat was purchased by the lawyer Charles C. Burlingham.

935 Park, southeast corner 81st Street, is a 1925 building by Sugarman Hess & Berger.

1111 Park, southeast corner 90th Street, was designed by Schwartz & Gross. Extending deep into the block toward Lexington, the building has six apartments per floor, each six to nine rooms, three to four baths, with drawing rooms 27' x 16', reception halls 16' x 16', and woodburning fireplaces. Apartments rented in 1925 for $285 to $600 per month. Recent co-op tenants have included the novelist Louis Auchincloss.

1160 Park, northwest corner 92nd Street, was designed by George Fred Pelham with suites of six to eleven rooms. It replaced the seven-story Quackenbush apartment house.

The *Real Estate Record*, in an editorial published in late September 1925, viewed with satisfaction the avenue's frenzy of building: "Park Avenue is now practically developed from the Grand Central to 96th Street and has few available corners left for apartment house projects. Those that are vacant have been already made into sites for de luxe multi-family skyscraping residences . . .

"The development of Park Avenue in the past twenty years has been one of the marvels of building progress in Manhattan. Where factories existed, where walk-up tenements lined the streets for miles, and where property was practically given away, the transformation into one of the most artistic thoroughfares in the world has taken place so quickly that even residents of the vicinity are astounded by the avenue's growth. . . Practically every operation along its extent has cost more than $1 million and some have even reached the $10 million mark." Al Jolson, then in his prime as the silent movie era flickered to an end, might have said, "You ain't seen nothin' yet."

Until now, most buildings on Park had been twelve or thirteen stories tall. With few exceptions, fourteen would now be the minimum.

Park Avenue buildings finished in 1926 include 820, 940, 975, 1035, 1040, 1085, 1088, 1125, 1172, 1225, and 1230 Park.

820 Park, northwest corner 75th Street, replaced the costly 1920 house of Mrs. Millbank Anderson, who had engaged John Mead Howells to design it and must have approved his plans but never moved into the limestone box he created—a house, in Andrew Alpern's words, "with minimalist articulation and almost no exterior embellishment. The traditional classical forms and detailing were so restrained that they were more a memory than a reality. The building was bloodless, lacking any of the charm or exuberance of good classical architecture." Alpern based his judgment on photographs, not being old enough to have seen the house, which remained vacant until 1924. Albert J. Kobler, a flamboyant young publisher, bought it, retained Howells to remodel and redecorate its interiors, and one year later had it torn down.

Kobler had come to New York from his native Vienna in 1906 at age twenty, worked in the textile business for eight years, and then become an advertising solicitor for the *New York Globe*. William Randolph Hearst had put him in charge of the *American Weekly* in 1917, and Kobler was on his way to increasing circulation of the Sunday supplement from 2 million to 25 million and boosting revenues from $35,000 per year to $13,000 per page.

Having bought three 75th Street row houses to enlarge his plot, Kobler engaged Harry Allan Jacobs to design a fourteen-story building for nine families who had closed their private houses and could afford rents of between $2,088 and $3,333 per month for apartments that, being on higher floors, were brighter and sunnier than most town houses. Tenants soon included Herbert H. Lehman and Carl H. Pforzheimer—Jewish, like Kobler, but both men of higher social standing. Suites at 820 ranged from fifteen to twenty rooms, duplexes and triplexes, with the top three floors—4,000 square feet—comprising what Alpern has called a "mansion in the sky" for Kobler.

From the entrance hall, with its low groin-vaulted ceiling, shallow stone arches, and carved doors, a stone stairway, embellished with wrought iron, led up to the library and down to the dining room. Walls of the dining room were stone, as was the massive fireplace; and the coffered ceiling was a copy of one in the Uffizi Palace. Off the entrance hall was the drawing room with its twenty-foot ceiling, "deeply carved and polychromed," to quote Alpern. Light from lead-and-stained-glass windows and a large chandelier illuminated Kobler's collection of rare French Gothic art and furniture, including a stone fireplace from the sixteenth century and a tapestry said to have belonged to Cardinal Wolsey and then to Henry VIII. Some of Kobler's furniture had purportedly come from the Strozzi and Barberini palaces. The tapestry, fireplace, and furniture in the drawing room could be seen from an oriel window in the library on the floor above, and the apartment had an eighteenth-century Venetian bedroom and baths finished in African onyx and gold. There was also an exclusive roof garden.

Kobler became publisher of Hearst's *New York Mirror* in 1928. A few years later he was able to settle a $500,000 debt for $150,000 in cash plus perhaps $25,000 from his $100,000 life insurance policy. He moved out of his luxurious aerie, and at the time of his death, on January 1, 1937 (he came down with the flu and died four days later), was living with his wife, Mignon, at the Madison Hotel, 10 East 58th Street. The triplex at 820 Park was shorn of its splendor and subdivided, as were most of the other apartments in the building at various times. The gray-shingled facing on the north section of the top three floors dates from 1940.

940 Park, northwest corner 81st Street, fifteen stories and penthouse, was designed by George and Edward Blum. It has two apartments per floor, those in the A line having eight rooms, three baths; those in the B line five rooms, two baths. The two penthouses are duplexes; Joseph Baum, the restaurateur, had the larger one in the 1960s and early '70s.

975 Park, southeast corner 83rd Street, replaced two four-story, multifamily stone houses with stores; the new building, commissioned by Michael E. Paterno and designed by J. M. Felson, was a co-op.

1035 Park, southeast corner 86th Street, was built on the site of the old Park Avenue Methodist Church, which had relocated to a new building adjoining 1035 in East 86th Street. Henry C. Pelton was the architect. The Park Avenue Synagogue, which had never been on Park but from the 1890s was in 86th Street to the east of the Methodist Church, moved out in 1927 to take up new quarters at 50 East 87th Street (Schneider & Herts, architects).

1040 Park, northwest corner 86th Street, replaced some frame houses dating to 1870 or earlier. Delano & Aldrich mixed Georgian and Art Deco styles and were persuaded by the publisher Condé Nast to create a glassed-in penthouse for him. A cooperative, 1040 offered apartments as large as twelve rooms, four baths, five master bedrooms, three servants' rooms.

1085 Park, northeast corner 88th Street, was designed by Schwartz & Gross with apartments of six to eight rooms.

1088 Park, southwest corner 89th Street, was put up by the publisher Robert J. Cuddihy, who in 1878, at age fifteen, had obtained a job as office boy in the publishing firm I. K. Funk & Co. founded the year before by a Protestant clergyman-bookseller, Isaac Kauffman Funk, and Adam Willis Wagnalls. Cuddihy was, in Stephen Birmingham's words, "tough, aggressive, and fiercely ambitious." By 1886 he was doing so well that he got married, and in 1890, after publishing a *Standard Dictionary of the English Language*, he helped launch *The Literary Digest*, a weekly that was not particularly literary but reprinted comment and opinion from other periodicals. Funk & Wagnalls, as it was called beginning in 1891, named Cuddihy publisher of the *Digest* in 1905, and in 1914 he acquired a controlling interest in the firm. Two years later, in 1916, the *Literary Digest's* new straw poll predicted the reelection of Woodrow Wilson, beginning a tradition that boomed circulation.

Small-boned, good-looking, Cuddihy took a dim view of drinking, smoking, and divorce. Employees who got divorced were quickly dismissed; books by divorced people were another matter. Publication in 1922 of *Etiquette—The Blue Book of Social Usage* by a forty-eight-year-old socially prominent New York divorcée, Emily Price Post, made Post rich and filled the coffers of Funk & Wagnalls as it went into repeated printings. The firm also published a *Standard Encyclopedia*—Cuddihy's idea—that sold more than 25 million copies between 1921 and 1952. But the great publishing phenomenon was the *Literary Digest*. By 1927 its circulation was 1.5 million, making it second only to the *Saturday Evening Post*; in 1930 it was selling 2.25 million copies of every issue. It had correctly predicted the elections of Harding, Coolidge, Hoover, and Franklin D. Roosevelt. Then, in 1936, it embarrassed itself by forecasting the easy election of Alf Landon, who, in the event, won only Maine and Vermont. That was the end of the *Literary Digest* but not of Funk & Wagnalls or the Cuddihys.

Cuddihy is said to have financed construction of 1088 Park because, as a Roman Catholic, he was unable to get into another Fifth or Park Avenue co-op. Whether or not that is true, Cuddihy and his son H. Lester, a friend of Robert Moses, engaged Mott B. Schmidt as architect. The building Schmidt designed occupies most of the blockfront between 88th and 89th streets; its central garden courtyard, with its fountains and Italian loggia, was Lester's idea. Each apartment overlooks the garden, which is nearly a quarter acre in size. Eighty-four apartments are a lot for a fifteen-story house, even one with so much blockfront, so there are no huge ones at 1088 Park (most are of six to nine rooms). It has, nevertheless, always been considered an elegant address, a favorite of families with children. Apartments of eight to nine rooms were offered in 1925, prior to completion, at $433 to $617 per month, rates so high that many of the building's initial tenants were Cuddihys, including MacGuires and Gillespies, who got lower rates. Another early tenant was Carl Van And, managing editor of the *New York Times*. By 1929 all had moved to other addresses.

When Cuddihy's wife died in June 1944 the couple was living in a more spacious apartment at 300 Park; but R. J. himself was back at 1088 Park at the time of his death, just short of his ninetieth birthday, in December 1952. Some of his thirty-five grandchildren lived at 1088 Park until the 1970s. Recent tenants have included the lawyer and politician Mark Green.

1125 Park, northeast corner 90th Street, was designed by Schwartz & Gross to have seventy apartments of from six to nine rooms and an Olympic-size lobby. Paul Wallahora, a high school dropout of sixteen, was hired as a doorman at $85 per month in January 1928 and was still on the job in 1989. Outwardly, his Park Avenue vista remained almost unchanged from 1939.

1172 Park, southwest corner 93rd Street just below the F. F. Palmer house that would soon become the George Baker house, was built by Michael E. Paterno and designed by Rosario Candela. It had living rooms 30' x 20', bedrooms 18' x 17', and woodburning fireplaces in each living room and library. Ceilings were advertised as being half a foot higher than the average at the time. Most apartments were of eleven or twelve rooms with five baths. The twelve-room penthouse had fourteen-foot ceilings and a living room thirty-two feet long; its first owner, Mrs. William Amory, sold it in the spring of 1927 to Mrs. Leonard K. Elmhirst, the former Mrs. Willard Straight (née Dorothy Whitney, sister of Harry Payne Whitney, sister-in-law of Gertrude Vanderbilt Whitney), who had sold her mansion on the corner of 94th Street and Fifth subject to a restriction that the house not be razed.

1225 Park, southeast corner 95th Street, was designed by George F. Pelham with five- to seven-room apartments. 1230 Park, southwest corner 94th Street, was by Gronenberg & Leuchtag.

Completed in 1927 were 660, 765-775, 812, 885, 888, 911, 983, and 1165 Park.

The New York Building Congress in 1927 conferred awards for exceptional craftsmanship on eight mechanics who had worked on 660 Park, northwest corner 67th Street. The New York chapter of the American Institute of Architects (A.I.A.) gave the building an honorable mention. Completed by Starrett Brothers from designs by York & Sawyer, 660 Park, according to Andrew Alpern, closely resembled Rouse & Goldstone's 760 Park. Nine apartments, each occupying a full floor, filled the upper stories of 660, and initial tenants included Darwin P. Kingsley, president of New York Life. What distinguishes the building, however, is its maisonette; set apart from 660 by architectural details on the building's facade, it has its own separate entrance, 666 Park, just west of the main entrance in 67th Street.

The maisonette takes up the building's entire first, second, and third floors, with each floor measuring 100' x 60', permitting as many as thirteen rooms per floor. A flight of marble steps from the street entrance leads to a foyer whose walls are carved Caen stone. On this level is a double-height living room measuring 22' x 49', a double-height dining room, a double-height library, a study, the kitchen, service pantries, and servants' hall. The second level has separate men's and women's coat rooms and six servants' rooms. On the third floor are the master suite (bedroom, sitting room, dressing room, and bath) plus two other master bedrooms, each with bath, as well as a sewing room, endless closets, and five more servants' rooms.

This twenty-seven-room maisonette would have at least three owners who were married women of independent means. It was first purchased for about

ABOVE: *Paul Wallahora, a doorman at 1125 Park since January 1928* (1989 photo)

$195,000 by Mrs. William K. Vanderbilt, Jr., the former Virginia ("Birdie") Graham Fair, daughter of James Graham Fair, the mining engineer. Together with two partners, Fair had opened the Bonanza silver vein of the Comstock Lode in February 1873; the vein yielded $150 million in silver, enabling Fair and John W. McKay to open the Bank of Nevada in San Francisco and Fair to buy his way into the U.S. Senate. Vanderbilt, whose sister Consuelo had married the duke of Marlborough, had dropped out of Harvard in his second year to marry Virginia Fair. That was in April 1899, but the couple had not lived together since 1909. Although Vanderbilt had, as noted, bought a maisonette across the avenue at 651 Park, he spent most of his time cruising aboard his 213-foot diesel yacht *Ara*, which he took to the Galápagos Islands in search of new marine specimens. When he returned to New York in June 1927 his wife left for Paris, where she obtained a divorce. Vanderbilt then married Rosalind Lancaster Warburton, ex-wife of the angler and painter Barclay Warburton—a grandson of John Wanamaker—with whom he had voyaged to the Galápagos.

Birdie Vanderbilt soon resold the 666 Park maisonette to Seton Porter, a socialite whose clubs included the Union, Yale, and Racquet & Tennis. Porter was an engineer who had cofounded National Distillers Corp. in 1924, anticipating the eventual repeal of Prohibition. In 1936 he married the former

LEFT: *The two-story windows of 666 Park (a twenty-seven-room maisonette in 660) face onto the avenue at 67th Street* (1929 photo courtesy Municipal Archive)
RIGHT: *The roaring twenties were boom times for builders* (April 1929 photo courtesy Municipal Archive)

Fredericka V. Berwind, daughter of the coal magnate Charles E. Berwind, who had once been called the most beautiful woman in Philadelphia. Porter was her third husband. Her first marriage had ended in divorce in 1911, whereupon she married Col. Henry H. Harjes, head of the Morgan Harjes Bank in Paris. During World War I, Mrs. Harjes had organized and endowed the first privately founded military hospital at the front, remaining there with a staff of trained nurses until the armistice, and then accompanying the French army into Germany. Col. Harjes died after a polo accident at Trouville in 1926 (as 660 and 666 Park were being completed), and his widow, as noted, married Seton Porter ten years later. The Porters made alterations to the maisonette and redecorated it.

Fan Fox and her husband, Leslie B. Samuels, took over in 1938 and made further renovations. Fox was an art collector and philanthropist, a descendant of Gershon Fox, whose Hartford dry goods store, founded in 1847, had grown into the department store G. Fox. She and Samuels are remembered for their benefactions to Lincoln Center that were used to renovate the New York State and Vivian Beaumont theaters. They paneled the library of their maisonette in Georgian style with a carved fireplace and pine overmantel taken from an eighteenth-century house in London. The dining room fireplace was surrounded with ceramic, and the room was given a large Russian chandelier with matching wall sconces. As for the huge living room, its walls were paneled with seventeenth-century pinewood originally used in a large English house. Corinthian pilasters were installed to flank the living room's fireplace, which was given an ornately carved mantelpiece and a complementary over-mantel.

Fan Fox (no kin to the stripper Fanne Foxe with whom Arkansas Congressman Wilbur Mills had recently come to grief) died in the late 1970s. Leslie Samuels put the maisonette on the market and moved, he told Andrew Alpern, into a suite in the Waldorf Towers. Imelda Marcos, wife of the dictator, inspected the place with her retinue, saying she wanted to buy the art and furniture for a museum in the Philippines; and after extensive negotiations she and Samuels cut a deal that evidently went through despite the overthrow of the Marcos regime. Samuels wanted $7 million for the maisonette itself, and the maintenance charges ran to more than $6,400 per month; that rather narrowed the market, especially for a co-op. The board of directors would not look with favor on an oil sheik, diplomat, or rock star. But when Sotheby's, after some months had passed, suggested that he lower the price, Samuels reportedly phoned his old friend Arthur M. Sackler. Principal owner of the William Douglas McAdams medical advertising agency, the publication *Medical Tribune*, and a pharmaceutical company, Sackler was also an art collector who, alone or with his brothers, had given Sackler wings to the Metropolitan (for which he imported the Temple of Dendur), the National Gallery, and Harvard's Fogg Museum, to say nothing of entire museums in Israel and China. Would Dr. Sackler be interested in the maisonette? He sure would. Sackler bought it, spent more than two years renovating and redecorating it, but did not live to enjoy it for long. He died in the spring of 1987. His widow, Gillian, still owned the maisonette as of early 1989.

765–775 Park fills the eastern blockfront between 72nd and 73rd streets. Michael E. Paterno had ten buildings razed to make room for his co-op apartment house. One, at the corner of 72nd Street, was the residence of Alma Gluck Zimbalist. Rosario Candela designed apartments with such generously proportioned rooms that there were only forty rooms to a floor instead of the usual forty-five. The forty-seven luxury apartments, simplexes and duplexes, ranged from nine to sixteen rooms with ceilings from 10′4″ to 13 feet high. Each apartment had from two to six woodburning fireplaces. Each of the four duplex maisonettes had its own private entrance and address. Four of the five roof garden penthouses were duplexes, the other a sixteen-room triplex with its own private, automatic elevator. Duplex and triplex apartments had separate stairways for the servants. Interviewed by the press, Paterno said, "I am convinced that Park Avenue is about the finest residential street in the city. It is certainly as good if not better than Fifth Avenue." Peter B. Schmidt, the Southampton-set lawyer-turned-entrepreneur who owned one of the duplex maisonettes, skipped the country early in 1988, allegedly with millions taken from trusting clients.

812 Park, southwest corner 75th Street, is a neo-Renaissance structure by J. E. R. Carpenter. A.I.A.'s New York chapter gave 812 its gold medal for the best-designed large residential building of 1927. Its cooperative duplex and triplex apartments, designed to accommodate thirty-six families, replaced nine row houses that had faced onto 75th Street. Duplexes typically had thirteen rooms, five baths.

885 Park, northeast corner 78th Street, and 888 Park, northwest corner 78th Street, are both by Schwartz & Gross. The first replaced three tenements on Park and four row houses in 78th Street; the second replaced six buildings on Park and five in 78th Street.

911 Park, southeast corner 80th Street, was designed by Schwartz & Gross to have apartments of ten to twelve high-ceilinged rooms, "log-burning" fireplaces, four to five baths. This structure replaced a seven-story apartment house, the Alvarado, and three four-story brick buildings.

983 Park, northeast corner 83rd Street, another Schwartz & Gross building, was designed to have apartments ranging from six rooms, three baths, to ten rooms, four baths.

1165 Park, northeast corner 92nd Street, by Schwartz & Gross, was designed to have apartments of eight to nine rooms with three to four baths. Recent tenants have included the investment banker Ira Haupt, whose firm was ruined in 1963 following the collapse of the Allied Crude Oil & Refining Co., which had obtained credit by using as collateral some Bayonne, New Jersey, storage tanks that turned out to be empty.

Park Avenue had supplanted Fifth as Millionaire's Row by 1927. Stuart Chase, writing in *The New Republic*, said, "Park Avenue on the island of Manhattan is the end of the American ladder of success. Higher one cannot go . . . The spoil of a continent, ay of the seven seas, is massed along this harsh stone canyon—the winnings from oil, steel, railroads, mining, lumber, motorcars, banking, real estate, moving pictures, foreign trade, speculating, the manufacturing of widgets, the marketing of toothpaste, the distribution of the assets of button kings . . . There are no more worlds to conquer. If America has a heaven this is it . . .

"The last ducal families are leaving Fifth—save for a strip opposite Central Park—and the palaces that they reared in the nineties are, after solemn public exhibition, being ignominiously destroyed . . . to give way to department stores, skyscraper office buildings, shops developed to the ultra-exquisite. It is to the social vacuum left by this desecration that Park Avenue has moved, but never, in its palmiest days, did Fifth Avenue boast such surried phalanxes of million-aires. More fashion it may have had, more individuality, more resplendent names bursting above the rooftops of an adolescent nation—Vanderbilts, Goulds, Astors . . . but never such solid, crushing and cascading wealth.

"We have, indeed, on Park Avenue the mass production of millionaires. It looks the part. The gaudy individual mansions of the handicraft era have given way to regimented, standardized and stupendous unit rectangles of quantity production. The Avenue, from Forty-sixth to Ninety-sixth street, is a succession of monolithic packing cases, each an apartment house twelve to twenty stories high, sitting by infinite solidity on a full city block. Hardly a terrace or garden or portico; nothing to break the relentless line of flat stone profiles; not an inch yielded for the property line that meets the sidewalk. One great cube of masonry after another in almost unendurable monotony . . . And yet it is a broad and noble street, lined like an arrow from north to south from the Grand Central to Fifty-seventh Street. The park space in its center, under which rumble the trains of the New York Central, burns its dull stone pavement without a touch of green, but from Fifty-seventh north it blossoms into a strip of formal garden with grass and shrubs. Thus there is, in places, a park on Park Avenue, contrary to the philology of most streets . . .

"The wealth and fashion of the nation lives, in perspective at least, in structures almost as gaunt as factories. Coming nearer, the differences in detail begin to register forcibly. Rolls-Royces parked along the curbings. Glimpses through carved doorways, past marvelously upholstered commissars, into entrance halls of marble, golden velour. Now and then a glimpse into an interior court, with pointed fir trees fighting for a sunless carbonated life. Governesses with exotic children; governesses with even more exotic dogs. On some of the monoliths set-backs above the fifteenth floor or so, promising sumptuous apartments with light from east and west, and the possibility of garden terrace."

Chase failed to mention that the new Park Avenue buildings had been built with cheap labor; pay scales in the building trades were the envy of many white-collar workers, but by modern standards they were paltry, as were those for people with jobs on Park Avenue. Each of the four elevator men at 898 Park, Andrew Alpern has written, was paid $20 a week in 1924—perhaps $140 in 1989 dollars—which was standard for the time, and the payroll for the entire building staff of nine was less than $10,000 per year.

1070 Park, southwest corner 88th Street (Schwartz & Gross), is a 1928 building. So is 1235 Park, southeast corner 96th Street (Gronenberg & Leuchtag).

1001 Park, northeast corner 84th Street, replaced Park Avenue's last remaining frame houses; they were torn down in 1928 to make way for a cooperative designed by Pleasants Pennington and Albert W. Lewis. It had taken three years to buy the property, because within its 100-foot avenue frontage was a one-foot-wide strip owned by the heirs to an old estate. This was believed to represent a faulty transfer of part of the land sometime in the past, but the deal could not go through until the heirs could be located. The new building was originally supposed to have one apartment per floor, each with thirteen rooms, five baths. It wound up with six-, nine-, and thirteen-room apartments.

No doubt some of the mercantile structures erected down on Fourth Avenue had greater architectural significance, but the real 1920s boom on Park Avenue was in residential towers for the rich.

480 Park, northwest corner 58th Street, is a good example. Commissioned by the developer Sam Minskoff, it was designed by Emery Roth and completed in 1929. Minskoff had paid about $3 million in April 1928 for the site on which stood the ten-story Hotel Clarendon and some old apartment houses; he said he would put up a building of twenty stories with penthouse containing suites of from three to ten rooms; he wound up with something slightly different. Constructed of buff brick and limestone with terra-cotta ornament, 480 Park's upper floors are stepped back in an assymetrical manner to resemble adobe pueblos of the Southwest. Apartments originally ranged from seven to fourteen rooms, some duplexes, all with high ceilings and woodburning fireplaces, a few with large terraces. Maid and butler services were available to all tenants, and meals were served in an elegant restaurant. An eleven-room simplex had a living room measuring 37'x 18', a 25' x 15' dining room, a 17' x 14' library, an 18' x 7' sunroom, and three terraces, the largest of which measured 50' x 14'. The master bedroom was 20' x 18' with adjacent dressing room and bath. There was a second bedroom, 17' x 14', with its own bath. Adjoining the 13' x 12' kitchen was a butler's pantry, and there were three small maids' rooms. Recent tenants have included the socialite publicist Jere Patterson, antique furniture dealer Alastair A. Stair, and William M. Backer of Backer Spielvogel Bates, the advertising agency.

720 Park, northwest corner 70th Street, is one of the posh apartment houses that were nearing completion all over town as the stock market headed for its peak in 1929. Presbyterian Hospital had just moved up to Morningside Heights, its medical pavilions were demolished, and 720 Park, designed by Cross & Cross with Rosario Candela, replaced some of them with a co-op built by Starrett Brothers. Apartments ranged in size from nine to fifteen rooms. Jesse Straus, head of the giant Macy's department store, took two floors; his home, Andrew Alpern has written, "included a 40-foot entrance gallery, a 36-foot library, separate wine and vegetable closets, a valeting room, a sewing room, and a kitchen larger than most modern living rooms." Recent tenants have included advertising executive Carl Spielvogel and his wife, Barbaralee Diamonstein-

Spielvogel, a writer and television producer who specializes in art and architecture.

730 Park, with its entrance in 71st Street, is a nineteen-story building by F. Burrall Hoffman, Jr. and Lafayette A. Goldstone that was finished in 1929 and occupies another corner of the old Presbyterian Hospital property. Apartments of seven to sixteen rooms include a sixteen-room duplex with six baths, six master bedrooms, and five servants' rooms. The duplex maisonettes each have thirteen rooms, five baths, an extra lavatory, four master bedrooms, and four servants' rooms. Recent tenants have included Robin Farkas of the retailing family (Alexander's), investment counselor John L. Loeb, and publishers (newspapers, Condé Nast, Random House, *Parade, Gourmet, Self, The New Yorker, Vanity Fair*) Donald and S. I. (Samuel Irving) Newhouse, Jr. According to *Forbes* the Newhouse brothers had holdings worth more than $5 billion in 1988. Toward the end of that year Si Newhouse bought a Jasper Johns painting for $17.1 million. In the 1920s that would have paid for at least half the new buildings north of 57th Street. In 1988 it was only money.

784 Park, southwest corner 74th Street, replaced four row houses and a Ramando Court, a small apartment house. Emery Roth, on commission from Bing & Bing, included duplexes on lower floors with fourteen rooms, six baths, four to five master bedrooms, and four servants' rooms. More typical are apartments of eleven rooms and five baths, but there are two triplexes of fourteen rooms, seven baths.

944 Park, midblock between 81st and 82nd streets, was finished in 1929 to designs of George Fred Pelham with apartments ranging from six to ten rooms.

1175 Park, southeast corner 93rd Street, is a 1929 Emery Roth building put up by the George Backer Construction Co. (Backer was married to a granddaughter of the banker Jacob H. Schiff) with apartments ranging from eight rooms, three baths to thirteen rooms, four baths. 1175 stands out today because of its brass mailbox and the evergreen hedge planted inside the low iron fence that lines its Park Avenue frontage; for more than half the year a profusion of bright flowers brightens the hedgerow.

1185 Park was the most ambitious of the projects underway as the market crashed in 1929: a 1,300-room house with accommodations for 180 families. Designed by Schwartz & Gross, it rose on Carnegie Hill just across 93rd Street from Roth's 1175 and across the avenue from George F. Baker's house. George Ehret, the brewer whose mansion had occupied the site since 1878, had died in January 1927 after amassing a fortune estimated at $40 million. His property took up the entire blockfront on the east side of the avenue between 93rd and 94th streets—201 feet on Park, 255 feet in 93rd Street (bringing it to within 100 feet of Lexington Avenue), and 230 feet in 94th Street. When the Bricken Construction Co. bought the property in April 1928 for nearly $3 million, its president, Abraham Bricken, said, "We have designed what we believe will be the sunniest apartment building in the city."

Bricken's company had erected 1085 Park, northeast corner 88th Street; 1111 Park, and 1165 Park, where Bricken occupied a specially built roof penthouse. All of these were fully rented, and Bricken was putting up 1070 Park, southwest corner 88th Street, which was to be finished in the fall of 1928 and was already 40 percent rented. He announced that 1185 would comprise six units, each with its own lobby and each with three entrances, each entrance having separate passenger and service elevators for the two apartments on every floor. There would be six-, seven-, eight-, and nine-room apartments. Nearly one-third of the plot would be given over to a drive-in garden court, 100 feet wide by 150 long, in the center of the building. Every apartment would have street or avenue frontage and would extend through to this wide courtyard for cross-ventilation.

Thus 1185 became the last of the large apartment houses built in the shape of a hollow square. (Graham Court, the Belnord, and the Apthorp are other survivors in this mode.) In the spring of 1929 Bricken had 300 masons and about 700 other workmen reporting for work daily at the building site. New contracts would go into effect beginning August 24, cutting the work week to five days (from five and a half) and raising wages by 10 percent. Bricken brought his project in ahead of schedule and saved money.

Suites at 1185 have spacious entrance galleries and sensible room arrangements. The duplex penthouse has a living room 32' x 20'6", a dining room 24' x 14', a library 27'8" x 16'8", a master bedroom 26' x 13'7", and three other bedrooms, sun parlor, two maids' rooms, and five baths upstairs. Downstairs are a servants' hall, two maids' rooms, and a lavatory off a circular staircase connecting the two floors. The building's high elevation meant that apartments did receive more sunshine than most, which in summer could make things uncomfortable: canvas awnings, used at windows to keep apartments cool before air conditioning, were eventually banned as a fire hazard. 1185 was converted to co-op ownership in 1953. Recent tenants have included advertising executive Laurel Cutler, publisher Helen Deutsch, and Wall Street broker Dennis Levine, who was convicted of inside trading.

Across the avenue, at the southwest corner of 94th Street, 1192 Park was completed in 1929 to plans by Rosario Candela. Recent tenants here have included Mrs. W. H. Vanderbilt.

Park Avenue's great building boom was far from over. As the Dow Jones Industrial Average hit giddy new heights, developers rushed to buy up sites that had been occupied by institutions or had simply seemed too pricey. Some of the city's most luxurious residential structures—on Central Park South and Central Park West as well as on Park Avenue—were nearing completion when the air went out of Wall Street's balloon in October 1929. By the time they were ready for occupancy, prospective tenants were scarce.

740 Park, northwest corner 71st Street, was finished in 1930, replacing three buildings that had faced on Park and a nurses' residence in 71st Street. Designed by Rosario Candela with Arthur Loomis Harmon and sheathed entirely in limestone, it has beautifully proportioned rooms and kitchens as large as many entire apartments. Early tenants included Marshall Field. The building originally contained an immense four-floor apartment for John D. Rockefeller, Jr. The

ABOVE: *1185 Park's gothic arches lead to a large inner courtyard* (1989 photo)

quadruplex had its own gymnasium, billiard room, and accommodations for five live-in servants. In December 1952, Rockefeller bought the entire building, then assessed at $2.8 million, of which $800,000 was for the land.

The *New York Times* architecture critic Paul Goldberger, in his 1979 book *The City Observed*, called 740 Park "a solid, sumptuous mass that sits on a corner with absolute authority." He noted that the hint of Art Deco in the fluted base and entrance detail was "made very, very tame for nothing would be worse than to have the gentry of Park Avenue think they were being given the style of Central Park West and the Grand Concourse." Two years earlier he had called 740 Park a "New York architectural Gibraltar, the limestone box that appears so solid that a bomb set off in one apartment conceivably could not be heard in the next. It is the epitome of New York apartment conservatism . . . There are vague hints of Art Deco visible, but they are subtle. The two entrances, one on Park Avenue and the other at 71 East 71st Street, are grandly if quietly expressed in granite . . . Rosario Candela designed or codesigned several buildings that rank among the jewels of the East Side and are nearly 740 Park's equals. Thirty-one apartments, generously proportioned. A typical living room is almost 40 feet long. Most are duplexes. Not long ago, the grandest of them all, 34 rooms on two floors, a carved-up remnant of Mrs. John D. Rockefeller Jr.'s original four-floor apartment, was on the market."

The purchaser was Saul P. Steinberg, who in 1961, at age twenty-two, had founded Leasco with $25,000 borrowed from his father. Steinberg had pioneered in computer leasing, taken Leasco public, and gone on to gain control of Reliance Insurance Group. Probably the second-richest man on Park Avenue (not counting people like Giovanni Agnelli of Fiat, whose Park Avenue penthouse, filled with art, was never meant for anything more than occasional use), Steinberg, according to *Forbes*, had a net worth of $660 million just before the October 1987 stock market crash. One year later he was worth a mere $400 million. He and his (third) wife, Gayfryd, and art collection still occupied the huge apartment at 740 Park. Somewhat smaller is the sixteen-room duplex in the same building acquired for $5.5 million in 1985 by leveraged buyout honcho Henry R. Kravis of Kohlberg Kravis Roberts and his fiancée, designer Carolyne Roehm, shortly before their wedding in the apartment. They managed to run the place with six servants, two of them sleep-in. Also at 740 are Steven Ross, CEO of Warner Communications, whose total 1988 compensation was reportedly $5.4 million, and Rand V. Araskog, CEO of ITT International, whose 1988 salary was reportedly $3 million.

770 Park, southwest corner 73rd Street, is another 1930 Rosario Candela building. A cooperative designed as a residence for forty families, it replaced the Sonora apartment house and seven row houses that had faced onto 73rd Street. Advertisements in the spring of 1930 offered a thirteen-room duplex with balcony, its windows facing on the avenue. A fourteen-room special duplex was advertised as having a living room 30' x 20' with a full-length balcony, windows on two sides. "Also master suite with corner boudoir. Simplexes of 11 and 13 rooms, duplexes from 7 to 15 rooms, terraces and loggias." Recent tenants have

included tobacco tycoon Edgar Cullman and investment banker David T. Schiff.

895 Park, southeast corner 79th Street, replaced a building on Park and eight row houses facing onto 79th Street. Sloan & Robertson, whose Chanin Building had just opened at 42nd Street, were the architects. A co-op with apartments of twelve to fifteen rooms simplex, duplex, and triplex, the building boasted a squash court and gymnasium facilities.

1021 Park, northeast corner 85th Street, was designed by Rosario Candela under the supervision of Kenneth M. Murchison and built by Anthony Campagna's sons Joseph A. and John J. This co-op adjoined the garden of Mrs. Reginald de Koven, widow of the composer, and backed up on the Park Avenue Methodist Church; since part of the garden was permanently restricted against building and the church was not about to come down, the apartments in 1021 were assured of sunlight. The new building, completed in 1930, replaced the Amos Pinchot house of 1906. Original owners included a partner in the investment banking house Brown Brothers, whose duplex of nineteen rooms and eight baths had been designed to meet his requirements. Most apartments are of eight rooms, four baths (A line), thirteen rooms, six baths (B line), or eleven rooms, four baths (C line).

The haut monde—and the haute bourgeoisie as well—had in the late 1920s been moving farther uptown to the 70s, 80s and even 90s. But Anthony Campagna was more attracted to a site farther south. In March 1929 he paid $4 million for a large plot on the west side of Park between 60th and 61st streets. The Brearley School occupied a nine-story structure on the 61st Street corner but was about to relocate to 610 East 83rd Street, near Carl Schurz Park. Also on the site was 520 Park, a twelve-story apartment house built only fifteen years earlier, which would be pulled down as soon as its leases expired. Campagna, who lived in a huge mansion up in Riverdale, told the press, "This is evidently one of the first occasions when a moderately new twelve-story apartment house that has always been well rented will give way in a short time to another similar building to meet the new requirements of city life."

Sixty years later, at 525 Park, across the avenue from Campagna's site, a major converter of such buildings to co-op ownership would be using air rights purchased from three adjoining buildings to construct three penthouses, each having about 4,000 square feet, counting terraces and balconies. The company, M. J. Raynes, had converted 970 Park to co-op ownership and was adding two triplex penthouses to the building's original twelve floors. They would have circular staircases, greenhouse studies, dens, libraries, huge terraces—and would sell for about $6 million each. A Chinese travel agency head had just had a rather shoddily-constructed triplex penthouse put up atop 470 Park at 58th Street.

Park Avenue sprouted penthouses as early as 1912, when 903 was built, but few such apartments existed in all of Manhattan until the 1920s. Three permits for penthouses were issued in 1918, and while this number had risen to ten by 1921 the great majority were for one-room structures. Some sources credit the publisher Condé Nast with popularizing penthouses for luxury residences when he had one built in 1926 atop a new building at 1040 Park. The number of penthouse permits leaped from twenty-three in 1922, to fifty-three in 1927, to seventy-three in 1928. But penthouses were often used for servants' quarters, as at 580 and 1133 Park in 1923, and for laundry equipment. Although steam dryers had been introduced early in the century, many people preferred to dry their wash in the sun; tenants in some buildings were allotted specific days of the week when they could have their maids use the rooftop laundry (if it rained, tough luck).

By 1929 the Buildings Department had given approval to 391 penthouses, and a good many were on Park Avenue. An eleven-room penthouse at 480 Park rented for $1,788 per month, then an enormous amount, and although most penthouses fetched under $100 per room per month, some rented for as much as $167 per room. Though penthouses brought higher rents than ordinary apartments, they were snapped up before anything else—usually from plans before buildings were completed. Improvements to the roof were generally left to individual tenants, who were free to plant trees and even vegetable gardens. Tenants of Park Avenue penthouses have included people of dubious probity, such as Ivar Kreuger. In recent years they have been owned by such celebrities as Fiat's boss Giovanni Agnelli and the tobacco heiress Doris Duke.

No other penthouse on the avenue can match the twenty-six-room triplex at 625 Park, a building completed in 1931 to plans by J. E. R. Carpenter. Huge terraces surround the living room, dining room, gallery, library, and kitchen, while other terraces surround the 68' x 17' recreation room. All of these rooms except the kitchen and gallery have woodburning fireplaces. The bedroom floor has six bedrooms and a maid's room. One bedroom is 33'6" x 18'2", another 29'8" x 20'6". Circular staircases connect the three floors. Helena Rubinstein, the cosmetic queen, owned this penthouse for thirty years and used its sixty-eight-foot-long salon for parties and chamber music recitals. A special room was designed to hold her collection of ultraminiature furniture in glass-enclosed dioramas, and another to house a set of Venetian shell furniture and a series of wall murals painted by Salvador Dali. Imperious and demanding, Mme. Rubinstein enjoyed breakfast in bed while hearing presentations from her advertising agency people (who were not even offered coffee). Charles Revson of Revlon, her major competitor in the cosmetics industry, took over the place after Rubinstein's death in 1965 and behaved in similar fashion. Revson himself died in 1975.

Recent tenants at 625 have included the onetime Wall Street whiz Marshall S. Cogan (whose automotive parts company Knoll International Holdings employs nearly 16,000 people); the Columbia Law School professor emeritus Milton Handler of Kaye, Scholer, Fierman, Hayes, and Handler; the art dealer Tibor de Nagy; and Marc Rich, the commodities trader who, with his associate Pincus Green, fled the country in 1983 before being indicted for tax evasion and fraud (they wound up paying the U.S. government $150 million plus $21 million in fines). According to *Forbes*, Rich and Green were worth at least $1.5 billion in 1988 but faced prison terms totaling 325 years if convicted.

Park Avenue has been home to the famous and the infamous. Few people today remember, perhaps few care, that its sidewalks and center mall were once much wider, its roadways narrower. Indeed the great building boom of the 1920s proceeded amid a stormy controversy over whether or not to make the avenue more accommodative to motor traffic.

9

The Traffic Artery

CARS AND TAXIS swoop up and down Park Avenue today at forty miles per hour and more. (Legal limit: thirty. No buses, please, and no trucks except for certain pickups and deliveries.) Third and Lex have been one-way since July 1960, Fifth and Madison since January 1966. Park is one of the few surviving two-way thoroughfares on the East Side. Traffic lights are not synchronized, and taxi drivers race to go twelve blocks before the lights change. Vehicles making left-hand turns sometimes pose a hazard. Its relatively smooth flow has nevertheless made Park a preferred north-south route for more than sixty years. Going south on the avenue's western roadway, vehicles ascend a ramp at 46th Street, whoosh through the base of 230 Park, zoom around Grand Central Terminal, whip across the busy crosstown traffic of 42nd Street, roar down to 32nd Street, and make their way on to Union Square.

Fifth Avenue was the major East Side traffic artery early in the century. Motor buses finally replaced horsecars on Fifth Avenue in 1907. (In those days, Lewis Mumford has written, a horse-drawn wagon traveled around New York at an average speed of eleven miles per hour, twice as fast as motor traffic a half century later).

In the early years of motorcars, when two-way traffic prevailed on all the avenues and city air still reeked of horse droppings, the divided roadways of Park favored it as potentially the most desirable route for anyone driving up- or downtown on the East Side. But after Grand Central opened in 1913 the avenue was a pedestrian mall north to 57th Street; to the south, between 32nd and 34th streets, the opening to the old Harlem Railroad tunnel, now used for streetcars, contributed to a traffic impasse compounded by steep grades on Park Avenue and the crosstown streets. A narrow rim on the west side of the avenue permitted passage of vehicles; it had no counterpart on the east side. Passengers transfering from the 34th Street crosstown car line to north- and southbound lines had to climb a series of steep stairs. Traffic in 33rd Street was blocked completely at Fourth Avenue. City engineers favored a plan designed by Lloyd Collis, a consulting engineer, which contemplated lowering the surface of 34th Street 6.22 feet at its intersection with Park Avenue, with consequent reductions of grade from 4.54 percent to 1.86 percent on 34th Street to a point 238 feet east of Park. In the block to the west toward Madison avenue the grade would be reduced from 2.13 to 0.79 percent, with readjustments of grades on Park Avenue itself.

When the Collis plan was adopted by the Board of Estimate in the fall of 1913, property owners who stood to suffer threatened to sue. The *Real Estate Record*, its crystal ball no clearer than anyone else's, said such owners were "cherishing an illusion . . . This part of Park Avenue is becoming very much more valuable for business than it is for residential purposes. No matter what steps are taken to do away with the present absurd grading of the intersection of 34th Street and Park Avenue, a large volume of traffic will move up and down the avenue. It will necessarily become much noisier than it is at present and much less desirable as a location for costly residences. Its inhabitants will begin to move out, and as they move out it will be difficult to replace them except with business firms. . . . That this part of Park Avenue will, as soon as it is freed, be rapidly transformed into a mercantile district cannot be doubted."

Meanwhile, traffic north and south of the terminal swelled—and slowed to a crawl. When a young auto salesman demonstrating a new Stutz was stopped in 1915 for going twenty-five miles an hour on Park Avenue, the cop was riding a bicycle.

Charles Reed's plan for viaducts around Grand Central Terminal remained a drawing-board concept for many years. Warren & Wetmore's designs for a viaduct across 42nd Street and around the westerly side of Grand Central were kept in a drawer in the office of the borough president until 1916, when the Fifth Avenue Association began agitating for a link between the upper and lower avenues. They finally prevailed, but work was delayed pending completion of the Lexington Avenue subway line into 42nd Street. Locations would have to be ascertained for the piers upon which the viaduct was to rest. Construction of the viaduct began in 1918, and work progressed rapidly despite wartime difficulties in securing labor and material. From Park and 40th Street, this viaduct—nearly 600 feet long—took two-way traffic and carried it around the west side of the terminal, depositing it at the corner of 45th Street and Vanderbilt Avenue. A spur ran along the east side of the terminal, providing parking space and forming an entrance to the new Commodore Hotel. But soon after the viaduct opened in 1919, it became clear that more would have to be done to prevent a traffic tieup at its northern end.

Southbound motorists encountered a bottleneck at 45th Street: diverted to

Vanderbilt, they could either go south three blocks on Vanderbilt to 42nd Street and then back onto Park, or they could go up the viaduct at 45th and Vanderbilt and onto Park again at 40th Street. Northbound cars could take one of three routes: they could turn right on 40th Street to Lexington Avenue, go up to 45th Street, and then go west onto Park; they could use the viaduct at 45th and Vanderbilt; or they could go up Park to 42nd, west to Vanderbilt, and up Vanderbilt to 45th (Vanderbilt was then a private thoroughfare above 45th Street). Thirteen lanes of traffic met at an intersection with outlets in only three directions.

Traffic congestion at Vanderbilt and 45th Street was probably the worst in the city. Park Avenue was crippled; the defile at 45th Street delayed traffic in the very heart of Manhattan's commercial district. In mid-February 1920 the city tried making Park Avenue one way northbound and Fifth Avenue southbound from 10 o'clock in the morning until 5 in the afternoon. Police predicted that a vehicle would be able to travel from 57th Street to 34th in less than ten minutes instead of the forty it sometimes took. The experiment was abandoned after a month, and the Fifth Avenue Association petitioned Mayor Hylan, suggesting a plan for permanent relief. The plan provided for an easterly roadway around the Grand Central Terminal into 45th Street at Depew Place. This would make the existing westerly viaduct a one-way road by taking northbound traffic around the opposite side of the terminal and depositing it at 45th Street, a block east of the congested Vanderbilt corner. City engineers in 1921 proposed to extend the east and west viaducts around the terminal to 45th Street and have them converge at 45th and Park.

New York Central engineers had other ideas. They proposed that Park Avenue be closed to all vehicular traffic at the 45th Street grade; new roadways would carry traffic around both sides of Grand Central between 40th and 46th streets. Easements for these roadways would be given to the city and Vanderbilt Avenue between 45th and 47th streets would be turned over to the city for public use. In return, the Central would obtain all remaining air rights, permitting construction of a monumental building on the site bounded by 45th and 46th streets between Vanderbilt Avenue and Depew Place. Borough President Julius Miller approved this plan and presented it to the Board of Estimate and Apportionment in January 1923. The board approved, the state legislature at Albany passed an enabling act that would permit the city to carry the plan into effect, and Governor Al Smith signed the bill into law. In the summer of 1923 the Board of Estimate appropriated $1,661,000 to cut eighteen feet from each side of the fifty-six-foot wide grass plots in the center of the avenue, thus widening the roadways in the blocks between 46th and 57th streets.

South of Grand Central, red-and-green traffic lights directed traffic by late 1925. Work to widen the avenue between 32nd and 34th streets had finally begun at the time construction began on 1 Park Avenue. Developers of the building had acquired an old carbarn site (formerly the stables of the New York & Harlem Railroad) occupying the full block bounded by Fourth and Lexington avenues between 32nd and 33rd streets; they persuaded the mayor and Board of Aldermen early in 1924 to let them have the 1 Park Avenue address instead of a Fourth Avenue address. South of 32nd Street the avenue would remain 100 feet wide. North of 32nd it was 140 feet wide: the Park Avenue and Vanderbilt hotels on the west wide lined up with Park Avenue buildings to the north, and on the east side twenty feet were being removed from the Park Avenue frontages of the carbarn site and of the 71st Regiment Armory between 33rd and 34th streets.

Martha Bacon and her neighbors opposed plans that would increase motor traffic on Park Avenue. In her fight to keep 1 Park Avenue at 34th Street, Mrs. Bacon enjoyed the support of H. Gordon Duval's Park Avenue Association. Duval, a young Englishman, had founded the association in 1922. Then only twenty-nine, he had arrived in New York just before World War I. It would later be said that he became a citizen and worked during the war as a "dollar a year" man on Liberty Loan campaigns. In 1924 he was sued by Ivy St. Clair, a dancer, for alleged breach of promise; and in February 1926, soon after raising the possibility that his Park Avenue Association might bring legal action to block extension of the avenue to 32nd Street, Duval married Hilda von Herrlich, daughter of a Connecticut clergyman. Duval installed his brother Montague as secretary of the Association, devoting his own efforts largely to publishing the *Park Avenue Social Review* and keeping the avenue free of commercialism and unwanted motor traffic.

Traffic was heavier on Fifth Avenue; seeking relief, the Fifth Avenue Association pressed to have Park Avenue widened so that it could share the growing burden. In the spring of 1925 the association released the results of a study showing that traffic on all the central avenues had increased by 20 percent in just one year. Despite its narrow twenty-seven-foot roadways, despite its Vanderbilt Avenue bottleneck, Park had overtaken Fifth as a traffic artery.

Construction of the new easterly roadway above Depew Place began in the early spring of 1926. It opened to traffic in January 1927, and contracts were let a few months later for widening Park from 46th Street, the northern end of the new viaducts, to 57th. Two viaducts, each 33'10" wide, would together provide nearly sixty-eight feet of elevated roadway across the congested Grand Central area. The central promenades on Park Avenue, formerly fifty-six feet wide, were cut down to twenty feet, increasing the width of the easterly and westerly roadways from twenty-seven feet to forty-five.

At 57th Street there was a problem. To accommodate switches in the tracks under Park Avenue at that point, a large overhead truss replaced the usual underground pillars, and this truss blocked any widening operation—as well as blocking the vision of "automobilists" going to and from the Queensboro Bridge and traveling up and down the avenue. Considerable engineering skill was needed to locate the necessary pillar supports in between the crisscross of tracks below and remove the truss. And the roadway four stories above the tracks required stronger pillars. Work progressed below street level, but the roadway south of 57th Street remained narrow in 1927. That was fine with Duval. Motor traffic on the residential avenue was anathema to him, and he opposed efforts by the rival Fifth Avenue Association to widen Park Avenue.

The avenue above Grand Central got its first traffic signals in May 1927, but only north of 59th Street. South of 59th the roadways were still too narrow to accommodate heavy traffic but they were widened by the end of 1927, and work began the following spring on the towering New York Central Building, an $8 million structure that spanned Park Avenue, with flanks touching on Vanderbilt Avenue and Depew Place. The extension of Depew Place permitted northbound traffic to pass through easily, and New Yorkers looked forward to the opening of the westerly roadway that would complete the project.

But if Park Avenue traffic were to flow smoothly, the avenue north of 72nd Street would have to be widened. And in the spring of 1928 Manhattan Borough President Miller issued orders that Park Avenue property owners between 57th and 72nd streets remove stoops, railings, and other projections preparatory to work that would narrow sidewalks and widen roadways. The Park Avenue Association circulated an appeal to its members to oppose this plan. Widening the avenue would be an invitation for more motor traffic, and that would "dangerously impair the many attractive features of Park Avenue's residential district."

The New York Central was cast as the villain. Directors of the Fifth Avenue Association had voted in favor of the street-widening program after being informed that the Central refused to close its ventilation gratings in Park Avenue's "center-mark strips." Members of the Park Avenue Association were told that the Central had tried to bargain for easements for two additional tracks under the avenue. When Borough President Miller learned that the Central would not cooperate in the improvement, he began negotiating with its officers. He also submitted to the Board of Estimate revised plans for the widening. He had originally recommended a plan for roadways forty-five feet on each side of the avenue, which would have been possible only by closing the vents. Then he found he could increase the roadway on each side to forty-three feet without closing the vents and altered his plans accordingly.

When the Board of Estimate held hearings on April 11, 1928, only one protest was registered against widening. It came, predictably, from the Park Avenue Association, which opposed the allotment of funds for such a purpose. The association's lawyer said his client did not object to widening the avenue at what he termed the "traffic" area between 57th and 61st streets. "There is no traffic congestion beyond this point," he said. "After 61st Street the traffic falls away. The district is regarded as residential." He concluded that 75 percent of the residents of Park Avenue who owned their own property were against the widening project and said there was no use making the improvement without removing the New York Central vents along Park Avenue. These, he noted, had been obsolete for twenty years, ever since the substitution of electric for steam operation on the line. The Board of Estimate, unmoved, voted public improvement expenditures estimated at $19,210,381, to be paid for through the issuance of one-year bonds, with $650,000 of the moneys to be spent on widening Park Avenue.

On June 6 Borough President Miller announced that he had persuaded Patrick E. Crowley, president of the New York Central, to close the railroad's openings in Park Avenue between 57th and 72nd streets at an expense of about $162,000 to the company. The openings would be roofed over with concrete and steel, with a few gratings left for ventilation and emergency use. Miller said that in the center of the avenue, where the openings existed, he would build a park similar to the center park in the avenue between 46th and 57th streets.

Would the roadways, then, be forty-five feet wide? Evidently not. Miller said he would widen the roadway to forty-three feet on each side of this center park, which would be twenty-four feet wide. The improvement was expected to double the avenue's traffic capacity. The grass plots in the center of Park Avenue, two to three feet above the roadway and surmounted by a three-foot fence, would be lowered to improve the vision of motorists and pedestrians at cross streets. Park Avenue would be repaved, and more than 100 trees would be planted along both sidewalks. Said a *Times* editorial, "Most persons agree that the new gardens in the center of the avenue are more sightly than the old ones which surrounded the air vents. Work on paving and the gardens is to begin as soon as possible. While it is in progress, traffic will be somewhat inconvenienced, as it was during the rearrangement of the lower portion of the avenue, but Borough President Miller and the officials of the railroad company, together with those organizations which have been urging the change, will receive the gratitude of residents and transients alike for making possible this new development of Park Avenue."

And suddenly Gordon Duval was dead. Just before five o'clock in the morning of June 29, three weeks after the *Times* editorial, Duval opened the door to the elevator shaft in the corridor of his penthouse apartment at 570 Park and plunged to his death. The elevator operator later said he had heard a heavy thud but had been unable to discover any cause. Hilda Duval awakened at seven-thirty, saw that her husband was not in the room, found the elevator door opened, and phoned the superintendent, who found the pajama-clad body atop the elevator cab. Police detectives called it an accident, remarking that the doors to the elevator shaft, a clothes closet, and a bathroom all looked alike; and although most elevator shaft doors could be opened only from the shaft side, this one could be opened from the corridor. Duval's widow later sued for $300,000, claiming negligence; the owners of 570 Park claimed that Duval had committed suicide; the plaintiff produced as a witness a woman who claimed that on the night before his fourteen-story plunge the Duvals had given a farewell party for her on the eve of a trip abroad. Duval had been in good spirits, she testified, and appeared to be in no mood to take his life. The widow, remarried to a Parisian interior decorator, was awarded $50,000 (soon reduced to $41,369, probably to save the building from having to bear legal costs), but at least a shadow of doubt remained. Had Duval perhaps been profoundly depressed at the loss of face suffered by his Park Avenue Association—and by the prospect of heavy traffic on Park Avenue?

The avenue might, in Captain Pendrick's words, be "one of the best routes for through traffic in the city," but it still had that bottleneck at 45th Street. Work was proceeding, however, to bring the easterly and westerly roadways around Grand Central Terminal and into the new New York Central Building, under construction at 45th Street. The skyscraper formed a gateway to upper Park Avenue from lower Manhattan. It was not yet finished when the new westerly roadway through it and around the terminal opened to traffic on September 6, 1928. Swinging toward each other at Park Avenue, the roadways descended from the tunnels into their respective lanes on Park Avenue at 46th Street. Southbound traffic had the entire western elevated ramp from the exit in the New York Central Building across 45th Street to the junction above the entrance to the terminal on 42nd Street. Traffic on Park Avenue could now, at last, flow smoothly and quickly. A parade of motorcars commemorated the event. Crosstown traffic in the highly congested Grand Central area was now eliminated. North and southbound traffic was carried by viaduct over 42nd and 45th streets, entirely unimpeded by crossstreets or stoplights between 40th and 46th streets. Crosstown traffic on 42nd and 45th streets passed unhindered beneath the flow of cars and taxis on Park Avenue.

Three and a half years later, the heavy traffic on Park Avenue was making some residents think that Gordon Duval might have been right. On February 11, 1932, the *Times* editorialized: "People who live in the apartments that face [Park

BELOW: *North of 86th Street the center mall was not narrowed until 1930* (1930 photo courtesy Municipal Archive)

Avenue] complain that they are experiencing increasing difficulty crossing the traffic stream now augmented by hundreds of cars seeking to take advantage of the viaduct over the congested streets of the Grand Central district. Park Avenue has another advantage which has turned out to be something of a disadvantage in the eyes of the pedestrian. It is twice as wide as the ordinary street, and the grass plot curbs afford but momentary sanctuary. The automobile is king. 'Beating the lights' quickly becomes a popular sport on so broad and tempting a highway. Left turns are winked at by the police; right turns are made—as they are everywhere else in the city, for that matter—without even the courtesy stop which the law requires." August Hecksher now headed the Park Avenue Association, but it was the rival Fifth Avenue Association that championed the cause of pedestrians against what the *Times* called "Park Avenue charioteers."

When Gordon Duval died in 1928 there were more than 22 million automobiles on American roads. Walter Chrysler in 1928 introduced the Plymouth, to compete with Ford and Chevrolet, and the DeSoto, soon widely used as a New York taxicab. While New York was not yet wholly committed to the automobile, Park Avenue, at least, was accepting the inevitable. But the boom times that had brought the avenue to flower were coming to an end. American factories turned out more than 5 million automobiles in 1929; not for another twenty years would they again reach that level of production. Meanwhile, taxis, private cars, and limousines would be pulling up at some swank new Park Avenue hotels.

BELOW: *Traffic moved freely right through the new New York Central Building* (January 1928 photo courtesy Municipal Archive)

10
.
Transients and Other Guests

THE RELIABLE *Mobil Travel Guide* has in recent years included two Park Avenue hotels (Regency and Waldorf-Astoria) and one just off Park (Inter-Continental) among the ten Manhattan hotels to which it awards four stars (only the Carlyle, on Madison at 77th Street, rates five). Mobil gives the Drake Swissôtel and Mayfair Regent three stars; the Doral Park Avenue, Kitano, and Park Sheraton two. Eugene Fodor's list of "super-deluxe" New York hotels has only one Park Avenue entry: "the 88 exclusive [Waldorf] Tower accommodations." He calls the Drake Swissôtel, Inter-Continental, Mayfair Regent, Regency, and Waldorf-Astoria merely "deluxe" and Kitano "first class." Arthur Frommer lists the Grand Hyatt New York, "Park Avenue at Grand Central Terminal," among the city's "new beauties" and includes the Drake Swissôtel and Waldorf-Astoria with other "classic standbys." David Yeadon ranks the Mayfair Regent third and the Waldorf-Astoria tenth in his list of the ten top hotels. You pays your money—a lot of it—and you takes your choice; but the Waldorf-Astoria, renovated and restored between 1982 and 1987 at a cost of $150 million, has regained its original Art Deco splendor and is again the best *large* New York hotel.

In addition to serving transients, hotels have offered some of the city's most comfortable places in which to live. The Beekman, Ritz Tower, Lombardy, Delmonico's, and Waldorf Towers are all prestigious residential addresses. Many hotels on Park—the Vanderbilt, Murray Hill, Marguery, Park Lane, Ambassador (the Sheraton East in its final years), and Sulgrave—disappeared between the late 1940s and mid-1960s, as did the Chatham on Vanderbilt Avenue. The Biltmore and Commodore continued into the late 1970s.

Murray Hill remains attractive to visitors, and three hotels still serve transients desiring the relative tranquility of this area. The Park Sheraton, at 45 Park, originally the Russell and later the Sheraton-Park Avenue and Sheraton-Russell before adopting its present name, was a residential hotel when it opened in the fall of 1923 at the southeast corner of 37th Street and Park. An "Italian style" structure designed by Rouse & Goldstone, it had eighty non-housekeeping suites of one to four rooms, some terraced, some with woodburning fireplaces. There was one housekeeping apartment with roof garden and, on the first floor, several doctors' suites. Bedrooms for personal maids and valets could be secured in the building. The hotel had a main dining room, two private dining rooms, and room service. The Bowery Savings Bank foreclosed on the Russell's mortgage in 1941 and sold the hotel in 1943 to Ernest Henderson. He had joined forces with a Harvard classmate ten years earlier to take over a Boston area hotel and begin Sheraton Hotel Corp. The Russell became New York's first Sheraton hotel.

Close neighbors to the Park Sheraton on Murray Hill are the Kitano and Doral Park Avenue. The Kitano, at 66 Park (southeast corner 38th Street), began life as the Murray apartment house in 1926, was acquired in 1970 by a Japanese construction firm, and reopened in 1973 as a 112-room transient hotel. More than 70 percent of its guests are Japanese businessmen, and it has a Japanese restaurant (a Tokyo restaurant owns the concession), but only two of its suites have Japanese-style living rooms, with tatami mats on the floors and deep, Japanese-style soaking tubs.

The Doral Park Avenue, opened by Alfred J. Kaskel in 1964 at 70 Park, northeast corner 38th Street, is a 204-room transient hotel with a penthouse for its owners, Doris and Alvin Kaskel, and two other penthouses. Alfred Kaskel's Carol Management Co. owned the Hotel 70 Park Avenue in the mid-1950s, took over the adjoining Dwight School, and used it to expand. In summer the Doral boasts a sidewalk café.

Several hotels rose above the tracks of the new Grand Central Terminal. The Biltmore opened on January 1, 1914, at the southwest corner of Vanderbilt and 44th Street, directly above Grand Central's brand-new room for incoming long-distance trains (the so-called "kissing gallery"). A guest could go from his Pullman seat to his room, take the subway downtown to transact business, and return to Chicago or wherever without ever going outdoors. Built by John McE. Bowman on land leased from the New York Central, the Biltmore was for most of its sixty-seven years (it closed in August 1981) true to its promise, a gracious refuge at the heart of the bustling city.

The Presidential Suite on the fourth floor consisted of a private salon, a dining room, reception rooms, and bedrooms. A private elevator brought the guest from Grand Central directly into his own apartment, which adjoined a large public salon and reception rooms. These could be used on special occasions to accommodate several hundred people. A man in public life could stop at the hotel, hold his receptions, and depart without attracting attention.

Private dining rooms and a special suite for private entertainments occupied the rest of the fourth floor. On the sixth was a roof garden with trees, flower beds, and shrubberies. A banquet hall three stories high was in the south wing of the 22nd floor, as was the main ballroom, which was two stories high. In summer the banquet hall's twenty-five-foot windows were removed on three sides to convert it into a "Skyline" Restaurant. The north wing of this floor was a hospital with nurses' rooms and suites for patients and their attendants. On the Madison Avenue blockfront were the Biltmore's main dining room and men's café. The hotel's north entrance on Vanderbilt Avenue led into the women's corridor, designed so that ladies could come and go without passing through the main lobby. There was a men's writing room and a women's writing room; ladies' hairdressing, reception, and cloakrooms; and a Turkish bath with plunge.

For nearly seven decades, preppies, college students, and young lovers met "under the clock"—the famous bronze clock in the Biltmore's elegant lobby so familiar to J. D. Salinger's fictional hero Holden Caulfield and to real-life middle-class couples. They dined at the lovely Palm Court, originally the tea terrace. Commuters relaxed at the Men's Bar, originally the Men's Café. Nobody remembered in 1973 that the hotel had once had many separate facilities for men and women, and the Men's Bar became a target of feminist ire; a suit was filed for violation of the Public Accommodations Law, and Human Rights Commissioner Eleanor Holmes Norton ordered the sign changed. The Biltmore was demolished in 1983 to make way for the atriumed Bank of America Plaza.

The Roosevelt Hotel, just north of the Biltmore, opened on September 22, 1924, with a dinner at which young Cornelius Vanderbilt IV sat on the dais along with Mayor Hylan and Carl Akley (an explorer friend of Teddy Roosevelt). The 1,100-room hotel had been built by Thompson Starrett on land owned by the New York Central. On its Madison Avenue side it replaced the Tiffany Studios, an old red-brick structure built by the Vanderbilt family to serve as the Railroad YMCA. By 1929, the Roosevelt was paying the New York Central $285,000 a year in rentals. Guy Lombardo and his Royal Canadians played for dancers in the Roosevelt Ballroom; their annual New Year's Eve radio broadcast of "Auld Lang Syne" became a national tradition.

Until the late 1940s, access from Grand Central was only by way of a steep flight of stairs. The hotel had spacious restaurants and private dining rooms, but like so many other hotels it was bankrupt at the end of 1933, and was bought for $25,000 on March 1, 1934. By November it was advertising rooms at $75 a month with a few singles at $60, swimming pool and bridge room privileges included. Six years later, in 1940, rooms were still available at $60, $75, and $90 a month. Conrad Hilton acquired a controlling interest in 1943 and ran the Roosevelt for a dozen years; an antitrust suit against Hilton Hotels ended in early 1956 with a consent decree under which Hilton agreed to sell the Roosevelt (Hotel Corporation of America was the buyer). In recent years Pakistani interests have operated the Roosevelt.

By far the largest of the hotels with Grand Central Terminal entrances was the thirty-three-story 2,000-room Commodore, which opened on January 28, 1919, on 42nd Street between Depew Place and Lexington Avenue. It was, in fact, the biggest hotel in the world at the time—named, of course, for the first Cornelius Vanderbilt. The Commodore rose on a site previously occupied by the Hospital for Ruptured and Crippled, purchased by the New York Central in 1911 as part of its program to buy property in the neighborhood of the new terminal then under construction. The Central's purpose was to secure subservice rights in order to build track loops under the station and to enjoy air rights for putting up various structures. A spur of the Third Avenue El ran along 42nd Street to a station at Grand Central just outside the huge new hotel. Hotel construction was delayed while engineers worked out the alignment of I.R.T. subway tracks extending under the site. The Commodore had a taxi entrance above Depew Place on the east side of Grand Central's circumferential drive; that entrance today serves the Grand Hyatt, sheathed in mirrored glass but built on the steel framework of the old Commodore.

John McE. Bowman put up the Commodore and advertised "A room and a bath for two and a half" (in September 1941 the minimum rose to $3.50 but in January 1949, when the hotel celebrated its thirtieth anniversary, the minimum was still only $4). The Commodore boasted the world's largest hotel lobby; laid out in the form of an Italian courtyard, it was designed and decorated to give the appearance of a garden. Surrounding it was an arcade and, above that, a gallery. At the west end of the lobby were public rooms for men: main offices, a porters' desk, cigar stand, telephone exchange, men's writing room, stock-broker's office, men's café, and washroom; at the east end were conveniences for women, including special dining rooms and a florist's stand. Ten passenger lobbies opened onto the lobby, and there were sixteen other elevators. Redcaps carried guests' bags direct from their trains (or by underground passage from the Baltimore & Ohio bus terminal across 42nd Street) to the lobby. The Commodore had three ballrooms. Its Grand Ballroom—100 feet long, seventy-eight wide, the largest in the country and perhaps in the world—seated 3,000 for a concert, 2,000 for a banquet.

When Zeckendorf Hotels took over the Commodore in September 1958, a room and bath still cost only $7. The bankruptcy of the Penn Central in 1968 sealed the hotel's doom. It was sold in 1975—the first sale of Penn Central property—to a brash, twenty-nine-year-old developer from Queens. Donald Trump's timing was perfect. The city had announced a new Business Investment Incentive Policy, with generous tax abatements, and this was the first venture under that program. The hotel had not paid its tax bills for four years and owed the city $6 million. Trump obtained an option to buy the Commodore, lined up Hyatt Hotels as a partner before putting down the $250,000 required to make the option binding, and then demanded fifty years' property tax abatement from the financially beleaguered city.

Another hotel operator offered to buy the Commodore for $2 million and spend a like amount on renovations but the Beame administration, trying to obtain the best possible deal for the city, agreed to negotiate with Trump. It was hoped that he would be persuaded to reduce his proposed fifty-year tax abatement to thirty-five years. Trump said he would be much less interested if the tax abatement offer was reduced. Several City Council members called the demand excessive: it would mean a tax savings of $56 million over fifty years. Trump insisted that he and potential investors would pull out of the deal if his demand was not met.

The Penn Central Transportation Company had sold only one of the twenty-four properties it had set out to unload in 1971; it was spending $4.5 million in 1976 on its three other hotels—the Barclay, Roosevelt, and Biltmore—but its biggest drain was the Commodore. Enough was enough: Penn Central announced that the Commodore would close on May 18 because of rising operating losses. The city's Board of Estimate was scheduled to vote May 20 on the Trump plan to rebuild the hotel, contingent on obtaining substantial tax relief. The board insisted on receiving elaborate justification for the tax incentives but finally gave the nod to Trump's plan, which involved having the New York State Urban Development Corporation facilitate transfer of the property from the bankrupt Penn Central to the developer.

Trump's original deal called for the city to forgo $4 million in yearly real estate taxes in exchange for a share in the new hotel's profits, plus payments beginning at $250,000 per year and rising in stages to $4.2 million after fifty years. The Trump Organization would convert the Commodore and own the new hotel. It proposed to pay the Penn Central $10 million, some of which would go to the city. Paul O'Dwyer, president of the City Council, hailed the project but suggested that the Board of Estimate examine what the city would get in exchange for tax forgiveness. Trump finally settled for forty years—a concession worth tens of millions of dollars. Moreover, instead of paying city sales tax on the building materials he needed for the Grand Hyatt, Trump made a deal to perform restoration work on the exterior of Grand Central. Although several hotel operators attacked the city's plan to forgo $4 million a year in property taxes, their protest fell on deaf ears. All the necessary approvals were obtained from the Board of Estimate and City Planning Commission; the Bowery Savings Bank and Equitable Life Assurance Society put up $80 million of the $100 million needed; Gruzen and Partners were retained as architects, and the Grand Hyatt opened in late September 1980. A double room went for $125 to $140, rates that would look cheap by the end of the decade.

North of Grand Central, where some of the city's finest transient and residential hotels still thrive, others have come and gone. Little more than memories survive to recall the Marguery, Chatham, Ambassador, Park Lane, and Sulgrave.

The Marguery, opened in 1918 at 270 Park, was part of the 719,000-square-foot residential complex covering the block between Park and Madison from 47th Street to 48th (where the fictional Lawrence Selden in Edith Wharton's 1905 novel *House of Mirth* had kept an apartment on the top floor of "The Benedick"). The hotel occupied an L-shaped segment at the northwest corner of the block at 47th Street. Beginning in 1948, with the closing of its hotel and restaurant, the Marguery began to change into an office building. The garden and grounds were converted to a parking lot in 1951, and by May of that year

ABOVE: *Donald Trump's Grand Prize for brass* (1989 photo)

the building was about 50 percent commercial. It was expected to be given over entirely to stores and offices by June but some residential tenants remained until 1955, two years before it came down to make way for a fifty-three-story office tower.

Northeast of the Marguery was the Chatham, on Vanderbilt at 48th Street, razed in 1965 for the west building of 280 Park (the Bankers Trust Building, completed in 1971). The Chatham opened in 1918 on a site formerly occupied by a railroad turntable before construction of Grand Central Terminal. The property was leased from the Central by the builder George Backer for a thirteen-story, 300-room hotel that catered at first exclusively to a residential clientele but later accepted some transients. Mayor Jimmy Walker and his second wife, the actress Betty Compton, had a suite at the Chatham which, in the 1930s, was one of the six most expensive hotels in the city; like the Biltmore, Park Lane, Roosevelt, and new Waldorf-Astoria, it charged $6 for a room and bath (only the nearby Ritz-Carlton, which charged $7, was more expensive). Chatham Walk, an outdoor restaurant and bar, opened in the early 1930s, and a French restaurant, the Divan Parisien, came along in the 1940s. The hotel was operated in its later years by Zeckendorf Hotels, a subsidiary of Webb & Knapp, a real estate company that went bankrupt in the 1960s. Long-term leases of blocks of rooms were arranged with big companies for the use of their executives, suppliers, customers, and other guests visiting New York.

A benefit dance (the Father Knickerbocker Ball) on April 19, 1921, marked the formal opening of the Ambassador Hotel, which wound up as the Sheraton East and came down in 1966. Located on the east side of Park between 51st and 52nd streets, it was designed by Warren & Wetmore, architects for Grand Central and for the splendid Ritz-Carlton (1910–56) on Madison Avenue between 46th and 47th streets. The firm had previously designed the Vanderbilt, Biltmore, and Commodore. Seventeen stories tall, the Ambassador had 600 rooms arranged in suites of one to five rooms, each with foyer and bath. A twelve-foot setback at the fourteenth floor complied with a new city zoning law, but the bare roof area running the length of the block at the fourteenth floor level was not left bare: a 28' x 12' area was planted with grass, flower beds, and shrubbery. Like almost every other New York hotel, however, the Ambassador went bankrupt in the Great Depression.

The Ambassador engaged Princess Rospigliosi, granddaughter of an American oil millionaire, who had married an Italian prince before World War I, to be its hostess. By 1941 the hotel was offering unfurnished and newly furnished suites of two, three, or four rooms, some with terrace, all with serving pantries and walk-in closets. After World War II, with a lavish ballroom and a supper club in its basement, the Ambassador was a smart society night spot. In 1958 the 475-room hotel announced plans to go co-op. The Seagram Building was going up just to its north, and its superb location made it a desirable place of residence. Prices per room, according to Col. Serge Obolensky, vice-chairman of Zeckendorf Hotels, would run from $6,619 to $11,235. But within eight years the Ambassador was gone. The Sheraton chain acquired it and in 1965 sold its lease to Rudin Management Corp., which acquired the entire block to put up an office tower, 345 Park.

The Park Lane, razed in 1965 to make way for the Westvaco Building, opened in 1924 on a site four blocks to the south of the Ambassador on a block of unused New York Central land between 48th and 49th Streets. Schultze & Weaver were the architects for the thirteen-story hotel. A syndicate headed by S. Fullerton Weaver announced in September 1922 that the new hotel would be of stone and brick in a Louis XVI architectural style that would harmonize with the general character of buildings in the Grand Central Terminal zone. The building's H shape would allow for maximum amounts of light and air, and every room would have outside exposure. There would be 600 rooms, divided into suites of from one to six rooms, with maids' quarters provided in the larger suites. Tenants of such suites could put up guests in single rooms set aside on each floor for that purpose. A two-room suite would consist of a living room 27' x 14', a bedroom 21' x 14', a bath, two closets, a foyer hall, and a serving pantry. Each suite would have a serving pantry equipped with refrigerator, china closet, and the like.

The Park Lane's restaurant, ballroom, and private dining room would also be in Louis XVI style. Meals would be served in apartments from the kitchen, situated between the ballroom and the restaurant, and no extra charge would be made for this service. Rents would cover such items as maid, valet, and lighting service. It was announced that Clarence M. Woolley, president of American Radiator Co., had leased a suite on the twelfth floor. The main dining room had a handsome florentine ceiling; decorated by Tiffany Studios, the room displayed an unusual amount of gold leaf and an impressive tapestry. In 1935 the Park Lane's six-room apartments were altered into smaller suites, and mechanically ventilated cooking spaces were provided. By August half of the suites had been converted to housekeeping apartments. To the rear of the hotel (on an alley called Park Lane that separated it from the Barclay), convenient parking space was available. By 1939, when the main dining room was renamed the Tapestry Room, the Park Lane had 500 rooms and apartments, 80 percent of them furnished. There were eighty transient rooms.

Not on Park Avenue but just east of the Park Lane is the Barclay, called the Inter-Continental through most of the 1980s. Its beginnings date to 1925, when a subsidiary of the New York Central leased the 205' x 200' "square block" bounded by Lexington Avenue and Park Lane, from 48th Street to 49th, to a syndicate formed to erect a hotel. Vanderbilt money was involved: heading the syndicate were J. Seward Webb, Jr., a grandson of William Henry Vanderbilt and brother of the lawyer Vanderbilt Webb, and Eliot Cross, the architect. Opened finally with a dinner dance on November 4, 1926, the Barclay had on its top (fourteenth) floor a seventeen-story apartment for Harold Stirling Vanderbilt, brother of the marine animal collector William K. Vanderbilt, Jr. and of Consuelo, and a cousin of Webb. Harold Vanderbilt was a director of the New York Central and liked living close to the boardroom in the New York Central Building. He had codified the rules of contract bridge while on a cruise in 1925;

he would go on to build and skipper the great J-class boats *Enterprise, Rainbow,* and *Ranger* that would defend the America's Cup in 1930, 1934, and 1937, respectively. A circular onyx-and-marble stairway from Vanderbilt's entrance hall ascended to the roof, where the millionaire had a gymnasium and squash court. Portraits of Vanderbilt ancestors hung on the drawing room walls, which, like those in the library, dining room, and bedrooms, were paneled with antique French oak. Vanderbilt lived here until 1942. Even larger than Vanderbilt's apartment was that of Perle Mesta, widow of an industrialist, who had homes elsewhere but took an entire floor of the Barclay soon after it opened, beginning her career as "hostess with the mostes'," although her large parties were given at the nearby Park Lane and other places about town.

By 1930, about two dozen families in the New York *Social Register* listed 111 East 48th Street as their principal residence. But while it originally had suites of from one to three rooms, expandable to larger suites, 505 rooms were furnished for a transient clientele, and within a few weeks of its opening the hotel was furnishing 100 additional rooms to make it nearly 75 percent transient. Gloria Swanson, Mary Pickford, Bette Davis, Zasu Pitts, Jimmy Durante, and David O. Selznick were among the Hollywood types who stayed here, knowing that the Barclay, unlike some other hotels, would not phone the gossip columnists. Ernest Hemingway was another occasional guest, and Henry Cabot Lodge, U.S. Ambassador to the United Nations in the Eisenhower administration, used the Barclay as his New York headquarters.

Stores, including the venerable Caswell-Massey pharmacy, occupy the hotel's Lexington Avenue side. Because it is recessed at the middle above the first floor, each of its 861 rooms has outside exposure, and handsomely patterned skylights flood the lobby with daylight. The lobby has pillars of imported Italian marble, with black marble trim for paneling. A long terrace near the main entrance was called the tea terrace; at one end was a door to the children's and nurses' dining room, served directly from the main kitchen. The main dining room, seating about 300, had an entrance from the tea terrace and another from 48th Street. For private functions, there were two private dining rooms on the second floor. In 1938 the Cornell Club, located since 1923 at 245 Madison Avenue, signed a twelve-year lease for the entire third floor of the hotel. A private entrance was installed at 107 East 48th Street for the club, which had a main dining room, three private dining rooms, grill, library, and lounges, card and billiard rooms, a ladies' department, and thirty-nine bedrooms and suites for resident members. In October 1938 the Wellesley and Bryn Mawr Clubs leased space on the Barclay's fourteenth floor and penthouse; Smith and Mount Holyoke soon followed. After the Cornell Club moved out in the early 1970s, nearly half the third floor was leased to the short-lived Manhattan Club, whose members included Mayor Abraham Beame, Senator Jacob K. Javits, former Mayor John V. Lindsay, and other politicians, judges, and lawyers.

The fountain in the center of the lobby facing the terrace and entrance to the main dining room dates to 1944, as does the large cage for the canaries that sing just below the terrace. But as the New York Central, and then the Penn Central, lost money in the 1960s, the Barclay went downhill along with the company's other hotels, the Biltmore, Roosevelt, and Commodore.

In 1978 a group of foreign investors, reportedly backed by Middle Eastern money, made a $50 million cash offer for the Barclay, Biltmore, and Roosevelt. Loews Corp., headed by Laurence and Robert Preston Tisch, had offered $45 million; they raised their offer to $55 million, and soon afterward, in a complicated "flip" transaction, sold the Barclay to Inter-Continental Hotels, a subsidiary of Pan American World Airways, and the other two hotels to the Milstein family. Loews received about $60 million, making a quick $5 million profit. Inter-Continental spent $32 million of Pan Am money to restore the hotel. Grand Metropolitan PLC, a British conglomerate, acquired the Inter-Continental chain of 100 hotels from Pan Am for $400 million in 1981, even before restoration work on the Inter-Continental New York was complete, and in 1985 it opened a Presidential Suite that has been used by France's President Mitterrand, President Aquino of the Philippines, and President Sarney of Brazil, among others. At $3,000 per night, it has in recent years been vacant only one night in four. By the late 1980s the hotel was virtually 100 percent transient, and in September 1988 a Japanese company acquired the Inter-Continental chain, including the old Barclay, for $2.27 billion.

The Lombardy, also east of Park rather than on the avenue, opened in the fall of 1927 at 111 East 56th Street and may, like the Barclay, owe its survival to the fact that it has no Park Avenue frontage suitable for an office tower. An apartment hotel put up by the developer Henry Mandel, it contained (and still contains) 175 units—330 rooms, singles and in suites, some with terraces. There were two three-bedroom triplex penthouses and a two-bedroom, two-bath flat. The publisher William Randolph Hearst, who had convinced himself that a bridge would soon span the Hudson at 57th Street, owned a good deal of property in the area and in July 1929 acquired the Lombardy from Mandel in a $4 million deal. But Hearst disposed of most of his Manhattan properties beginning in 1938, and by November 1941 the Lombardy was bankrupt; it was bid in at $50,000 and acquired by the Central Hanover Bank and Trust, which did not find a buyer until after World War II.

The Lombardy went co-op in the early 1950s. Buyers, who paid what now seems like a song, did well. Most, in fact, bought for investment purposes, not to obtain a residence, and about 100 of the 175 units are now rented to transients by the day, week, or month. The restaurant Laurent and its "Bar Americain" have been in the Lombardy for decades. It is open for lunch and dinner and, although independently owned, provides guests with all meals via room service. With a staff that includes many old-timers, the hotel offers a personalized service and prides itself on knowing the wishes of its guests, most of whom are regulars.

The clientele has included producers, directors, actors, and others in the entertainment world who like being able to come and go without being annoyed by autograph seekers. Bette Davis lived here for long periods of time. Richard Burton lived at the Lombardy when he was appearing on Broadway in *Equus* and at other times (including a period shortly before his divorce when Elizabeth

Taylor was also at the Lombardy and Burton was courting Susan Hunt). Other show business guests have included Phyllis Diller, Lena Horne, Jaclyn Smith, and Jack Weston. A one-bedroom apartment at the Lombardy sold for $275,000 in 1988. Monthly maintenance was between $1,600 and $1,800.

The Ritz Tower at 465 Park, which has also had its share of show biz types, opened for occupancy on October 8, 1926, at the northeast corner of Park and 57th Street. Stuart Chase, writing in 1927, noted that for Park Avenue residents whose children had "married and departed" there was the apartment hotel, "of which the Ritz Tower is the outstanding exhibit this year. In these, instead of maintaining ten or twelve rooms for the corps of one's own servants, one might live with equal luxury in three or four rooms, the house providing all services including those of maid and butler, with meals served in one's rooms or the exquisite restaurant below. For this snug home life one pays in the neighborhood of $3,000 per room per year in rental alone."

Novelist Cornelius Vanderbilt's hero in *Park Avenue* was "Schuyler Van Courtlandt," a young man about town who had evidently forsaken his family home on Fifth Avenue: "While young Van Courtlandt thought it jolly to have a Park Avenue address, most of those who resided about him in the three square miles of exclusive clubs, recherché hotels, and towering apartments thought it chic to live there. Had they changed their mind they might have turned the city upside down from the point of view of several wealthy realtors.

"Schuyler's bachelor suite was atop the Ritz Tower—that imposing structure at 57th Street and Park Avenue—which a national newspaper-editorial writer was said to have built out of his savings. Either someone had not told Schuyler the truth about the remuneration of newspapermen, or the renting-agent had permitted his colorful narrative to wander lackadaisically astray the boundaries of credulity. Schuyler's suite, thirty-three stories above the street which he had chosen as his abode . . ."

In fact it *was* Hearst's editor, Arthur Brisbane, who had assembled the 130' x 80' corner plot in 1924 and announced that he was going to raze its seven four- and five-story brownstone dwellings to put up a twenty-seven-story apartment house. Brisbane filed plans early in 1925 to build a thirty-three-story building and promptly leased the property for twenty-one years to the Ritz-Carlton Hotel interests, receiving a fixed rent to be paid at no less than $1,000 per day, $365,000 a year. The Ritz Tower was the first residential skyscraper designed to meet the requirements of the 1916 zoning law. Mayor Jimmy Walker and a crowd of city officials, publishers, and businessmen attended the opening banquet on November 15, 1926. Also present were the building's architect, Emery Roth, and his associate, Thomas A. Hastings of Carrère & Hastings.

By one account, Brisbane borrowed $4 million to finance the project and was able to maintain the burden of mortgage payments for only three years. By another account he had built the Ritz Tower in partnership with William Randolph Hearst, who owned the rest of the Park Avenue blockfront. (Hearst also owned the property at the southeast corner of 60th and Park.) Brisbane reportedly found his financial commitment too heavy and offered in 1928 to sell the building to Hearst, who accepted. Another story has it that Hearst acquired ownership for $17 million in November 1927.

In any event, the Ritz Tower was hailed at its opening as the tallest inhabited building in the world—590 feet high, forty-two stories overall (it actually has thirty-seven stories), an exclusive apartment hotel with three floors reserved for a selected transient clientele. Promoters said there were 449 furnished and unfurnished rooms, all of unusual size, some having the dimensions of miniature ballrooms with suite arrangements ranging from two rooms (living room and bedroom) to ten rooms with serving pantry in each suite and a bathroom with tub and shower for each bedroom. In addition, there were nine large duplex suites on the nineteenth-twentieth floor. Setback terraces opened off apartments on the nineteenth and twenty-fifth floors. The lobby had walls of a warm walnut, with beautifully carved paneling throughout and marble floors in all public rooms. Off the foyer was an Italian tea garden, entered at two sides by handsome Florentine gateways, with a French restaurant—the Ritz Tower's main dining room—adjacent to it through two archways. The hotel's kitchen served three hotel restaurants, a large two-level grill room (leased to bridge players of the Cavendish Club for many years beginning in August 1950), and all the private apartments except Arthur Brisbane's.

Occupying part of the nineteenth and twentieth floors, Brisbane had a specially designed eighteen-room duplex with a double-height living room 20'x

BELOW: *The Ritz Tower was once the world's tallest inhabited structure* (May 1928 photo courtesy Municipal Archive)

20' designed to resemble the great hall of a Renaissance palazzo. It had heavy iron chandeliers, leaded glass windows, and an allegorical multi-colored painted canvas ceiling modeled after one in a Venetian palace. This apartment ran the entire seventy-foot length of the hotel's Park Avenue frontage and was the only one in the building to have a full-size kitchen and accommodations for the owner's domestic staff (other tenants quartered their servants downstairs on the second or third floor). Floors above Brisbane's apartment from the twenty-first floor to the top contained apartments of from four to twelve rooms each. Living rooms were typically 24' x 15', bedrooms 17' x 13'. Each bedroom had its own bath and each apartment its own private vault. A thirty-seventh-floor suite was taken in 1927 by the flamboyant English author Elinor Glyn, then sixty-two, whose short story "It" had been the basis of the Hollywood hit starring Clara Bow.

Plans were announced early in 1929 to build a fifty-five story Ritz Tower annex on a site extending north to 58th Street. Then came Wall Street's collapse, aborting the idea and dooming Park Avenue to the white-brick apartment house at 475, built on the shell of a 1909 apartment house. In the 1930s Hearst moved into the old Brisbane apartment with his good friend Marion Davies; they remained at the Ritz Tower until 1938, occupying rooms comparable to those at Hearst's California castle, San Simeon.

The hotel's restaurants had a public entrance on the 57th side and occupied space that was used from the late 1950s until its closing in 1972 for what was unquestionably New York's best restaurant, Henri Soulé's Le Pavillon. (Soulé, who died early in 1966, had reportedly been backed by then Ambassador Joseph P. Kennedy in starting the restaurant after the New York World's Fair of 1939–1940. Originally located at 5 East 55th Street, it was an overnight success and served for more than a quarter of a century as the training ground for New York's best chefs, maître d's, captains, and waiters.) A basement kitchen still provides three meals a day through room service, but the Ritz Tower's only restaurant in the 1980s was Mitsukoshi, in the basement of the Japanese store by that name. Mitsukoshi, which had its beginnings in a seventeenth-century store founded by the Mitsui family, is Japan's largest department store chain. Its president, Shigeru Okada, occupied the an eleven-room remainder of the old Hearst apartment in the late 1970s, paying $4,000 in monthly maintenance for the place with its wraparound terrace.

Le Pavillon was converted into the First Women's Bank at 111 East 57th Street. A much larger bank was breathing down the Ritz Tower's neck when Arthur Brisbane died on Christmas Day, 1936. His high-rise dream had been losing money for years. The Hearst interests paid taxes on the property through 1937, after which Continental Bank and Trust began administering it for the benefit of its bondholders. Hearst and Davies were evicted from their suite in 1938 and prepared to return to California. When the Ritz Tower passed from Hearst's ownership, the sale was said to be the first part of a program calling for a gradual liquidation of almost all of Hearst's Manhattan real estate holdings outside of his newspaper properties. The Sonnabend hotel chain bought the building in January 1952 and a few years later engaged Dorothy Draper to redecorate its rooms.

In 1955, a year before it went co-op, some New Yorkers learned there was a three-story building occupying the Ritz Tower's Park Avenue frontage to a depth of 17.6 feet and architecturally blended into the main hotel structure. The lease on this corner building was extended in April 1955 until 2018. The hotel's second and third floors were given over to offices in the co-op conversion; the Bridge and Whist Club had space on the third floor. Plans of the upper floors showed the largest living room to be 24' x 16', the largest bedroom 15'11" x 15'10". Instead of nine duplexes there were now only three, and although most apartments had two or three bedrooms there were five or six studios. Chambermaids or valets were available on alternate floors, and Charles of the Ritz (which got its name from the old Ritz-Carlton on Madison Avenue, then recently closed) had a beauty salon at the corner, space later taken by Mitsukoshi. Women living at the Ritz Tower could sometimes be seen emerging from elevators in their housecoats for a quick dash through the lobby to the beauty shop.

Glitz rather than social status has distinguished tenants of the Ritz Tower. Frank Crowninshield, the publisher, had a duplex in the 1930s. Greta Garbo and Sigmund Romberg moved in a little later. Recent tenants have included the actress and radio-TV personality Arlene Francis (*née* Kazanjian) and her late husband, the actor-producer Martin Gabel, who moved into an eighth-floor apartment in the late 1950s. It was from a window in this apartment that an eight-pound exercise dumbbell toppled to the street on June 30, 1960, striking Alvin R. Rodecker, a vacationing Detroit businessman who had just emerged with his wife from Le Pavillon after a gala luncheon to celebrate his sixtieth birthday (he died the next day). Francis was in Westport, Connecticut, for a role in a play; an air-conditioner had been temporarily removed from the window, and a hotel maid had accidentally dislodged the dumbbell, which fell on Rodecker. His widow sued; a jury awarded her $175,000 from the Gabels and $10,000 from the hotel.

Other recent tenants include Paulette Goddard, Claire Trevor (who actually lived at the Sherry-Netherland on Fifth Avenue but kept a studio at the Ritz Tower for painting), the designer Valentino, the literary agent Irving ("Swifty") Lazar, the record company executive Clyde Davis, and the publisher Frances Lear, who started her magazine, *Lear's*, from her apartment. She had received $110 million as a divorce settlement from her ex-husband Norman Lear, a television producer (*All in the Family* was his idea). Most apartments have two bedrooms, although some have three and four. Norman Lear put together several apartments on the sixteenth and seventeenth floors to create a large duplex that included living room, large kitchen, pantry, dining area, two bedrooms, dressing room, four and a half baths, study, library, and guest quarters consisting of living room, two bedrooms, and two baths. It was offered for sale early in 1988 at $2.5 million, with monthly maintenance of $10,000, including hotel services.

When playwright Neil Simon was a youngster working for the radio comedian Goodman Ace, he sometimes visited Ace at his apartment in the Ritz Tower and vowed that he, too, would live here if he could ever afford it. By the mid-1970s he could afford it; he and his wife, Marsha Mason, bought a small apartment—living room, bedroom, and den—and spent roughly a third of their time here for about a decade. Said Simon of the Ritz Tower, "The location is perfect, the service is wonderful, and the people are first class."

Not all Ritz Tower employees are celebrity-minded. The hotel locks its door at midnight, and guests must ring to be admitted. When a woman guest rang one night a few years ago, the night man was a little slow in answering. The woman's escort, Frank Sinatra, banged on the door, and when the door was finally opened he was irate. "Do you know who I am?" The night man answered in his Irish brogue, "The face is familiar. Tony Curtis?"

When today's traveler walks into the Ritz Tower, plunks down his suitcases, and announces that he has a reservation, he is politely directed to a hotel over on Central Park South—either the St. Moritz or the old Navarro, which reopened as the Ritz-Carlton in 1983 (and was bankrupt a few years later but continued to operate at inflated prices). Before the Ritz Tower went co-op it did accept transients, and until August 1987 co-op owners, many of whom spend much of the year abroad or in warmer climes, could rent their apartments to transients ($135 to $160 single, $150 to $180 double per day) and receive an income on their investment. A new policy limiting rentals to periods of at least thirty days caused several owners to put their apartments up for sale.

The Ritz Tower was only four years old when Cornelius Vanderbilt's novel *Park Avenue* appeared; Park Avenue hotels north of Grand Central included the Marguery, Chatham, Ambassador, Park Lane, Barclay, Lombardy, Drake, Mayfair House, Beekman, and Sulgrave. The Waldorf-Astoria was still a-building. And while a few office buildings rose among the hotels and apartment houses just north of Grand Central, Park Avenue was still almost exclusively residential.

The Drake, designed by Emery Roth and erected by Bing & Bing in 1927 on a plot 105' x 67' at 440 Park, northwest corner 56th Street, was acquired in 1981 by Swissair and Nestlé S.A., which operate it almost entirely as a transient hotel, the Drake Swissôtel. Zoning restrictions prevented Roth from making the Drake soar, as did his Dorset at 30 West 54th Street, but the two are similar in materials and styling. The Drake's first three floors, clad in limestone, serve as a base for the brown brick superstructure that rises above it. Built at a cost of about $5.5 million, the hotel originally had 477 rooms (the small, homey wood-paneled lobby belied its size) laid out in suites of one to three rooms, smaller than those at the Dorset, with serving pantries in the two- and three-room suites. Suites on the tenth, twelfth, fifteenth, seventeenth, and twentieth floors have roof terraces. When it opened, the Drake had apartments of luxurious dimensions on its upper floors. Living rooms from the seventeenth to nineteenth floors were as large as 26'5" x 20', bedrooms as large as 20' x 14'; on the twentieth and twenty-first floors, living rooms were as large as 25' x 17' and 27'7" x 16'4" with open fireplaces, dining rooms 18'8" x 12', a bedroom 16' x 15'3", and another 16' x 16'.

In receivership by 1937, the Drake rebounded after World War II. Residents soon included the grain merchant Michel Fribourg (who later bought a town house off Park in the 70s), the former silent screen star Constance Talmadge, and the film star Debbie Reynolds. Maurice Chevalier stayed here when he had a Broadway engagement.

Zeckendorf Hotels bought the Drake in 1958, acquired a row of old houses just to the east, replaced them with an annex containing 150 rooms (the total is now 634), and in August 1958 announced plans to go co-op, although a substantial number of rooms would be kept for transient use after the conversion. Permanent residents—the self-styled "saloonkeeper" Toots Shor was one—would be able to buy their apartments at prices ranging from $6,619 to $11,235. In fact, the co-op conversion plan was aborted. A restaurant-discotheque, Shepheards, took over the corner in the 1960s and continued for many years until it was replaced by a shoe store. Loews Hotels, bought the Drake in 1971, turned most of its large suites into singles, and sold it in 1981 to Swissôtel, which replaced the old Drake Room restaurant with the Café Suisse as an extension of the lobby and in July 1986 opened a fine restaurant, the Lafayette, under the operation of a Swiss chef. The *New York Times* restaurant critic, Bryan Miller, rated the Lafayette "extraordinary" in April 1988, thus placing it in the pantheon of the city's six four-star restaurants.

By 1986 the Drake Swissôtel had only one permanent guest, although some corporations still leased a few suites on a permanent basis. None of the fireplaces worked, but there were more than fifty suites, with a few two-bedroom units on the upper floors remaining pretty much as they had in the 1920s; one—with a large marble foyer, a very large living room, two bedrooms, and two baths on a high floor at the corner of Park and 56th—was redecorated by Swissôtel in 1987 at a cost of $120,000 and rented for $750 a night.

Delmonico's, at 502 Park, northwest corner 59th Street, is another survivor, entirely residential except for some offices. Demolition of a few small buildings to make way for the hotel—originally to be called the Viceroy, then the Cromwell Arms—got underway in 1926. Its first four floors were to be devoted to offices, the 487 rooms on the upper twenty-six to be arranged in one- to five-room suites. Delmonico's opened on October 1, 1929, just before the stock market crash, with a formal eight-course dinner for 400 guests. Thirty-two stories tall, the building inspired the American painter Charles Sheeler to sketch its soaring lines; it had 525 rooms in suites of various sizes, including one that was called the highest-priced apartment in the world, a fifteen-room triplex occupying the three top floors and renting for $3,750 a month. There were terraced suites in the tower, and all suites were equipped with serving pantries and electric refrigeration. Many were furnished by leading decorators. Delmonico's had a two-story-high dining room, a three-story-high ballroom, and a grill. The name Delmonico's was that of a famous restaurant which, as the *Times* said on September 8, 1929, "for almost a century was the brilliant center of the city's social life" (in January 1937 a White Plains, New York, court upheld the hotel's right to use the name). Nicolas Sabatini, chef at Delmonico's restuarant from 1912 to its last midnight supper on May 21, 1923, was an employee of the new Delmonico's.

By July 1932 Delmonico's was in default of interest on $3.8 million in bonds and on taxes but continued to operate. Tenants in October 1935 included former New York Governor and Mrs. Charles S. Whitman, Mr. and Mrs. Oliver Harriman, Mr. and Mrs. George H. Sloane, and the humorist Finley Peter Dunne ("Mr. Dooley"). In March 1936 the building—built at a cost of $5 million—was bought at auction for $1.8 million. William Zeckendorf, Jr., converted the hotel into a rental apartment house in 1975 and replaced Delmonico's restaurant on the Park Avenue side of the building with the showrooms and gallery of Christie's, the London art auction house. Regine's, the French discotheque operated by Regine Choukroun, her sister Evelyne, and her husband, Roger, opened at Delmonico's in 1975. The building soon went co-op. In addition to its apartments, it also has a good many offices, including those of Fred Wilpon, part owner of the Mets.

The Beekman Hotel at 575 Park, southeast corner 63rd Street, opened early

LEFT: *The Swissôtel Drake boasts one of the city's best restaurants* (1989 photo)   RIGHT: *Delmonico's famous restaurant has given way to an art auction house* (1989 photo)

in 1927, with 130 apartments, 349 rooms, 218 baths. Apartments each had one, two, or three bedrooms with high ceilings, woodburning fireplaces, serving pantries, and one to three baths, although there was one six-room apartment with three baths, kitchen, and maid's room. The largest living room was 25'5" x 16'8", the largest bedroom 22'4" x 12'5". Built from plans by George F. Pelham in Italian Renaissance style, the Beekman's exterior finish is of limestone on the first three floors, topped by dark buff brick with terra-cotta trim. An adjoining building, in 63rd Street, was soon joined to the original structure; apartments off the avenue have kitchens but no fireplaces.

Douglas Fairbanks, Jr., kept a pied-à-terre at the Beekman for many years. The owner of the Tailored Woman shops lived there, as did Sara Fredericks, whose dress shop survives at 508 Park, and Ann Folger of the Folger's Coffee family. Other recent tenants have included the lawyer who defended Lucky Luciano, the political leader Stanley Steingut, former New York attorney general Louis Lefkowitz, a nonagenarian real estate broker, Steve Lawrence and Eydie Gorme, Fred Pierce (who headed American Broadcasting before its takeover by Capital Cities), the Wall Street seer Henry Kaufman, and an assortment of Wall Street and real estate types who like the location and appreciate the Beekman's services. Room service was provided by the stuffy and expensive restaurant, Le Perigord Park, until it was replaced in 1988 by Hubert's, which moved uptown from its pricey but imaginative twenty-table dining spot at 102 East 22nd Street, off Park Avenue South. Karen Hubert, a writer specializing in education, and Len Allison, who worked in video and films, lived together in Brooklyn in the mid-1970s and shared the cooking in their small house. From serving weekend meals at home they graduated to a landmarked tavern with twenty-two-foot ceilings in the Boerum Hill section, and early in 1983 moved to East 22nd Street, where they built their reputation.

The Mayfair Regent at 610 Park, southwest corner 65th Street, opened as Mayfair House on November 9, 1925. Designed by J. E. R. Carpenter, it originally had 450 guest rooms, lobby, dining room, and lounges, many of them beautifully decorated and luxuriously furnished, although unfurnished suites were also available. Valet and maid service were optional. The management announced its intention of making Mayfair House "a socially exclusive type of town house, still *en règle* in London. The sort of house that will look after you when you're in town and look after itself when you're out of town." The opening of Le Cirque restaurant in March 1974 made the hotel a fashionable jet-set gathering place (prix fixe luncheon early in 1989 was $27). Mayfair House was acquired in the 1980s by the Hong Kong-based chain Regent International Hotels, hence the name Mayfair Regent.

Gone now is the Sulgrave, an apartment hotel that opened in December 1924 at 60 East 67th Street, just off the southwest corner of Park. The Emigrant Bank foreclosed on the Sulgrave's $1,405,000 mortgage at the end of 1931, and it was acquired in 1945 by the managing director of the Sherry-Netherland on Fifth Avenue, who brought in a good deal of transient business. The hotel was razed

ABOVE: *The Beekman: an impeccable residential address* (1989 photo)

ABOVE: *Café society meets at the Mayfair Regent's Le Cirque Restaurant* (1989 photo)

in the early 1960s and replaced with a white, glazed brick apartment house, 650 Park.

The Regency at 540 Park, northwest corner 61st Street, opened in 1963 with 500 rooms. Built and operated by Loews Hotels, the hostelry is probably better known as the place for "power breakfasts" than for its accommodations, although its 111 suites and 250 other luxury guest rooms are popular with government figures, business leaders, and entertainment names (some call it "Hollywood East," and its big California suite, occupying about 1,000 square feet, is always in demand).

What most people associate with the Regency is its power breakfast. Most of the Japanese and other foreign businessmen who stay here take breakfast in their rooms. The film and rock stars sleep to noon. But from before 8 o'clock in the morning until after 9 each business day, limousines are double- and triple-parked outside, creating a traffic bottleneck as Wall Street dealmakers and politicians break croissants in the clubby atmosphere of the Regency.

Preston Robert Tisch, president of Loews Hotels, celebrated the tenth anniversary of the power breakfast in March 1986, saying, "We really started something." Others credit Gerald (Jerry) Tsai, Jr. with having started it all. Tsai, the dealmaker who later turned American Can Co. into Primerica Inc., began coming down from Boston and staying at the Regency in the 1960s. He had built a reputation at Boston's Fidelity Funds, was putting together a mutual fund of his own, and soon attracted other dealmakers. By 1969 the dining room entrance was clogged by 7:54 in the morning with lawyers and financiers from the upper East Side angling for tables in spots where they might overhear something from the mouths of the movers and shakers, who included the Lazard Frères investment banker Felix Rohatyn (who a few years later became chairman of the Municipal Assistance Corporation and was credited by many with keeping the city out of bankruptcy). Other regulars have included Mark M. Kaplan (who united Burnham & Co. with Drexel Firestone & Co. over a Saturday breakfast at the Regency to create Drexel Burnham Lambert); the lawyers Martin Lipton (of Wachtel, Lipton, Rosen, and Katz) and Joseph Flom (of Skadden Arps Slate Meagher and Flom); and Jerome Kohlberg, Jr., who left Bear Stearns & Co. to start his own investment banking firm (Kohlberg Kravis Roberts) and did some of his first deals over breakfast at the Regency, selling divisions of large, troubled companies to groups of investors organized by Kohlberg and his associates. There is also former Postmaster General Preston Robert Tisch and his brother Laurence, who together own the Regency along with other Loews Hotels.

By 1988, breakfast for two averaged about $30 plus tip. This was a pittance to Jonathan M. Tisch, Preston Robert's son, who was himself president of Loews Hotels when, in April 1988, he married Laura S. Steinberg, the twenty-five-year-old daughter of financier Saul P. Steinberg. The *Times* called it a "Wall Street wedding" that joined "two billionaire families." There were jokes that the Securities and Exchange Commission would have to approve the marriage.

None of the hotels listed above quite compares with the Waldorf-Astoria, called for many years the "new" Waldorf-Astoria. The old one had been an

ABOVE: *Power brokers breakfast at the Regency* (1989 photo)

amalgam of the thirteen-story Waldorf and the seventeen-story Astor House at 34th Street and Fifth Avenue. In May 1929, five months before the stock market crash, wreckers began razing the thirty-two-year-old hotel to make way for the Empire State Building.

By 1929 the American Express Building, located on the Lexington Avenue side of the plot, had been entirely demolished; about half of the Central YMCA on Park Avenue had also been torn down, and the main portion of the Central's powerhouse was gone, although its two giant smokestacks still stood. The huge steel columns needed to support the Waldorf would be driven down between the subterranean railroad tracks and rest on solid rock. The substructure would require 2,000 tons of steel, the superstructure another 25,000 tons.

"New Waldorf Gets Own Rail Siding," reported the *New York Times* in 1929. Since the tracks of the New York Central ran directly beneath the block (whose air rights had been obtained on a sixty-three-year lease from the railroad), guests with private rail cars would be able to have them routed directly to the hotel instead of to Penn Station or Grand Central and could leave them on Track 61 beside a special elevator which would take them directly to their suites or to the lobby. (General Pershing once availed himself of this convenience, and President Roosevelt once employed it for a discreet exit to Hyde Park after a Waldorf dinner; aside from that, the Waldorf siding has been used only to carry materials and equipment down to track level for work on skyscrapers that went up in the 1960s.)

Trains, it was announced in 1929, would run on the hotel's main basement level, while two subbasement levels would extend far into the ground below the tracks. The Waldorf's cellar would include a large vacuum cleaning room, the hotel ice plant, locker rooms for the staff, a butcher shop, a bakery, laundries, and the china service. There would be thirty-one elevators including service. The main kitchen would be located on the second floor three stories above the street, an unusual arrangement made necessary by the fact that the basement was occupied by the railroad. On January 1, 1930, the Hotel Waldorf-Astoria Corporation, builder and owner, leased the plot on which the hotel was to be erected from the New York Central. The twenty-year lease contained clauses for renewal, and the railroad put up $10 million to back the project, this amount to be amortized over a period of years.

The new Waldorf-Astoria opened on October 1, 1931, occupying the entire block from Park Avenue to Lexington between 49th and 50th streets. The old Waldorf-Astoria had been 198'6" wide x 350' long; the new one was 200'10" wide x 405' long. The old Waldorf-Astoria had been seventeen stories tall and about 225' high at its highest point; the new one had forty-seven stories in its twin towers, reaching to a maximum height of 625'7". Designed by Schultze & Weaver, built by Thompson Starrett Co. in just two years, the new Waldorf-Astoria incorporated more than 3,000 cubic feet of cut Swensen pink granite in its base. More than 80,000 cubic feet of selected light silver-gray Indiana limestone made up the main shaft of the hotel, which was faced with more than 3 million ordinary-size bricks specially made to harmonize with the limestone. In addition to the face brick, eight million ordinary bricks went into the building. A private driveway 90' wide and 200' long bisected the building between 49th and 50th streets, enabling patrons to go directly from their automobiles to their rooms or to functions in the hotel via conveniently located entrances.

The new Waldorf was originally expected to have about 2,200 guest rooms, the tower apartments having eighteen-foot ceilings, boudoirs, and bathrooms, with living rooms 25' x 45'. The hotel did not, in the end, have 2,200 rooms, and in that respect was not the world's largest hotel, but it did have some 2,000 rooms, including 300 residential suites, numerous ballrooms, dining rooms, restaurants, kitchens, foyers, lounges, clubrooms, and private entertaining suites. Decorators from America, England, France, and Sweden collaborated to furnish it and avoid stereotyped hotel atmosphere; early American, eighteenth-century English, Adam Brothers, Chippendale, Sheraton, Hepplewhite, Louis XV, and Louis XVI styles were all represented. Suites were decorator-designed to have the individual manner of a private residence. Each comprised a foyer, living room, dining room, and boudoir with three or four bedrooms and baths. Living and dining rooms had open fireplaces with Louis XV or XVI antique marble mantles.

Ordinary guest rooms were also planned to have individual character. The average room was said to be larger than corresponding rooms in many other hotels of comparable size and spaciousness. Guest rooms averaged over 9,500 cubic feet. Radio, television (in 1931!), and public address facilities were installed throughout the building. Patrons were also able to listen at will and in the privacy of their own rooms to speeches and music from the hotel's various public rooms. Portable movietones were available for private use. Public rooms were air-conditioned and kept at an even temperature the year round by Carrier cooling, dehumidifying, and humidifying equipment. For all its modern conveniences, the new Waldorf-Astoria retained many of the traditional features of the old Waldorf—Peacock Alley, the Empire Room, and the Astor Gallery, with paintings and other decorative details having special significance for patrons of the old Waldorf.

The private Canadian Club on the eighteenth floor (it had been at the old Belmont Hotel and later moved into the Metropolitan Club on Fifth Avenue) contained a foyer, dining rooms, a lounge, library, billiard room, and card room designed in Georgian and Tudor styles. Terraces extended to the nineteenth floor where private bedrooms and baths were reserved for club members. Also on the nineteenth floor were the general offices of the Junior League, Inc., which still has guest rooms at the Waldorf that include a large outdoor dining terrace, dining rooms and lounge, and private bedrooms. The twentieth-floor roof was given over to recreation and dining. This floor also had a children's playroom plus an outdoor-terrace playground. A special home-cooking kitchen on the twentieth floor was set aside for preparing and cooking meals just as in a typical American home, served by room service.

Prohibition was still in effect when the Waldorf-Astoria opened, but the builders, seeing Repeal just around the corner, soon put in an air-conditioned wine cellar (on the fifth floor) large enough to cradle 37,000 gallons of wine. The Men's Bar opened in 1934 with a stand-up bar sixty feet long and seating facilities for about 200 patrons. A dry martini cost thirty-five cents, champagne $1 a glass, a bottle of Louis Roederer Brut 1926 champagne $8.50. Women were not permitted, and the Men's Bar was one of the few places left where a man ordering whiskey had a bottle placed on his table. Bronze statues of a bull and a bear from the old Waldorf, a reminder of the patronage of the great financiers of years ago, were conspicuously displayed. The Palm Bar on the eighteenth floor was opened in the early summer of 1934 and named for its characteristic decoration—palms with trunks of copper and widely spreading copper leaves, silvered on their underside; it was popular in summer and in winter was frequently used in connection with meetings, dinners, and other functions held in the Starlight Roof. The hotel was supposed to be able to hold dozens of functions at the same time, doing it so discreetly that a guest not invited to a party would be quite unaware that it was going on.

B. C. (Bertie Charles) Forbes, a young publisher, was later quoted as saying, "I would invest my savings in living at the Waldorf and doing my utmost to rub shoulders with the financial and business great . . . It was the best investment I have ever made in my life." Elsa Maxwell, the professional hostess, moved into the Waldorf Towers when they opened. To cultivate her connections, she organized a yearly party in the hotel. Frank Crowninshield edited a promotional book about the Waldorf, published in 1939 as *The Unofficial Palace of New York*.

The Duke of Windsor brewed his own tea at the Waldorf after abdicating the British throne in 1936 (he and his duchess lived in the Towers at various times for half a century). The Maharajah of Indore arrived in 1937 with a large retinue carrying vast supplies of native vegetables and spices. He took over nearly a whole floor and an entire corner of the Waldorf kitchens.

It all cost a great deal of money, and the Great Depression had so reduced revenues that the New York Central agreed to let the corporation stop its amortization payments in 1932 and 1933, with the amounts to be paid, with interest, when business was better. The Central also agreed to a modification of the land lease calling for the railroad to receive hotel revenues (after payment of taxes but before payment of interest and other charges) and apply whatever revenues there were up to the amounts of the lease rentals as part payment of the rentals. This gave the hotel a new lease on life until conditions could improve (other hotels built on Central-owned property received similar leniency).

But the hotel operated in the red for a dozen years. Then, on Easter Sunday 1949, it broke all occupancy records. The Waldorf-Astoria leasehold was sold in October 1949 to the Hilton chain for $3 million. Purchases made personally by Conrad Hilton, Hilton Hotels Corp., and Col. Henry Crown, chairman of the board of Materials Service Corp. of Chicago and a Hilton director, accounted for 30 percent of the shares, a controlling interest. At the time of the sale, single rooms went for $7 to $12 per day with bath; suites with boudoir, $32 to $35, single or double occupancy.

The Empire Room, which had given way to the Wedgwood Room, was redecorated in 1951 to become once again the Empire Room supper club. The Grand Ballroom could be set up for 2,000 people, and adjoining quarters opened for another 1,000 at sales conventions or for meetings of professional groups or learned societies, testimonials, charity balls, or fetes of all kinds. The hotel had nine restaurants ranging from a coffee shop to the Empire Room and Starlight Roof, which offer big-name entertainment for dinner and the aftertheater crowd.

The Waldorf's Presidential Suite, 35A in the Towers, was inaugurated in 1954 when President Eisenhower came to address the annual spring dinner of the American Newspaper Publishers Association, held in the hotel. Ike was the first official to occupy the refurbished four-bedroom suite, which is not reserved for heads of state but may be booked by anyone with the wherewithal ($3,000 per night in late 1988). Waldorf Towers guests have included every president of the United States since Herbert Hoover; and the Presidential Suite has been used also by such monarchs and heads of state as Britain's Elizabeth II, France's Charles de Gaulle and Valéry Giscard d'Estaing, Israel's David Ben-Gurion and Menachem Begin, Japan's Hirohito, Jordan's Hussein, Norway's Olaf V, Romania's Nicolae Ceausescu, Saudi Arabia's Saud and Faisal, the Sultan of Brunei, the Soviet Union's Nikita Khruschchev, and Spain's Juan Carlos I. In addition to the Presidential Suite there is Suite 42A, the only American ambassadorial residence not owned by the U.S. Government. George Bush lived in this Towers suite when he was ambassador to the United Nations, as did General Vernon A. Walters and other U.S. ambassadors to the UN. The 3,200-square-foot Royal

ABOVE: *The Waldorf-Astoria has few peers anywhere* (1988 photo)

Suite in the Towers was created for Elizabeth II when she and Prince Faisal were both booked into the Presidential Suite on overlapping visits. The Towers go from the 28th floor to the 42nd and contain 115 suites (of which 30 to 40 percent are leased by private tenants) and ninety rooms, of which the cheapest went in late 1988 for $275 per night. Towers residents have included former President Hoover; General Douglas MacArthur (whose widow was still a resident in 1989); a former secretary of the treasury, who kept on his wall a framed sheet of dollar bills signed "C. Douglas Dillon"; Consolidated Foods chairman Nathan Cummings, whose suite contained paintings by Degas, Gauguin, Monet, Van Gogh, and other impressionist masters (Cummings died in February 1982 at age eighty-eight); Lee Iacocca; and Frank Sinatra. Tenants have sometimes had their own chefs, butlers, and phone systems. Guests including Imelda Marcos, Elizabeth Taylor, and Bob Hope have enjoyed such luxuries as bowls of fresh flowers, changed daily; four elevators manned twenty-four hours a day; a private entrance in 50th Street; and a concierge.

By 1956, normal occupancy of the Waldorf, both resident and transient, was 2,200, and the ratio of employees to patrons was almost one to one, about that of a steamship at the time. Twenty years later, in October 1976, Hilton Hotels agreed to buy the Waldorf-Astoria for $35 million—about $10 million more than the hotel had cost in 1931, albeit in inflated dollars—from the bankrupt Penn Central Transportation Co. which owned the land. The sale was approved by a federal court in Philadelphia over the objections of New York City, which said $9.75 million in real estate taxes were due on the property and should be paid in full. (A federal district judge in Philadelphia ordered trustees of the Penn Central to pay the city $2.5 million.) By early 1988, after its five-year, $150 million renovation program, the Waldorf was said to be worth $700 million. That estimate looked modest after Donald Trump paid $400 million for the Plaza in the summer of 1988, and the Gotham (later, briefly, Maxim's, then the Peninsula) went for a price that seemed similarly irrational.

But when the new Waldorf opened in 1931, prices for everything were deeply depressed, and so was the mood of the country. The whole world, in fact, was in the depths of what is still recalled as the Great Depression.

11

■

Coming Down to Earth

ON JULY 28, 1932, Wall Street's Dow Jones Industrial Average sank to 41.22, down from its high of 381.1 on September 2, 1929. Millions of once prosperous businessmen and lawyers were out of work, and hopes of a quick recovery had long since faded. Hotels, obliged to lower their rates, were driven into bankruptcy. The building trades suffered severely, and the market for Park Avenue apartments was in disarray.

Caught short by the collapse in Wall Street, Anthony Campagna sold the northwest corner of 60th Street to the Methodist Church, which engaged the distinguished Boston architect Ralph Adams Cram to design Christ Church, completed in 1932 at 520 Park. Cram was noted for his work at Rice University, Princeton, St. Thomas Church on Fifth Avenue, and numerous cathedrals, including the Cathedral of St. John the Divine on New York's upper West Side. Rather less able was George F. Pelham, Jr., retained by Campagna Construction Co. to design 530 Park, southwest corner 61st Street; originally intended to be a large cooperative apartment house with suites of six to eighteen rooms, it was completed in a modified form in 1930.

Other 1930 buildings, all of them started before the crash, are 7, 10, 740, 770, 784, 895, 1021, 1100, 1120, and 1220 Park Avenue.

7 Park, with suites of one and a half to three rooms, wrapped around Martha Bacon's residence at the northeast corner of 34th Street (the house was razed decades later and the apartment house enlarged). Robert T. Lyons was the architect of the original 7 Park, David Moed of the later section. Opposite is the Hotel Ten Park Avenue, northwest corner 34th Street, designed by Helmle,

Corbett, and Harrison. Owned by the Community Church of New York City from 1943 to 1973, the residential hotel was converted to co-op ownership early in 1974. According to the Reverend Donald S. Harrington, it was more profitable to go co-op than to sell the building to an investor.

740, 770, 784, 895, and 1021 Park were discussed in Chapter 8.

1100 Park, northwest corner 89th Street, was by DePace & Juster, its first three stories clad in a warm brown stone. 1120 Park, northwest corner 90th Street, was by George Fred Pelham. 1220 Park, overlooking the Squadron A Armory at the northwest corner of 95th Street, was a co-op with simplex and duplex apartments ranging in size from seven to fourteen rooms; many had terraces. Rosario Candela was the architect, Joseph Paterno the builder. The building replaced four five-story tenements on Park and three in East 94th Street. Apartments were large—up to fourteen rooms, six baths, with an extra lavatory, four master bedrooms, four servants' rooms.

778 Park, northwest corner 73rd Street was completed in 1931. Designed by Rosario Candela for the real estate operator Charles Newmark, it replaced a small apartment house, the Sunnyside, and was sometimes itself called the Sunnyside. It has a four-story limestone base and, like its neighbor 770 Park to the south, is topped with a castlelike housing for its water tank. Also finished in 1931 was 891 Park, between 78th and 79th streets, a twenty-six-foot-wide

BELOW: *Begun when times were good, 1220 opened in the teeth of the Depression* (February 1930 photo courtesy Municipal Archive)

structure by Arthur Paul Hess that replaced two narrow buildings facing onto the avenue. This was the only new rental apartment house on the avenue. Built of granite, limestone, brick, and terra-cotta, with one apartment per floor (the largest are six rooms, three baths), it occupied the site of the former Frederick Dwight residence.

Paradoxically, the 1930s actually saw an increase in the number of families living on Park Avenue. Not only could fifteen families live where only one had, as at 891, but large apartments were being broken up into smaller ones. A case in point was 405 Park, at 54th Street, which after being reduced to smaller units was fully rented by 1935. The building at 320-330 Park, between 50th and 51st streets opposite St. Bartholomew's, was transformed by Schultze & Weaver to have units of between three and eight rooms, and retail shops were cut into its Park Avenue facade.

Some property owners upgraded their buildings in a bid for tenants; 400 Park became the first apartment house in America to have every room air-conditioned, this in 1936 (it also had its eleven- and twelve-room suites converted into apartments of five and six rooms). Wherever they could, landlords divided large apartments into suites with more reasonable rents. Too often that proved impossible, in which case owners might opt to reduce their taxes by demolishing their buildings: Robert Walton Goelet took down the structures on the west side of Park between 53d and 54th streets, just north of the Racquet & Tennis Club, and replaced them with a "taxpayer," a one-story row of shops with an arcade leading to a movie theater. Such a commercial intrusion no doubt had Gordon Duval turning in his grave, and a lawsuit was filed to block Goelet's project; the appellate court rejected the suit and gave its go-ahead late in 1936. To the south, at 39th Street, open-air pay-for-play tennis courts replaced some buildings on the east side of the avenue. These survived into the 1950s.

Compare lists of tenants in Park Avenue apartment houses in 1936 with those in 1929 and there are obvious changes. To be sure, some names were replaced because financial reverses forced certain families to find less prestigious places of residence. But tenants come and go even in the best of times; to a remarkable extent Park Avenue's 1929 occupants were still to be found at the same addresses seven years later. Still, a glance at the real estate pages of the newspapers in the early 1930s shows that many co-op apartments were put on the market at sacrifice prices, and some co-op buildings went to a rental basis. Rents were slashed, construction of new buildings came almost to a halt, and although even in the teeth of the Great Depression the very rich carried on pretty much as usual, the glory days of Park Avenue were gone.

From 57th Street north to 96th, Park Avenue in 1936 would look very nearly the same for the next fifty years. Some remaining private houses would be replaced by apartment buildings in the next few decades, and the Squadron A Armory would be replaced by a school; but for the most part the churches, hotels, clubhouses, apartment buildings, and apartment hotels of

1936 would for the most part still be there more than a half century later. Reading the society pages in the 1930s, one would never have guessed that the country was hurting. Whatever might be happening elsewhere, Park Avenue debutantes still had their coming out parties, and their parents still attended benefits. Two exclusive men's clubs actually built new clubhouses on the avenue.

12
■

Sanctums of Privilege

PRIVATE CLUBS are by nature exclusionary, undemocratic, discriminatory, at complete variance with traditional American principles, and they are entrenched fixtures of modern American life—bastions of the political, social, and financial establishment whose membership is usually white, Protestant, and by invitation only. Men's clubs existed in New York even before 1836, when the Union Club was founded, and for more than eighty years there have been exclusive women's clubs as well.

The city's most lavish clubhouse is that of the Metropolitan Club on Fifth Avenue at 60th Street, which also provides quarters for the Canadian Club. The Metropolitan,* often called the Millionaires' Club even back when millionaires were few and far between, is, like so many others, an offshoot of the Union.

Also on Fifth Avenue are the University, founded in 1865, mainly by Yale men, and the Knickerbocker, started in 1871 because the Union Club had too long a waiting list. The Yale Club on Vanderbilt Avenue has towered over Grand Central's Park Avenue viaduct since 1915, and the city's most notable men's clubs and a leading women's club have had their houses on Park since as early as 1918. The Colony Club, at the northwest corner of Park and 64th Street, was

---

* J.P. Morgan organized the Metropolitan after the governors of the Union declined to admit one of his associates; infuriated, he rounded up some friends and had Stanford White design a gleaming white Italian Renaissance palace on Fifth Avenue adjoining the pink château of Elbridge T. Gerry, designed by Richard Morris Hunt and razed in the late 1920s to make way for the Hotel Pierre. Morgan retained his membership in the Union Club and later returned to it, conceding ruefully that his associate was every bit as obnoxious as the governors had judged him.

completed in the early 1920s, and the Racquet & Tennis Club went up about five years earlier on the west blockfront between 52nd and 53rd Streets. The Princeton Club occupied a building at the northwest corner of Park and 39th Street from 1923 until 1961. The Union League Club moved into its new clubhouse at the southwest corner of Park and 37th Street in 1931; and the Union Club—oldest of the city's surviving clubs—moved into new quarters at the northeast corner of Park and 69th Street in 1933.

Like the clubs founded earlier in London, New York's clubs emerged from convivial groups that met at taverns, men who began in the 1830s and '40s to have their own clubhouses. Although the city's oldest club as such is the Union, a member of the Century Association (such as Louis Auchincloss) might protest that the Union was preceded by the Sketch Club, organized in 1829, which became part of the Century when that club was created in 1846. (The Sketch evidently dissolved after its first year in order to rid itself of one objectionable member, but it was promptly reorganized.)

The Knickerbocker and Brook are offshoots of the Union, founded in part because the Union had a waiting list with 800 names (it took ten years for a man to reach the top). The Union may have taken its name from that of a London club. It started at 343 Broadway and moved by stages further and further uptown. By the 1890s the club had 1,500 members; the initiation fee was $300, annual dues $75. Ward McAllister, the social arbiter, was a member, as was his successor, Harry Lehr.

The Union remained at Fifth and 51st until 1933. Members at that time included Nicolas Murray Butler, Alfred Lee Loomis, Clarence H. McKay, W. Kingsland Macy, Ogden Livingston Mills, J. Pierrepont Morgan, Ogden Mills Reid, and Edward T. Stotesbury. "More typical," *Fortune* magazine said in 1932, were Anthony J. Drexel Biddle, Jr., Francis Higginson Cabot, R. Stuyvesant Pierrepont, Percy R. Pyne II, Dallas Bache Pratt, Alfred Coster Schermerhorn, Cornelius Vanderbilt, Courtlandt F. Van Rensellaer, Jr., Ten Eyck Wendell, Jr., Lucius Wilmerding, Henry James, Adrian Iselin, Phoenix Ingram, Robert Goelet, and Albert Eugene Gallatin. "These," observed the editors, "are names you are more likely to find in the society notes than in the headlines, names that represent great families rather than great individuals."

Union Club membership in 1987 included more than three dozen Park Avenue residents with *Social Register* names: Michael Nash Ambler, Thomas H. Barton, Allen F. Blanchard, Marshall P. Blankarn, Gerard Boardman, E. Michael Bradley, Clifford Brokaw III, Charles F. Brush III, William B. Chapell, Jr., Walter J. Curley, Howard B. Dean, John W. Espy, Kruger G.D. Fowler, Jr., George A. Fowlkes (President), J. Winston Fowlkes III, Peter Frelinghuysen, DeWitt Hornor, John K. Howat, Francis L. Kellogg, Richard A. Kimball, Jr., Henry L. King, Paul C. Lambert, Donald M. Linnell, John E. McCracken, Alexander Y. McFerran, Ranald H. MacDonald, John D.W. Macomber, Keith M. Moffat, George C. Montgomery, John G. Ogilvie, Courtlandt Otis, Jere W. Patterson, George B. Reese, H. Alexander Salm, Walter H. Saunders, William J. Schieffelin, Richard Schumacher, Robert W. Sheehan, Dixon F. Stanton, and Vance Van

Dine. "As in most first-rate clubs," said *Fortune* in 1932, "the Union's membership charges are extremely reasonable. Initiation is $300, dues $200 a year. It is only the *nouveau riche* clubs which inflate initiation fees and dues to fantastic figures." By 1989 the initiation fee was $2,000, annual dues as high as $1,550 (for a senior New York resident).

The Yale Club was the first to erect a clubhouse on (or at least overlooking) Park Avenue. Founded in 1897 with nearly a thousand members (far less exclusive than the Union, Union League, or Racquet & Tennis, the Yale was soon the world's largest club), it was made to pay and had grown enormously.* It soon built what seemed a capacious clubhouse at 30 West 44th Street opposite the Harvard Club, whose first section, designed by McKim, Mead & White, had been finished in 1894. This second clubhouse was constructed in such a way that if the club should fail the building could be turned into bachelor apartments like the nearby Royalton Hotel. The Yalies need not have worried: within a few years the club had outgrown the building (it later became part of Touro College). Leasing a site at 50 Vanderbilt Avenue from the New York Central, it retained James Gamble Rogers, the Yale campus architect, to design a structure suitable to such a large membership.

Rogers had to concern himself with more than aesthetic considerations. Because two stories of railroad tracks would run under the building, the supporting columns had to be placed where they would not interfere with the clearance needed for trains. To compensate for vibration, Rogers placed a three-quarter-inch space of mastic material just a few inches above the sidewalk; this also allowed for movement caused by the expansion and contraction of steel. The front of the clubhouse was carried on columns inside the building, more than five and a half feet behind its facade.

Rogers overcame a number of problems. Not only would there have to be an extensive system of small rooms used for bedrooms and minor offices, but the club also required a number of large assembly rooms that could accommodate crowds. These had to be without columns, which meant the superstructure had to be carried by tremendous spans which, in turn, had to be carried on beams and girders, those in the basement being about eleven feet deep. The New York Central would have to approve the height of the structure, the material used, the cornice line (it had to be about eighty-one feet above street level), and so forth. Twenty-one stories high, the Yale Club is comparable to a city hotel. Its entrance is on Vanderbilt Avenue (an underground entrance from the subway and that part of Grand Central extending below Vanderbilt Avenue was closed in the early 1960s). A service entrance opens onto 44th Street, and all service departments are in the western part of the house, with a separate service elevator system.

Off the low-ceilinged entrance hall is an office, a large cloakroom, telephone

---

* By 1988 membership was 9,233, with 30 percent of it living in the city. Dues ranged from $200 to $700 per year for city residents, $124 to $440 for suburbanites, $244 to $360 for out-of-towners; there was a $100 initiation fee.

booths, and elevators. A very short flight of stairs (or the elevator) takes one to the second floor with its large, high-ceilinged living room or "lounge," a big room that has been called "a large-scale replica of some room in a private house half remembered or in the Palazzo Mycenae in Rome." The lounge has nine windows and deep embrasures. The Grill Room is on the second mezzanine; the billiard room on the third floor; the library on the fourth; Turkish baths, swimming pool, and locker rooms on the fifth; gymnasium and squash courts on the sixth; bedrooms on all floors from the seventh to the seventeenth inclusive; private dining rooms on the eighteenth; a kitchen on the nineteenth; a restaurant (the main dining room) on the twentieth; the wine "cellar" together with storage rooms on the twenty-first. Above is the roof garden, which in 1915 commanded a superb view of Manhattan and the surrounding country beyond the rivers. With the exception of the wood floors in the dining room and lounge, there is practically no wood in any part of the Yale Club. Floors throughout are of marble, terrazzo, tile, or cement.

Women were first admitted to membership in the 1960s, and the club's small swimming pool, the Plunge, was finally opened to them in 1987; until then men had swum nude in the Plunge. It has since declined in popularity, and so few women have availed themselves of the facility that its costly conversion to unisex use is generally considered a monumental blunder.

The Princeton Club, founded in 1875, never approached its Yale or Harvard counterparts in membership or munificence. Eight years after the Yale Club opened on Vanderbilt Avenue, the Princeton Club moved into the old Austin Fox residence, a Victorian brownstone at 39 East 39th Street, northwest corner Park, on Murray Hill, where it remained for thirty-eight years. In the 1950s it tried to sell the property and finally, in July 1960, found a buyer. In November it announced that it had bought a 95' by 100' property at 15–21 West 43rd Street, a parking lot that adjoined the Century Association clubhouse (a McKim, Mead & White structure completed in 1891) and faced what was then still the Columbia University Club (later acquired by the Unification Church of Sun Myung Moon). The Princeton Club had 3,000 members; its president announced that the new building, with bedrooms, a taproom, and squash courts, would accommodate a membership of 6,000.

Still for men only is the Racquet & Tennis Club at 370 Park Avenue. This Florentine Renaissance palazzo, completed in 1918, fills the west blockfront between 52nd and 53rd streets. Robert Goelet, who owned the property, persuaded the club to let him put up the building and lease it from him. Paul Goldberger has called it "very mediocre McKim, Mead & White. This time the Italian palazzo has come out looking rather like a warehouse, and one yearns for the delicate touch of Stanford White whose death twelve years before this commission put an end to what sprightliness this great firm's work might have had." Even if one agrees, "mediocre" McKim, Mead & White is more pleasing than the design seen in many of the Racquet Club's latter-day office tower neighbors; loss of this building would occasion much lamentation. What started the trend to modern office buildings on Park Avenue was Lever House. As that

ABOVE: *The Yale Club, as big as a hotel* (1989 photo)

graceful glass box went up just to the north of the Racquet Club in the summer of 1951, Douglas L. Elliman, chairman of the house committee, decided that the club's private dining rooms had become very valuable for commercial purposes and could be rented for a fairly handsome sum. McKim, Mead & White was brought in to draw up plans with a view to relocating these private dining rooms. There was also talk of putting a couple of doubles courts for squash on the roof and, despite widespread opposition to admitting "ladies," making some provision for accommodating women visitors, possibly by cutting a door to the south of the main entrance into the existing Strangers' Room, which would be given appropriate toilet facilities and a snack bar. Consideration was given, too, to buying a building just to the west of the clubhouse and making it into a separate ladies' annex. But when members saw the bill submitted for McKim, Mead & White's plans and the estimates for the work there was such an outcry that nothing was done.

Eventually, an air-conditioning machine was mounted in the air space above the service alley that runs through the west side of the clubhouse. The first-floor mezzanine continued to be used for the club's kitchen, refrigeration, wine storage, linen room, and tailor shop. The main dining room and pantry are on the second floor. Along with the usual dining rooms, bedrooms, and squash courts the clubhouse contains one of the few existing courts for the game of court tennis (sometimes called "Louis Quatorze").

Founded as such in 1890 at 27 West 43rd Street, with the stated purpose of

BELOW: *The Racquet & Tennis Club: for men only* (1989 photo)

"encouraging all manly sports" among its members, the club is an outgrowth of the Racquet Court Club, begun in 1875, which had in turn absorbed the Racquet Club, started in 1868—well before lawn tennis was introduced to America. Only one early member had a Park Avenue address: E. (for Evander) Berry Wall, of 43 Park, a dandy with a reputation for changing his costume innumerable times in the course of a day (in later years William Randolph Hearst's Cholly Knickerbocker always put Wall at the head of his list of best-dressed men).

The initiation fee was raised late in 1988 to $5,000, annual dues to as much as $1,550 (for a senior New York resident). The Racquet & Tennis Club had more than thirty *Social Register* members with Park Avenue addresses: Stanford H. Brainerd, Dr. van Vechten Burger, Jr., Amory S. Carhart, Beverly Corbin, Jr., Arthur H. Diedrich, Christopher A. Forster, Robert A. Gale, Warren B. Idsal, George S. Johnston, Donald D. Lamont, Gerit L. Lansing, Lewis H. Lehrman, Winslow M. Lovejoy, Jr., Thomas N. McCarter III, Roman Martinez, Richard E. Metz, Alex E. Pagel, Anthony Pantaleoni, Jeffrey Pettit, Peter V. N. Philip, Ogden Phipps, John S. Pyne, Willis Reese, Frank E. Richardson, James H. Ripley, Donald O. Ross, Edward Russell, Jr., Winthrop Rutherfurd, Truman M. Talley, S. Staley Tregallas, and Roger W. Tuckerman.

Of these, Johnston, Metz, Pagel, and Rutherfurd had wives who belonged to the Colony Club, which in 1987 had at least eighty-five members living on Park. The Colony Club was founded in 1903. Its genesis was in the mind of Mrs. J. (Jefferson) Borden Harriman (*née* Florence Jaffray Jones), a thirty-two-year-old matron who in the summer of 1902 was obliged to leave Newport to run some errands in the city. She found the Harriman town house full of painters and plasterers, and it was unheard of for a woman to check into a hotel alone. New York had no women's club; there were women's leagues and women's associations, but the word "club" had connotations of something other than public service. Mrs. Harriman persuaded Mrs. John Jacob Astor, Mrs. Payne Whitney, and some other women to join her in building a clubhouse with all the comforts of the Union Club. They fixed an initiation fee of $150 and annual dues at $100, putting the Colony Club on the level of the most expensive men's club, and set exclusive admission standards.

Members were asked for contributions to finance construction of the clubhouse. J. P. Morgan, whose three daughters were all members, agreed to subscribe $10,000 if nine other men would do the same. William C. Whitney offered to put up $25,000 if the women built a clubhouse as large as that of the Metropolitan Club. Stanford White was commissioned to design the clubhouse, which was smaller than the Metropolitan but seemingly quite large enough. White came to an untimely end in June 1906; the building was completed eight months later at 120 Madison Avenue, between 30th and 31st Streets, where it is now home to the American Academy of Dramatic Arts; Elsie DeWolfe (later to become Lady Mendl) interrupted her stage career to design the interiors.

Mrs. Harriman, who served as president from 1904 to 1916, wrote in the *Century* magazine in 1924, "When we were building, it was depressing to learn that the Princeton Club had put its house plans in abeyance on the ground that the Colony Club would soon fail and be for sale cheap. . . .

"When I told Mr. Morgan that members of the Princeton Club hoped to take over the Colony Club when it failed, he sniffed as if he had looked into a crystal and knew that within three years after we had opened at Madison Avenue we would already be planning larger quarters and that in twelve years the house charges would show an increase of 513 percent., and would be nearly half a million dollars in 1922. . . .

"The club-house formally opened March 11, 1907. We had opened with 498 members and in 1908 had 819. By 1918 we had more than two thousand members and a waiting list of over a thousand. It had become the custom for members to put up their daughters while they were yet in kindergarten. In the new club there are two charming ballrooms . . . Renting the ballrooms has helped in financing the club."

The club announced in 1914 that it would give up its Madison Avenue clubhouse for a new one that would be built as "the finest club-house in the world." The new house, to be designed by Delano & Aldrich, would cost an estimated $400,000; the club obtained a $500,000 loan to cover building and land. Delayed by the war (brass window fixtures had been ordered from France and the chandeliers from Germany), the new Colony clubhouse finally opened in 1923 at the northwest corner of Park and 63rd Street (its marble base now makes it appear to be a continuation of 570 Park at 64th Street). The red brick-and-marble Georgian-style building, apparently a four-story residence with a mansard roof, is in fact 130 feet high and filled with sybaritic luxuries quite unknown at the old club house or even at the best men's clubs. A 20' x 60' marble-and-tile swimming pool is in the basement, together with massage baths, mud baths, and sulfur baths similar to those at European spas. A special elevator links the basement with the fully equipped oak-paneled gymnasium on the fifth floor and the squash courts above. There was originally a kennel where members could leave their dogs.

Caen stone lines the walls of the Colony Club's round entrance hall, while its one-and-a-half-story high ballroom has walls with brocatelle hangings. On the second floor are two dining rooms, the library, a cardroom, and a seventy-foot-long lounge paneled in American butternut. There are forty bedrooms—and a guests' room where anxious applicants are interviewed for membership. Privacy is jealously guarded. The New York Times carried a story on April 29, 1930, that said, in part, "For two weeks it has been a secret that police were called by the Colony Club on Park Avenue at 62nd Street, socially rated as one of the most important clubs for women in New York. It was explained to the police that it was a very disagreeable experience for the Colony Club to have dealings with them and that nothing must be said about it. The police have deferred to this wish, even though they have not yet been able to gratify the request of the club for the arrest of Basil Allaway, a clerk to whom the club entrusted its bankbook and whose accounts appear to be $11,000 short." (Allaway was arrested in Portland, Oregon, on August 16, 1932.) Less community minded than its younger cousin, the Cosmopolitan (or Cos) Club, and more expensive, the Colony has annual dues of about $1,400 with a monthly minimum for food and beverages.

The *Social Register* does not indicate membership in the Union League Club, which has traditionally put more emphasis on Republican party affiliation than on social standing. (Its unwritten rule for years was No dogs, no women, no Democrats, and no journalists.) In 1988 the club had about 1,600 members, who paid (or whose employers paid) annual dues of about $1,500, up from about $875 in 1975. There is an initiation fee of about $1,000. Organized early in 1863 with a seriousness of purpose not notable in other clubs, the Union League Club in its early years forbade card-playing and similar games. The circumstances of the club's founding are in mild dispute. By one account, it was founded by Republican members of the Union Club. When the Civil War broke out, the Union Club had more than seventy Southern members, including Judah P. Benjamin, Confederate secretary of war. Some Union Club members wanted Benjamin expelled as "a traitor and rebel." The governors took the view that Southern members were gentlemen first, traitors and rebels second, and allowed them to resign honorably. When a group of Republican Union Club members, flushed with patriotism, tried to have the governors declare the club Republican in politics, they failed; it was these men who formed the Union League Club.

By another account, the club was an outgrowth of the U.S. Sanitary Commission, which dates to June 1861 and also spawned the American Red Cross. A small nucleus of Union supporters decided that the Union League Club should be something more than just an association whose members had a common purpose: it should have permanent quarters, a "wine room," a restaurant, billiard rooms, and all the other conventional comforts and luxuries of a club. Members performed significant service to the Union cause during the war.

In 1868 the club moved into a house at 26th Street and Madison Avenue that had been occupied until 1866 by Leonard W. Jerome, the sometime ally of Commodore Vanderbilt whose daughter Jenny would be the mother of Winston Churchill. On March 5, 1881, more than six months before club member Chester A. Arthur became the nation's president, the club moved into a house of its own on Fifth Avenue at 39th Street, where it remained for fifty years. It had by then established "artistic memberships": recipients paid dues by contributing paintings to the club's collection. Albert Bierstadt, Francis B. Carpenter, Jaspar F. Cropsey, and Thomas Nast are among those represented.

The club reached its peak of political influence and prestige in 1897. For another ten years or more, any high Republican official who could afford it sought membership as a matter of course. One of the oldest members in 1929 was George F. Baker, Jr., chairman of First National Bank, who had joined in 1878 when he was thirty-eight. On July 26, 1929, the club's finance committee met at the bank's building downtown; a telegram was read from the eighty-nine-year-old Baker: "Sorry I cannot attend club meeting today but unless market is very weak think that securities had probably better be sold and proceeds deposited with First National Bank to be drawn upon as needed.

LEFT: *The Colony Club: for women of the Old Guard* (1989 photo)   RIGHT: *The Union League Club, bastion of Republicanism* (1989 photo)

George F. Baker." The market did not peak for another five weeks, but by early August the club's sinking fund had sold all its stocks and bonds for $1,113,326.18. There was still nine years left on the lease at 39th Street and Fifth Avenue, with the privilege of renewal for another twenty-one years from 1938. Selling the lease brought in upwards of $1 million. The market crash that came in October would have reduced substantially the sum netted by taking Baker's advice. Terminally ill at his country house in Tuxedo (he lived nearly two more years and profited handsomely from the crash), Baker had saved the club from a disaster that might well have doomed it.

Flush with funds at a time when property was being thrown on the market at sacrifice prices, the Union League Club voted to move. It bought some houses at the southwest corner of Park Avenue and 37th Street, had them demolished, and on June 4, 1930, laid the cornerstone for its new building. Albert N. Connete and Benjamin Wistar Morris (Morris had designed the annex to the nearby Morgan Library) followed the plan of the old clubhouse as much as possible and came up with an eight-story Georgian brick structure which had a setback at its fifth floor and a three-story penthouse on its roof. The entrance, in 37th Street, was flanked on either side by narrow grass plots behind wrought-iron fences. Into this new building the club moved on February 2, 1931.

Inside the clubhouse, center stairs lead to a ground floor on which are located checkroom and office. At the left of the entrance is the club's art gallery and a small visitors' room, on the right an alcove for the doorman and necessary telephones. A sweeping circular marble stairway leads from this front entrance to the first floor, where a lounge runs the length of the building, ninety-five feet on the Park Avenue side. The billiard parlor and its café occupy this floor toward the west. Above the lounge, on the second floor, is the Great Hall, and the library is above the café. The main dining room and kitchen occupy the third floor; on the fourth are the ladies' dining room and cocktail lounge, which run the length of the building along Park Avenue. The remaining space on this floor is taken up by a barbershop and three squash courts. On upper floors are located the gymnasium and living quarters—sixty-five bedrooms, each with a private bath. Downstairs are the wine cellar, pastry kitchen, storage pantries, and a huge refrigerator used exclusively for storing cheese. There is also a printing shop, carpentry shop, and the like.

The ladies' dining room, paneled in natural mahogany, was the subject of acrimonious discussion which came to a head in a dinner meeting called by some members to protest the presence of women. The male chauvinists got nowhere, but while wives and daughters of members could use the club, no woman could become a member in her own right for nearly sixty years.

While Union League Club members were moving to their new Park Avenue palace, the Union Club still occupied the palazzo at Fifth Avenue and 51st street that it had owned since 1904. The site had cost $700,000 in 1903 and the clubhouse another $1,235,000. In 1927 the members had voted to sell this clubhouse to Jeremiah Milbank, who had offered $4 million for it, and build a new one on lower-taxed land. A building committee made a survey of every available corner on Fifth and Park avenues between 50th and 72nd streets and finally selected the Redmond house at the northeast corner of Park and 69th. A twenty-day option was secured to buy the house and property for $1.2 million. But how to assemble on such short notice a quorum of members to approve the purchase? As luck would have it, Charles A. Lindbergh was due to arrive home from Paris that Saturday, and a great welcoming parade was scheduled to move up the avenue past the club at 3:30 in the afternoon. The meeting was called for 4 o'clock. Far more than the required number were present, and the purchase was duly voted.

Later, after the deal had been struck, it was said that a certain real estate operator who had long had his eye on the Redmond plot for a big apartment house offered the club $800,000 profit if it would resell to him. Nothing doing. After buying the Redmond property, adding a smaller plot next to it for $148,000, and paying off the mortgage on its old building, the Union Club found it would have left from Milbank's $4 million some $1.5 million with which to build its new home. Delano & Aldrich, the architects, called for bids in the fall of 1931 but postponed letting any contracts. The wage agreements of most of the building trades unions expired May 1, 1932, they knew, and these agreements would inevitably be renewed at lower levels. The architects also foresaw the continued decline in the price of building materials. Contracts, therefore, were let one by one, "each at the last possible moment in the construction schedule," to quote *Fortune* magazine. "The structural steel, first to be awarded, went to McClintic-Marshall in January, the elevators to Otis in February, the granite and limestone in April, etc. This Fabian policy has saved the club a pretty penny."

Some 500 members used the Fifth Avenue clubhouse every day, said *Fortune* in December 1932. The club had about 900 running accounts, 22 percent of its members lived outside the city, there was no waiting list ("You're elected instanter—or not at all"), members averaged fifty years of age.

The new clubhouse opened in August 1933—a Georgian granite-and-limestone pile with a mansard roof but with nothing more than a UC over the door to identify it. A reporter for the *New York Telegram* wrote: "The Union Club, conservatism's townhouse, opened its new home today at Park Avenue and 69th Street and the 35 members who had gathered on its steps before the door swung officially ajar at 7 A.M. went in to be confronted by a main lounge in which the chairs faced away from the windows, by squash courts, living quarters, air conditioning, and trick lighting.

"There wasn't any ceremony. There was a lot of talk about the club house being the 'most modern in existence,' and certainly this seemed justified. Should London call a member while he is bound in elevator to the fifth floor squash courts he can receive the call right in the car, possibly complete his business before he steps out.

"The squash courts—there are three—are themselves an innovation. The Union Club heretofore did not go in for exercise on the premises. Adjacent is a huge wicker-furnished lounge, with a series of dressing cubicles.

"On the floor below are bedrooms. The bathrooms are lumined by a new baselight system to insure the perfect shave. The building is air conditioned. The third floor houses the balcony, the library with its 16,000 volumes, and also the club's 'eternal light' memorial to its war dead.

"On the second floor are banquet and dining rooms, a lounge, assembly rooms. The main floor, with its turned-from-the-window chairs and the famous Washington portrait, also contains the backgammon room. As a matter of fact, even did the lounge chairs face the window, as in the old building at Fifth Avenue and 51st Street, it would be difficult for even the most avid window gazer to see out, due to the elevation. In the basement are billiard and pool rooms, a barbershop—and the bar. True, for the moment it is called merely 'The Oyster Bar,' but it is quite seaworthy enough to fulfill its larger calling, with Ratification."

The old Union Club on Fifth Avenue had closed on May 19, 1933 (it was replaced by Best's, a department store that came down to make way for the Olympic Tower apartment building completed in 1976 at 645 Fifth).

In the late 1960s, Hunter College students were caught up in the turmoil that was sweeping campuses that was infecting their counterparts around the world. One day a small crowd of undergraduates barged into the neighboring Union

ABOVE: *The Union Club, oldest of all, still strictly for men* (1989 photo)

Club, having no idea what it was (who knew what the UC over the door might mean?) and asked about the nature of the institution. Someone, thinking fast, informed the intruders that they had entered a home for aging lepers; the students beat a hasty retreat.

Pretensions to grandeur still abound in New York society, but exclusionary club rules are no longer accepted as the natural order of things. In his 1974 memoir, *A Writer's Capital*, the Park Avenue lawyer-novelist Louis Auchincloss wrote of his childhood, "With other children I took the anti-Semitism which then characterized the Protestant society of New York for granted. Most of the schools and clubs admitted no Jews at all unless they were converted or unless they had married Christians. Brearley was considered 'liberal' because it took one Jewish girl per class, yet I can never recall thinking that my parents or their friends had any particular animus against Jews. Their attitude was simply an arbitrary 'grown-up' thing . . . I can even remember explaining to cousins at a Christmas party that father had sold our house in Cedarhurst because Cedarhurst had become 'too Jewish,' and this being accepted as impassively as if I had spoken of the pollution of air by a factory. I suspect that the lack of emotion connected with this prejudice may have been the reason that it was so easy for me and most of my contemporaries to drop it altogether when we grew up.

"The same thing may be said about the prejudice against Roman Catholics. This certainly existed, though, like the anti-Semitism it was snobbish rather than religious in nature. Catholicism was associated in our minds with the poor, ignorant Irish maids who worked such long hours and slept in often unheated areas on the top of brownstone houses. So far as blacks were concerned, however, there was no prejudice at all, because blacks did not exist for us. Nobody that I knew even had a black servant. They lived up in Harlem, presumably because they liked it, and our paths never crossed. If any particular fact of dreadful poverty or discrimination was impressed upon us, I think our attitude was probably that we had fought a war to free them and that that should be enough."

Most of the people in Auchincloss' set have presumably risen above the prejudices with which they may have been reared—most but not all. The City Commission on Human Rights held hearings a year after publication of the Auchincloss memoir and found there was "stubborn persistence of 'white only' or 'male only' policies in private clubs." This, it observed, was "attributable in part to the fact that very little of what takes place in the sanctum of the club is overtly or openly discussed. Membership determination is generally made in secret, membership lists are confidential, and activities are not publicized in advance other than to members. This privacy is deemed by clubs to be within their rights, arising from constitutional guarantees of privacy and free association. Although exclusion of minorities and women may not be the reason for secret determinations, the lack of public scrutiny permits the continuance of categorical exclusions no longer acceptable in other settings. The Elks and the Moose have deleted the racial restrictions in their membership requirements, girls can now play on Little League baseball teams, women may be seated at the tables down at Mory's, and the League of Women Voters will need a new name now that its long-standing policy of barring full membership to men has ended. We need a climate in this city," the commission concluded, "that will not tolerate clubs where no women, no blacks, and no Jews are allowed."

Gloria Steinem, then editor of the feminist *Ms.* magazine, testified at the hearings that clubs were "an important part of the decision-making structure in this country, more important than the boardrooms, the executive suites, the union halls or courts or state legislatures where the decisions are supposed to be made."

An unpublished report based on the May 1975 hearings by the City Commission declared that clubs and membership organizations in general were "white male Protestant strongholds. Their membership policies have been unaffected by shifts in national attitudes and unresponsive to changes in the policies and structures of major social institutions that have taken place during the past twenty years. Although assessments of the degree to which all forms of ethnic and sex discrimination has decreased in the United States obviously will vary, it will be conceded, at the least, that overt discrimination has been very much on the wane."

The report quoted Samuel Friedman, director of the Social Discrimination in Business and Industry Division of the American Jewish Committee, who had in his testimony cited a 1973 survey of several hundred clubs made by the A.J.C., which found the barriers of forty years before still in place with only a few exceptions. Based on this and other testimony, the report stated that "Club policies are self perpetuating. Control is passed by one group to the next by selecting those they perceive to be 'their kind,' and new blood seldom is infused. Most policy questions are settled in small, secret meetings. Applicants are rejected without any stated reason, and those excluded tend to keep their feelings private, rarely electing to publicize what they construe as embarrassing and humiliating estimations of individual worth. The fact that discrimination is largely de facto rather than de jure, or in accordance with stated policy, permits most clubs to deny the existence of racial or ethnic criteria for selection.

"To what extent employers subsidize club membership for important executives or others can only be estimated but there is no doubt that it exists. What proportion of the costs represent genuine business expense is also unanswerable. The true value of club membership is known only to those who are members. . . . Bringing about change is slow when the excluded population has accepted exclusion, a problem no more evident than in the case of women who have traditionally been excluded or allowed limited access to the sanctum of the male club."

In earlier years, when midtown Manhattan abounded with good restaurants at which any professional or business person could entertain a client, there was no compelling need for a man or woman to belong to a club. As high rents and other factors reduced the number of white-tablecloth restaurants, club membership assumed a growing importance.

The Marco Polo Club at the Waldorf-Astoria, founded in October 1959 and opened early in 1960, is a private club that pays rent to the Waldorf (whose Norse Grill had previously occupied the space), uses part of the Waldorf kitchens, has a Waldorf chef assigned to it, and prides itself on being able to offer the best food of any club in the city. Originally for men only, although women were permitted at dinner, the club now invites women to join; Mrs. Douglas MacArthur, a resident of the Waldorf Towers, was on the club's board of governors in the late 1980s, when membership was between 750 and 800. The club is open for lunch and dinner, and serves breakfast in its private rooms. There are three private rooms, seating up to twelve each; total seating capacity, including the private rooms, is about 135. A member may rent the club for a wedding or other function on a weekend. Club activities include theater, ballet, opera parties, and even a day at the races in conjunction with the Union League and Sky clubs. Resident, nonresident, suburban, and international memberships are offered; there are also diplomatic memberships for UN members, and dinner memberships, which cost less than the normally steep fee (close to $2,000) of regular membership.

The Sky Club, on the fifty-sixth floor of the Pan Am Building (200 Park Avenue), opened in 1963 to rival the much older Cloud Club atop the Chrysler Building.

The Board Room Club, on the forty-first floor of the Bankers Trust Building addition, 280 Park, was founded in 1969 when the building opened, designed by the same people as the Sky Club, if in a less conservative style. Members and their guests have sweeping views to the south, east, and west—the Statue of Liberty, planes taking off from Newark Airport. Membership is about 1,000 (perhaps 100 are women), and close to 400 can be seated for a meal. There are no facilities other than for eating and drinking. An applicant must be sponsored by five different members, must buy a capital certificate, and must pay annual dues said to be about $2,000. Such fees and dues are generally paid for by companies, not individuals.

Newest of the clubs is Club 101, which opened in 1982 in the brand-new 101 Park building between 40th and 41st streets. The building's public cafeteria does 1,100 to 1,200 lunches per day (often to employees subsidized to some extent by companies in the neighborhood); and an Italian restaurant, CI, with a sea of white tablecloths at the southeast corner of 41st Street, lures passersby with the promise of civility—but Club 101 is strictly private. Located at street level in space specifically designed for it, the club, which has 1,300 members, seats 135 in a spaciously configured main dining room. Private dining rooms seat another 100. The club serves lunch five days a week, and arrangements can be made for breakfasts, cocktail parties, or dinners. If approved by the Club 101 board, an applicant pays a $1,500 initiation fee and annual dues of $1,000—$500 if he or she lives at least forty miles away. Companies must have one assigned member; other employees may be authorized to use the facilities.

Like the Colony, Racquet, and Union clubs, the Marco Polo, Sky, and Board Room clubs are, in the code language of lawyers, "distinctly private clubs," as is Club 101; they do not obtain revenues from nonmembers "for the furtherance of trade or business." This distinction made the Union League Club, the University Club, the New York Athletic Club, and the Century Association subject to the city's Local Law 63, enacted in 1984 to ban discrimination in clubs that have more than 400 members, provide regular meal service, and regularly receive "payment for dues, fees, use of space, facilities, services, meals or beverages directly from or on behalf of non-members for the furtherance of trade or business." Dues payment by employers subjected a club to the law.

Lawyers for the New York State Club Association argued that Local Law 63 violated "the fundamental right of our citizens . . . to choose who their friends will be." But in the case of *New York State Club Association, Inc.* v. *The City of New York*, the U.S. Supreme Court ruled unanimously in June 1988 that there was nothing unconstitutional about Local Law 63; the ruling, cheered by women and minority groups, made some people distinctly unhappy.

13

Literary Park Avenue

IT USED TO BE SAID (with only a little truth) that just one book was to be found in the typical Park Avenue apartment, the *Social Register*. As for writers, serious ones lived in Greenwich Village, in Chelsea, or on the upper West Side. Park Avenue was for lawyers, stockbrokers, corporation brass, advertising executives. Whoever heard of a writer—other than a copywriter—living on Park Avenue?

Louis Auchincloss, whose novels are often peopled with Park Avenue types, might take exception to such talk. Auchincloss, born in 1917, has lived for years at 1111 Park and is married to a descendant of Commodore Vanderbilt. As a boy, he enrolled in the Knickerbocker Grays. "Two afternoons a week I and a couple of hundred other boys dressed in gray uniforms learned close-order drill in the Park Avenue Armory. I remember protesting to Mother the impropriety of having to get into the Madison Avenue trolley in full uniform accompanied by a nurse." Later he attended Mrs. Hubbell's dancing class, "which met on Thursday afternoons in the ballroom of the Colony Club." This was before Groton, Yale, University of Virginia Law School, the U.S. Navy, and two Wall Street law firms. As noted earlier, Auchincloss grew up in a world of snobbery and prejudice, attitudes still found among some of his fictional characters. He wrote his first novel at twenty-three and was so disappointed by Scribner's rejection notice that he went to law school. He was more successful at thirty, when he finally had a novel published. Some critics would protest that Louis Auchincloss is a Wall Street lawyer who just happens to write entertaining novels. Anyway, they would say, isn't he rather an exception in having a Park Avenue address?

Perhaps. But Tom Wolfe, who may often be seen strolling the avenue with his dogs has long lived just off Park, the playwright Neil Simon lived for some years at the Ritz Tower, and a number of prominent women writers have had apartments on the avenue—Willa Cather, Edna Ferber, Mary Roberts Rinehart, Janet Flanner, and Lillian Hellman, among others.

Edith Wharton, who would later live on Park in the Seventies, was born just off what later would be called Park Avenue South and was baptized at Calvary Church, northeast corner 22nd Street, early in 1862. Mention should also be made of Herman Melville, perhaps the greatest novelist this country has ever had. The name Park Avenue had not yet been applied even to the upper reaches of Fourth when Melville, whose novels *Omoo* and *Typee* were enjoying some modest success, moved in September 1847 into a house at 103 Fourth Avenue that would be his home for the next fifteen years (Cooper Station of the U.S. Postal Service now occupies the site).

The author had just turned twenty-eight when, in August 1847, he was married in Boston to Elizabeth Shaw, daughter of Judge Lemuel Shaw. His younger brother Allan was married September 22, and the two benedicts obtained the house at 103 Fourth Avenue. They and their wives moved in along with their mother, Maria Gansevoort Melville, and four unmarried sisters. The house was close to that of Evert Duyckinck, Melville's editor at Wiley & Putnam, American publisher of *Typee*.

Redburn, written in ten weeks and published in 1849, and *White-Jacket*, written in two months and published in 1850, were produced at 103 Fourth Avenue. There Melville wrote the first chapters of his masterpiece, *Moby-Dick*, after returning on February 1, 1850, from a trip to Europe. Published in 1851, the novel had a poor reception, with fewer than fifty copies sold in the author's lifetime. Melville worked through the summer of 1850 in the Berkshires, and in September purchased a 160-acre farm near Lenox, Massachusetts. In October 1863 he moved back to New York, buying a house from his brother Allan at 104 East 26th Street (60 East by earlier numbering), close to the two railroad depots built six years earlier. The Melville house was torn down and replaced with an office building that is now 357 Park Avenue South. Street signs on the avenue between 26th and 27th streets identify the block as Herman Melville Square. Just west of the Armory at 104 East 26th Street a plaque on the side of a building reads: "Herman Melville/ the American author/ resided from 1863–1891 at this site where he wrote *Billy Budd* among other works."

Billy Budd, Foretopman, was not finished until the year of his death and not published until 1924. But Melville's writing career was about finished by the time he moved into 26th Street; he earned his living as a customs inspector. Sitting on his back porch in 1875, smoking his pipe and looking across his garden, he could see the rear of 111 East 25th Street, a house in which Henry James occupied two rooms. James, then thirty-one, was the author of the novel *Roderick Hudson* then being serialized in the *Atlantic Monthly*, which paid him $100 a month. He received a like amount for the reviews he wrote for the *Nation*. James would spend most of his life abroad and receive far more remuneration for his writing than Melville, who was forever embittered by the commercial failure of *Moby-Dick*. The house in which James lived for a while was razed in 1905 for the construction of the 69th Regiment Armory. A year or two later the young poet Ezra Pound resided at 270 Fourth Avenue before going abroad in 1908 to become an expatriate.

The area south of Union Square where Melville had shared a house from 1847 to 1863 was becoming the city's cultural center: the Academy of Music had opened in 1854 at 14th Street and Irving Place, Cooper Union in 1859 in Astor Place. Wallack's Theater was on the west side of Fourth at 13th Street.

This section included the part of Fourth Avenue which later had so many secondhand bookdealers that it came to be known as Booksellers Row, or Book Row, a mecca for seekers of out-of-print volumes. The first dealers were Jacob Abrahams (who had come from Poland in the 1880s) and Peter Stammer. Abrahams established himself in 1893 at 80 Fourth Avenue, Stammer came along seven years later at No. 95. Herbert Hammond opened The Book Mart in 1901 at No. 105, and before long there were Alexander Hall at 89, Andrew McLaren at 86, and Pincus Wachstetter at 123, a stall that Stammer himself would later occupy.

Jacob Abrahams had moved in 1898 to 145 Fourth Avenue, where he remained until he died in the late 1930s. He sold old magazines as well as used books. The "Black Tom" explosion of July 30, 1916, blew up some Jersey City docks loading munitions; seven men were killed, thirty-five injured, and $40 million worth of property destroyed. German saboteurs were blamed and somehow Abrahams' store was implicated. His partner Herman Meyers was called before a governmental committee to tell what he knew. He could say only that he had noticed a well-dressed man dropping in from time to time and browsing in the deserted, dimly lit rear of the bookshop. The man was evidently a German agent who passed on military secrets by slipping them into old copies of *Saturday Evening Post* where they were later picked up by a confederate.

Bookshops proliferated on Fourth Avenue: M. A. Gropper at 97, Edward Adams at 136, Joseph Rosenbaum at 83. "Empty your purse into your head," Peter Stammer advertised. Stammer's, which closed in late 1969, began in a basement at 95 Fourth Avenue, moved shortly to 123, moved again a few years later to 120 East 23rd Street, and by 1910 was back on Booksellers Row at 61 Fourth Avenue. *Pearson's* magazine for June 1919 called Stammer "the original New York book hunter." Yale professors came down from New Haven to browse and buy at Stammer's; Harvard added to its economics collection from the shop; N.Y.U. purchased its journalism library there. Helping out was Stammer's nephew Nat Pine, who had come from Russia in 1905 and gone to work for his uncle at $3 a week. By the end of World War I Stammer's cousin Samuel Dauber had opened a shop in the same building. Dauber later went into business with Pine; their shop, Dauber & Pine, moved to Fifth Avenue, where it remained until the 1970s.

Much larger than any of these was Theodore E. Schulte, who opened at 80 Fourth and remained there for more than half a century. Schulte had started in the book trade at age twelve. O. Henry used to browse at his shop. Other famous customers included Fritz Kreisler, Marlene Dietrich, and Marion Davies, who bought books on the Quakers for a forthcoming movie role.

In the mid-1920s came David Kirschenbaum's Bargain Books and Max Breslow's Bookshop for Bookish People. The Bible House building, built in 1853 at 45 Fourth (New York's first structure to be erected on a framework of cast-iron columns), was home to a number of booksellers. The American Bible Society owned the building and was understanding when a tenant couldn't pay his rent on time. Louis Cohen's Argosy bookshop (now in East 59th Street near Bloomingdale's) was in the Bible House, as was Sam Scheinbaum's Parnassus Shop.

When the New York Telephone Company published its first classified directory in 1928, it listed a number of Fourth Avenue booksellers: J. Abrahams at 145, American Bible Society at 8th Street, Argosy at Bible House, Bargain Book Store at 79, Frank Bender at 84, Norman W. Cohen at 87, Samuel Fechter at 114, A. Geffen at 112, T. M. Moore at 333, Parnassus at Bible House, Romm's at 110, Schulte's at 80, P. Stammer at 61, Harry Stone at 137, Samuel Weiser at 116, and Wex at 65—most of them overcrowded, musty shops, some smelling of cat, seemingly disorganized, but with the possibility of undetected treasure lurking on the next shelf.

Rents dropped during the Depression to levels that even used bookdealers could afford. George Rubinowitz and his wife Jean started the Fourth Avenue Book Store at 138 Fourth in 1940. Thornton Wilder and Zero Mostel were good customers. The Anchor Book Shop at 114 also began in 1940, and the Corner Bookshop, formerly at 120, moved to new quarters at 102—not at a corner but across the street from one. Part of Booksellers Row was on nearby Broadway between 8th and 14th streets, once the heart of the theater district.

Normally fierce competitors, the shops joined forces in May 1942 to form the Fourth Avenue Booksellers Association. City officials had issued an order that all dealers remove their bargain stands from the sidewalks in front of their stores. Some twenty-five dealers met and established headquarters at 73 Fourth Avenue (later moved to 113 East 9th Street). Theodore Schulte went to City Hall and got the order rescinded.

The Pageant Book and Print Shop, in recent years at 109 East 9th Street, opened in 1945 as the Pageant Book Company at 59 Fourth Avenue, where it remained until 1980. Run by Henry ("Chips") Chafetz and Sidney Solomon (both had worked for George Rubin at the Fourth Avenue Bookshop), Pageant stocked more than 100,000 books in 3,000 square feet of selling space.

When Herbert Oxer opened the Vanity Fair bookshop at 108 Fourth in 1950, Book Row compared favorably with London's Charing Cross Road and the banks of the Seine. But the closing of Wanamaker's, which had drawn traffic to the Astor Place area, came as a blow in December 1954. Then developers pulled down old buildings to put up apartment houses such as 145 Fourth. Bookshops were displaced but carried on, some moving to Broadway or Third Avenue. In 1969 a request was made to the city that street signs on Fourth between 8th Street and 14th be changed to read: "4th Ave-Book Row." Plans to hold a book fair on the avenue at the same time as the art fair on Washington Square never got beyond the talking stage.

Book Row once had three dozen shops. Now it has none, and the Fourth Avenue Booksellers Association is only a memory. Samuel Weiser, specializing in the metaphysical, has moved to 132 East 24th Street. The major survivor is Strand, at 828 Broadway. Founded by Ben Bass on 8th Street in 1928, Strand later moved to 81 Fourth Avenue before taking up its present location at 12th and Broadway. Huge and well-stocked, the store has 50,000 square feet of space with more than 2 million books. Ben Bass's son Fred has a staff of 150 to keep the store—and its satellites—humming.

If the Fourth Avenue blocks below Union Square were Book Row, those north of 23rd Street were for many years Publishers Row. A few remained even in the late 1980s: Crown at 225 Park Avenue South, Franklin Watts at 387 Park Avenue South, Facts on File at 460 Park Avenue South, E. P. Dutton and Hawthorn Books at 2 Park Avenue, and some lesser-known firms here and there in the neighborhood. Doubleday, indeed, was for many years on Park Avenue north of Grand Central (at 277 from 1966 to 1972, at 245 from 1972 until late in 1988), but only the most successful houses can afford midtown rents.

Offices of the Social Register Association were for decades at 341 Fourth Avenue. In recent years they have been on the tenth floor of 381 Park Avenue South. Louis Keller, who published the first *Social Register* in 1887, sold his book for $1.75. Fifty years later the price was up to $7 ($50 for the entire multi-city collection); in 1989 the price for the national *Social Register* was $75. Anyone can buy a copy. A small staff reads the application forms which all candidates are required to file, looks over endorsements from friends already listed, accepts or rejects on the basis of mysterious criteria, and eliminates names of those who make "inappropriate" marriages (whatever that may mean) or in other ways offend. Cornelius Vanderbilt, Jr. (IV) was dropped after publication of his 1935 book *Farewell to Fifth Avenue.*

Publishers Row developed over the course of twenty-five years. John Wiley and Sons moved into the Silk Center Building at 432 Fourth before 1905, and Funk & Wagnalls took two floors at 44-60 East 23rd Street, corner of Fourth. By 1910 Dodd, Mead had completed its own building at 441 Fourth. Longmans Green, long extinct, moved into the new Dodd, Mead building early in 1910. In 1913, the year before R. J. Cuddihy acquired majority control, Funk & Wagnalls took new quarters in the twenty-story Hess Building, 354 Fourth Avenue. And in 1914 Harper and Brothers became the last major publisher to leave lower Manhattan. After 106 years at Franklin Square, the firm established itself in a new building at 49 East 33rd Street, corner Fourth Avenue where it remained until Harper & Row moved uptown in July 1972.

By 1920, virtually all of the major book publishers had moved from lower Manhattan to the area either of 23rd Street (Scribners; Dodd, Mead; Putnams; and Dutton), 33rd Street (Oxford Press, Doubleday Page, Appleton, and others), or Fourth Avenue above 25th Street. Scribners, Putnams, and Dutton specialized in nonfiction and prospered largely on their backlists. Other kinds of business, notably the silk trade, were invading the area, and Longmans Green moved in 1922 to Fifth, but Fourth still rivaled Fifth as Publishers Row, even after many companies had moved north to the 40s and 50s. In 1925 Henry Holt left 44th Street after fourteen years and moved to 1 Park Avenue, where it remained for some years. Other houses were still on Fourth Avenue just to the south.

Houghton Mifflin, William Morrow, Yale University Press, and others all had offices in the New York Life Building at 386 Fourth in 1928. Coward-McCann moved in across the street at 425. E. P. Dutton was about to occupy offices in the Guardian Life Insurance Building at 300 Fourth Avenue, where it would remain for decades; and in 1929 D. Van Nostrand moved to 250 Fourth after nearly a decade at 8 Warren Street.

These publishers were all still on Fourth Avenue or Park when Willa Cather moved to Park Avenue in 1932. Her 1931 novel *Shadows on the Rock* had put her into the top ten of fiction best sellers for the first time. Cather is best known for her novels about early days in Nebraska (*My Antonia, O Pioneers!*) and the Southwest (*Death Comes for the Archbishop*), but she was born (1873) in western Virginia and spent more than half her life in New York City. Visiting Lincoln, Nebraska, in the summer of 1903, she had met a local girl, Edith Lewis, who became her lifelong lover and companion. They were together for more than four decades, and although most of those years were spent in Greenwich Village, where lesbian relationships were tolerated at a time when such things created problems elsewhere, the couple moved in December 1932 to a big apartment at 570 Park, the building in whose elevator shaft H. Gordon Duval had met his death a few years earlier.

In Greenwich Village, writes Cather's biographer Phyllis Robinson, "she had looked out at the world with pleasure and anticipation. The windows of the Bank Street apartment had opened to the street and the rooms seemed always to be flooded with sunlight. The Park Avenue apartment was in the rear of the building and the heavily curtained windows all faced the blank wall of the exclusive Colony Club next door. The apartment turned its back on the fashionable avenue below just as Willa shut herself off from the life around her. Even in the last years at Bank Street she had rented an empty apartment above hers so that she would not be disturbed by noise overhead.

"Having an apartment of her own again [after several years at the Grosvenor Hotel on Fifth Avenue] seemed to release Willa's energies," Robinson writes. "It pleased her to be able to receive her friends in dignified surroundings and she and Edith began to entertain at small dinners. The space, the silence, the sense of peace and privacy were just what Willa needed for her work. In the spring following the move to Park Avenue she began her new book, working on it over the next months in New York" and elsewhere. *Lucy Gayheart* came out in February 1935 and the next month began serial publication in *Woman's Home Companion*. Cather's final novel, *Saphhira and the Slave Girl*, appeared at the end of 1940. On the afternoon of April 24, 1947, alone in her room at 570 Park, Willa

Cather suffered a cerebral hemorrhage. She was dead by the time Edith arrived home.

Early in 1932 the Swedish mountebank Ivar Kreuger shot himself in his Paris apartment, leaving behind a mountain of debt and a New York penthouse at 791 Park. It lay vacant for two years before being rented by Edna Ferber, a Midwestern writer of forty-eight who had lived for years on the West Side. Her novels included *So Big* (which won the Pulitzer prize), *Cimarron*, and *Show Boat* (basis of the 1929 Jerome Kern-Oscar Hammerstein II musical), the women's magazines paid handsomely for her short stories and for serializing her novels, and she had collaborated with George S. Kaufman on a number of Broadway hits, including *The Royal Family* and *Dinner at Eight*. Ferber wrote about the former Kreuger apartment in her 1938 autobiography *A Peculiar Treasure*, saying that she had lived in it for three years (1933–36).

It was, she said, the "only really quiet apartment" she had ever seen in New York. Traffic noises bounced off its high brick penthouse parapet, over which "unbelievable willow trees," planted by Kreuger, tossed "great leafy hoopskirts in careless abandon." The apartment itself lay empty and "dilapidated" in the wake of its previous owner's suicide. "I, renting it at a surprisingly low price, became Kreuger's sole heiress, really, for I alone benefited by his going." Ferber wrote of pulling down partitions and building "great French windows that let in the sun." She recalled a grape arbor thirty feet long, a peach tree eighteen inches in circumference, espaliered apple trees, "rhododendrons, wisteria, ivy, roses, lilac bushes, iris, forsythia, privet all growing on a penthouse sixteen stories high on Park Avenue. There were three fountains, a rock garden . . . with . . . flagstone paths."

In her 1963 memoir *A Kind of Magic*, Ferber said she had "come upon this unbelievable country house in the air." (Her friend Dorothy Rodgers, wife of the composer Richard Rodgers, had evidently found the "sky-house.") "It was offered me for rental at an unbelievably low figure. . . ." Ferber now recalled that she had lived there for five years (until May 1939), not three, and the willow trees described earlier as being twenty-four inches in circumference and fully forty feet high were now remembered as "fifteen feet high and as thick in circumference as an elephant's leg. [They] cascaded their liquid green branches over the parapet. Peach trees, espaliered apple trees, grape arbors and strawberry plants and rhubarb actually bore fruit in this bizarre Eden. Two fountains tinkled annoyingly. Jonquils popped their golden heads in the spring. . . ."

Ferber moved from Park Avenue to a house in Connecticut but returned in 1953 to another Manhattan apartment at 730 Park. Here she wrote the novels *Giant* and *Ice Palace*, and here she died, in 1968, at age eighty-three.

While Ferber was in Connecticut, the gossip columnist Dorothy Kilgallen of the *Evening Journal* and her husband Richard Kollmar took an apartment at 630 Park, southwest corner 66th Street. Nobody would call Kilgallen a serious writer but she deserves mention. (The same might be said of Finley Peter Dunne, "Mr. Dooley," the Chicago humorist of the late 1890s who moved to New York in 1900 and died in the spring of 1936 in his suite at Delmonico's Hotel, seven blocks south of Kilgallen's apartment.)

Born in Chicago in 1913, the daughter of a Hearst newspaperman, Kilgallen had emulated Nelly Bly (Elizabeth Cochrane), who in November 1889 had been sent around the world by Pulitzer's *New York World* to beat Jules Verne's fictional Phileas Fogg. In September 1936, Kilgallen, twenty-three (the same age that Cochrane had been), set off on the German dirigible *Hindenburg*, which had inaugurated regular transatlantic air service four months earlier. Racing against Bud Ekins of the *Telegram* and Leo Kieran of the *Times*, she took Pan American's China Clipper from Manila to San Francisco via Guam, Wake, Midway, and Honolulu, covering 8,200 miles in five days. Ekins won the race, breaking the record by circling the earth in eighteen days, fourteen hours, fifty-six minutes and becoming the first man to do it entirely by air over passenger routes that had barely been established.

After a sojourn in Hollywood, Kilgallen returned to New York to write a Broadway gossip column, "The Voice of Broadway," in November 1938. *Knickerbocker Holiday*, the Kurt Weill-Maxwell Anderson musical, had opened in October with a twenty-seven-year-old baritone, Richard Kollmar, in the cast. Kilgallen married Kollmar in April 1939, and in 1941, after the birth of their first child, they moved into a seven-room apartment at 630 Park Avenue. Kollmar was known to WOR radio listeners as the voice of "Boston Blackie." In 1945 "Breakfast With Dorothy and Dick" debuted on WOR, giving the illusion that the program emanated from a country cottage.

A writer for *The New Yorker* magazine visited the Kollmar apartment one August morning in 1946. Naturally, he wrote, referring to the homey front-porch-rocker material prepared by the station, "I was impatient to see the little vine-covered cottage in which Dick has installed Dorothy. I was disappointed to find that they lived in a sixteen-room apartment on Park Avenue at 66th Street. The door was opened by an elderly Negro butler wearing a white jacket. I entered a long marble hallway, at the far end of which I could dimly see Mrs. Kollmar waiting to greet me in a floor-length hostess gown. By the time I had walked the length of the hall Mr. Kollmar, having left his rocker and come in off the front porch, was at her side. Mrs. Kollmar is a slim, young brunette with immobile features. Mr. Kollmar is a stocky, boyish looking man . . ."

Kollmar was also a drunk, and Kilgallen became the family's breadwinner. On February 2, 1950, she appeared in the premiere performance of "What's My Line?" a CBS TV game show moderated by John Daly. Kilgallen would continue as a regular on the show until her death, in November 1965, from acute alcohol and barbiturate intoxication. Lee Israel, her biographer, suggests that Kilgallen was killed in connection with a gigantic cover-up of facts associated with President John F. Kennedy's assassination at Dallas two years earlier; but he produces no real evidence for such a suggestion. Nor is there any evidence that Dorothy Kilgallen had literary talent. Park Avenue had better writers.

Still living at 630 Park at the time of Kilgallen's death was Mary Roberts

Rinehart, author of the 1908 best seller *The Circular Staircase* and of its 1920 Broadway adaptation, *The Bat*. The writer Geoffrey T. Hellman had visited Rinehart and profiled her for *Life* magazine. Less gifted than Cather or even Ferber, she made a lot more money than either from her sixty-odd books (serious novels as well as murder mysteries) and numerous magazine stories and serials, all written, Hellman noted, "in long-hand with a fat fountain pen."

Her eighteen-room Park Avenue apartment, Hellman wrote, included "a dining room-drawing room-living room suite with a ninety-foot vista, a working study with a more modest vista, a billiard room, and an eight-room servants' wing occupied by three domestics and several dozen filing cabinets crammed with affectionate fan mail, voluminous income tax reports, and other stigmata of a successful, popular writer . . . Her apartment is embellished with Gainsboroughs, Raeburns, Chinese-Chippendale chairs, Adam side tables, inlaid Spanish cabinets, Austrian Aubusson rugs, and a carved dining-room table from the collection of the Duke of Cleveland (England)."

The Rineharts' sons Stanley M., Jr. and Theodore left Doubleday Doran in 1929 and started Farrar and Rinehart, which later became Rinehart and Co. and in 1960 merged with two other houses to become Holt Rinehart Winston (now Henry Holt). Mrs. Rinehart evidently provided some financial support and wrote a mystery novel, *The Door*, for her sons' firm. George Horace Lorimer, the famous *Saturday Evening Post* editor, paid $60,000 for serial rights. In the 1930s, when millions of Americans were struggling to survive, Rinehart was averaging $100,000 a year. Magazines paid between $45,000 and $65,000 for her mysteries, depending on their length, and *Good Housekeeping* put up $75,000 (the largest amount she ever received for serial rights) to run installments of *The Doctor*, written after the death of Dr. Stanley Rinehart, Mary's husband, in October 1932.

Rinehart moved into the fifth-floor Park Avenue apartment in February 1935. She was fifty-eight and getting richer as readers kept eating up her words. Settled in at 630 Park, she resumed work on *The Doctor. A Light in the Window* was published in 1948. Rinehart published only two short stories in 1949 and two more in 1950 (three of the four appeared in the *Post*), but by 1951 she was completing another mystery novel, *The Swimming Pool*, which appeared in 1952. It was her last full-length work. A novella, *The Frightened Wife*, was finished for serialization early in 1953. Written when she was seventy-seven, it ended her career with the *Saturday Evening Post*, which had turned down *The Swimming Pool*. Rinehart died in September 1958 at eighty-two, a Park Avenue dowager unlike most of the blue-haired breed, in that her fortune had come entirely from her own efforts.

Three years earlier, in August 1955, Kathleen Winsor, the sexy young author of the sexy best seller *Forever Amber*, had bought a penthouse apartment at 895 Park. Whether she ever wrote anything there is doubtful.

A more serious writer was Janet Flanner. In October 1925, while Willa Cather was writing *Death Comes for the Archbishop*, a seven-month-old weekly magazine, *The New Yorker*, began publishing articles headed "Letter from Paris" and signed "Genêt." "Genêt" was Flanner, who lived in Paris and—except for the war period, when she was in the United States—would be there for fifty years. Flanner was forty-eight and living in New York when she met another independent working woman, the Italian-born editor, Natalia Denesi Murray, ten years her junior, in early January 1940. Flanner had divorced her husband and made a life for herself in Paris; Denesi had married William Murray and settled in New York, but by the time she met Flanner and began a relationship she, too, was divorced.

In 1966 Mrs. Murray became a vice-president of Rizzoli Editore. Flanner came to visit for three months, her longest visit since the early 1940s, and "we decided to move into a new apartment more suited to our needs." They took a flat at 785 Park, northeast corner 73rd Street. "It was there that Janet was to live permanently for three years, the last ones of her life." Flanner returned to New York on February 24, 1972, turned eighty a few weeks later, and then flew off to Paris. At the end of January 1974 she was back in New York, where she wrote several long articles. "She had a studio equipped with a desk full of drawers for her clippings, where she could work undisturbed," Mrs. Murray writes. Flanner's final "Letter from Paris" appeared in the September 16, 1975, *New Yorker*. Thereafter, beginning on October 10, 1975, Flanner lived in the apartment at 785 Park with Mrs. Murray. On November 7, 1978, she was rushed to the emergency room of Lenox Hill Hospital and died there of an aneurism.

Residing a few blocks south at the time was Lillian Hellman. Hellman's hit play *The Children's Hour*, with a plot suggested by her lover Dashiell Hammett, opened in November 1934. Hellman soon began writing for Samuel Goldwyn, commuting from Greenwich Village to Pacific Palisades, California. *The Little Foxes* opened in 1939, *Watch on the Rhine* in 1941. In 1942, with *Watch on the Rhine* playing to capacity Broadway audiences and *The Little Foxes* made into a movie, Hellman bought a town house at 63 East 82nd Street, keeping two floors for her own use and renting out the rest.

That house remained her New York base for more than a quarter of a century. It was there that she threw a party for the cast of *The Children's Hour* when the play was revived in 1952, and where she lived when she went down to Washington in May of that year to testify before the House Un-American Affairs Committee, telling the congressmen that she was not a "Red" (but refusing to say whether or not she had been three or four years earlier, because such testimony "would hurt innocent people in order to save myself . . . I cannot and will not cut my conscience to fit this year's fashion," Hellman declared).

Hellman sold the 82nd Street house in 1969 and moved the following spring into a tenth floor co-op apartment at 630 Park. According to Hellman's biographer William Wright, the place "had a large living room, a full dining room, and two bedrooms, one of which Hellman turned into a workroom. She decorated the rooms with the same highly personal meld of period furniture, family items, relics from her plays and her travels, books everywhere, and many photographs, most conspicuously in the living room, one of herself as a child, one of Sophrona (Sophrona Mason, a black woman who had been her first nurse in New Orleans), and a large framed one of Dashiell Hammett at his most dashing." In 1982, still smoking heavily as she had done from an early age, Hellman suffered a mild heart attack and had a pacemaker installed. She had painful arthritis and, despite several operations, her eyesight was nearly gone. Wracked by emphysema, nearly blind and severely crippled, Hellman died in 1984.

None of the writers discussed above had anything much in common beyond a Park Avenue address. In fact, Edna Ferber once told her niece, "I always know how to vote on any board that Lillian Hellman is on. Whichever way she votes, I simply vote the opposite." Nor does their residence on Park Avenue give it any literary distinction. It merely attests to the truth that women of a certain age and ample means naturally gravitate to havens of sedate gentility, where the "space, the silence, the sense of peace and privacy" cherished by Willa Cather are prized above the bustling excitement available elsewhere. The cachet of a Park Avenue address may also have a certain appeal.

Unexciting it may be, but the security of staid and proper Park Avenue has definite charms for those of advancing years, whatever their literary tastes or abilities. To Louis Auchincloss, to writers whose work has not yet brought them public acclaim, to all who can afford it and who need only memory and imagination to activate their muse, the avenue has presented a bland, quiet background against which to work.

14
.
Commercial Incursions

WHEN Martha Bacon fought the extension of Park Avenue south to 32nd Street she was not only trying to block usurpation of her address; she was also resisting the intrusion of an office building into her residential enclave. Never mind that Rose Hill and Murray Hill had lost some of their old residential panache: putting up an office building and calling it 1 Park Avenue was simply not to be tolerated. H. Gordon Duval's Park Avenue Association supported Mrs. Bacon in her opposition to further commercialization. By the time their battle was lost in the political arena and the courts, 2 Park Avenue had replaced the old Park Avenue Hotel, and the framework of an even taller office tower loomed above the avenue between 45th and 46th streets. The Architects Building at 101 Park had stood since 1912, the Pershing Square Building at 42nd Street since 1922. Otherwise the avenue remained almost untouched by commercial taint.

Not so the blocks south of 32nd Street: Fourth Avenue fairly bristled with office and loft buildings. 403, northeast corner 23rd Street, had been there as long as anyone could remember. 230, southwest corner 19th Street, dated to 1895; 304, southwest corner 23rd Street, to 1904. The panic of 1907 interrupted only briefly the transformation of what later would be Park Avenue South to commercial use. Completed in 1908 at 346 Fourth, northwest corner 25th Street, was the headquarters of the Provident Loan Society, a not-for-profit corporation founded in 1894 soon after the start of a four-year economic depression. Wall Street stock prices had collapsed in June 1893, 600 banks had closed their doors, and 15,000 business firms had failed. A local philanthropist had written in 1892, "There is no merchant in this community who would not be driven into bankruptcy if his unsecured bills payable bore the rate of interest which the poor have to pay on the most undoubted security. Borrowing is often the greatest necessity; let the Anglo-Saxons learn from the Latins and build up in New York a Mont-de-Piété [municipal pawnshop] where it shall not be shame and ruin to borrow, and where self-respect need not make part of every pledge." Thirty-one men, including Cornelius Vanderbilt III, responded to Alfred Bishop Mason's plea. The philanthropists formed the Provident Loan Society "for the purpose of aiding such persons as said Society shall deem in need of pecuniary assistance, by loans of money at interest, upon the pledge or mortgage of personal property." In short, they set up a pawnshop. It expanded, and its sponsors engaged Renwick, Aspinwall & Tucker to design a handsome office building for its growing operations.

More and more developers after 1908 were pulling down old Fourth Avenue houses with their street-level shops and blasting out excavations for great loft and office buildings. In 1909 the old Everett House hotel was replaced by the Everett Building, 200 Fourth Avenue, and the American Woollen Building was finished across the avenue in the next block at 225, replacing the Florence House. (In recent years Baruch College has leased seven floors at 225, Crown Publishing four floors).

Also dating to 1909 are 233 and 251 Park Avenue South. At Madison Square and 23rd Street, the new forty-eight-story Metropolitan Life Insurance Company tower (with a forty-first-floor observation platform) attracted visitors in 1909 to the world's tallest building, which it remained until completion of the Woolworth Building in 1913. Napoleon LeBrun & Sons, who had designed the original 1896 building, also designed the tower. In two years it was looking down on the new Germania Life Insurance Building by D'Oench & Yost at 201 Fourth Avenue, northeast corner 17th Street (the company would change its name to Guardian Life in 1917).

Owners of these new buildings refused to rent space to manufacturers. Wholesalers, who had often shared buildings with manufacturers in earlier years, were now refusing to do so. Manufacturers, they said, employed cheap labor which tended to congregate in the halls and on the sidewalks, crowding the elevators at certain hours and lowering the tone. The wholesalers generally operated on wider profit margins, employed a better class of help, and could pay higher rents; Fourth Avenue building owners were happy to oblige them by excluding manufacturers.

300 Park Avenue South, northwest corner 22nd Street, was finished in 1910. Other 1910 buildings include 381, 386, and 401. 381, southeast corner 27th Street, was designed by Charles A. Valentine. 386, northwest corner 27th Street, is the Mills & Gibb Building, designed by Clinton & Russell; it was selected by the American Institute of Architects as the finest structure of its type. At 401, southeast corner 28th Street, recent tenants have included Health Management Systems and Sterling Software. Park Avenue South buildings of 1911 vintage include, in addition to 201 (Guardian Life), 250, 315, 373, and 390. At 250, recent tenants have included the Calet Hirsch & Spector advertising agency,

which has had three floors and its name over the building's door. Positano Restaurant has been at the corner; the Art Directors' Club has also been on the ground floor. 315 has in recent years leased twelve of its twenty floors to the New York State College of Optometry. Carrère & Hastings designed 373. 390 has been taken over by New York Life.

Dating to 1912, with a magnificent marble-walled, ornate-ceilinged lobby, is 257 Park Avenue South, southeast corner 21st Street; this office and salesroom structure (originally the Eagle Building, now the Gramercy Park Building) by Warren & Wetmore replaced the New Amsterdam Hotel, which had stood for a generation. Recent tenants have included the Traphagen School, the Better Business Bureau, Dr. Arthur Sackler's *Medical Tribune*, and Werner (est) Erhard & Associates.

Also of 1912 vintage are 345, 352, 450–60, and 470. 345, originally the Armory Building, fills the eastern blockfront between 25th and 26th streets, just west of the 69th Regiment Armory; recent tenants have included Levine, Huntley, Schmidt & Beaver, the advertising agency. 352 wraps itself around the small Provident Loan Society building at 25th Street. At 450–60, southwest corner 31st Street, recent tenants have included direct mail operations of Ogilvy & Mather, the advertising agency, which has six floors, and Facts on File, the publisher, which has two. 468 occupies the northwest corner of 31st Street; 470, filling the blockfront between 31st and 32nd streets just south of the Park Avenue Hotel, was designed by Mulliken & Moeller and acquired in 1920 by Schwartzenbach, Huber & Co., a major silk manufacturer. Quite a few of these buildings were for silk firms; formerly centered in the area of Broome, Mercer, and Greene streets, the silk district had moved in 1911 and 1912 up to Fourth and Madison avenues between 17th and 32nd streets.

260 Park Avenue South, southwest corner 21st Street, was erected in 1913 to designs by Neville & Bagge (the United Federation of Teachers union has long been the sole tenant). Other 1913 buildings include 440, southwest corner 30th Street; Cross & Cross, the architects, topped it with a grandiose temple of Corinthian columns.

A 1914 building is 215 Park Avenue South, southeast corner 18th Street. Another is 432, northwest corner 29th Street; Warren & Wetmore designed it with Robert T. Lyons. Six four- and five-story buildings occupied the northwest corner of 28th Street; they were pulled down in 1916 and replaced by 404, a store and loft building designed by Walter Haefeli. By 1917, when 404 was completed, the blocks beteen Union Square and 32nd Street formed a canyon of twelve- to twenty-story office and loft buildings, all of them handy to the subway. 270 Park Avenue South, northwest corner 21st Street, may have been the first such building to go up after World War I. Designed by George and Edward Blum for a firm of wool merchants, it opened in 1921.

Still bare earth at the start of 1921 was the Park Avenue blockfront between 41st and 42nd street, where the old Grand Union Hotel had stood until 1914. The Victory Hall Association tried unsuccessfully to raise $20 million for an amphitheater to memorialize the war dead, and a syndicate headed by

Henry Mandel took over the site and engaged the architect John Sloan; in 1922 it opened the Pershing Square Building, 100 East 42nd Street. This was the same syndicate that paid $1.6 billion for the block bounded by Park and Lexington avenues between 32nd and 33rd streets—with assurances from the Board of Aldermen and mayor that its new building could be called 1 Park Avenue. York & Sawyer were the architects for 1 Park, which was finished in 1925. Recent tenants have included Loews Corp., a conglomerate put together by Laurence and Preston Robert Tisch, and the publisher Ziff-Davis (each has five floors; together they occupy nearly half the space). Lorillard Inc., the name on the building, is an old tobacco company owned by Loews Corp.

To the south, 386 and 419 Park Avenue South date to 1927. The latter, designed by Walter Haefeli, is at the southeast corner of 29th Street. Tammany Hall, whose "Wigwam" had stood for decades in 14th Street and whose Democratic leaders still ruled New York, moved in 1928 into a new marble building at 100 East 17th Street, corner of Fourth Avenue. (In recent years it has housed the International Ladies Garment Workers Union Local 99-105, and its 499-seat auditorium has been used by the Roundabout Theater Company, a group with 20,000 subscribers).

Between 26th and 27th streets, New York Life Insurance Company had moved in 1928 into a pyramid-topped tower designed by Cass Gilbert with an imposing three-story lobby on a site formerly occupied by Madison Square Garden (and, before that, by the old New York & Harlem Railroad terminal). Work began in 1929 on a new north building for Metropolitan Life, with great vaulted entrances at each of its four corners on 24th and 25th streets. The creation of Harvey Wiley Corbett and D. Everett Waid, it would not be finished until 1932.

Far surpassing most of these in the opinion of Lewis Mumford was 2 Park Avenue, northwest corner 32nd Street. In this skyscraper, completed in 1927 and originally called the Park Avenue Building, the architect Ely Jacques Kahn achieved, said Mumford, "almost complete success . . . With a warm buff brick as a foundation, [it] works up into bands of sunny terra-cotta broken and accentuated with red, green, bright sky-blue. The pattern is abstract; and every part, down to the lighting fixtures, has the same finish, rigor, swiftness, perfection. In this building, structure and feeling are at last one: the directness and simplicity of the first have not been forfeited to the decoration; the warmth and human satisfaction of the decorative forms have not been overpowered in the structure itself, for they are expressed there, too. . . . One building like this, which faces the entire problem of design, and has a clean, unflinching answer for each question, might well serve to crystallize all the fumbling and uncertain elements in present-day architecture. The success of the Park Avenue Building is not due to the fact that it is a tall tower or that it is a set-back building. It is not a tower and the set-back is trifling. Its success is due to its unique synthesis of the constructive and the feeling elements. . . . The Park Avenue Building shows the limit of the architect's skill, to date, under urban conditions, where

LEFT: *1 Park Avenue, controversial in the 1920s* (1989 photo)   RIGHT: *New York Life* (1989 photo)

the programme is inflexibly laid down by the businessman and the engineer, and where the site is too costly to be played with."

Sites north of Grand Central were costlier. The only Park Avenue commercial structures before World War II were two office buildings on opposite sides of the avenue between 46th and 47th streets and the New York Central Building that towered astride the avenue immediately to their south.

Anchoring the residential structures that now extended up the avenue, 245 Park and 250 Park were built above the railroad tracks. The Park-Lexington Building at 247, finished in 1922, connected with Grand Central Palace (built in 1913), home to the annual flower, auto, boat, and sportsman's shows (it would be the major New York area induction center for draftees in World War II and the city's exhibition hall until 1956; both buildings would be replaced in the 1960s by 245 Park). Mrs. Katherine M. Gibbs, who lived at 280 Park, had her secretarial school at 247 in the 1920s; the publicist Benjamin Sonnenberg, who in 1931 would acquire the old Stuyvesant Fish mansion in Gramercy Park, had a private elevator to his floor at 247 Park; his chauffered car—a tan Rolls-Royce in winter, a green Packard touring car in summer—was always waiting outside. Other tenants included *Liberty* magazine and some advertising agencies, notably Kenyon & Eckhardt and the much larger Lord & Thomas (it

LEFT: *Metropolitan Life, North Building* (1989 photo)   RIGHT: *2 Park Avenue* (1989 photo)

became Foote Cone & Belding in 1943) headed by Albert Lasker, whose home office was in Chicago. American Tobacco (Lucky Strike cigarettes) was Lasker's biggest account.

The Postum Building, at 250 Park, was right across the way. Designed by Cross & Cross and completed in 1924, it still stood in 1989, occupying the site originally earmarked for a new Metropolitan Opera House. Marjorie Merriweather Post, head of Postum Cereal Co., was only twenty-seven when her father, the Post Toasties king Charles Post, committed suicide in 1914 at Santa Barbara. An only child, she incorporated the company in 1922 and went on to acquire Jell-O, Minute Tapioca, Maxwell House, Igleheart Brothers (Swans Down cake flour), Log Cabin, and Frosted Foods (not yet called Birdseye), out of which General Foods Corp. was created in 1929. The Listerine king, Gerard Lambert, soon had his office at the top of 250 Park. Recent tenants have included Sullivan & Cromwell, a Wall Street law firm.

Soaring above these structures in Beaux Arts majesty, the New York Central Building opened in 1929 at 230 Park, bestriding the avenue like a colossus. Warren & Wetmore, architects for Grand Central, designed this tower with east and west roadways for Park Avenue's swelling traffic, east and west pedestrian passageways to connect 45th and 46th streets, classical statuary flanking the clock on its north facade, a fabulous copper cupola, and an ornately detailed lobby. Like Grand Central itself, the New York Central Building symbolized power and affluence. It could be seen by anyone looking down Park Avenue from the north or up the avenue from below Murray Hill. *McCall's* magazine and other tenants enjoyed a certain status of location.

No longer is the New York Central Building called by that name (it became the New York General Building and was renamed again after Harry B. Helmsley acquired it in 1977), it is invisible from the south of Grand Central, and it has long since ceased to stand out against the sky when seen from the north. Otherwise, upper Park Avenue today appears much as it has for a decade, but the look of permanence may be deceiving. At the end of World War II, before it had any office buildings north of 47th Street, Park Avenue also looked complete and permanent—a sparkling canyon of luxury apartment houses, clubs, and hotels. Only a clairvoyant could have known that the blocks from 47th to 59th would soon reflect not individual prestige but rather corporate ostentation; that north of Grand Central the once homogeneous boulevard would be radically altered.

At the time of H. Gordon Duval's death in 1928 the avenue was still purely residential above 47th Street. Then, in November 1929, over the objections of

BELOW: *The New York Central (later Helmsley) Building was the avenue's tallest office structure north of Grand Central until 1959* (photo courtesy New-York Historical Society)

the Park Avenue Association, the Board of Estimate rezoned the thoroughfare between 50th and 57th streets. As early as April 1930, when Wall Street seemed to be recovering from its October 1929 plunge, some builders announced plans for a fifty-story tower at the northeast corner of Park and 53rd Street. Schwartz & Gross had been engaged to design the new structure, and negotiations were reportedly underway to lease the ground floor and fourteen upper floors to a leading department store. Apartment houses of fifteen, thirteen, and eight stories, including the posh Montana at 375 Park, would be demolished, and the new tower would be completed by the spring of 1932. If grim economic realities had not forced a cancellation of these plans, Park Avenue below 57th Street might have lost its residential character long before it did.

Owners of other luxury apartment houses—383, 399, 400, 410, and 420-430 Park, to name a few—prepared to replace them with office towers. Tenants, hearing predictions that the avenue below 57th Street would soon become a business district, moved out, increasing the vacancy rate in many buildings. But the economic downturn became a collapse and office-building projects were aborted. The New York Central, which owned some of the largest residential structures on the avenue, regained possession from lessees. Deciding that the city had no shortage of commercial space, the railroad brought its properties up to snuff and again offered long leases.

A few apartment house owners tore their buildings down to save on taxes. Others spent money to modernize; when rents were slashed by as much as 75 percent, residential tenants gradually returned. At 300 Park, eighteen-room apartments had rented for more than $2,000 per month, which in the 1930s was more than most New Yorkers paid per year; those rents came down to between $500 and $550. Rents on six-room suites dropped from $650 to between $300 and $330. The numbers would subsequently have climbed back to the stratosphere had it not been for rent control restrictions that went into effect late in 1943. After the war, in those blocks where zoning regulations permitted commercial development, owners of rental apartment houses on Park Avenue were eager to sell. The only available buyers would tear down the rent-controlled structures and put up much larger ones in which corporations would pay fancy prices to rent space.

Thus did it happen that New York's postwar office building boom began on Park Avenue. It had been widely expected that many business firms would relocate to the suburbs after the war, and in later years many did; in the immediate postwar era, however, most chose Manhattan for their corporate headquarters, and the first choice was Park Avenue.

In 1947, Tishman Brothers put up the Universal Pictures Building at 445 Park, southeast corner 57th Street, more recently called the MCA Building. Jordan Case & McGrath, an advertising agency, has had four floors in this building, which replaced a structure with 100 apartments. This first postwar office building was hailed by Lewis Mumford in his *New Yorker* "Skyline" column as "a technical milestone." In the December 13, 1947, issue, Mumford criticized the developers for using every cubic foot of ground and air space permitted under the zoning law but said of the architecture, "The fenestration is . . . conspicuously good . . . The utilization of the continuous, horizontal strip-window . . . provides for the maximum amount of daylight for the interior and permits the most flexible use of the outer wall space. The device that the firm of Kahn & Jacobs has worked out for 445 Park Avenue is so adroit that one regrets that we have had to wait so long for it. The columns of the exterior walls are much slenderer than usual—a mere twelve inches wide on the exterior face and fourteen inches on the interior—and they are therefore only about ten feet apart, instead of the customary twenty feet. The wind stresses, instead of being borne by the columns in the wall, are taken up by columns set well back in the structure. This is an exceedingly neat solution to this hitherto baffling problem. The windows, set in stainless-steel frames, form continuous bands, visually interrupted only by the slim columns, so that the facade, up to the final setback, consists of bands of glass and metal alternating with bands of limestone."

In 1948 came the Arabian-American Oil Company Building at 505 Park; designed by the newly created firm of Emery Roth & Sons, it curves around the northeast corner of 59th Street.

At 390 Park, on the west side of the avenue between 53rd and 54th streets, the taxpayer put up by Robert W. Goelet in 1936 was acquired by Lever Brothers, whose chief executive officer Charles Luckman soon left to pursue a career in architecture. In place of the taxpayer, Lever erected a sparkling glass-walled building that took up far less of its site than the law permitted. Lever House, designed by Gordon Bunshaft of Skidmore, Owings & Merrill, opened on April 29, 1952, at a time when every other building on the avenue was masonry, like the Racquet & Tennis Club facing it to the south. Critics hailed the building for its aesthetics; passersby gaped. A traveling gondola suspended from the roof enabled window cleaners to wash the structure's 1,404 panes of heat-resistant blue-green glass, but the windows were sealed, and the centrally air-conditioned building was profligate in its use of energy.

Still an aesthetic jewel with its metal-and-glass curtain walls, Lever House is not without its critics. "The break with the street wall of Park Avenue, so liberating in the 1950s, now seems needless and not a little narcissistic," writes Paul Goldberger. "And the premise of 'structural honesty' on which the building was said to be based is, of course, an exaggeration: the double slab form is a pure composition, and the use of spandrel glass—the glass that covers the structure between the floors, making the entire outside look like a window—is not structural honesty at all, but merely a modernist brand of ornament."

A more serious criticism is that Lever House inspired construction of similar energy-wasting extravaganzas all over the world. Many are on Park Avenue. Curtain-wall construction did not begin with Lever House. Its principle dates to the nineteenth century, when curtain walls were made of masonry. Relatively new was the idea of lightweight, factory-made curtain-wall panels of glass, metal, or porcelain that could be fitted together like a jigsaw puzzle—quickly, easily, and cheaply. Unhappily, even tinted glass transmits heat and cold far more readily than does masonry; to keep the new buildings cool in summer and

ABOVE: *Lever House started a revolutionary change* (1988 photo)

warm in winter required enormous amounts of energy; when power was shut off late at night, hardworking bankers, lawyers, advertising people, and office personnel discovered that the glittering towers could be damned uncomfortable. When a water shortage forced a shutdown of air conditioning in the summer of 1966, office workers suffered even from 9 to 5.

Economy took precedence over aesthetics in the beige glass-and-aluminum Colgate-Palmolive Building at 300 Park, put up soon after Lever House by a major competitor of Lever Brothers. It replaced the apartment house where Louis Sherry's Restaurant had been. In 1922 the land and building at 300 Park had represented an investment of nearly $8.5 million; in 1951 it was sold for about $3.5 million. And where once there had been more than 100 luxury apartments, now there was a pedestrian office building designed by Emery Roth and Sons. Also by Emery Roth and Sons but finished earlier is 430 Park, an office tower (the Bank of Montreal Building) between 55th and 56th streets. Completed in 1955, it replaced a thirty-family apartment house and other structures. The little Mercedes-Benz showroom at 430, originally a Jaguar showroom, was the first New York design by Frank Lloyd Wright and not a distinguished one.

What everybody loved to hate in 1955 was the Davies Building at 460 Park, northwest corner 57th Street. Financed by William Randolph Hearst's protégée Marion Davies, still only fifty-five but destined to die six years later, the building was sheathed in prefabricated aluminum panels and erected in record time. Emery Roth and Sons, who designed 460 Park, also designed the 225,000-square-foot General Reinsurance Building, 400 Park, which opened in 1957 at the northwest corner of 54th Street, supplanting forty-eight apartments; across the avenue, at 405 Park, a building designed by Herbert Tannenbaum had gone up in 1956, supplanting thirty apartments.

Demolition of several four-story apartment houses on the eastern blockfront between 55th and 56th streets, just north of 417 Park, began in June 1955. Built in 1871 by Robert Goelet, father of Robert W., they dated to the post-bellum period when Steinway made pianos and Schaefer brewed beer a few blocks to the south, the railroad still ran at grade level, and the area abounded with tenements. These small, French château style stucco structures with their narrow iron balconies and street-level shops were economic anachronisms, souvenirs of old Robert Goelet's prediction that this would one day be a site of office structures. When less patient investors put up twelve- and fourteen-story apartment houses on their Park Avenue sites to rent at $1,000 per room per year in the 1920s, Goelet sat tight. His heirs now owned the blockfront, extending 201 feet on Park Avenue, 146 in 55th Street, 132 in 56th. Kahn & Jacobs designed 425 Park to fill the site, and National Biscuit Company leased six floors from the plans (thirteen floors have in recent years been occupied by the law firm Kaye Scholer Fierman Hays & Handler).

None of these stepped-back, "wedding-cake" structures (their design was dictated in part by zoning law considerations) can hold an aesthetic candle to the Seagram Building at 375 Park, an austere bronze-and-glass shaft designed by Mies van der Rohe in association with Philip Johnson. Called Seagram House (as in Lever House) before its completion, this handsome structure replaced the Montana apartment house, which, in its time, had replaced the old Steinway piano factory with more than 100 luxury apartments. The Seagram Building was Mies's first executed office building commission, and its handsome plaza, landscaped with trees and fountains, was as revolutionary in 1957 as was its understated bronze dignity.

Samuel Bronfman, the Canadian distiller who had prospered during Prohibition and acquired Joseph E. Seagram & Sons in 1927, had not intended to beautify New York. Bronfman's taste was in his mouth (a notoriously foul mouth). His daughter Phyllis Bronfman Lambert, who had studied architecture at Vassar, persuaded Sam to use someone with an international reputation rather than a commercial firm. After considering Wright and Le Corbusier, Lambert selected Mies van der Rohe, and her father allowed him to design something more than a building that would make maximum use of its real estate. "You might think this austere strength, this ugly beauty, is terribly severe," Lambert has said about the $36 million building. "It is, and yet all the more beauty in it."

Few people knew it, but when the Seagram Building opened in the midst of the cold war it possessed one of the city's few atomic bomb shelters. Its Four Seasons Restaurant set new standards of culinary excellence, and its twenty-four-hour Brasserie Café won an immediate following. The weeping beeches on its terrace drooped, and were quickly replaced with gingkos, which proved hardier. (The building was sold in 1979 to the Teachers Insurance and Annuity Association-College Retirement Equities Fund. Joseph E. Seagram and Sons Inc. received $70.5 million for the building, $15 million for the land.)

If the Seagram Building represents a triumph of taste over money, the opposite may be said of the high rise immediately to its north. Vincent Astor, something of a high rise himself (he stood six feet four and was once described as a "gaunt, stoop-shouldered giant" with "grasshopper legs") was just about Sam Bronfman's age, sixty-five, in 1956. His grandmother was the Mrs. Astor whose nineteenth-century ballroom, at Fifth Avenue and 34th Street, could accommodate only 400; his father, Col. John Jacob Astor IV, the second-largest individual owner of New York property, had gone down with the *Titanic*, leaving Vincent $70 million, of which $60 million was in real estate. Young Vincent doubled this inheritance. He soon began to take an active interest in his real estate holdings and was shocked to learn that some were slum tenements—and that some of the houses were not homes.

Vincent Astor began getting rid of his slum properties. When Fiorello La Guardia was mayor, Astor sold his remaining slum properties to the Municipal Housing Authority, receiving less than their land value. In 1933 Astor was married, for the third and last time, to Mrs. Brooke Russell Marshall, daughter of a major general who commanded the Marine Corps from 1934 to 1936. When he announced in September 1956 that he was going to develop the block to the north of where Bronfman was putting up the Seagram Building, Astor's project made headlines.

Astor's tower, across the avenue from Lever House, would occupy the block

ABOVE: *Seagram's austere bronze tower no longer belongs to Seagram* (1989 photo)

194 | COMMERCIAL INCURSIONS

bounded by Park and Lexington avenues from 53rd Street to 54th. That meant tearing down twenty-two apartment buildings, brownstone walk-ups, and stores. Carson & Lundin, architects, had designed a forty-six-story metal-and-glass tower that would rise from "Astor Plaza," a garden sunk below street level and surrounded by shops, restaurants, and a bank. Landscaping atop an adjoining two-story glass house would allow for tenant displays; this landscaping, plus the sunken garden of Astor Plaza, would match the floral and pool setting of the Seagram Building, or Seagram House (which was then expected to reach forty-one stories) and would blend with the garden setting of Lever House. A subbasement garage would accommodate 400 cars, and tunnels would connect the structure to subways and adjoining buildings, thus reducing pedestrian traffic in a building whose one million square feet of office space would house a population of more than 10,000. There would be a helicopter landing pad on the roof. This monument to Astor would cost an estimated $75 million. Other stockholders in the venture were William S. Paley and Frank M. Stanton of CBS, Astor's banker-adviser Hoyt Ammidon, and two Astor executive employees, all as private investors. They had joined Astor in acquiring the site from the English branch of the Astor family once headed by William Waldorf Astor, a cousin of Vincent's father and for many years far and away New York's largest taxpayer. "This project," Astor said, "confirms my belief in the future of Manhattan real estate and, more particularly, my conviction that the once-fine residential section on Park Avenue has become an equally distinguished business section. We believe it will provide the finest headquarters for business and industrial firms in the world."

Indeed, Park Avenue was aquiring a whole new ambience: it had fully a dozen commercial structures completed or under construction. Widely praised was the small Pepsi-Cola Building of 1958 at 500 Park, southwest corner 59th Street (Skidmore, Owings & Merrill). An elegant prism set on its own elevated plaza, it had a big lobby for exhibits, a new one every two weeks. One of Andy Warhol's first shows was here, and Monsanto surfaced the floor with AstroTurf to demonstrate its new grass substitute. (Olivetti Corp. bought the building in 1970 and used the lobby for sales offices. Olivetti sold in 1980 and the building was taken over by a Dutch bank and Walt Disney, Inc.)

Astor Plaza was not among the new megastructures. Vincent Astor and his partners had their block cleared but were unable to secure financing; they finally sold the excavated site at a loss to Citibank, still called First National City Bank (it had been created in March 1955 by a merger of National City and First National). Astor died, childless, shortly afterward, in 1959. (His widow wound up with one piece of Manhattan property, the co-op apartment where she lived.) First National City put up an undistinguished structure, also designed by Carson & Lundin (with Kahn & Jacobs), that filled the block, with no open plaza or sunken garden, although there is some greenery on the terrace of the setback on the building's south side.

On the west side of the avenue, at 410 Park, southwest corner 55th Street, Chase Manhattan Bank (created in March 1955 by a merger of Chase National

Bank with the Bank of the Manhattan Company) occupied the first two floors of a building designed by Emery Roth and Sons (Skidmore, Owings & Merrill designed the bank, whose second-floor banking room boasts an Alexander Calder mobile). This was completed in 1959 (same year as the Seagram Building), two years before Citibank's building could open its doors at 399 Park.

Dwarfing both of these paeans to commercial banking is Manufacturers Hanover Plaza, a fifty-three-story black metal and stainless steel tower, originally the Union Carbide Building, at 270 Park. Designed by Skidmore, Owings & Merrill and opened in 1960, it replaced the old Marguery, which was torn down in 1957. Time Inc. had originally planned to build in the block between 47th and 48th streets but opted instead for Rockefeller Center, whereupon Union Carbide acquired the Park Avenue site. Because of the railyards beneath it, the ground floor had to be used for elevator equipment; elevators start at the second floor, reached by escalators from street level. Critics complained that the new structure did not relate to its site, that the placement of its tower was conspicuously cockeyed, that its pedestrian passage to Vanderbilt Avenue was poorly designed, and that despite its generous setback it had no greenery to relieve its man-made planes. In the 1980s, Manufacturers Hanover installed fountains to give the building's sterile exterior more character.

Other 1960 buildings are 320 Park, ITT World Headquarters, and 350 Park, originally the Manufacturers Hanover Trust Building. 320 Park, facing the Waldorf-Astoria, came to have a BMW automobile and motorcycle showroom on its 51st Street corner. Both 320 and 350 were designed by Emery Roth and Sons. Richard and Julian Roth, who had taken over their father's business in 1947, were now by far the most prolific creators of Park Avenue office towers and were being asked to design more. Developers selected the firm not because its buildings were beautiful but because it had adapted thin-skinned, curtain-wall facades that squeezed more rentable space out of a building lot than anyone else in the business—usually 80 to 90 percent of the interior space. And they had developed an almost uncanny knack for estimating construction cost, accurate to within 2 percent.

But many architects and city planners expressed dismay at what was happening on Park Avenue. One writer spoke disparagingly of "Rothscrapers." Bertram Goldberg, the Chicago architect who would gain fame in 1964 with his sixty-story twin Marina City towers, voiced a socio-economic concern. In a speech to the Chicago Real Estate Board in February 1961, he said, "I am overwhelmed by the lack of sensitivity among the planners in New York in their reshaping of Park Avenue. These glass curtain walls are for me the eyes of the blind. Apartment buildings are being torn down and replaced by offices. . . . This is the real estate man's answer to a need for additional income. Space, which as apartments, is returning $3 a square foot, is being replaced by space, which as offices, is returning $8 a square foot—a very simple arithmetic improvement."

Park Avenue office rents would rise in the next three decades to six or eight times the $8 a square foot cited by Goldberg. What really bothered him, though, was the idea of "a twenty-four-hour-day population . . . being replaced by a seven-hour-day population for a period of only a five-day week. . . . The thirty-hour week is not too far from our present economic concepts. We therefore have to look at this expensive machine—Park Avenue—headed by the Grand Central Station, being developed for usage only thirty hours per week. Can our economy stand this kind of specialized development? . . . Twenty years from now, it is conceivable that Park Avenue during half the week will look like Wall Street on Sunday. . . . Our tax structure demands the two-shift central city."

The critic Jane Jacobs, in her 1961 book *The Death and Life of Great American Cities*, spoke of areas that "go ominously dead at night . . . The stretch of new office buildings centering on Park Avenue between Grand Central Station and Fifty-ninth Street is such a territory," she said. "The area just south of Grand Central is another. . . . Many a once vital district, having lost in the past a mixture of primary uses which brought attraction, popularity and high economic value, has declined sadly. . . . The new office stretch of . . . Park Avenue is far more standardized in content than Fifth Avenue. Park Avenue has the advantage of containing among its new office buildings several which, in themselves, are masterpieces of modern design (Lever House, Seagram, Pepsi-Cola, and Union Carbide). But does homogeneity of use or homogeneity of age help Park Avenue esthetically? On the contrary, the office blocks of Park Avenue are wretchedly disorganized in appearance, and far more given than Fifth Avenue to a total effect of chaotic architectural wilfulness, overlaid on boredom."

Nobody paid much attention. Another financial institution, Bankers Trust Company, leased the building that was about to rise at 280 Park, 48th Street to 49th, on the blockfront to the north of the Union Carbide tower. Designed by Henry Dreyfuss with Emery Roth and Sons and completed in 1963 (the addition at the rear was built in 1971), 280 Park replaced two luxury apartment houses. Bankers Trust occupies fifteen of the thirty floors, plus nineteen in the forty-three-floor annex.

Not to be outdone by its rivals, Chemical Bank (created in 1954 by a merger of Chemical Bank and Trust with the Corn Exchange Bank) leased ground-floor space in the new fifty-story skyscraper going up at 277 Park, 47th to 48th Street, where the Hecksher Apartments with their "acre of garden" had stood until late 1958. Stahl Equities Corp. leased the block from the New York Central and New Haven Railroads and engaged Emery Roth and Sons to design a new 277 Park, a $45 million building that opened late in 1964 with 1.5 million square feet of space. Its atrium, or conservatory, with some 1,500 plants on Park Avenue dates to 1983, by which time a dozen foreign banks had taken space in Park Avenue's towers. The pop art sculpture *"Taxi!"* at the north entrance is by J. Seward Johnson, Jr.

Thanks to a change in the zoning law, which took effect in the summer of 1965, designers were given more latitude in the shapes they gave to new skyscrapers. The change came too late for 245 Park. Designed by Shreve, Lamb & Harmon and completed in 1966, this hulk, occupying an entire block, replaced the old Park-Lexington Building and Grand Central Palace.

Erecting 245 Park presented formidable engineering problems for Uris

ABOVE *Atrium of 277 Park* (1989 photo)

Brothers, the builders. Uris not only acquired the air rights above the tracks but also rented the railroad's 100-ton crane, rolling it into place on a convenient track. New York Central flatcars and gondolas were engaged for hauling material. The old Grand Central Palace exhibition hall on the Lexington Avenue side of the block had been the only building along the avenue whose steel was an integral part of the railroad structure below. The columns of other Park Avenue buildings, such as 277 Park, went down past the tracks and were not attached to the actual railroad tunnel frame. Uris used many of the old Grand Cental Palace underpinnings; to eliminate the vibration of the two tiers of trains passing below, engineers insulated the bases of the column supports in mats of lead and asbestos. The skyscraper's columns go down into bedrock about six feet below Grand Central's three levels at 47th Street. In some cases the steel contractor came within two inches of track beds. Engineers had to memorize train schedules in order not to dispatch a steel column downward at the same time that the stationmaster was dispatching a local to White Plains. Workers, many hired because they had had experience on 277 Park, took pains to avoid the live third rail of the forty railroad tracks among which they had to dig and weld and rivet. Uris engineers learned from the veterans of 277 Park how to use the elevator under the Waldorf-Astoria garage to carry equipment down to track level at 49th Street.

To make things even more difficult, the U.S. Post Office mail shuttle service took up three platforms of the railroad terminal directly beneath the site. This shuttle system, with its bulky conveyor belt, occupied ground needed for several major "legs" of the skyscraper, and it could not be moved. Its operation, in fact, could not be interrupted even for half a day. James Rudderman, the building's structural designer, solved the problem by designing seven steel trusses, the strongest being more than forty feet across and a story high, to serve as a bridge within the building to distribute the weight across the mail shuttle. Doors in the trusses permitted access to the center of the building.

245 Park was originally the American Tobacco Building, then—after the company changed its name—the American Brands Building. American Brands moved its headquarters in June 1986 to Old Greenwich, Connecticut and the building became, simply 245 Park. Bear, Stearns, investment bankers, have been the major tenants since then.

Just north of 277 Park, the Park Lane Hotel that had stood since 1924 came down in 1965 to make way for 299 Park, between 48th and 49th streets. Designed by Emery Roth and Sons with 900,000 square feet, it opened in 1967 for Westvaco (originally West Virginia Pulp and Paper Company).

Another hotel, the Sheraton East (formerly the Ambassador), was demolished in 1966 to make way for 345 Park, which occupies the 51st to 52nd street blockfront. To make way for his new office building, the developer Samuel Rudin bought not only the Sheraton East lease but also that of the small Gladstone Hotel. He paid prices not seen since the 1920s: $2 million for an East 52nd Street building that housed nuns who taught at Cathedral High School, $1.6 million for Al Schacht's Restaurant. Designed by Emery Roth and Sons with an elevated main lobby reached from an L-shaped plaza, 345 Park, sheathed with pre-cast stone, occupies a full block and rises higher than its more elegant Seagram Building neighbor to the north.

At the southwest corner of 57th Street, where the American Bible Society (once in the old Bible House at 45 Fourth Avenue) occupied a handsome six-story red-brick building, the fashion designer Florence Lustig acquired neighboring properties in 1963 and in 1965 acquired the Bible Society Building itself, thus obtaining one of the most valuable corners in the city and enough space to put up a skyscraper that would front on both Park Avenue and 57th Street. The bronze-sheathed Franklin National Bank Building, 450 Park, was completed in 1972—two years before the bank failed in a major scandal. Emery Roth and Sons were the architects.

I. M. Pei and Partners designed 499 Park, southeast corner 59th Street. The gleaming black tower was completed in 1980.

These new Park Avenue office towers took the place of stately if architecturally undistinguished masonry apartment houses and hotels and are in many cases themselves thoroughly undistinguished. Others, with their blue, green, black, brown, or gray tinted glass, gave the avenue a glamorous (some said garish) new look as, in Ada Louise Huxtable's phrase, "business palaces replaced private palaces, soap aristocracies supplanted social aristocracy. . . . This latest breed of skyscraper included the most important examples of architecture's revolutionary new style, a style that was fast becoming the symbol of business success and prosperity (even though the vitreous facades were often greeted with horror by the man in the street, who deplored these sterile glass boxes bereft of ornament and lacking in the shops, cafés, and other amenities that had made the avenue seem livable)."

Where individuals had once flaunted their wealth in what Thorstein Veblen called "conspicuous waste," corporate America now erected "noncompetitive" office buildings that sacrificed rentable space for the sake of prestige. Never mind that new luxury apartments were smaller and shoddier than prewar apartments: business and professional people now spent their days (often far into the night) in bright, spacious, air-conditioned surroundings that made prewar offices look positively antediluvian. Law firms moved uptown from Wall Street, taking suites in the new Park Avenue towers even though it meant signing leases at more money per square foot than almost anywhere else in the city.

Money seemed no object in the inflationary mood of the late 1970s and early '80s. Developers had tenants eager to rent space at fancy prices. But where to find Park Avenue real estate below 59th Street that was not already built up with an office tower or hotel? The five remaining apartment houses—417, 470, 475, 480, and 485 Park—were co-ops whose owners seemed to have no interest in moving. The same seemed to be true of the Ritz Tower. And St. Bartholomew's Episcopal Church just north of the Waldorf could hardly be for sale, could it?

New Yorkers were startled to read in their morning *Times* on September 19, 1980, that St. Bart's might indeed be sold. Some unnamed corporation had offered $100 million for the site and its buildings, nearly three times per square foot what someone had paid a year earlier for a parcel in the neighborhood. It was, in fact, more than anyone had ever paid for Manhattan real estate. And although the church had not accepted the offer, neither had it said no, which in itself shocked many New Yorkers, including more than a few St. Bart's parishioners. Whether St. Bartholomew's and its community house would survive had not yet been decided when *The Battle of St. Bart's*, Brent C. Brolin's study of the case, was published in 1988; it will probably not have been resolved when this book appears. But a Park Avenue location such as that of St. Bart's is sure to make developers salivate.

Fisher Brothers, developers of 299 and 400 Park, found a way to exploit the name Park Avenue without building on the avenue itself. In 1981, while the parishioners of St. Bart's were taking sides in the battle over whether to sell all or part of their church site, Park Avenue Plaza opened at 55 East 52nd Street, shoe-horned into the space west of the Racquet & Tennis Club and replacing a forty-year-old French restaurant, Pierre's, along with some other low structures. Designed by Skidmore, Owings & Merrill, the green glass tower has 1,050,000 square feet. Its three-story landscaped atrium contains shops (including Chartwell Booksellers) and, in front of a waterfall, a modest "Café Marguery" whose name, at least, memorializes the famous restaurant that once attracted gastronomes to the avenue between 47th and 48th streets. No such amenity graces the lobby of Park Avenue Tower, the Helmut Jahn creation that opened in 1987 immediately to the west of 410 Park at 65 East 55th Street. But the Park Avenue Atrium, designed by Edward Durell Stone, that opened in 1981 just east of Depew Place in 46th Street, has, as its name suggests, a planted atrium which preceded the one at 277 Park. It also has some restaurants. To number the building 237 Park, however, took a certain amount of nerve.

More than a few moderate-priced restaurants disappeared in the rush to develop the blocks off Park Avenue. Clubs opened in some buildings to satisfy the demand for exclusive luncheon facilities. Banks and some corporate clients installed their own private kitchens, chefs (some receive $50,000 per year and more), and executive dining rooms. Bob Posch, chef for Continental Grain's boss Michel Fribourg at 277 Park, left restaurant work for the corporate world. Now his cuisine was reserved for the likes of Henry Kissinger, lawyer Arthur Liman, bankers, and grain buyers from foreign governments, although there were days when Posch prepared *déjeuner* for Fribourg alone—with a waiter and printed menu. Posch prided himself on his "negative-cholesterol" oat and wheat bran muffins.

While Park Avenue from Grand Central to 59th Street had become almost entirely commercial it retained an air of upper-class privilege and elegance. So, arguably, did the Murray Hill area south of 42nd Street, where office buildings had existed on Park Avenue long before there were any north of 47th Street; here, too, the avenue in the postwar years changed from primarily residential to primarily commercial. In 1953, after more of Murray Hill's Park Avenue residences had given way to apartment houses of little architectural merit, Tishman Brothers put up 99 Park, an office tower that fills the blockfront between 39th and 40th streets. Emery Roth and Sons were the architects, and their original plans called for a masonry building. When the developers saw the new aluminum-clad Pittsburgh headquarters building of the Aluminum Company of America (Alcoa), however, and the results of tests conducted by General Bronze Company in Long Island City, they saw a way to save money. The facade of 99 Park consists of roughly 1,800 die-pressed aluminum wall-window panels, each about two stories high and set and containing two large windows, that are bolted to the building's framework. These geometrically patterned panels permitted application of the exterior at the rate of two floors per day, an economical if unaesthetic idea that yielded even more spectacular time saving two years later in the Davies Building at 460 Park.

In 1959, when the avenue above Grand Central was seeing a flurry of office construction, the major building activity to the south was a church going up at 59 Park, southeast corner 38th Street. The Roman Catholic Church of Our Saviour, a Romanesque house of worship designed by Paul C. Reilly, has air conditioning equipment where the carillon would ordinarily be.

The Princeton Club was torn down in 1961 and replaced by 90 Park. A bronze tower designed by Emery Roth and Sons, it was finished in 1964 and occupies the entire blockfront between 39th and 40th streets opposite 99 Park.

Park Avenue South languished. Despite its new name, vacancies had increased in office buildings which had formerly housed publishing, furniture, and office equipment firms. Prosperity in those fields had prompted the companies to take more prestigious space in midtown. Comparatively low rents attracted charitable organizations, government and municipal agencies, newly formed companies, architects, and engineering firms to take up the slack, but nobody put up any new Park Avenue South office buildings in the 1950s and '60s.

475 Park, at the southeast corner of 32nd Street, was completed in 1970, a bronze, glass, and steel tower. The sculpture out front, *Triad*, is by Irving Marantz.

Shreve, Lamb & Harmon Associates, architects for 475, went on to design 3 Park Avenue in the block to the north. 3 Park is a brick tower, financed with bonds issued by the Educational Construction Fund; it replaced the 71st Regiment Armory which for years was Martha Bacon's southerly neighbor (a bronze plaque, on the 33rd Street terrace wall, is all that remains to remind us of what once was). Its top bathed at night in orange light, 3 Park stands out also by being set at an angle to the street; its upper floors have provided offices for Blue Cross & Blue Shield, United Medical Service, and the New York State Housing Finance Agency; its first nine floors are occupied by the Norman Thomas High School, which replaced the Central Commercial High School at 214 East 42nd Street. (Some local residents took exception to having the new school named for the perennial Socialist candidate for president.)

Construction began in the fall of 1980 on another tower, designed by Eli Atia and Associates at 101 Park, between 40th and 41st streets. Peter Kalikow of H. K. Kalikow and Co., the developers, had torn down the Architects Building of 1912 and were replacing it with one having 1,285,055 square feet of rentable space. Recent tenants have included some Wall Street law firms; Booz Allen & Hamilton, the management consultants, with six floors; and Philip Morris, with five.

The Philip Morris Building at 120 Park, between 41st and 42nd streets, is a comparatively low tower designed by Ulrich Franzen and Associates and finished in 1983. It contains a Whitney Museum gallery that is open to the public; this 5,000-square-foot gallery, like Grand Central Terminal across the street, was soon taken over by vagrants and other homeless people. Urine damage required frequent repairs.

Luxury and squalor have coexisted for years on Park Avenue, although the crowded corridor now mostly offers something in between. Retail establishments have ranged from the most exquisite to the most egalitarian. A. T. Stewart's eight-story department store at 10th Street, between Broadway and Fourth avenues, was the world's largest building with a cast-iron front when it opened in 1862 with a huge skylight to illuminate its center court. John Wanamaker took over the store in 1896 and supplemented it in 1903 with a fifteen-story establishment that filled the block between 8th and 9th streets, Broadway to Fourth Avenue, with no inner courtyards. Daniel Burnham, the Chicago architect whose Flatiron Building had opened in 1902 at 23rd Street between Fifth and Broadway, designed this Wanamaker annex, used today by the Federal government (it contains as much space as the Empire State Building). The old cast-iron Wanamaker store to its north went up in flames on July 15, 1956, and was replaced in 1970 by Stewart House, an unlovely white brick apartment building at 70 East 10th Street.

For many years the avenue's (and the city's, perhaps even the world's) biggest retailer of women's coats and dresses was S. Klein on Union Square, a rambling series of small buildings, dwarfed by their overhead signs, that stretched from 14th Street to beyond 15th (one of the haphazard structures was said to have housed the saloon in which "The Face on the Barroom Floor" was written). This warren was the outgrowth of a single store opened in 1912 by a twenty-five-year-old Russian immigrant, Samuel Klein. In 1931, despite the Depression, S. Klein sold 3 million dresses, 1.5 million coats, and 750,000 women's tailored suits, taking in about $25 million (Bloomingdale's, including all departments, grossed $22 million). Up to 11,000 meals a day were served at the store's restaurant. The bare-floored store had practically no private dressing rooms or salespeople, sold strictly for cash, did not deliver, and advertised only to announce that the store would be closed for a legal or Jewish holiday. It had stopped advertising sales in the 1920s because the ads brought out women in such hordes that subway service was disrupted, Union Square was jammed, windows were broken, and mounted police had to be rushed in to keep order.

Klein's big idea from day one was to sell clothing as cheaply and quickly as possible, and in the greatest volume. He bought 5,000 dresses at a time on average—and often 20,000 or 30,000—and by paying spot cash obtained a price advantage of 5 to 10 percent over other buyers. Girls at twelve IBM duplicating keypunch machines punched holes in tabulating cards according to data on tags. Anything not sold at the end of two weeks was marked down, and drastic reductions were made until the merchandise was gone. Although the quality of goods varied, even matrons from upper Park Avenue were among the 100,000 customers who shopped on an average day at Klein's. S. Klein buyers, all men, received $40 to $200 per week in 1932, but most of the store's 1,500-odd employees were paid the going wage on Union Square—$10 to $25 per week, with the vast majority receiving $10 to $15. Times were hard. Customers crammed their purses down the front of their blouses to free both hands to pluck dresses off the racks. When a shoplifter was apprehended she was immediately placed on display in one of the store's "crying" rooms—glass-enclosed booths upstairs.

On the other hand, Klein's made it easy to get one's money back, even for a moth-eaten garment bought eight months earlier. The customer was always right. *Fortune* magazine, writing about the store in 1932, told of a "large Jewish lady" who once "brought back a fur coat saying she found she couldn't afford it. Klein, strolling through the store, observed the tears, asked the woman a few questions, and finally told the clerk to refund the money, 'and let her keep the coat, too.' News of this sort of thing have stored up for Klein goodwill more valuable than pearls or rubies."

Klein's was taken over by McCrory's and closed in August 1975. William Zeckendorf acquired its site in a tax-advantaged financing deal reportedly engineered with the help of Stephen Lefkowitz, a lawyer with Patterson Belknap and the son of a former state attorney general. Zeckendorf tore down S. Klein's eleven buildings and erected Zeckendorf Towers, a mixed-use building designed by Daniel E. Dougherty of Davis Brody and Associates. Occupying the block between Union Square East and Irving Place from 14th to 15th streets, it opened late in 1987 with 650 apartments and 375,000 square feet of office space. Integrated Resources, a financial services company, moved into the offices in September 1988.

Quite another order of retail operation than Klein's is Martha's, located since 1966 at 475 Park, southeast corner 58th Street. Born in Brooklyn, Martha Phillips sold lace blouses at age eight in her father's store, The Star, which specialized in hand-tailored suits and riding costumes. At eighteen she married Phillip R. Phillips, a ready-to-wear maker who died in 1981, and in 1934 launched a fashion career of her own, renting space on the twelfth floor of 501 Madison Avenue and laying down a red runner from the elevator to the door of her shop. Right from the start she attracted customers such as Marjorie Merriweather Post, to whom price was not important; even in the Depression, Martha's sold nothing for less than $100, and its monthly rental for a whole floor was $1,200. Martha's opened a Palm Beach shop near the end of World War II in 1945 but remained in its Madison Avenue location until the building was emptied for demolition in 1954, whereupon it moved to the old Savoy Plaza Hotel on Fifth Avenue (demolished in the late 1960s for the General Motors Building). Martha and her daughter, Lynn Manulis, made annual buying trips to Europe and are wholly or partially credited with having brought to prominence in America such designers as Laura Biagiotti, Halston, Carolina Herrera, Mary McFadden, Zandra Rhodes, and Valentino.

Customers such as Brooke Astor, Doris Duke, Diana Ross, and Gloria Vanderbilt come to Martha's for designer costumes with fancy price tags. A hand-embroidered evening gown may fetch $20,000. Bill Blass, James Galanos, and Oscar de la Renta are among the designers who have appeared at Martha's with samples and models. When Blass came in the spring of 1984, Martha took orders over a four-day period for $400,000 worth of merchandise. The Park Avenue salon employs fifteen alterations people, five fitters, ten salespeople, one or two models, and a couple of people to press clothes and sew on Martha's labels. Annual sales, including those at the Palm Beach, Bal Harbour, and Trump Tower shops, run to about $25 million.

Sulka's, the men's haberdashery founded in 1895, has been on Park Avenue for more then thirty years, most recently at 55th Street.

Two decades before Martha's and one block north, at 59th Street, there was a Park Avenue Theatre. This Walter Reade cinema opened at the end of October 1946 on a subscription basis. Patrons who bought fifty-two-week "memberships" at fees ranging from $124.80 to $187.20 were entitled to see two features per week in the same seats at the same time, with no waiting. Programs were mailed weekly to keep subscribers advised, and the management provided checkrooms, lounge rooms, wheelchair facilities, hearing aids, makeup, and

ABOVE: *Where the well-heeled go to be well dressed* (1989 photo)

telephone service for physicians. Unfortunately, the theater was not able to book first-run films and the experiment lasted barely a month. Some $90,000 was returned to subscribers on a pro rata basis, and Universal Pictures took over just before Christmas.

Whatever H. Gordon Duval might have thought of the movie theater or of Martha's, his disdain for commercialism—or at least for certain forms of it—is still very much alive on upper Park Avenue. In early 1984, when a Korean grocer named Kyu-Sung Choi wanted to open a delicatessen at the northeast corner of Park and 75th Street, some local residents—notably Shirley Bernstein—hit the ceiling. This, they said, was an infringement on the most exclusive of residential neighborhoods. Nobody had objected to the "nice little" flower shop that had occupied the site before it went out of business (the owners pleaded guilty to selling heroin and to firebombing a competitor's shop). But a delicatessen was different. Racism may also have played a part. Opponents got two city agencies to issue stop work orders to thwart Choi's remodeling project. They enlisted the support of local politicians, who came out against the deli, and threatened lawsuits. Engineers, lawyers, and architects studied zoning codes and plumbing diagrams in search of technical infractions.

But some politicians championed Choi's cause. Johnny Carson told jokes about people on Park Avenue having to look at vegetables. Choi paid what must have been a whopping rent and opened his Park Avenue Gourmet Foods, selling endive from Belgium, peppers from the Netherlands, and asparagus from France. William Geist, writing in the New York Times in February 1985, quoted one customer, Susan Spence, who had initially opposed the deli, but "when the chips were down and she had to have brandied apricots at 11:30 P.M., 'by golly, Mr. Choi had them.' " Stuffier local residents refused to shop at the deli as a matter of principle. An elderly woman in a mink stole who walked past with the aid of a cane told Geist that she "would not think of shopping at the deli. I don't like it being here. But then I don't have to do the food shopping. One has someone to do such things."

No such conflict exists in the unique mix of commercial and residential use that characterizes the avenue (including Park Avenue South and Fourth Avenue) extending south of Grand Central. Where retailers once lived in rooms above their stores, office buildings now stand cheek by jowl with churches and apartment houses (some of which once were office buildings). Perhaps nowhere else in the city does there exist a comparable mile and a half of integrated urban land use, commingling vintage and last-word architecture that serves, side by side, the demand for office space (by government agencies, labor organizations, and philanthropic groups as well as business corporations), religious activities, retail operations, and living quarters.

While new office towers were transforming the blocks immediately to the south and north of Grand Central, developers continued to find sites for new Park Avenue apartment houses. They might encounter initial resistance to high prices (or rents), but in the end there were always tenants in buildings with Park Avenue addresses.

15

The Right Address

EVEN AS office towers rose on the blockfronts below 59th Street, Park Avenue retained its cachet as a sought-after place of residence. And as New Yorkers moved from economic depression to postwar affluence, developers again began to put up apartment houses that would find ready acceptance almost without regard to the price (or rents) of their units.

Economic conditions were still far from robust in 1938, when construction resumed in a small way on the lower avenue. The entire blockfront between 35th and 36th streets, occupied by structures that included a four-story 1895 building which had housed the Women's City Club (the Protestant Church of the Covenant had been on the site earlier), was demolished to make way for 20-30 Park, a functional building designed by Emery Roth. It was completed in 1939 with apartments of one to four rooms and a built-in scale in every bathroom. 50 Park, northwest corner 37th Street, is a 1940 building of similar character by George Fred Pelham, Jr.

Far to the north, the Brick Presbyterian Church (York & Sawyer) had just gone up at the northwest corner of 93rd Street, replacing some four-story houses.

Sylvan Bien designed 737 Park, an Art Deco apartment house built by Sam Minskoff and Sons in 1940 to replace seven row houses that had faced onto 71st Street. Also built in 1940 was 785 Park, designed by George F. Pelham, Jr. for Sam Minskoff and Sons at the northeast corner of 73rd Street; it replaced three structures that had faced onto the avenue including a handsome limestone residence acquired for $90,000 (it had been assessed at $245,000). 1150 Park, southwest corner 82nd Street, also by George F. Pelham, Jr., was finished in 1940. Completed in 1941 was 1130 Park, southwest corner 91st Street opposite the Brick Church (George F. Pelham, Jr.). It replaced two old five-story apartment houses. Recent tenants here have included the investment adviser Fred M. Alger.

World War II caused another interruption. The first postwar Park Avenue apartment house is probably 710 Park, on the corner site once used by the Union Theological Seminary and then for the mansion of George Blumenthal. Sylvan Bien designed 710 for Sam Minskoff and Sons. Across the street is 715 Park by Emery Roth and Sons, completed in 1949 on a corner site where row houses built in the early 1880s had been replaced by a couple of turn-of-the-century buildings, including the former Robert S. Brewster mansion. Recent tenants have included the real estate broker Edward Lee Cave, whose clients mostly prefer prewar buildings. Cave founded Sotheby's real estate division before starting his own firm.

Emery Roth and Sons also designed 40 Park, a 1950 apartment house that replaced four faded old residences at the northwest corner of 36th Street and a vacant strip that bordered on the Morgan Library. One of the houses was the old Herbert L. Satterlee residence, whose contents had once included a Gainsborough painting of the duchess of Devonshire for which the financier J. P. Morgan, Mrs. Satterlee's father, had paid $150,000. Where four families had lived, there would now be 156 plebeian suites of from one to five rooms each. Samuel Rudin, the developer who assembled the property, did not obtain the five-story house at 56 Park, once the residence of the Reverend C. R. Stetson, which later housed the consulate and UN mission of El Salvador.

Across the avenue at 41 Park a similarly unremarkable apartment house went up in 1953 to designs by Sylvan Bien. Erected at the northwest corner of 36th Street by the two sons of the veteran builder Anthony Campagna, 41 Park replaced five houses that had stood immediately to the north of the Advertising Club—the 1898 J. Hampden Robb house. It may have been the first apartment house on the avenue to have a garage in its basement. 35 Park, put up by Anthony Campagna and Sons and designed by Sylvan and Robert L. Bien, opened in 1956 at the southeast corner of 36th Street. 80 Park, southwest corner 39th Street, is a 1956 building designed by Kahn & Jacobs with Paul Resnik with 232 two- to five-room suites; rentals started at $175 per month, including electricity. Despite predictions that heavy traffic would make Murray Hill suitable only for commercial use, it was still attracting residential tenants.

750 Park, southwest corner 72nd Street, opened in 1951 (Horace Ginsbern & Associates), replacing the old Wiborg house. Sylvan Bien is responsible for 605 Park, southeast corner of 65th Street. Completed in 1954, it replaced eight row houses, two of them facing onto Park Avenue and six facing onto 65th Street. The building's first floor is faced with polished granite, above which it is glazed white brick with corner balconies. Recent tenants have included the banker-economist Herbert J. Stein.

1095 Park, southeast corner 89th Street, was completed in 1953 to designs by Schwartz & Gross, whose brick structure with casement windows harmonized with the 1920s buildings in the neighborhood. 1036 Park, southwest corner 86th Street, opened early in 1957 with eighty apartments; architect Gustave Wiser's mixture of green ceramic and red brick contrasted sharply with the 1920s masonry of its neighbors.

If some of the avenue's new office towers employed the framework of previous structures, so could an apartment house. 475 Park, completed in 1958 at the southeast corner of 58th Street, was built in part over the girders of a 1909 building, one of the avenue's first co-ops. William Randolph Hearst had once owned the building, which was later acquired, along with some adjoining houses in 57th and 58th streets, by Aluminum Company of America, which was going to erect a thirty-story tower for its New York headquarters. Unable to evict some legal tenants, Alcoa abandoned the project and sold out in 1950. Henry Goelet engaged Charles N. and Selig Whinston, architects, to design the white brick structure, which wrapped around the Ritz Tower. This is the house whose street-level corner premises were taken over in 1966 by Martha's.

In 1959 the Arthur Curtiss James mansion at 700 Park, northwest corner 69th Street opposite the Union Club, gave way to an apartment house of gray glazed brick atop a two-story polished granite base. Kahn & Jacobs, Paul Resnik, and Harry F. Green were the architects. Recent tenants have included Jack Aron of Sherry Wine and Spirits.

799 Park, northeast corner 74th Street, came in 1961, perpetrated by H. I. Feldman with glazed white brick facing; it replaced two tenement houses, one of which had in, turn, replaced three stables. 650 Park, also faced with white glazed brick, is similar in its incongruity; designed by John M. Kokkins, it was completed in 1963 at the southwest corner of 67th Street, replacing four five-story tenements and an eight-story apartment house on Park Avenue and the Sulgrave Hotel plus two row houses in 67th Street. Recent tenants have included the financier Albert List and the lawyer Fred Fishman of Kaye Scholer. 1199 Park, northeast corner 94th Street, is a 1961 building by Robert Bien.

1020 Park, northwest corner 85th Street, was completed in 1962 just south of 1036 and with far more Park Avenue frontage (Wechsler & Schimenti). Apartments were offered on a rental basis only briefly; co-op conversion took place in September 1965.

Still a rental building at the beginning of 1989, and still boasting manned elevators long after most apartment houses had switched to automatic, was 920 Park, completed in 1964 at the northwest corner of 80th Street where a pet shop and liquor store had occupied the street level of some old houses. Lyras, Galvin & Ayana were the architects.

1245 Park, northeast corner 96th Street, is a 1967 building by Pomerance & Breines. Never successful, it was taken over in 1977 by Mount Sinai Hospital for use as a staff residence.

About the best that can be said of these buildings is that many have basement garages. And it is better to be inside one looking out at the avenue's old glories than to be in one of the latter and have one's view polluted. Older buildings have

ABOVE: *700 Park replaced the Arthur Curtis James mansion* (1989 photo)

the advantage of prewar construction that assures them of quieter apartments with higher ceilings and larger rooms.

Of the avenue's postwar buildings, only 733 Park, southeast corner 71st Street, presumed to vie with the great luxury houses of earlier decades in the size of its apartments. It was completed in 1971 on the site of the mansion put up for Elihu Root when "nobody" lived on Park, This thirty-story bulding was designed by Kahn & Jacobs with Harry F. Green to contain only twenty-eight apartments. Andrew Alpern says it "represents a style of luxuriously exclusive urban living that has almost vanished from the city." Paul Goldberger, less charitably, calls it "nothing more than a tower of red brick. The apartments within are generously laid out but there is little except a few showy entrance details—travertine, chandeliers, and the like—to tell us that this place is something special." A typical unit consisted of nine rooms, four and a half baths. Recent tenants have included the venture capitalist Lionel Pincus of E. M. Warburg, Pincus and Co.

Goldberger's biggest criticism of 733 Park is its violation of the street line. "This building stands aloof while 740, which has a much greater right to do so, acts as a willing and gracious neighbor." He concedes that it was the 1961 zoning law, which he ascribes to the success of the Seagram Building, that caused buildings like 733 Park to be designed "as sheer towers rather than masses built onto the street lest they break with the spirit of the avenue."

In Goldberger's view 900 Park is a more serious violation of that spirit because "it creates a sense of void at a crucial intersection," the northwest corner of 79th Street. Built in 1973, this twenty-eight-story tower replaced the old Sherman Hoyt house. Goldberger identifies its architect, Philip Birnbaum, as the man who designed "most of the boring Second Avenue highrise towers." Birnbaum, who in recent years has lived at 799 Park, had also designed 1 Lincoln Tower near Lincoln Center and would later do Tower 67, also on the West Side. In 900 Park, Goldberger observes, Birnbaum went "arty, and the results are dismal indeed."

More obscure but no more imaginative an architect was Stephen Lyras, responsible for 1065 Park, northeast corner 87th Street; put up in 1974, it is a tower of caramel brick—quite out of scale with anything for more than half a mile to the north or south—that once called itself Carlton Park.

Only sixteen upper Park Avenue apartment houses have been built since World War II, which is perhaps why they seem so out of place. The avenue's conservative architectural tone was established before World War I; about three dozen of its best buildings date to the second two decades of the century, about six dozen, including hotels, to the years between the wars, mostly the 1920s.

Like developers of commercial property, residential developers found ways to capitalize on Park Avenue's name even when they could not obtain sites on the avenue. 500 Park Avenue Tower, completed in 1983 to designs by James Stewart Polshek, is a forty-story condominium on the south side of 59th Street, cantilevered over the western side of 500 Park (the old Pepsi-Cola Building) with offices on its first eleven floors (it replaced the Hotel Nassau). When

ABOVE: *733 Park replaced the Elihu Root mansion* (1989 photo)

developers ran out of possibilities on Park Avenue proper, they turned to Park Avenue South and even what remained of Fourth Avenue south of Union Square. At the northwest corner of 20th Street, an old office-and-loft building, 254, was converted in 1978 into 240 studio and one-bedroom apartments. Soon thereafter a twenty-story commercial structure finished in 1927 at the northeast corner 29th Street, was converted to residential use: Park South Tower at 425 Park Avenue South has four 1,100-square-foot apartments per floor, with just two apartments on the top floor that have their own private roof gardens; other tenants share a larger common roof garden.

Peter Kalikow's Ascot apartment house, a co-op at 407 Park Avenue South, northeast corner 28th Street, opened in 1983. Designed by Philip Birnbaum, it replaced the all-night Bellmore Cafeteria that had once offered free seltzer and was a popular haunt of taxi drivers working the graveyard shift.

A New Jersey firm took over the old Bank for Savings at the southwest corner of 22nd Street, engaged Philip Birnbaum (with Beyer, Blinder & Belle), and late in 1988 opened Gramercy Place, complete with health club. The ground floor of the bank building became a supermarket.

145 Fourth Avenue, southeast corner 14th Street, was completed in 1963, a rental building that called itself the Village Mayfair. 70 and 77 East 12th Street, south- and northwest corners of Fourth Avenue, are about the same age. The law was changed with regard to living in former loft buildings, and addresses such as 65, 80, 111 (Starrett & Van Vleck; built at the southeast corner of Fourth and 12th Street in 1920 for the International Tailoring Company), 115, and 127 Fourth were converted to rental and tenant-owned residential use (conversion of 115 into the Petersfield came in the mid-1980s).

As speculators bid up the value of Manhattan property, and developers sought financing for one residential or office project after another, more New Yorkers began to worry that the city's heritage was being sacrificed to individuals bent on fattening their own net worth at the community's expense.

16.

Develop or Preserve?

"New york is a series of experiments," said *Harper's Weekly* in 1869, "and everything which has lived its life and played its part is held to be dead, and is buried, and over it grows a new world." Edith Wharton, writing in her seventies, echoed the thought when she spoke in her 1934 book *A Backward Glance* about New York becoming "as much a vanished city as Atlantis or the lowest layer of Schliemann's Troy."

To few parts of New York do the statements apply more than to Park Avenue, which is quite unrecognizable today from its "Railroad Alley" incarnation. Between 46th and 59th streets it has changed dramatically since the late 1940s, when it was still almost exclusively residential. Yet the avenue north of 59th, which saw wholesale changes in the two decades before Wharton's book, has not seen many since. While other sections of the city were transformed in the postwar years, upper Park Avenue changed hardly at all.

As more and more of old New York fell to the wrecker's ball, concern increased that commercial interests, guided only by the profit motive, were determining the city's future. By the late 1950s, a private group calling itself the New York Community Trust was placing plaques on buildings it considered of outstanding historic or architectural importance, and the Municipal Art Society was compiling a citywide list of buildings it considered to have special architectural merit. What nobody knew was that in December 1954 the beleaguered Pennsylvania Railroad had sold to William Zeckendorf's Webb & Knapp an option for the development of air rights between Seventh and Eighth avenues where Penn Station stood. Six months later, Zeckendorf had signed an agreement with James Symes, president of the Pennsy, to buy the air rights and build a new station below street level. Nothing of this was leaked to the public. The world still came and marveled at the colossal, yet graceful, edifice, hardly suspecting that the building designed to last forever was about to be taken away.

Pennsylvania Railroad stockholders were told in May 1960 that the station was in terrible shape and operated at a loss of $1.5 milion each year. That same year, the Madison Square Garden Corporation was formed and began putting together a plan to sell to the public. Air and highway travel had reduced demand for passenger rail service, and Penn Station's location was no longer convenient to the center of the city, but sixty-four long-distance trains still operated in and out of the station in addition to the Long Island Rail Road. The number of redcaps had been cut nearly in half; arriving passengers now had to search for someone to help them with their baggage. Because of "deferred maintenance" (the traditional railroad method of saving money) the majestic station's pink walls, once sparkling, were now covered with grime.

Finally, in July 1961, the Pennsy came clean about its plans. But the story in the New York Times downplayed the loss of the old station and went on about the new Madison Square Garden complex—designed by Charles Luckman Associates with a 20,000-seat sports arena, 1,000-seat "forum," 500-seat movie theater, forty-eight-lane bowling alley, and twenty-nine-story office building—that would rise atop the new station.

The City Planning Commission held hearings on the proposal in January 1963. Paris, coincidentally, adopted its landmarks preservation law at just about that time, and New York Landmarks, edited by Alan Burnham, was published. Grace Church, which backs up on Fourth Avenue at 10th Street, is the chief landmark listed, a structure "of national import to be preserved at all cost." Designed by James Renwick, Jr., and built in 1846, it was far superior, said Burnham, to Renwick's Calvary Church on Park Avenue South at 21st Street (and to his St. Patrick's Cathedral of 1879).

The other Park Avenue landmarks included by Burnham were the 71st Regiment Armory at 34th Street (torn down a decade later), the Racquet & Tennis Club, the George F. Baker residence, the Church of St. Ignatius Loyola, the Park Avenue Christian Church, St. Bartholomew's, Grand Central Terminal, the 7th Regiment Armory, the Vanderbilt Hotel (closed a year later and turned into apartments and offices), Regis High School (between Park and Madison avenues, 84th to 85th streets), the Henry P. Davison and Percy R. Pyne residences, the Elihu Root residence at 71st Street (replaced a few years later by 733 Park), and the Church Missions house at 22nd Street (taken over by Protestant Welfare Agencies in 1963). About Penn Station, Burnham wrote, "It may soon be demolished to make way for a remodeled station."

And so it was. New York's Planning Commission has no jurisdiction over the preservation of architecture, nor can it determine whether a company has the right to tear down its building and sell the land. The Planning Commission could decide only whether or not to grant a zoning variance for a sports arena to be built on the site. (The Madison Square Garden complex opened in 1968. It never showed a profit, and beginning in March 1982 it needed huge subsidies from the city to stay afloat. Those who headed the Madison Square Garden Corporation had political connections: real estate taxes were cut by 75 percent in the summer of 1982 and a bill was passed providing a tax break totaling $50 million for the current year; the city also agreed to subsidize the Garden's energy costs.)

On October 10, 1963, as demolition began, the *Times* lamented the "vandalism" of the great station's destruction. "Any city," the *Times* philosophized, "gets what it admires, will pay for, and ultimately deserves. We want and deserve tin-can architecture in a tin-horn culture. And we will probably be judged not by the monuments we build but by those we have destroyed." The Pennsy's president replied with bottom-line mentality, "Does it make any sense to preserve a building merely as a monument?"

Penn Station still has eleven platforms for its twenty-one tracks, it still occupies twenty-five acres between Seventh and Eighth avenues from 32nd Street to 34th, but it has been shorn of its glory. Reduced in scale, bereft of human dimension, lighted even on the brightest days only by flickering fluorescent bulbs, it is a dim, depressing point of arrival and departure, a grubby stop for passengers en route to New England or destinations in the South and West. The great Pennsylvania Station of 1910 is gone. Little men of small vision allowed it to be razed in the interest of short-term gain for private individuals.

Enraged by the destruction of Penn Station in 1963, caring New Yorkers pushed the City Council to pass America's first landmarks preservation bill. In the preceding forty years, many states and hundreds of municipalities had enacted laws to encourage or require the preservation of buildings and areas of historic or aesthetic importance. In addition to these efforts, Congress determined that "the historical and cultural foundations" of the nation should be preserved as a living part of its community life and development in order to give a sense of orientation to the American people. The National Historic Preservation Act of 1966 enacted a series of measures designed to encourage preservation of sites and structures of historic architectural or cultural significance. New York City, acting pursuant to a New York State enabling act, adopted its Landmarks Preservation Law in 1965. The city acted from the conviction that its standing "as a world-wide tourist center and world capital of business, culture and government" would be threatened if legislation were not enacted to protect historic landmarks and neighborhoods from precipitate decisions to destroy or fundamentally alter their character. The Landmarks Preservation Commission could under the law designate a building to be a "landmark" on a particular "landmark site" or could designate an area to be a "historic district." The Board of Estimate could thereafter modify or disapprove the designation, and the owner could seek judicial review of the final designation decision.

The Carnegie Hill Historic District, established in 1974, protects buildings in side streets and in midblock but has irregular boundaries; when nominated to the National Register of Historic Places it was rejected, presumably because of those irregular boundaries. The Metropolitan Museum Historic District, established in 1977, also comprises mostly side streets. But the Upper East Side

Historic District, designated in 1981, does include at least that stretch of Park Avenue between 62nd and 79th streets. Efforts to extend landmark protection to buildings elsewhere on the avenue inevitably encounter resistance.

Park Avenue landmarks as of 1988 were the following (south to north; date of landmark designation in brackets):

57 Park (Guatemalan Permanent Mission to the United Nations), [September 1979]; Pershing Square viaduct [September 1980]; Grand Central Terminal [September 1967; interior September 1980]; Helmsley Building (formerly New York Central Building) [March 1987]; St. Bartholomew's [March 1967]; Racquet & Tennis Club [May 1979]; Lever House [November 1982]; 680-690 Park houses [November 1970]; 7th Regiment Armory [June 1967]; Church of St. Ignatius Loyola [March 1969]; former Lewis G. Morris house [April 1973]; former George F. Baker house complex [January 1969].

The owner of a designated landmark is obliged to keep his building's exterior "in good repair" and has to secure the commission's approval before making exterior alterations. The city administrative code Chapter 8-A 1976 requires that the selected landmark be at least thirty years old and possess "a special character or special historic or aesthetic interest or value as part of the development, heritage or cultural characteristics of the city, state, or nation." Under two separate ordinances, owners of landmark sites can transfer development rights from a landmarked parcel to proximate lots, a provision that affords relief on occasion from what some landmark owners consider a terrible economic hardship.

Not all landmark owners. So proud were the Bronfmans of their building at 375 Park that in 1976 they asked the city to change the law and make the Seagram Building elegible for landmark status before December 1987, when it would turn thirty. (As of early 1989 it was still not landmarked.)

Lever House was designated a landmark about seven months after it turned thirty. Fisher Brothers and another realty company wanted to tear it down and replace it with a skyscraper. Andrew Stein, then Manhattan's borough president, led a fight in 1983 to have the Board of Estimate overturn the landmark designation. He (and the other four borough presidents) very nearly won: the board voted by a scant six to five to sustain the landmark status. Reportedly it was Brendan Gill, the *New Yorker* magazine architecture specialist, former Municipal Art Society chairman, and chairman of the New York Landmarks Conservancy, who made the difference. Knowing that the city comptroller Harrison Goldin held two swing votes, and that Goldin was always eager for publicity, Gill telephoned Jacqueline Onassis. She agreed to meet with Goldin at Lever House, press photographers snapped her planting a kiss on Goldin's cheek, and about three weeks later Goldin joined with Mayor Koch and Carol Bellamy (then president of the City Council) to block any change in Lever House's landmark designation.

Developers can play rough when they want to avoid restrictions. In 1980, workmen with jackhammers, acting on orders from the developer Paul Milstein, destroyed the Biltmore Hotel's Palm Court's architectural features in order to thwart efforts to have the room landmarked. Milstein and his brother Seymour had obtained zoning variances and made a fortune building apartment houses in the Lincoln Center area; they had also wangled a twenty-year real estate tax abatement to convert an empty old Eighth Avenue hotel into the 1,310-room Milford Plaza, which opened at the end of July 1980. The Milsteins had purchased the Biltmore from the bankrupt Penn Central in July 1978 for about $30 million in a package deal that included the Roosevelt. They leased the Roosevelt and, at the beginning of 1980, filed plans to demolish the Biltmore and replace it with a twenty-eight-story office tower.

The Landmarks Preservation Commission balked at plans that called for escalator pits that would touch upon a room in the landmarked Grand Central Terminal. Paul Milstein had signed a lease in July with the Bank of America for most of the space in a building he was going to build in place of the Biltmore, and he said he was bound to deliver the space as promised. He could not accommodate the wishes of preservationists, he said, and when he learned that moves were afoot to preserve parts of the Biltmore, including the Palm Court, he simply had his men demolish the architectural features that gave the room its distinction. Fearing that the landmarks commission might cost him a fortune by delaying his plans, Milstein struck a deal with the Landmarks Conservancy, headed by Brendan Gill. Milstein guaranteed in writing that he would recreate the Palm Court in his new lobby, and the preservationists agreed not to pursue the official landmarking of any parts of the Biltmore. After some further demolition, the conservancy, a nonprofit organization, considered suing Milstein but wound up settling out of court for $500,000. "The Milsteins were acting in bad faith from the beginning," Gill told *Avenue* magazine writer Jonathan Greenberg. "It was a classic case of how not to save your city. [The Milsteins] never really wanted to recreate the Palm Court. That they paid the $500,000 was an acknowledgement that they had sinned."

Two years earlier, in 1978, the landmark status of Grand Central Terminal itself—and the very legality of New York's Landmarks Preservations Law—had been tested in a case decided by the highest court in the land.

17

Save Grand Central!

IT MAY NOT BE FINISHED until 1998, but the $51 million renovation project to restore Grand Central has already made the place look a lot more like its original self.

This rejuvenation is a credit not to capitalist enterprise but rather to state socialism. Chauncey Depew, could he hear these words, would no doubt enter a lawyerly demurrer. Do the Penn Central Corporation and its stockholders not still own the terminal? Ownership by a corporation is hardly consistent with socialism. Depew was a smart man who lived to ninety-four, joking that he got his exercise "acting as pallbearer to my friends who exercise." And he would be right about Penn Central, successor to the New York Central, New Haven, and Pennsylvania railroad companies, owning Grand Central. But since 1983 the terminal has been leased for a nominal $1 a year to the New York Metropolitan Transportation Authority (MTA) and managed by its new subsidiary, Metro-North Commuter Railroad. It is to all intents and purposes a creature of the state.

Such a development would have astonished the heirs to Commodore Vanderbilt's fortune. In 1913 the terminal was a monument to the power of raw capitalism, an economic system that still makes its presence felt all the way up Park Avenue. But the profit motive was not sufficient to maintain passenger rail service in and out of Grand Central, and as the century wore on Adam Smith's "invisible hand" was not able to save the terminal from desolation and imminent death.

Grand Central's importance began to fade only four years after its completion. At 1 o'clock in the morning of April 1, 1917, two sections of the Federal Express, one from Boston and the other from Washington, rumbled across the new Hell Gate Bridge connecting Queens and Ward's Island in the East River. No ceremony marked the opening of the New York Connecting Railway, but the crossing of these two trains, within minutes of each other, was a historic event (it was overshadowed by President Wilson's war message to the Senate as America entered World War I; newspapers buried the railroad story on back pages). Passengers traveling between the South and New England could remain in their seats without having to navigate the streets between Penn Station and Grand Central. The dream of the Pennsy's late president, Alexander Cassatt, was fulfilled.

The New York Connecting Bridge did more than shorten the trip between Boston and Washington from fifteen hours to about twelve: it reduced traffic at Grand Central and increased it at Penn Station.

A *Times* editorial hailed the event: "The Connecting Railway, over which the first trains are passing this week . . . connects two railways of the first class. . . .

"The Grand Central Terminal is overworked, and the Pennsylvania terminal [sic] has capacity to spare. The change in their relations marks the difference in their conception."

To charges that Penn Station was too large the president of the Pennsylvania Railroad had recently responded that it had been built for "the future"; the *Times* editorial noted that Grand Central would hardly have been possible without "the real estate conception which put to use the great area of costly real estate" and

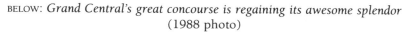

BELOW: *Grand Central's great concourse is regaining its awesome splendor* (1988 photo)

that the Pennsylvania had plowed more than $100 million into its station, tunnels, and bridge ("the greatest single steel span in the world, a bridge costing some $27 million"). American railroads, the editorial suggested, were already in decline.

"The . . . Connecting Railway . . . was conceived in the days when there was money in the railway business, and it was not thought good for the nation to starve them. These operations would not be undertaken in conditions like the present and could not be carried through. If they had been delayed a few years they might have brought embarrassment even to the rich railways which executed them. In that case the city would have suffered as now the city and the railways benefit together."

Use of Grand Central still expanded. In 1946, 63 million passengers passed through its gates—little more than a third of the number that used Penn Station in 1936 but the high-water mark for Grand Central. Every day, 550 regular trains entered or left the terminal, arriving or departing on average one minute apart during the evening rush hour. Nearly 3,100 people were needed to run Grand Central—dispatchers, trainmasters, car repairmen, gatemen, ticket sellers, 285 redcaps (Penn Station had 335), sixty parcel room attendants, 335 janitors, window washers, and cleaning women; thirty-eight train reservation clerks to handle as many as 2,000 telephone calls an hour; sixteen information clerks (Penn Station had twenty) to answer as many as 20,000 questions a day; a locksmith, a clock repairman, and two physicians to staff the station's emergency hospital.

Three years later, in 1949, the Central felt it had to boost revenue: it began to broadcast advertising messages over the terminal's public address system, stopping only after the *New Yorker* magazine's legendary editor Harold Ross led a vociferous protest. Not to be denied, the Central came back the following year and installed on the terminal's east balcony the Eastman Kodak Colorama, a 1,080-square-foot color transparency, eighteen feet high, sixty feet in length, that was changed every month. It was backlighted by 600 arc lamps that burned twenty-four hours a day. Other commercial displays followed, including a Merrill Lynch stockbroker booth, automobile exhibits, and publicity gimmicks on the main concourse. More of the same intruded on the lower-level concourse; kiosks, vending machines, telephone booths, and coin-operated lockers clogged the main waiting room.

New York Central lawyers had been trying for years to make the State of New York refund taxes that the railroad had paid on its right-of-way under Park Avenue. A referee ruled against the railroad in 1950 and was upheld by the courts, a financial setback for the Central. Robert Young, a brash Texas stock manipulator who had gained control of the Chesapeake & Ohio and other roads, was demanding a seat on the Central's board. With America in an economic recession, the battle for control reached a climax. The railroad reported a deficit of $2.5 million, and Young started a proxy fight. He sent agents door to door soliciting votes of stockholders, and won by more than a million proxies. There were no longer any Vanderbilts on the board when Young took over in mid-

1954. He named Alfred Perlman of the Denver & Rio Grande Western as chief executive officer of the Central. Perlman, who had been graduated from MIT at age twenty, brought a new ruthlessness to management, cutting the Central's work force by some 15,000. Commuter cars were not maintained, commuters' complaints were ignored.

And still the financial drain of passenger services continued. In 1954 the railroad claimed it was losing $25 million a year on the terminal's operations. It sold the New York Central Building (it became, first, the New York General Building, then the Helmsley Building). William Zeckendorf, Jr., head of Webb & Knapp, proposed an eighty-story skyscraper that would swallow up Grand Central. Robert Young liked the idea; in September 1954 he announced plans to tear down the terminal and replace it with an office tower more than 500 feet taller than the Empire State Building. New Yorkers objected strenuously.

Erwin S. Wolfson had a more subtle proposal. A prominent promoter, contractor, and building owner whose Diesel Construction Co. was probably the city's biggest, Wolfson suggested in February 1955 that a sixty-five-story office tower be erected above the shed area north of the terminal and south of the New York General Building. By 1957 he had engaged Richard Roth of Emery Roth and Sons and, as design consultants, Walter Gropius, chairman of Harvard's School of Architecture and founder of Germany's Bauhaus in 1918, and Pietro Belluschi, dean of MIT's School of Architecture and Planning. Critics faulted their plans: huge horizontal breaks at the twenty-second and forty-fifth floors would take the soaring height out of its tower and make it look like three huge building blocks.

The New York Central, meanwhile, continued to lose money. Day coaches were added to the once glamorous 20th Century Limited in 1957 (it would be discontinued altogether ten years later), and still the money hemorrhaged away. The New York Thruway and St. Lawrence Seaway, both built with government subsidies, were draining railroad freight revenues. Alfred Perlman testified at congressional hearings, saying the government owed some help to the railroads; Congress turned a deaf ear. Robert Young held meetings with James Symes, chairman of the Pennsy, and they seemed to be making some progress toward a merger.

Then, on January 25, 1958, Young killed himself with a shotgun in the study of his Palm Beach mansion. The Interstate Commerce Commission was insisting that the bankrupt New York, New Haven & Hartford be included in any merger. Neither the Central nor the Pennsy wanted to take in the New Haven, whose position had been weakened by stock raiders—and by the Connecticut Turnpike. Its commuter rail service to New York City was essential but unprofitable. Merger talks broke off.

Criticism of his Grand Central City project did not deter Erwin Wolfson. Neither did a walkout by steelworkers in mid-July 1959, beginning a strike that would last for more than three months and delay materials. Wolfson went abroad and returned quickly with $25 million—perhaps 20 percent of what he needed—from the English investor Jack Cotton.

The railroad was still trying to get more revenue out of Grand Central. New Yorkers protested in 1960 when they learned that bowling alleys and a restaurant might be installed in the vaulted space under the fifty-foot ceiling of Grand Central's main waiting room. Forty lanes could be built in that "wasted" space, and the revenue would help to offset the terminal's losses. The bowling alleys would be installed in three tiers and would lower the waiting room ceiling from fifty feet to fifteen. The first level would contain a 200-seat restaurant and a 600-seat four-lane tournament arena with built-in telecasting equipment for the Gothams, the New York team in a new professional national bowling league. Upper tiers would have thirty-six additional lanes. All three tiers would consist of concrete slabs floated on a steel structure spanning the sixty-foot-wide waiting room so interior spaces would be free of columns.

An editorial in the *Times* noted that the recent fiftieth anniversary of Pennsylvania Station had been ignored and said, "We can understand why. It must be because it is ashamed of what has happened in the past few years inside that great structure once considered among the classic buildings of America. If bowling alleys are put up in Grand Central, we are sure that its owners will soon feel the same way. Surely the citizens of New York will."

John Crosby, critic-at-large for the *Herald Tribune*, called attention to a hearing scheduled by the Board of Standards and Appeals to consider an application for a variance that would pave the way for the proposed bowlers' accommodations. Said Crosby, "I hope somebody will show up to protest this vandalism to our railroad station . . . We don't need bowling alleys in Grand Central. Besides, once the waiting room is sacrificed to greed, the [120-foot] ceiling of the main concourse would be eyed greedily by some speculator too. The whole thing ought to be stopped in its tracks."

The New York Chapter of the American Institute of Architects (A.I.A.) organized a special group to oppose the project. Heading the Municipal Art Society was the architect Harmon H. Goldstone, who joined in the protest, as did the designer Victor Gruen and other leading figures in architecture and design. In October 1961, at a public hearing before the Board of Standards and Appeals, opponents argued that it would be "a shocking desecration of a nobly designed room, constructed of excellent materials and of excellent workmanship, and also an infringement of public interests and the public good" to lower the ceiling height from fifty feet to fifteen.

Said one critic, "Grand Central is *de facto*, if not necessarily legally, a public building . . . In 1964 New York will play host at its world's fair to millions of visitors who will pass through Grand Central and it is of vital concern to the city that they get an impressive greeting, unmarred by overcrowding and honkytonk. . . . It seems paradoxical, if railroad companies expect subventions, tax advantages, state loans for new railroad cars (as just received by the New York Central) in order to improve and enlarge their passenger business, that they should simultaneously engage in measures which diminish the convenience, efficiency, and beauty of their terminal facilities."

The board voted 4–0 to reject the Central's application. Its decision was not, however, based on anything as frivolous as aesthetics or loss of grandeur. An existing zoning ordinance, and a new one to become effective in December, specifically barred bowling alleys in a restricted retail zone. The terminal's location was in such a zone, and although the Board of Standards and Appeals refused to approve the requested variance, it left the terminal owners free to use the waiting room's air space for some other purpose; they could also seek a court order to reverse the board, or they could try to have the zoning changed. The Central decided not to pursue the matter; it was now busy with plans for alterations to the terminal's north-side interior.

Harper's magazine for May 1960 carried an article by Edgar Kaufman, Jr., a former Museum of Modern Art staff member and department store heir who lived outside Pittsburgh in the famous 1937 Frank Lloyd Wright house "Falling Water." Billboarding Kaufman's article were these words by a *Harper's* editor: "Into one of the most congested half miles in the world, a new building of colossal size will bring another 50,000 people each day. Why was it allowed to happen? What will it do to New York?"

Wrote Kaufman: "From now on, as you enter or leave Manhattan on any one of the 500 trains scheduled daily on the tracks of the New York Central and New Haven railroads, you will be passing inside and under one of the most extraordinary structural enterprises ever undertaken. This is a huge skyscraper beginning to be built from the tracks up, athwart Park Avenue just north of Grand Central Terminal. So far as anyone now knows it will be called Grand Central City, although the name could easily change before the building is finished some time in 1962 or 1963. . . .

"Grand Central station, New York's most familiar gateway for rail traffic, spans Park Avenue at Forty-second Street. To the north, at Forty-sixth Street, Park Avenue is similiarly straddled by a tower, the New York General Building that extends south to Forty-fifth Street. From Forty-fifth Street clear to Forty-second no cross streets penetrate a continuous mass of rather low buildings linked to the station. It is on this site, from Forty-fifth down to the north wall of the terminal, thus more than two blocks long, and extending in width from Vanderbilt Avenue to Depew Place, that the new skyscraper will be built. Grand Central Terminal itself, the big concourse, will remain, as will the New York General tower. Only some low office structures will be stripped to their steel and skeletally incorporated into the new Grand Central City.

"The building site, so tucked away within its crowded neighborhood, is in fact the biggest single undivided parcel of mid-Manhattan real estate not hitherto developed. Thus the largest uninterrupted floors of any new building could be built one on top of the other. The building code (since changed) permitted a tower of unlimited height to be erected over 25 percent of this site; that is, the opportunity was present for a truly mammoth skyscraper in a uniquely public spot.

"The most spectacular accumulation of new Manhattan skyscrapers built since the last world war is along Park Avenue just north of the New York General Tower. For blocks on both sides of the avenue metal-framed glass facades—thin curtain walls hung outside the structures—shimmer back the big lights and shadows of the urban view, making an icy, craggily irregular canyon unlike any city ever built or dreamed before. . . . Now the surprising terminus to this crystal chasm has been designed by two famous architects. . . . Their Grand Central City . . . will stand on Park Avenue massively, dwarfing the New York General Tower as well as everything else in view. . . . Unlike most recent skyscrapers, this building (according to present plans) will be a white cliff of rough quartz, sharply patterned by vertical and horizontal shadows. Thus the colorful, generally feminine sleekness of the glass canyon to the north will be closed by a great, grainy masculine slab. From the south this same slab will arise in strange contradiction to the sumptuous academic stone arcades of the station. . . . Seen from either main approach, Grand Central will sit adamantly eccentric among its neighbors. . . .

"The world's largest office building is . . . not only not grand; it's uncomfortably out of human scale and downright ugly."

Kaufman wrote about the "staggering complications" for planning and construction presented by the railroad tracks and about the necessity of using costly space for food counters, shops, machinery, storage, and the like, which in a normal building would be placed in basement areas. He cited planners' objections that to congest any further the already "choked" Grand Central district, with its crowded subways and eating facilities, was immoral, "a dangerous but fully legal disregard for human decencies."

"With shrewd purchasing and construction, Grand Central City expects to compete advantageously in rentals despite such extraordinary features as large thirty-two-foot bays between columns, hollow steel floors liberally sprinkled with every kind of utility outlet, the most and fastest elevators and escalators yet, a garage for 400 cars that will be a miracle of automation, the very best lighting and ventilating available, and lobbies, telephone, and restaurant accommodations that, expertly calculated, will relieve many tenants of economic burdens commonly shouldered by them in other buildings. Grand Central is generally careless of its influence on a crowded Grand Central district, taking more from it than contributing to it. That expresses itself regardless of its neighbors. It blocks the view, it shares no whit of style. When Commodore Vanderbilt, surely a champion of free enterprise, organized the Grand Central area, enterprise was free enough to create order in the grand manner of Versailles on the grand scale of the railway age. What is happening now is hardly more than what happened in Rome in the Dark Ages—men tear down great works to put up the best they can. Grand Central City is a sincere effort but in the very middle of the ruins of a short-lived grandeur it has failed to grasp the spirit of what is grand. Infinitely larger than any work that stood or stands nearby, its design shows none of the scale of urban grandness that is still exemplified in the station next door."

By 1961 the project under construction had been renamed the Pan Am Building and its height scaled back from sixty-five stories to fifty-nine. The biggest mortgage placed up to that time on a single commercial building—$70 million—had been arranged by Wolfson with a pension fund. (In the spring of 1980 the Pan Am Building was assessed at between $86 and $93 million; it was actually worth a lot more. In late July of that year Pan American World Airways, losing money copiously, would reach a preliminary agreement to sell the Pan Am Building to Metropolitan Life for about $400 million, reportedly the highest price paid up to that time for a single building. Since the buyer would turn over stock instead of paying cash, the city would realize little in the way of sales tax.)

When the Pan Am Building opened in 1963, with 2.4 million square feet of office space, it was the world's largest commercial office building. Its 17,000 tenants and 25,000 daily transients imposed a terrible burden on Grand Central's already overcrowded space and services. And it changed forever the look of Park Avenue, totally blocking that boulevard's vista where the New York General Building had merely interrupted it. Ada Louis Huxtable, the *Times* architecture critic, refused to be awed by the names of Gropius and Belluschi. While a $100 million building could "not really be called cheap," she wrote, "Pan Am is a colossal collection of minimums. Its exterior and its public spaces, in particular, use minimum good materials of minimum acceptable quality executed with a minimum of imagination (always an expensive commodity), or distinction (which comes high), or finesse (which costs more). Pan Am is gigantically second-rate." But compared to some later midtown buildings Pan Am is not all that bad, aesthetically. Its big faults are simply its monstrous size and the congestion it produces.

A heliport opened on the roof late in 1965, over protests that an accident in midtown Manhattan would be disastrous. New York Airways continued operations for twenty-eight months, over protests that its helicopters were far too noisy and served far too few people to justify the disturbance. The facility closed in February 1968, mainly because it was not profitable, and nothing was heard of it until May 23, 1974, when a young man bent on extorting $2 million commandeered an executive helicopter at the 34th Street heliport on the East River and wound up on the 800-foot perch atop the Pan Am Building, where he was captured. Commercial flights resumed on February 1, 1977, with fifty-foot-long Sikorsky S-61 helicopters that carried thirty passengers, whisking them to and from Kennedy Airport in ten minutes or less for $22.15 ($15 for passengers holding tickets on flights of Pan Am or other airlines).

Then, just after 5 o'clock on the afternoon of May 16, 1977, New York Airways Flight 972 arrived from Kennedy and set down on the landing pad at the northeast corner of the Pan Am Building's roof. Its twenty passengers deplaned, a dozen of twenty-one new passengers boarded, and the rest were waiting to board when the craft's right front landing gear suddenly collapsed. One of the four twenty-foot blades of its rotor, idling at 1,000 revolutions per minute, snapped off, slashed four people to death on the roof, plunged over the side, smashed into a window on the thirty-sixth floor (the office of an advertising account executive at Foote Cone & Belding who had just left to change for a softball game), and broke in two. A shower of glass descended upon rush-hour pedestrians on Vanderbilt and Madison avenues, and part of the rotor blade fell to earth on Madison Avenue, killing a woman at 43rd Street. Severed limbs were found on the roof of the Pan Am Building after the bloody carnage, and helicopter flights were never resumed.

So preoccupied were many New Yorkers with the monster rising athwart Park Avenue in the early 1960s that they paid little attention to what was happening to Penn Station; its fate, as we have seen, was actually sealed before the public knew what had happened. Only after the original Penn Station's rose marble had been replaced by metal and plastic did travelers realize what had been lost. The new materials did not hold up, and by 1984 a rehabilitation program was begun to make conditions less noxious for the 235,000 Long Island Rail Road passengers (and 15,000 long-distance travelers) who used the facility every day.

In August 1967, under the Landmarks Law, Grand Central Terminal was designated a landmark and the block it occupies a landmark site. Had the law been enacted earlier, Penn Station would probably have enjoyed the same protection. But as Paul Goldberger, an admirer of the old Penn Station, has said, Grand Central's use of space is more expeditious. "Grand Central has that extraordinary natural procession, where you get off a train and all you do is walk. Penn Station was never as natural and simple a thing as Grand Central."

Landmark designation effectively barred any further construction on the property and any alteration of the huge terminal's exterior. The Pan Am Building, completed several years earlier, rose above the shed area on the northern side of the Grand Central block; it would almost certainly have been disallowed under the new law. The financially pressed Penn Central had opposed landmark designation in hearings before the commission but did not seek judicial review of the final decision. Instead, it entered on January 22, 1968, into a fifty-year lease and sublease agreement with UGP Properties, headed by the English developer Morris Saady. UGP contracted to erect a fifty-nine-story office tower over the terminal's waiting room; UGP would pay Penn Central $1 million a year while the new building was under construction and $3 million a year thereafter.

Marcel Breuer, the Hungarian-born architect who had worked at the Bauhaus before coming to America in 1937, designed the new tower. Breuer's trademark was cast stone; his credits included the Whitney Museum at Madison Avenue and 75th Street, opened in 1966. But the monster that was to rise above Grand Central was, in Ada Louise Huxtable's term, a "grotesquerie." Wrote Huxtable, "A picture of the proposed commercial tower . . . is like a slap in the eye. The design shows a waffle-faced slab, obliterating the terminal's facade, supported by giant cant legs from the elevated roadway. The new tower would form one side of a huge sandwich board (the Pan Am Building would be the other side) and together they would squeeze the old building in a brutally arrogant embrace. The grand civic gesture has been replaced by the grim economic gesture."

Three plans were submitted to the landmarks commission for approval in 1968 and 1969. The first, Breuer I, provided for construction of a fifty-five-story office building to be cantilevered above the existing facade and to rest on the roof of the terminal. The second, Breuer II revised, called for tearing down a portion of the terminal that included the 42nd Street facade, stripping off some of its remaining features, and erecting a fifty-three-story office building. The landmarks commission denied a certificate of no exterior effect on September 20, 1968. Penn Central and UGP then applied for a certificate of appropriateness for both proposals. After four days of hearings the commission denied this application as to both proposals. "To protect a landmark," said the commission, "one does not tear it down. To perpetuate its architectural features, one does not strip them off." In conclusion, the commission stated, "[We] have no fixed rule against additions to designated buildings—it all depends on how they are done. . . . But to balance a fifty-five-story office tower above a flamboyant Beaux-Arts facade seems nothing more than an aesthetic joke. Quite simply, the tower would overwhelm the terminal by its sheer mass. The 'addition' would be four times as high as the existing structure and would reduce the landmark itself to the status of a curiosity."

Without seeking judicial review of the commission's turndown, Penn Central and UGP brought suit in state court, claiming that the application of the landmarks law had "taken" their property for public use without just compensation, thus violating the Fifth and Fourteenth amendments, and arbitrarily deprived them of their property without due process of law, another Fourteenth Amendment violation. The trial court granted relief, bringing dismay to all who loved Grand Central.

By this time Central and Pennsy executives had reluctantly agreed to include the New Haven in their merger—called in 1968 the largest corporate merger up to that point. (It was actually an absorption of the Central by the Pennsy rather than a true merger.) The newly formed Pennsylvania New York Central Transportation Company (Penn Central) was in financial straits almost from the start, although Metroliner service between New York and Washington continued to be popular and fully booked.

On June 23, 1970, the Penn Central entered reorganization proceedings under the federal bankruptcy law. Amtrak came into existence on May 1, 1971, and essentially nationalized long-distance passenger rail travel. Only massive federal subsidies keep it running. Under the provisions of the act that created Amtrak, railroads could give up their best passenger equipment to Amtrak in exchange for permission to discontinue their long-distance passenger service. The Penn Central had no objection to that. By 1976 its assets had been turned over to the Consolidated Rail Corporation, or Conrail; it was no longer in the railroad business.

Grand Central Terminal, meanwhile, echoed with complaints. Commuter train service was declining, advertising displays crowded the concourse, and at the end of July 1974 the Oyster Bar closed. Operated by the Union News Company since the terminal opened, and renowned for its oyster stew, the restaurant was said to be squeezed between rising prices and consumer resistance. Fortunately, the restaurateur Jerome Brody, who had worked with Joe

Baum at Restaurant Associates and gone on to revitalize Gallagher's Steak House, took over Grand Central's Oyster Bar and gave it a new lease on life. By May 1975 his menu was featuring raw herring flown in from the Netherlands.

A rally outside the terminal in April 1977, a few weeks before the grisly accident atop the Pan Am Building, aroused public opposition to the proposed UGP-Breuer building that would further congest the subway platforms, sidewalks, and concourse of the Grand Central area. The New York Court of Appeals then reviewed the lower court's decision and concluded that there had been no "taking": the landmarks law had not transferred control of the property to the city but merely restricted exploitation of it; and there was no denial of due process because (1) the same use of the terminal was permitted as before; (2) the appellants had not shown that they could not earn a reasonable return on their investment in the terminal itself; (3) even if the terminal proper could never operate at a reasonable profit, some of the income from Penn Central's extensive real estate holdings in the area must realistically be imputed to the terminal; and (4) the development rights above the terminal, which were transferable to numerous sites in the vicinity, provided significant compensation for loss of rights above the terminal itself.

Historic preservationists cheered the decision; many owners of landmarked property, and property with a potential for being landmarked, hoped for a reversal by the U.S. Supreme Court, which agreed in September 1977 to hear the case. By taking jurisdiction, the justices set the stage for a decision on what

BELOW *Since 1912, the Oyster Bar has been one of the city's best seafood houses* (1989 photo)

the state must pay a property owner when it blocks development of any property by designating it as a historic site.

On June 26, 1978, the high court ruled six to three that the application of the landmarks law to the Terminal property did not constitute a "taking" of the property "within the meaning of the Fifth Amendment as made applicable to the States by the Fourteenth Amendment. In a wide variety of contexts, the government may execute laws or programs that adversely affect recognized economic values without its action constituting a 'taking' . . .

"In deciding whether a particular governmental action has effected a 'taking,' the character of the action and the nature and extent of the interference with property rights (here the City tax block designated as the 'landmark site') are at focus upon rather than discrete segments thereof. Consequently, appellants cannot establish a 'taking' simply by showing that they have been denied the ability to exploit the adjacent air space, irrespective of the remainder of the appellants' parcel . . .

"That the Landmarks Law affects some landowners more severely than others does not itself result in 'taking,' for that is often the case with general welfare and zoning legislation. Nor, contrary to appellants' contention, are they solely burdened and unbenefited by the Landmarks Law, which has been extensively applied and was enacted on the basis of the legislative judgment that the preservation of landmarks benefits the citizen both economically and by improving the overall quality of city life . . .

"The question presented is whether a city may, under a comprehensive program to preserve historic landmarks and historic districts, place restrictions on the development of individual historic landmarks—in addition to those imposed by applicable zoning ordinances—without effecting 'taking' requiring the payment of just compensation . . .

"Landmarks cannot be divorced from aesthetics—particularly when the setting is a dramatic and integral part of the original concept. The terminal in its setting is a great example of urban design. Such examples are not so plentiful in New York City that we can afford to lose any of the few we have, and we must preserve them in a meaningful way—with alterations and additions of such character, scale and materials and mass as will enhance, protect and perpetuate the original design rather than overwhelm it."

Justice William J. Brennan, Jr., wrote the opinion. Dissenting were Justice (later Chief Justice) William Rehnquist, Chief Justice Burger and Justice Stevens. Wrote Rehnquist, "Of the over 1 million buildings and structures in the City of New York the appellees have singled out 400 for designation as official Landmarks."* The owner of a building might be pleased at first that his property had been singled out for such a distinction, but he might well discover, as did the Penn Central, that landmark designation imposed upon

* A large percentage of New York's designated landmarks are public structures such as the Brooklyn Bridge, City Hall, the Statue of Liberty, and the Municipal Asphalt Plant and thus can never raise Fifth Amendment "taking" questions.

him a substantial cost with little or no offsetting benefit except for the honor.

The question, said Rehnquist, was whether the cost associated with preserving designated landmarks had to be borne by all of the city's taxpayers or could, instead, be imposed entirely upon the owners of the landmarked property. "In August 1967 Grand Central Terminal was designated a Landmark over the objections of its owner Penn Central. Immediately upon this designation Penn Central, like all owners of a Landmark site, was placed under an affirmative duty, backed by criminal fines and penalties, to keep 'exterior portions' of the Landmark 'in good repair.' Even more burdensome, however, were the strict limitations thereupon imposed on Penn Central's use of its property."

Substantial property rights, said Rehnquist, had been taken—"in a literal sense"—from Penn Central. "The courts have held that the deprivation of the former owner rather than the accretion of a right or interest to the sovereign constitutes a 'taking.'"

Of all the terms used in the Taking Clause, wrote Rehnquist, "just compensation" has the strictest meaning. The Fifth Amendment did not allow simply an approximate compensation but required "a full and perfect equivalent for the property taken . . . If the adjective 'just' had been omitted, and the provision was simply that property should not be taken without compensation, the natural import of the language would be that the compensation should be the equivalent of the property, and this is made emphatic by the adjective 'just.' There can, in view of the combination of those two words, be no doubt that the compensation must be full and perfect equivalent for the property taken."

Invoking words written by Justice Holmes more than fifty years earlier, Rehnquist warned that courts were "in danger of forgetting that a strong public desire to improve the public condition is not enough to warrant achieving the desire by a shorter cut than the constitutional way of paying for the change." The Court's opinion in the Penn Central case, said Rehnquist, demonstrated that "the danger thus foreseen has not abated. The City of New York is in a precarious financial state and some may believe that the costs of Landmark Preservation will be more easily borne by corporations such as Penn Central than the overburdened individual taxpayers of New York. Such concerns do not allow us to ignore past precedents construing the eminent domain clause to the end that the desire to improve the public condition is, indeed, achieved by a shorter cut than the constitutional way of paying for the change."

Since 1978 the Court has moved closer to Rehnquist's position. In *First English Evangelical Lutheran Church of Glendale* v. *County of Los Angeles*, it held that even a temporary land-use regulation (for flood control) that took away all rights to private use would require compensation, although the monetary damage in this case may have been less than that suffered in many other permanent "regulatory takings." In *Nollan* v. *California Coastal Commission*, the Court held in June 1987 that it was a taking to require as a condition for a building permit that the owner give public beach access over his land. This was a five to four decision, and Justice Brennan, in his dissent, said the opinion written by Justice Antonin Scalia gave the plaintiffs "a windfall at the expense of the public." Both rulings suggested a shift in the Court's approach in takings cases to one more sympathetic toward property owners. The record is not consistent: in February 1988 the Court upheld a San Jose, California, rent control law. Chief Justice Rehnquist wrote the opinion, which was considered a setback for landlords and champions of property rights. Still, as Peter Finley Dunne, long before he moved to Park Avenue, had his Mr. Dooley say, "No matter whether the constitution follows the flag, th' supreme coort follows th' iliction returns."

In July 1988, ten years after the Court's Penn Central decision, Amtrak announced that it would stop using Grand Central "as early as" 1990. (Amtrak's Hell's Gate Connecting Bridge was then discovered to have been dangerously neglected, but that is another story.) The federally financed long-haul passenger rail system was running eight or nine trains a day into Grand Central and another eight or nine trains out of the terminal, as compared with 100 trains using Penn Station.

Amtrak trains leaving Grand Central in early 1989 included the following:

7:30 A.M.: #57 The Bear Mountain to Albany (Rensselaer); daily except Friday, Saturday, and Sunday

8:45 A.M.: #63 The Maple Leaf to Toronto; daily

10:45 A.M.: #69 The Adirondack to Montreal; daily

12:45 P.M.: #73 The Empire State Express to Albany (it had once gone all the way to Buffalo); daily

1:55 P.M.: #65 The Niagara Rainbow to Niagara Falls; daily except Friday (on Fridays #33, also the Niagara Rainbow, but with a slower schedule)

3:00 P.M.: #71 The Sleepy Hollow to Albany; daily except Sunday (on Sundays #31)

4:35 P.M.: #77 The Hudson Highlander to Schenectady; Monday to Friday

5:40 P.M.: #75 The Electric City Express to Schenectady; Sundays only

7:35 P.M.: #49 The Lake Shore Limited to Buffalo (it then diverged west on the old Twentieth Century Limited line to Chicago); daily

Only the Lake Shore Limited offered sleeping-car service. All these trains would soon depart from Penn Station, said Amtrak. It was building a ten-mile track extension over an abandoned West Side freight-track bed that would bypass Grand Central and connect with the Spuyten Duyvil Bridge, closed since 1982—the year that Amtrak began planning to bypass Grand Central—but scheduled to reopen. For the first time since the construction of New York's great railroad tunnels, there would be a direct rail route through the city to and from the Hudson River Valley.

The new Jacob K. Javits Center had agreed to let Amtrak tunnel under property it owned between Penn Station and the West Side track bed, which belonged to Conrail, the federal freight system. Unless opposition from West

Side community groups succeeded in derailing the Amtrak plan, trains that had once traveled underground from Grand Central would now emerge from a tunnel under the Convention Center and travel aboveground along the Hudson to the Spuyten Duyvil Bridge over the Harlem River.

Metro-North, whose annual budget was $447 million, would hardly feel the loss of $600,000 in annual revenues from electricity (standby power for trains during layovers) and services (trash removal and yard switching) provided on an avoidable-cost basis to Amtrak. Those who suffered would be long-haul passengers, who would be obliged to use the demeaning facilities of Penn Station instead of Grand Central's spacious and thrilling splendor.

The glory of Grand Central would now be enjoyed only by commuters fortunate enough to live in Westchester or Connecticut (rather than Long Island or New Jersey)—and, unhappily, by vagrants with nowhere else to go. Property rights take precedence over human needs on Park Avenue and, sometimes, in the minds of judges; the values brought by Justice Rehnquist to the issue of saving Grand Central are very much like those that permitted the demolition of single-room occupancy hotels, traditional residence of last resort before the streets.

Writing in the *Times* in November 1987, Jane Gross remarked about the

LEFT: *Amtrak's use of Grand Central may be nearing an end* (1988 photo)   RIGHT: *Shame of the city: sad times for Grand Central's waiting room* (1989 photo)

homeless who "congregate in a pair of waiting rooms near the entrance at 42nd Street and Park Avenue. Sometimes, they fill the scarred wooden benches, with shopping carts and bundles at their feet and the litter of fast-food meals around them. Even when there is room for others to sit, the stale stench of unwashed clothing and the ranting of the mentally ill discourage travelers who once waited for trains under these vaulted ceilings and grand chandeliers."

18

The Other Park Avenue

ON A COLD NIGHT in early January 1989 a homeless man could be seen sleeping under a blanket on Park Avenue's grassy median opposite St. Bartholomew's. Other men, women, and children without addresses sought shelter at Grace Church, in Grand Central Terminal, in the Whitney Museum gallery at 120 Park, at St. Bart's, in the 7th Regiment Armory, even in the steam-pipe passages under Park Avenue. If imminent bankruptcy was New York's overwhelming concern in the mid-1970s, its seemingly intractable problem in the late 1980s was homelessness.

A *Times* reporter in 1977 had revealed the existence of a "hobo colony" living in the steam tunnels six levels beneath Park Avenue from Grand Central to the Waldorf-Astoria. Wrote Doris Kleimann, "Living in the darkness, relieved only by an occasional overhanging bulb, amid hissing steam pipes, oppressive heat, and dripping water, as many as 40 tramps have lived for years in dungeons of filth where days are measured by the rumble of passing commuter trains and dangers abound for the uninitiated. They range in age from 17 to 70. Many once had families, homes, jobs, and responsibilities but now they have sidestepped the more conventional life to live underground . . . They're all men. Women are forbidden."

By the 1980s a few women lived among the men in these lower depths. Metro-North had taken over Grand Central and was calling the vagrants "a threat to public safety." Efforts were made to stop the terminal from being turned into a flophouse: doors were closed at 1:30 each morning, forcing everyone except employees to leave. Nearly all the benches were removed from the great waiting room. The terminal's 300 lockers were also removed.

Metro-North forbade shaving and clothes laundering in the men's room. It barred a fast-food chain from distributing unsold doughnuts lest it draw more hungry people. When evictees camped on the ramp leading to 42nd Street, terminal janitors mopped the ramp with a strong ammonia mixture. When the vagrants obtained cardboard boxes and newspapers to shield them from the noxious fumes, Metro-North chained the 42nd Street doors open, even in 10° cold. An elderly woman, who had been living on one of the surviving benches in the waiting room, was repeatedly removed by police in the first weeks of December 1985. On Christmas Eve, even though clearly ill, she was compelled to move outside. And although "Mama Doe" was allowed to come back inside at dawn and resume her position on the bench, she died of pneumonia on Christmas morning.

Buses appeared after dark each day to take people to city shelters where they would receive food and cots, but many considered the shelters more dangerous than the streets and refused to go. They welcomed the nightly arrival of a van with volunteers from the Coalition for the Homeless Grand Central Feeding Project; it pulled up to 43rd Street and Vanderbilt Avenue with sandwiches, fruit, and milk for some 600 persons. To discourage their presence, the 42nd Street ramp was fenced off early in 1987; thereafter the waiting room benches were cordoned off with yellow tape at 9 o'clock each evening. Police patrolled the area with a dog.

Wrote Jonathan Kozol in 1987, "Telephones in Grand Central are aligned in recessed areas outside the main concourse. On almost any night, before one-thirty, visitors could see a score of people stuffed into these booths with their belongings . . . One night, I saw three people—a man, a woman, and a child—jammed into a single booth. All three were asleep."

When the waiting room reopened in October 1988, tiny white lights dangled from eight artificial maple trees. Most of the benches had been restored and were promptly monopolized by vagrants, who continued to be drawn to Grand Central. Until these unfortunates could be otherwise accommodated (conditions in the city shelters were unspeakable), their presence would hamper efforts to return the great terminal to its original splendor.

There had always been homeless people; they had just never before been so numerous, or so visible. Except for a sharp recession in 1982 the Reagan years were not starving times. Why, then, such hordes of homeless men, women, and children? Many on Park Avenue prefer to blame it on court decisions that released mental patients unprepared to cope with freedom and made it impossible to enforce vagrancy laws. Or they may just not want to think about it. Residents who never venture north of 96th Street ("Ghastly idea. Why should we?") incline toward denial. Poverty does not exist. Harlem does not exist.

When Harlem landowners succeeded in having New York's first public transit started in 1831 they could hardly have known that their railroad tracks

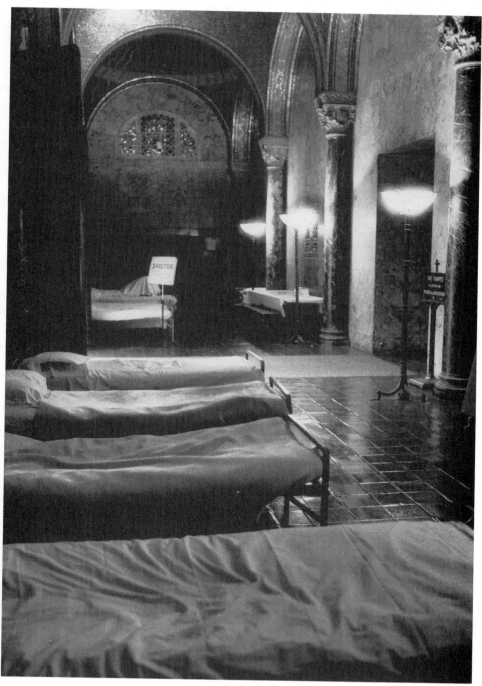

ABOVE: *St. Bartholomew's sets up cots for the homeless* (1989 photo)

ABOVE: *Vagrants with nowhere else to go sleep in the terminal and in tunnels under Park Avenue* (1989 photo)

would one day run beneath some of the world's most expensive real estate—and run for two miles above some of Manhattan's most squalid neighborhoods.

The New York & Harlem Railroad was intended to enhance property values by giving this remote area a rail link to the city's commercial center. It did just that. The steam cars put Harlem within easy commuting distance of downtown sections; and in an era of malaria, yellow fever, and tuberculosis, houses in the fresh, clean air of Harlem Heights were highly prized. The railroad tracks were eventually placed in a trench practically to the Harlem River; at 125th Street, commuters had modest waiting rooms recessed into the rock flanking the railroad's leased right-of-way.

But as rail and waterway traffic increased, the New York Central's low turntable bridge over the Harlem River became a bottleneck. Sharing the bridge with the Central were the New Haven Railroad and, briefly, the New York & Northern, which had leasehold rights and which, in 1890, complained to Washington that the bridge's low clearance made it hazardous. The War Department, which had jurisdiction over navigable waterways, forced the Central to build a new, higher bridge. This meant elevating the tracks and building a new 125th Street station. Neighboring property owners sought to block construction of the new bridge, viaduct, and station; Chauncey Depew threatened to eliminate the 125th Street stop altogether, saying it had never been profitable. Finally, in 1897, his New York Central completed the new bridge and viaduct; and, yielding to pressure, erected a new 125th Street station with a street-level waiting room described by the *Times* as having an interior "finished entirely in antique oak. The ticket agent's box is an elaborate piece of furniture in carved oak and ground glass. The main entrance is guarded by handsome steel gates of unique design. The new station is one of the finest in the city." Beneath the waiting room, a basement was created out of the space formerly used for a station in the old cut between 125th and 126th streets. Upstairs above the waiting room were open-air platforms.

Harlem was still a prosperous white community in 1897. Oscar Hammerstein, the German-American cigarmaker and theatrical impresario who had built the Harlem Opera House in 1889, lived in a fine house at 145 West 136th Street. Jacob Riis, in his 1890 book *How the Other Half Lives*, spoke with respect and compassion of the city's black population, which had more than doubled in the previous decade with the overflow from Southern cities: "There is no more clean and orderly community in New York than the new settlement of colored people that is growing up on the East Side from Yorkville to Harlem. . . . Cleanliness is the characteristic of the negro in his new surroundings, as it was his virtue in the old. . . . Nevertheless, he has always had to pay higher rents . . . for the poorest and most stinted rooms. The reason advanced for this systematic robbery is that white people will not live in the same house with colored tenants, or even in a house recently occupied by negroes, and that consequently its selling value is injured."

Roughly 70 percent of New Yorkers in 1901 lived in 83,000 tenement houses—five-, six-, even seven-story wood and masonry structures, each ninety feet long, in 100' x 25' lots with only tiny air shafts to provide light and air (they were often blocked by refuse), and provided with minimal indoor plumbing only because outhouses would have taken too much space. In 1901 a law was passed to prevent further construction of such buildings, which quickly were called "old law" tenements. Black New Yorkers in 1901 were concentrated in the Tenderloin area west of Herald Square, where some tenements had recently been displaced by a new store put up for R. H. Macy Co. Other tenements were coming down to make way for lofts, hotels, office buildings, and Pennsylvania Station. Where were the old slum dwellers to go?

As it happened, excavation was under way in Harlem at the time for the new I.R.T. subway under Lenox Avenue. Developers were putting up so many new Harlem apartment houses in anticipation of the subway that within a few years there was a tremendous oversupply. On block after block stood virtually empty buildings. Seeing all those displaced blacks downtown in the Tenderloin section and all those vacant apartments uptown, Philip A. Payton, a black real estate operator, recognized an opportunity: he approached landlords and guaranteed premium rents on condition that they accept black tenants. Many landlords balked; others leapt at the chance to increase their rents, and for the first time in its history New York had decent housing available to black residents.

Harlem's good neighborhoods never did include upper Park Avenue, part of the working-class East Harlem section whose tenements housed successive generations of immigrant German, Irish, Jewish, Italian, Scandinavian, and—ultimately—Puerto Rican families. Politicians appealed to them with promises to remove the New York Central tracks above the avenue north of 96th Street. On October 24, 1929, as Wall Street took its dive, a firm of Philadelphia traffic engineers submitted to Mayor Walker a $1 billion plan for traffic relief that called, among other things, for decking over Park Avenue north of 96th Street. From building line to building line, a through highway at the fourth-story level would carry cars and trucks above the railroad viaduct and across the Harlem River up to Gun Hill Road in the Bronx and beyond. Beneath the highway would be space for storage, garages, kitchens, and the like. The engineers of Day & Zimmerman predicted that such a project would lead to construction of buildings like those that flanked the avenue south of 96th Street.

Fiorello H. La Guardia, Republican-Fusion candidate for mayor, attacked the plan in a fiery City Club luncheon speech. The city's bonded indebtedness already amounted to $750 million, he said, and it had committed itself to $400 to $500 million more. "Where are the funds coming from for this proposed traffic plan? . . . It is all very well to bring out a traffic relief plan on paper in October before election but what does the present administration plan to do with it? Place it in a drawer after election to bring out again in a slightly different form four years hence?"

Mass meetings protested the decking of upper Park Avenue. A priest said it would produce a "gloomy cavern" illuminated by artificial light, an ideal nesting place for gangsters and thugs. Charles A. Gristede, the grocer, was named chairman of a citizens' committee to campaign against the elevated highway project. The Harlem Board of Commerce asked the Board of Estimate to take no steps to carry out the proposal. Decking the avenue would create an "outrageous" condition in which buildings on upper Park Avenue would be unrentable below the fourth story. A more feasible plan would be to place the tracks in a tunnel and tear down the viaduct north of 96th Street. A bill to prepare for condemnation of the overhead structure was introduced in the legislature in February 1930. Mayor Walker, at a 1931 meeting of the Board of Estimate, rejected a proposal that the city and the New York Central jointly share the cost of tearing down the viaduct; the city, he said, could not afford to meet its part of the expense. Engineers estimated that placing the tracks in a tunnel would cost $100 to $200 million.

Eugene A. Walsh, chairman of the Real Estate Committee of the Harlem Board of Commerce, blamed the railroad viaduct for depressed property values on upper Park Avenue. The city, he said, was losing nearly $9 million a year in taxes as compared with assessments south of 96th Street. On the 1927 tax rate of 2.72 percent of assessed valuation, the city collected $10,286,946 in taxes on Park Avenue area south from 96th Street to 57th and only $1,453,628 from the stretch of territory to the north. For the New York Central to operate its trains practically on the doorsteps of the residents of upper Park Avenue discouraged improvements in that section. Assessed valuations on land and improvements on both sides of Park from 96th to 135th streets in 1931 were $11,405,505, as compared with $181,414,692 for an area of identical size between 57th and 96th streets.

"Let us assume that the city's share of the cost reaches $100 million," said Walsh. "If at the end of ten years the removal of the viaduct resulted in the improvement of the upper section of Park Avenue amounting to one half the value of the buildings erected south of 96th Street during the past ten years, the additional return to the city in taxes would be nearly $5 million annually, or almost twice as much as would be required for interest and amortization on the city's investment."

Two months later, Manhattan's new borough president, Samuel Levy, announced a proposal to put the railroad tracks north of 96th Street into a $200 million extension to the Park Avenue tunnel that would dip under the bed of the Harlem River as far as Mott Haven in the Bronx. "I am not prepared to say how this might be divided between the city and the railroad," said Levy. "The money is an important factor, of course, but this improvement must come." He mentioned the possibility of state aid, but with none forthcoming, talk of extending the tunnel under upper Park Avenue faded once again.

More pressing was the need to clear Harlem's slums. The City Housing Authority, established in 1934, had little money with which to construct new buildings. Harlem suffered riots in 1935 as the need for livable low-cost housing grew more desperate. On December 3, 1935, Mayor La Guardia, Governor Lehman, and Eleanor Roosevelt opened the nation's first public housing. The eight-building City Housing Authority complex with 123 apartments was on the lower East Side (between 2nd and 3rd streets, Avenue A and First Avenue), not in Harlem. It marked the start, nevertheless, of a citywide program that would grow to have 178,801 apartments in 318 projects housing 560,000 people— about the population of New Orleans.

The Harlem River Houses (seven red brick structures, four and five stories high, with trees, plazas, a nursery, a health clinic, and social rooms) opened on October 1, 1937, at 151st Street and the Harlem River Drive—the city's first federally financed, federally constructed public housing. Would-be tenants of the 577 apartments were carefully screened. East Harlem from 97th to 133rd Street remained a warren of old-law tenements in which black, white, and Hispanic families existed in mutual squalor.

Less to make life easier for Harlem residents than to clear the streets of pushcart peddlers and put a roof over their heads, Mayor La Guardia built food markets (later called La Marqueta) under the railroad tracks between 111th and 116th streets. As East Harlem became El Barrio ("the district") and Spanish became its lingua franca, the produce at La Marqueta came to have a Caribbean character, with breadfruit, chayote, cherimoya, and mangoes seen in great profusion.

East Harlem was still racially mixed when slum clearance finally began in the summer of 1946 with ground-breaking ceremonies for the first of nine developments that would face on Park Avenue. James Weldon Johnson—lawyer, author, civil rights leader—had with his younger brother John Rosamond written "Lift Every Voice and Sing," an 1899 song that became known as the black national anthem. The James Weldon Johnson Houses were state financed. Governor Thomas E. Dewey, Mayor William F. O'Dwyer, and city construction co-ordinator Robert Moses helped dig up the first spadeful of earth as neighborhood schoolchildren, black and white, looked on.

Moses, in many ways the most powerful man present, had not yet embarked on his wholesale destruction of communities to make way for the Cross-Bronx Expressway and Lincoln Center; his autocratic ways were just beginning to draw heat from community leaders. Moses asked the public for patience and co-operation. People who protested evictions, he said, faced a choice between "a three- to four-year program" or a "ten-year program" of slum clearance. Building on vacant land, he said, meant that slums would stay.

The Johnson project would house 1,310 families, eight or nine families to a floor, in ten six-, ten- and fourteen-story buildings between Third and Park avenues from 112th Street to 115th. Originally tenanted primarily by poor Italian and Hispanic families, the houses would by 1988 have 1,736 Puerto Ricans, 1,552 blacks, 31 whites, and 94 "others," mostly Hispanic, whose overall gross incomes averaged $10,865.

Two days after the Johnson Houses opened in December 1948, the Abraham Lincoln Houses opened between Park and Fifth avenues, 132nd Street to 135th. This project, replacing a slum area in which the writer James Baldwin had grown up, accommodates 1,286 families, most of them Puerto Rican. When the statue *Lincoln and Boy* by Charles Keck was dedicated in February 1949 on a play-

ABOVE: *At the end of the tunnel, the beginning of squalor* (1988 photo)

ABOVE: *Tenants in the Johnson Houses and other projects look down on Metro-North trains* (1988 photo)

ground in the project, an official said the proportion of white families was "hardly any." (There were eight in 1988.)

Voters in November 1949 approved three housing propositions, making another $300 million in loan funds available for public housing. By that time the City Housing authority had spent roughly $600 million on projects in the various boroughs and about 41,000 families lived in public housing; the authority hoped to have 500,000 families in public housing by 1957.

There was still talk of widening Park Avenue north of 96th Street to the Harlem River and eliminating the overhead railroad tracks. As late as May 1956 Mayor Robert F. Wagner, Jr. said the city had plans to widen Park Avenue for two miles south of the river; the project would be undertaken "sometime in the future." "Park Avenue is up to 96th Street one of our greatest thoroughfares, a symbol all over the world of the urban living that is New York. And yet, north of 96th Street, where the railroad runs above ground, there are slums and some decay." Plans for improving the avenue, said Wagner, depended to some extent on what the railroad intended to do about Grand Central Terminal (the New York Central had said it might make the newly opened Mott Haven station in the Bronx its main depot in the city because of the high cost of operating Grand Central). "In the meantime," Wagner went on, "as housing projects bordering on upper Park Avenue are being built, they are being set back from the present street lines to permit the future development of Park Avenue whenever it occurs."

Within a year of these remarks the Housing Authority was razing 137 acres of East Harlem tenements—some of the city's worst slums—in the blocks between Madison Avenue and the East River from 97th Street to 115th. Where blocks of musty old tenements had stood, sunlight and air were pouring in for the first time in decades. A dozen projects, four of them in a strip of superblocks that combined normal city blocks, were going to house 13,500 families in the city's largest concentration of public housing. Scarcely a street in the area was untouched. Structures worth saving were left as an invitation to rehabilitation by private enterprise. The 448-family Lexington Houses, opened in May 1951, are between 98th and 99th streets from Park to Third avenues. The George Washington Carver Houses, opened early in 1958, occupy most of the seven blocks between 99th and 106th streets from Madison Avenue to Park.

In the state-financed Carver Houses, 5 percent of the units were designed for the elderly, 1 percent for the handicapped. And although the project was named for the famous black botanist of Alabama's Tuskegee Insitute, the first tenants were white. Jacob Rosenberg, seventy-two, and his wife, Anna, sixty-nine, were tickled pink with their new home, which had an electric range, a seven-cubic-foot refrigerator, doorways without sills, radiators that gave out 10 percent more heat than ordinary radiators, mechanical openers for windows, nonslip ceramic tile in the bathroom, and grab bars along the wall by the tub and sink. The bedroom had double exposure for more air and sunlight.

In September 1963, six weeks before President Kennedy's assassination, Herbert H. Lehman Village was dedicated at 108th Street between Madison and Park avenues. The Kennedy administration had just launched a campaign to induce Congress to approve new funds for low-rent public housing, and Robert C. Weaver, administrator of the Housing and Home Financing Agency and the president's chief advisor on housing, warned that a halt in the program would mean "the continued shame of needless poverty and misery in the richest land the world has ever known."

Work was progressing at the time on the federally-funded DeWitt Clinton Houses, which extend from Park Avenue to Lexington on the two blocks between 104th and 106th streets and the two between 108th and 110th. Dividing the site were some sound apartment structures; these were preserved. Work was also going forward on the city-financed Sen. Robert A. Taft Houses, named for the Ohio solon who had sponsored the 1949 housing act that provided federal funds for slum-clearance projects. This project rose between Fifth and Park avenues from 112th to 115th streets. Both the Clinton and Taft houses were finished late in 1965. Incomes of tenants in the Clinton Houses in 1988 averaged $12,213, in the Taft Houses $13,198.

Low rents made housing available to many middle-income families that private builders could not reach. Annual income limits for large families were originally $6,900 in projects financed by the city, $5,900 for state-aided apartments, $4,000 plus $100 allowance for each child in federally aided projects. Income limits for small families were lower. (Nearly all the projects were federalized over the years, says Val Coleman, a spokesman for the City Housing

Authority, and all public housing is subject to the same rule. "There are no class distinctions between the city, state, and federal projects. We try desperately to maintain a mix in each project. Tenants all pay 30 percent of their income on rent.")

While the bright, airy, hygienic new high-rise projects seemed an improvement over the vile tenements, some critics, including Lewis Mumford, suggested that it might have been more humane—and more economical—to rehabilitate buildings that were still "decently habitable" rather than resettle most of their occupants in even worse quarters.

Jane Jacobs questioned the whole idea of projects in a world of crime-ridden cities. She maintained that cities were safer and more pleasant when they consisted of neighborhood communities where people lived in relatively small, low-priced buildings, knew their neighbors, and hung out on stoops rather than in the depersonalized environment characteristic of housing projects. "In some rich city neighborhoods where there is the do-it-yourself surveillance such as residential Park Avenue . . . street watchers are hired," wrote Jacobs. "The monotonous sidewalks of residential Park Avenue . . . are surprisingly little used; their putative users are populating, instead, the interesting store-, bar-, and restaurant-filled sidewalks of Lexington Avenue and Madison Avenue to east and west, and the cross streets leading to these. A network of doormen and superintendents, of delivery boys and nursemaids, a form of hired neighborhood, keeps residential Park Avenue supplied with eyes. At night, with the security of the doorman as bulwark, dog walkers safely venture forth and supplement the doormen. But this street is so blank of built-in eyes, so devoid of concrete reasons for using or watching it instead of turning the first corner off of it, that if its rents were to slip below the point where they could support a plentiful hired neighborhood of doormen and elevator men, it would undoubtedly become a woefully dangerous street." Slums have "built-in eyes." Projects do not.

But wasn't Jacobs being simplistic? Lewis Mumford thought so. "Everything that Jane Jacobs has said in condemnation of the sterile and inhumanly hostile projects is true," he wrote, "but I hasten to add they would not be any better if on her pet formula the designers had multiplied the number of streets and lined them with shops, and thus produced even more stifling and strangulating forms of congestion. The rapes, the robberies, the destructive delinquencies, the ever-threatening violence, for which she naively believes she has found a simple planning antidote, would still be there, since these are symptoms, not just of bad planning, or even of poverty, but of a radically deficient and depleted mode of life, a life from which the most destitute slum dwellers and the most affluent suburbanites equally, though in different ways, suffer. There is no planning cure for this machine-centered existence which produces only psychotic stresses, meaningless 'happenings,' and murderous fantasies of revenge . . . If this remedy were a sound one, 18th century London, which met all of Mrs. Jacobs' planning prescriptions, would not have been the nest of violence and delinquency it actually was . . .

"Jane Jacobs pointed out a fact to which many planners and administrators had been indifferent—that a neighborhood is not just a collection of buildings but a tissue of social relations and a cluster of warm, personal sentiments, associated with the familiar faces of the doctor, the priest, the butcher and the baker and the candlestickmaker, not least with the idea of 'home.' Sanitary, steam-heated apartments, she observed, are no substitute for warm-hearted neighbors. Even if they live in verminous cold-water flats and chat across the air shaft, the little changes of scene as a woman walks her baby or tells her troubles with her husband to the druggist, the little flirtations that often attend the purchase of a few oranges or potatoes, all season a housewife's day and mean more than mere physical shelter. It is no real gain to supplant this. . . .

"Mrs. Jacobs gave firm shape to a misgiving that many people had begun to express, for she saw more deeply into the plight of both those who were evicted and those who came back to living in a . . . sterilized barracks. These barracks had been conceived in terms of bureaucratic regimentation, financial finagling, and administrative convenience, without sufficient thought to the diversities of personal and family life, thus producing a human void that matched the new architectural void. In this process, even valuable buildings, though cherished landmarks in the life of the community, are often destroyed so that the operation may 'start clean' without any encumbrances."

Park Avenue's encumbrance north of 96th Street was the railroad viaduct. Beginning in the summer of 1986 there was an added encumbrance: crack, a cheap, easily accessible, smokable cocaine derivative that also wreaked havoc in some Park Avenue families south of 96th. Even as the projects were clearing out East Harlem's slums, narcotics had begun their sinister invasion of the inner city. Jack Gelber's 1959 off-Broadway play *The Connection* about drug addiction enjoyed a run of 755 performances; Michael Gazzo's 1955 play on the same subject, *A Hatful of Rain*, had pioneered the genre. Addicts burglarized, robbed, and even killed to support their expensive habits. Locksmiths did a brisk business installing multiple burglar guards. But the plague had scarcely begun. Tenements in the shadow of the Park Avenue viaduct became infested with shooting galleries, crack parlors, and other vice dens. The city demolished them in the 1980s. Project residents started tenant patrols to protect their communities from drug dealers.

A federal project with ninety apartments had opened in the spring of 1970 on the east side of Park between 122nd and 123rd streets, and one for 150 families, built with funds left in the pipeline after the Carter administration, opened in June 1986 on the same side of the avenue between 119th and 122nd streets. But northern Park Avenue remained largely a wasteland.

On the east side of the avenue between 108th and 109th streets one hears the chatter and laughter of schoolchildren outside P.S. 108 (the Peter Minuit School). Farther north, in the mean street that is Park Avenue, a bleak scene confronts the nervous passerby. From 115th Street to 116th (Luis Muñoz Marin Boulevard) is a steep hill, icy in winter. Between 118th and 119th streets, on the west side of the avenue, someone lives in a mobile home. From 120th to 121st

This, too, is Park Avenue: an abandoned house in a vacant lot in East Harlem (1988 photo)

on the same side is the Center for Multiply Handicapped Children (the Robert D. Frost School). Grassy lawns with a deserted house mark the southwest corner of Park and 122nd Street. From 123rd to 124th is the parking lot of the North General Hospital ("We Serve Our Community") with its Helen Fuld School of Nursing. (Helen Fuld, who lived at 28 West 128th Street, was a major East Harlem property owner before and after World War I. In 1920 she raised rents and was fined for not supplying tenants with enough heat and water.) At 125th Street are the remnants of a small hotel, the Grand Union. The Arthur A. Schomburg Intermediate School is on the west blockfront between 127th and 128th streets; facing it across the avenue is a drug rehabilitation center in what once was a warehouse. Hookers patrol outside.

Clark & Wilkins, established in 1870, has a yard at the southeast corner of 128th Street with fencing, ironwork, and masonry. (A Bronx yard supplies Park Avenue residents south of 96th with firewood.) From 129th Street to 130th, on the east side of Park is a moving and storage company in a blocklong turn-of-the-century building. A six-story factory building is at the northwest corner of 130th Street. A few blocks farther on is Exit 20 off the FDR Drive. Filling stations, a police precinct house, hospital ambulances, prostitution, and open drug dealing dominate this part of Park Avenue. Not a pretty place in which to raise children, it is where many hardworking New Yorkers must live.

Only a third of East Harlem's project tenants in the late 1980s were welfare recipients; scarcely 27 percent (mostly women with dependent children) depended entirely on welfare, as compared with 23 percent in projects citywide. The vast majority of people living on Park Avenue north of 96th Street were decent, industrious, working-class citizens, some of whose incomes had risen close to the point where they would have to move out of city housing.

Thirty percent of income for rent is too much, says Val Coleman of the Housing Authority. "That's an increase from a more reasonable 25 percent before Reagan. The higher percentage has done enormous damage to public housing because it tends to drive out the working families. Without the working families public housing deteriorates. The kids don't have role models, and the whole thing crumbles as it has in much of the country. In other cities they've made no efforts toward economic integration of the developments. As the ethnicity of the neighborhoods has changed, the projects have changed—which means they're doing their job. They should be more racially integrated but that's not an easy thing to accomplish."

Between 111th and 116th streets, La Marqueta in 1988 was being used by junkies. The city had turned this and some other muncipal markets over to merchants' associations in the fiscal crisis of the 1970s. From roughly 1977 to 1986 the merchants managed La Marqueta, and they let the old buildings deteriorate. The city still made capital repairs to the sheds, but the repairs did not keep up with the decline. Conditions finally became so bad that the city decided to seek private development money to refurbish the market. The

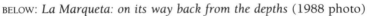

BELOW: *La Marqueta: on its way back from the depths* (1988 photo)

ABOVE: *Breadfruit? Chayotes? Cherimoyas? Mangoes? La Marqueta has them all* (1988 photo)

Department of Ports and Terminals selected a developer, SanJames Realty, headed by a man with experience in the South Bronx and other Hispanic areas. Jim Sanchez assured the city that he could obtain $7 million in private funds to rehabilitate La Marqueta as a community marketplace, retaining its neighborhood flavor and expanding it.

But tenants obliged to pay 30 percent of their small incomes on rent have little left to buy other necessities, much less luxuries. While some New Yorkers paid even larger percentages, few Park Avenue residents south of 96th Street spent that much of their income on shelter. At 98th Street and Park a developer early in 1989 was offering one-bedroom co-ops in the Carnegie Terrace, an "elegantly renovated 19th Century building," for $99,000. One-bedroom co-ops a few blocks to the south sold for three and four times as much.

19

Prestige at a Price

The appalling figures came popping up into his brain. Last year his income had been $980,000. But he had to pay out $21,000 a month for the $1.8 million loan he had taken out to buy the apartment. What was $21,000 a month to someone making a million a year? That was the way he had thought of it at the time—and in fact, it was merely a *crushing, grinding burden*—that was all! It came to $252,000 a year, none of it deductible, because it was a personal loan, not a mortgage. (The cooperative boards in Good Park Avenue Buildings like his didn't allow you to take out a mortgage on your apartment.) So, considering the taxes, it required $424,000 in income to pay the $252,000. Of the $560,000 remaining of his income last year, $44,400 was required for the apartment's monthly maintenance fees. . . . There was no getting out from under the $1.8 million loan, the crushing $21,000-a-month nut, without paying it off or selling the apartment and moving into one far smaller and more modest—*an impossibility*! There was no turning back! Once you had lived in a $2.6 million apartment on Park Avenue—it was impossible to live in a $1 million apartment. . . . What did a million get you today? At most, at most, at *most*: a three-bedroom apartment—no servants' rooms, no guest rooms, let alone dressing rooms and a sunroom—in a white-brick high-rise built east of Park Avenue in the 1960s with 8 ½-foot ceilings, a dining room but no library, an entry gallery the size of a closet, no fireplace, skimpy lumberyard moldings, if any, plasterboard walls that transmit whispers, and no private elevator stop.

—*The Bonfire of the Vanities* (1987)

POOR SHERMAN MCCOY is not alone. Tom Wolfe's protagonist has his counterpart, if on a less grandiose scale, up and down Park Avenue.

Money worries are not supposed to trouble Park Avenue. It has developed a reputation for affluence that is sometimes at odds with reality. Sixty years before Wolfe, in its July 2, 1927, issue, R. J. Cuddihy's *Literary Digest* ran a piece entitled "How Our Cliff-Dwelling Plutocrats Roost in Park Avenue."

Citing the Park Avenue Association as its authority, the article rhapsodized, "From 34th to 96th Street, a distance of about three miles, no less than 16,000 persons, roughly 4,000 families. For 1927 the Association expects them to spend the staggering total of $280 million, or $70,000 per family. The average income, after allowing for savings and reinvestments, is probably in excess of $100,000. Well may the Association say that 'Park Avenue leads the world in concentrated buying power.' Nothing like it has ever been seen on earth before. The Association discreetly refrains from estimating the total spent for liquor, but the *New York World*, following the same statistical analysis, computes an outlay of $15 million, or just under $4,000 per family, as compared to $15,000 for rent, furnishings, including pictures and antiques, $8,000 for food and restaurants, $5,000 for jewelry, $4,000 for motorcars and garaging, $4,500 for men's clothes, $21,000 for women's clothes (one mother and one daughter). To live on or near the Avenue places one automatically on the key sucker list of the country as one of the responsibilities of the office."

The chief source for the piece was Stuart Chase's May 25th *New Republic* article. "There are in the United States today," Chase had written, "more than 15,000 millionaires; 207 individuals paid taxes on incomes of $1 million or more in 1926—the greatest number on record. Even the fabulous earnings during the war did not produce such a crop of million-dollar incomes.

"Of the 15,000 millionaires, nearly 4,000 live in Greater New York, such an unparalleled concentration that it is safe to estimate that the overwhelming majority live on Park Avenue or its immediate vicinity. We know of apartment houses with 60 millionaires under a single roof! Along the whole stretch of the avenue, perhaps 3,000 are on exhibition, while another 1,000 have the spending of the income on $1 million—$50,000 and upwards a year. And spend it. For here live the ultimate Joneses; if we can keep up with them, life has no further crowns, no further penalties. Through the service entrances, and up the service elevators, pour the quintessence of what money can buy. Lorelei Lee, we remember, turned back contemptuously from all the capitals of Europe, and headed straight for Park Avenue, the only spot from which shopping could be conducted properly. Nor could one ask for a sounder judge of values. . . .

"The Avenue spends $280 million a year, according to a recent conservative estimate, and the income of its average family probably exceeds $100,000. . . .

"Within the limits of standardized steel and veneer masonry construction, the apartments do what they can. One hears of a single bathroom in jade and gold costing $35,000. One hears of 'duplex roof' apartments, which are really separate houses perched on the tops of the monoliths, with light on four sides, renting as high as $40,000 a year. Mr. Adolph Zukor leases nine rooms at $4,000 per room. Twenty thousand dollars a year for space below the roof is a common figure. For the most exclusive section of the avenue, the average rental is in the neighborhood of $1,500 per room per year. The 'co-operative' apartment house, so-called, is here the order of the day. In a co-operative, one buys one's apartment outright. The residents then own the building, the roof and walls complete, while the speculative builder, not, it is said, without a smile, steps out of the picture altogether. It costs about $7,500 per room to buy into a co-operative—say $75,000 for a family home. This is obviously less costly than paying the current rentals, but one bears the not inconsiderable risks of the future of New York real estate. After all, there is a limit to the number of sardines which can be packed in a can.

"Even at these princely figures the Park Avenue resident pays only from five to ten percent of his income for rent or its equivalent, in contrast with the twenty-five to thirty-five percent paid by the wage earner. But a man who needs, according to current market quotations, twenty-five thousand dollars to finance a debutante daughter through one season, must save somewhere.

"The most luxurious apartment on the avenue is held by a bachelor, it is on the roof, it contains a ballroom eighty by forty feet, and a living room two-thirds as spacious. For its lordly floors, rare rugs have been especially woven, while all dressing cabinets have been built into the walls of the bedrooms . . . .

"By and large, the important factor is not the outlay for rent but for furnishings. One simply is not settled if the decorations do not reach $100,000—the operation being frequently on the principle of giving the interior decorator *carte blanche*. For the fauna of the Avenue is perhaps equally compounded of real swells, and of butter-and-egg men whose children are destined to be real swells. (Not to mention a liberal sprinkling of apartments reigned over by that particular variety of blonde which gentlemen are said to prefer.) . . . Of servants' bedrooms, the average size is 6 x 8 feet.

"To many dwellers on the avenue, success has come from a spirited sales-manship. . . . Here the American dollar reaches its dizziest point. For the towering and relentless rectangles of this street, the richest nation which the world has ever seen consecrates its cash balance, develops its personality in ten easy lessons, reads the confessions of those who have climbed to the stars from one suspender, improves its table manners, learns the rite of the cocktail, consolidates button factories . . . and dedicates its life."

At the time Pease & Elliman, real estate brokers, were promoting co-op apartments at 812 Park. A co-op, said the advertisements, was a better buy than a private house: a four-story private house on Park Avenue would require a cash investment of at least $125,000 in addition to a mortgage of $100,000 and yearly maintenance—including taxes, interest on the mortgage, operating costs, and heat—of $13,000. Annual maintenance charges on a $66,000 duplex of eleven rooms on the seventh and eighth floors of 812 Park would come to only $6,600. Also available: nine-room duplexes at $25,000 to $48,000; ten-room duplexes at $37,00 to $55,000; eleven-room duplexes at $45,000 to $76,000; thirteen-room duplexes at $69,000 to $90,000; nine-room maisonettes at $36,000; and twelve- to sixteen-room roof garden triplexes at $78,000 to $118,000. The numbers, quaint today, were whopping big prices in a time when clerks earned $18 per week and few executives had salaries as high as $10,000 per year.

Translating dollar amounts of earlier years into today's terms is a treacherous business, but even when multiplied by 7 to bring them into line with the 1989 Consumer Price Index the apartment prices look cheap.

In his book *A Writer's Capital*, Louis Auchincloss said, "One never gets far discussing who is rich and who isn't. We can only state the facts. By 1927, when I was ten, we lived in the winter in a brownstone house on 91st Street with two nurses, a cook, a kitchen maid, a waitress, and a chambermaid. We had a summer house on Long Island which a caretaker later kept open for winter weekends. For July and August we rented a large shingled cottage in Bar Harbor. We had a chauffeur and two cars which rose to four as the children learned to drive. My parents belonged to half a dozen clubs and all this was maintained on an annual income of less than $100,000 out of which Father was able to make substantial savings."

By 1988 some salaried executives on Park Avenue received in excess of $5 million per year. (Others on the avenue had higher incomes based on larger net worth, but few commanded salary-and-bonus packages to match those of Steven Ross or Rand Araskog.) Instead of having 15,000 millionaires as in 1927, America had well over a million; thousands were millionaires in the classic sense of having annual incomes of $1 million or more, and some of these owned Park Avenue co-ops.

Cooperative ownership began in the mid-1880s, partly as a way to keep out undesirable tenants. Co-op plans languished in 1908, when a glut in apartment houses made rents comparatively cheap and landlords offered one or two months' free rent to lure tenants. Before 1920 there were probably no more than twenty-five cooperative apartment houses in the city, according to the *Real Estate Record*. The only co-ops on Park Avenue at the beginning of 1920 were 471 (replaced in 1958 by 475), 563, 823, 850, 863, 925, and 969.

Eight years later, as New York roared through the decade of bathtub gin, rental apartments abounded on Park Avenue despite an increase in cooperative plans. An apartment of eight rooms and three baths at 1133 Park, overlooking the avenue and decorated to order, was advertised at $425 per month. A spacious Park Avenue flat of seven rooms, three baths, with a twenty-four-foot living room and sixteen-foot gallery was offered at $300 per month. A sunny eight-room duplex, three baths, on an outside corner in the 70s rented for $358 per month.

In August 1928 apartments at 277 Park Avenue "Around an Acre of Garden" were offered "at surprisingly moderate rentals to complete the early renting of this large building": seven rooms, three baths at $408 per month; six rooms, two baths at $275; five rooms, two baths at $250. Across the avenue at the Marguery, 270 Park, a fourteen-room apartment with four baths rented for $833 per month, one with six rooms and three baths for $542 and up. Douglas L. Elliman advertised a four-room, one-bath apartment at 631 Park at $215 per month; eleven rooms, four baths at 830 Park for $633; eight rooms, three baths at 935 Park for $458; eight rooms, three baths at 1035 Park at $433; four rooms, one bath at 1225 Park for $212.50 and seven rooms, four baths at the same address for $320. A Buick sedan sold in 1928 for $2,045, a seven-passenger limousine for $2,145.

By the spring of 1930, when it looked as if the stock market crash six months earlier might have been an aberration, a seven-room apartment at 277 Park was offered at $350 instead of $408; eight rooms at 1035 Park at $416 instead of $433; five rooms and three baths at 1225 at $279.

Lack of demand would bring these rentals down further, and co-op prices would be slow to recover. In 1949, when two-bedroom houses in America sold, typically, for $10,000, a four-bedroom duplex off Park Avenue in the 60s, an apartment with a two-story living room and a woodburning fireplace in its 21' x 16' library, could be bought for $8,250 with monthly maintenance under $250.

Cooperative ownership plans of the 1920s and '30s had turned out to have what real estate people called "objectionable features," but by the early 1950s these had been eliminated and there was less chance of owners being stuck. If a tenant-owner could not meet his obligations, he did not have to forfeit his stock or lose his share of equity in the building; he had the right under his proprietary lease either to sell his stock or sublet his apartment, subject to approval by the co-op board of the sublessee. And instead of having nine to eighteen rooms, most buildings now had three- to six-room units, which not only made them more marketable in lean years but also made it possible to split the maintenance expenses, including mortgage and tax payments, among many more tenant-owners. In the late 1940s and early '50s, therefore, many Park Avenue buildings that had been co-ops before the Depression went co-op again. And many rental buildings became co-ops as the Korean War reminded New Yorkers how scarce housing had been during World War II. Prices crept up but hardly went through the roof.

In autumn 1958, the author bought a modest eight-room, four-bath duplex penthouse at Park and 81st Street for $51,500, with monthly maintenance just short of $400. A smaller Park Avenue apartment on a high floor in the 70s with two master bedrooms, two baths, large living room was on the market at $25,000 ("seller will accept terms") with monthly maintenance of $275.50. Advertisements included such offerings as "Park Ave 12 rooms for rent $800 per month outstanding bldg corner high floor 4 master brs and library," "1120 Park, 3 ½ rms spacious high ceiling 9th floor luxury suite living room 18' x 18', excellent dining area, $241.67 monthly," and "Park Ave luxury 6, 3 baths, perfect condition $28,000."

Let it be noted, though, that America's economy was in recession; unemployment was at a postwar high, the median U.S. family income was still only $5,087 per year. A Brooks Brothers cotton oxford shirt sold for $6.50 ($7 in blue). In thirty years the median family income would rise to about $30,000, and the Brooks Brothers shirt that had sold for $6.50 would be $42 (and would go to $45 in early 1989). The subway ride that cost fifteen cents from 1953 to 1966 would be $1. And the daily *Times* would cost thirty-five cents. But not even college tuitions and doctor bills would escalate by the same factor as prices of apartments on Park Avenue and other favored sections of Manhattan.

Even in relatively good times there can be economic setbacks, and they hit some people harder than others. In the Nixon recession of 1969–70, the first Wall Street brokerage house to come acropper was McDonnell and Co., a prestigious sixty-five-year-old firm whose principal uptown office was at street level in the Postum Building, 250 Park Avenue. McDonnell's chief executive officer was T. Murray McDonnell. His sister Anne had married Henry Ford II in what was described as the "wedding of the century," and the McDonnells— part of what Stephen Birmingham has called "the McDonnell-Murray-Cuddihy Irish mafia clan" that had made Southampton such a fashionable Long Island summer resort—had at one point owned New York's largest apartment: a duplex and simplex combined at 910 Fifth Avenue to accommodate the fourteen children of James Francis McDonnell and his wife, the former Anna Murray. Unfortunately, Murray McDonnell had proved a better salesman than manager. According to Birmingham, after the collapse of the firm on March 12, 1970, one of McDonnell's sisters confided to a friend that she might, in some discreet manner, have to take in boarders to help pay the maintenance and upkeep on her big, antique-filled apartment at 660 Park. "But no matter what has happened," she said, "nothing will ever persuade me to to get rid of my butler Paul." Paul stood behind Madame's chair at dinner, announcing in French the name of each course as it was served.

When 733 Park was finished in 1971 the least expensive unit carried an initial price of $270,000. A typical apartment consisted (and still consists) of nine rooms and four and a half baths. The duplex penthouse, also nine rooms but more grandly laid out, was priced at $526,500, with a monthly maintenance of $3,137. Those were hellishly high prices in the early 1970s, and it was a long time before all the apartments were sold. Condominiums, whose tenant-owners can finance their purchases and need not be approved by a board as in a co-op, were unknown in Manhattan until the 1970s and, on Park Avenue, until the 1980s. In a condo building one had no idea who one's neighbors might be. Condo prices, though, could be at least as high as co-op prices.

In 1973, as U.S. troops pulled out of South Vietnam, the petroleum-producing cartel cut off sales of oil to Europe, Japan, and America. Soviet purchases of American grain triggered a spiraling in food costs. Prices began a steep ascent, the world was plunged into the worst economic recession seen since the 1930s, and a devaluation of the dollar (to boost exports) increased prices of imports, including oil, and, soon, of everything else. Instead of the deflation experienced in the 1930s, there was inflation. By 1977 apartments at 417 Park were selling for between $12,000 and $14,000 per room, with monthly maintenance charges of more than $162 per room. There were occasional bargains; one family had reportedly paid only about half the asking price for their apartment because the Southern woman who was selling it was in a hurry to move back South.

City police, firemen, teachers, transit workers, and other employees demanded better pay; the easiest way to get money for higher wages and salaries was to boost real estate taxes. Those taxes have not risen as much as most other things. In June 1954 the City Council set the basic real estate tax at $3.68 for each $100,000 in property valuation, the highest it had ever been. By 1989 it was a little more than $9. The higher tax meant higher maintenance charges and higher commercial rents (passed along in higher restaurant tabs, higher doctor bills, and the like). Higher commercial rents forced more than a few business concerns to leave the city. Landlords complained of higher fuel bills, but they could not fairly blame the higher rents they charged on higher property taxes which had not even tripled in a quarter century. After reducing expenses by putting in automatic elevators and slashing payrolls, landlords were simply "maximizing returns," boosting rents to ten and fifteen times their 1954 levels.

And a benign city administration did nothing to stem the avarice that was forcing more and more businesses to seek space in the long-neglected teens and twenties, where rents were lower, and even out of the city, where rents were lower still and there was no occupancy tax. At the same time, new technologies (computers, modems, fax machines) were threatening to make urban concentration of office personnel less essential.

Higher property taxes have nothing to do with higher apartment prices. What drove prices up in the 1970s and '80s was simply rising demand and, as the stock market soared, growing affluence. By early 1984, a two-bedroom, two-bath apartment in a new building sold for close to $300,000 or rented for $2,000 per month. This assumed standard "luxury" amenities such as a doorman and a laundry room in a building located in almost any decent Manhattan neighborhood. By year's end co-op and condominium prices were pushing $380,000, and when they dipped to $350,000 in 1985 there was some distress among developers and brokers. Would the astronomical increases of the early 1980s now give way to astronomical decreases? But between January and July 1987 the average price of a "typical luxury two-bedroom unit" jumped from $387,000 to $430,000. Park Avenue apartments often cost more; and for extra-large apartments, always in short supply, the prices could be stupendous.

In July 1987 a four-bedroom penthouse co-op on Park between 92nd and 95th Streets sold for $3.8 million. In September 1987 a sixteen-room co-op in a prewar building on Park between 70th and 73rd Streets sold for $5 million. Cooperatives made up 86 percent of the market, as compared to 14 percent for condominiums. The average asking price per room was $63,762 for a co-op studio, $83,100 for a condo studio; $71,705 in a co-op one-bedroom, $99,149 in a comparable condo; $82,908 to $104,445 in a co-op two-bedroom, $127,569 to $129,795 in a comparable condo; $216,898 in a co-op apartment of more than two bedrooms, $284,427 in a comparable condo apartment. Thus in October 1987 a nine-room co-op on Park between 86th and 89th streets sold for $1,675,000 through Douglas Elliman.

In more than a few instances, such large apartments were occupied by only one person. And because part of their monthly maintenance was tax-deductible as interest on a mortgage, co-op owners were being subsidized to an even greater extent than tenants in the projects north of 96th Street, virtually all of whom paid a much higher perentage of their income on shelter than did owners of posh co-ops.

After the October 1987 stock market meltdown many apartments went begging, but the high end of the market remained strong. In February 1988 a nine-room co-op on Park at 78th Street was reportedly sold for $2.5 million through Elizabeth Stribling and Associates. A six-room co-op at 84th and Park was sold soon afterward for $1 million through Corcoran Group. In May 1988 a seven-room co-op between 76th and 79th streets sold for $2.9 million through Halstead Properties. In June 1988 a fourteen-room co-op at Park and 66th Street sold for $3.5 million through William B. May. In July a ten-room apartment on Park in the low 60s sold for $3.3 million through Douglas Elliman-Gibbons & Ives. In August 1988 an eight-room co-op on Park in the low 70s sold for $2.6 million through William B. May, and one of comparable size in the high 80s sold for $1,269,000 through M. J. Raynes.

In the fall of 1988 Sotheby's advertised an 8,000-square-foot Park Avenue duplex penthouse in the 60s, "the ultimate penthouse . . . 5 woodburning fireplaces. Sunny, large terrace. Asking $9,200,000." No prices were given for a ten-room triplex penthouse in the 70s or for the "baronial splendor" of twelve rooms with twelve-foot ceilings listed by William B. May in "one of Park Ave's finest prewar buildings."

Most Park Avenue residents had bought at much lower prices and felt themselves rich when they looked at such numbers. Offers from the 6 percenters were certainly tempting, but, as Sherman McCoy said, where could one move? "What did a million get you today?"

2O.

Afterwords

PARK AVENUE'S PLANTED MEDIAN STRIPS, once more than fifty feet wide, have all been twenty-two feet wide since the early 1930s. (The median strips of Park Avenue South, installed in the spring of 1962, scarcely span five feet.) Writing about the avenue in 1927, Stuart Chase said, "The park space in its center, under which rumble the trains of the New York Central, burns its dull stone pavement without a touch of green, but from Fifty-seventh north it blossoms into a strip of formal garden with grass and shrubs. Thus there is, in places, a park on Park Avenue, contrary to the philology of most streets."

Whether or not it can accurately be said to have a park, photographs of the avenue south of 57th Street taken before 1927 show small trees in tubs on grassy strips threaded with broad footpaths and park benches. What Chase had seen was the center malls in the process of being narrowed, after which they were resodded, landscaped, and eventually planted in season with flowers.

"Misty days like this created a peculiar ashy blue light on Park Avenue," wrote Tom Wolfe in *The Bonfire of the Vanities*. "But once they stepped out from under the awning over the entrance . . . such radiance! The median strip on Park was a swath of yellow tulips . . . There were thousands of them, thanks to the dues apartment owners like Sherman paid to a gardening service . . . There was something heavenly about the yellow glow of all the tulips."

Those tulips began with Mary Lasker, who never lived on Park Avenue but had a lot to do with making it burst into bloom each spring and remain in flower much of the year.

Mary Woodard, Radcliffe '23, was hired by Reinhardt Galleries, married

Paul Reinhardt in 1926, and became the only art dealer on 57th Street with a degree in art history. After a divorce, she developed the idea of "Hollywood Patterns," inexpensive dress patterns with the cachet of *Vogue* magazine and the glamour of movie stars. When she met Albert Lasker in 1939 she was well established in a business career and living in a penthouse at 400 East 52nd Street. Lasker was a Chicago advertising mogul, head of the big Lord & Thomas agency, who had made a fortune promoting Lucky Strike, Kleenex, Kotex, and Pepsodent. He was sixty, Mary less than forty when they were married in June 1940. They soon set up residence in Beekman Place, Lasker doing business out of the Lord & Thomas offices at 247 Park Avenue; in 1942 he quit advertising altogether (Lord & Thomas became Foote, Cone & Belding).

As a memorial to her mother, who had died the year before, Mrs. Lasker in 1941 purchased two or three million winter chrysanthemum seeds and presented the plants to the city for planting in Central Park and elsewhere. She then got the idea of planting bulbs in the center mall of Park Avenue south of Grand Central and in the late 1940s imported 40,000 bulbs from Holland. City officials told her there was too much soot and grime north of

BELOW: *Park Avenue's center mall once offered a pleasant promenade past St. Bart's and the Ambassador Hotel* (1922 photo from *Old New York, Yesterday and Today* courtesy New-York Historical Society)

the terminal for the plantings to flourish, but Mary and her sister, Mrs. Allmon Fordyce, were not easily discouraged. They persuaded the city to make test plantings, obtained cooperation from Mayor Wagner and Parks Commissioner Moses, and paid for the initial planting. Other donors financed the planting of two additional blocks, the city took over where Mrs. Lasker had begun; and by 1960, as Lasker's biographer John Gunther wrote that year, "twenty-two blocks of the plaisance of Park Avenue are transformed into a glowing carpet of tulips every spring." City officials took over the Park Avenue Malls Planting Project with continuing gifts from private citizens, including 500 trees from Mrs. Lasker.

The Park Avenue Association founded in 1922 by H. Gordon Duval persuaded the city to edge the avenue's center malls with ornamental fences. The fences, which may still be seen in the avenue's Murray Hill blocks, were hardly an improvement. In December 1966 Thomas P. F. Hoving, administrator of recreation and cultural affairs in the Lindsay administration (his father was a longtime Park Avenue resident), announced that the fences around the center mall of one block would be removed. Said Hoving, "Traffic Commissioner Henry Barnes and I do not see eye to eye on some matters, and I was trying to figure out some way to propose this to him when I got a letter from him a few days ago. He said he felt the fences were a traffic hazard and should be removed. We're going to try one block soon."

As Hoving spoke to reporters, Christmas trees up and down the avenue were about to be lighted for the twenty-second year, beginning with an almost ecumenical ceremony outside the Brick Church. Part of Park Avenue South is blocked off each spring for a street fair, but upper Park will countenance nothing of the sort. Only for the Christmas tree lighting—with appropriate words from the minister and singing of carols—is a block or two ever closed to traffic. Building residents may exchange greetings, but this community sing is the closest that this part of Park Avenue ever comes to the sort of neighborhood spirit found in many of the city's other sections. Still, if there is "something heavenly" about the flowers that brighten Park Avenue each spring, the same may be said about the glow of Christmas tree and Hanukkah lights on its malls each December, an echo of the festive holiday parties and balls that go on almost nightly in apartments and hotels lining the avenue—and in houses just to the east and west.

The tree lighting began in 1945 when families who had lost sons or brothers in the war planted cherry trees in the avenue's islands and lighted them at Christmas as a memorial. Evergreens soon supplemented the cherry trees. When the original contributors ran short of money, Mrs. Lasker helped to continue the project. By 1983, however, the original group was defunct. At that point Peter O. Price of 550 Park, president of the Carey Bus Company, created the Avenue Association. "We got a lot of new people involved and raised $180,000," he told an interviewer. "It sounds like a lot of money, but most is labor—trimming, lighting, maintaining, and keeping the trees safe." With help from Mrs. Lasker,

ABOVE: *Christmas caroling outside the Brick Church is the upper avenue's only community get-together* (1988 photo)

the Lauder Foundation, Citibank, and private contributors,* the association lighted trees between 53rd and 96th streets.

For a retailer on Park Avenue, Christmas may account for more than a third of annual sales. Such retailers include elegant dress shops (Martha's, Sara Fredericks), luggage shops, jewelers (Seaman Shepps, founded in 1913, has been on the avenue since the mid-1950s), haberdashers (Sulka), German motorcar dealerships, and—in Delmonico's Hotel—Christie's, the New York branch of the auction house founded at London in 1766, where a bidder may sometimes pick up a French impressionist painting for only a few million dollars.

There is also, to be sure, a Korean delicatessen and—at the northeast corner of 96th Street, a supermarket. But from 46th Street to 96th what the world thinks of when it hears "Park Avenue" is still the street of dreams. Especially for those who dream of money. In offices on Park in the 40s and 50s, over power breakfasts on Park in the 60s and power lunches at the Four Seasons, are hatched billion-dollar deals that may on occasion benefit others besides the dealmakers whose limousines are double-parked outside. Farther uptown families raise children. Mothers—yes, and nannies, too—march their children to and from private schools where the annual tuition may easily exceed $10,000, wait for the school bus to bring the young master in his blazer (or Sis in hers) home from one of the good West Side schools or from Riverdale. In what the world thinks of as Park Avenue there are still maids and even butlers to handle such tiresome details as ordering the groceries and dealing with the dry cleaner. Milkmen still arrive at service entrances early in the morning to deliver milk in glass bottles. Masseurs, dog walkers, exercise trainers, hairdressers, manicurists, terrace gardeners are but a phone call away.

Park Avenue can be charitable (charity affairs are the basis of society from the Junior League on up), but it casts a nervous glance at its counterpart north of 96th Street and keeps its sidewalks clear of hoi polloi. Having the underclass underfoot is more than Park Avenue is prepared to accept.

Park Avenue can be narrow-minded. The cooperative apartment (there is little else on the avenue today) originated in part for reasons other than economic. In the spring of 1963 the City Commission on Human Rights heard complaints that some of the higher-priced co-op buildings on the avenue (and on Fifth) did not permit theater people, diplomats, or Jews to buy apartments. 720 Park was cited as an example. Daniel and Joanna S. Rose of 215 East 79th Street, expecting their fourth child, had sought to buy a twelve-room apartment (price: $157,500; monthly maintenance: $1,100). Daniel was a Yale graduate, an Air Force veteran, and a real estate professional—a partner in Rose Associ-

---

* The Avenue Association runs advertisements asking for contributions. A gift of $500 will fund a fully lighted cherry tree, $1500 will purchase a lighted Christmas tree, $3,000 will illuminate a whole block's mall of two Christmas trees or six cherry trees. The cherry trees are usually lighted in early December to celebrate Hanukkah, the Christmas trees a week or so later at the Brick Church ceremony.

ABOVE: *Park Avenue South, less stuffy, enjoys annual street fairs* (1988 photo)

ates. Joanna, a Bryn Mawr alumna and former student at Oxford, testified that a broker had told her that being Jewish would be no problem but that another broker had subsequently said, "You'll never get in there." She submitted several social references, including one from an Oxford don and one from an assistant secretary of state. There were three Jewish apartment owners at 720. Frederick S. Lane, a lawyer and former director of the Waterfront Commission told the commission that a representative of the co-op's management had informed him that the board could reject Mr. Rose without explanation on any grounds it chose, including "the way he wears his necktie or parts his hair." The man was Jewish himself and said he was embarrassed by the rejection. Two licensed real estate brokers, both women, denied that being Jewish figured in the acceptance of a prospect as a purchaser of an apartment at 720 Park. The Roses withdrew their complaint a few weeks later, giving no reason.

Then, in October 1963, Alfred R. Bochroch and his wife, Alice, filed suit in Supreme Court against the 1001 Park Tenants Corp. A senior partner in an accounting firm and president of Temple Emanu-El, Bochroch said he had made a $10,000 down payment on an apartment in April 1960; three months later he was denied the right to pay the balance on the $33,850 apartment through "the device of having one director of the Tenants' Corp. move that the application not be approved." Charging that he and his wife had been refused the right to buy the co-op because they were Jewish, Bochroch asked the courts to impose $250,000 in punitive damages and $70,000 in other damages. The defendants denied the allegations and moved for dismissal. Bochroch received court permission at year's end to sue the Park Avenue Realty Corp., but the action was subsequently aborted. Whispers about discrimination at certain buildings continue, and real estate agents are known to steer Jewish, diplomatic, and theatrical prospects away from those buildings.

At Christmas and Easter the lights in the Helmsley Building at 46th Street create a cross. Once mostly Irish Catholic and German Lutheran, Park Avenue became predominantly white Anglo-Saxon Protestant. Today it is predominantly white, and rich. But to believe that even a third of the families on Park Avenue below 96th Street have country houses and winter in Palm Beach is to buy a Hollywood fantasy. The collective net worth of avenue residents is no doubt in the tens of billions, and they spend a billion or two each year, but the wealth is hardly homogeneous. More than a few people with Park Avenue addresses cut corners on other items in their budget in order to meet their monthly maintenance bills. Some even send their children to public school.

Snobbery flourishes here. It always has. Triplex looks down its nose at duplex, duplex at simplex, co-op at condo, triple-numbered building at quadruple-numbered, old money at new, WASP at non-WASP, Sephardic and German Jew at Eastern European Jew. And the Joneses always seem to have more of everything.

Another foolish misconception about Park Avenue is the idea that its solid look of permanence will never change. The blocks between 47th and 59th streets have long since been transformed into headquarters for world business. Such

ABOVE *The Helmsley Building's lights make the sign of the cross at Christmas and Easter (Pan Am Building in background)* 1988 photo)

fixtures as St. Bart's, the Racquet Club, Lever House, the 7th Regiment Armory, and even Grand Central may be endangered species despite their landmark status. Height restrictions have been junked since the time when many Park Avenue structures were built. Such things can be modified. Little more than the individual wealth and collective determination of present co-op owners prevents old twelve-story houses from being supplanted by towers that can accommodate more of the families eager for the prestige of a Park Avenue address.

Candela, Carpenter, Delano & Aldrich, McKim, Mead & White, Roth, Schwartz & Gross, Schultz & Weaver, and the rest have left their marks here. No one can predict how long the doughty beauties they created will remain. Most of Park Avenue's apartment houses are now sixty to eighty years old, not in the least bit ancient by European standards but certifiably antique in America, and tempting targets for developers whose only criterion is potential profit.

Timeless in its apparent serenity, the avenue is a dandy in aspic—flush, comfortable, hiding its vitality beneath a gloss of dignity, looking appalled from the quiet, restrained grandeur of its old buildings at the florid architectural excrescences that have erupted virtually without control on other avenues. That so unpromising a piece of real estate as Railroad Alley could have become so desirable would no doubt have astonished Commodore Vanderbilt. William Wilgus and Chauncey Depew, could they see it now, would goggle. Martha Bacon would sniff, H. Gordon Duval beam with satisfaction. Vanderbilt would order his statue turned to face north and demand a piece of the action.

ACKNOWLEDGMENTS

∎

The author is grateful for valuable help received from Andrew Alpern; Joseph Androvich of 7 Park Avenue; Dara Asken of the New York Department of Ports, International Trade and Commerce; Fred Bass of Strand Books; R. Clifford Black IV and John Jacobsen of Amtrak; Charles Brescher of the Citizens' Budget Commission; Candice Burtis of Park Tower Realty Corp.; Joseph Cavalieri of Conforti Construction Co.; Kenneth Cobb of the Municipal Archives; Val Coleman of the City Housing Authority; Maxwell Davidson of 970 Park; Daniel E. Dougherty of Davis Brody and Associates; John Fava of the City Tax Study Commission; Gaylord Fenton, John Pryor, and Stephen Quinn of the Ritz Tower; Richard Fisher of Fisher Brothers; Ethna Flaherty of the New World Foundation; Arlene Francis of the Ritz Tower; Tom Frank of 1111 Park; Joan Franklin; Morton Freund; David Gibbons of the Drake Swissôtel; Christopher Gray; John Hempel of 500 Park; Donna Hunt of Lawrence Properties; Mike Isepp of Club 101; Mark Itzkowitz of the Inter-Continental Hotel; James P. Kevelle of the Provident Loan Society; Peter Laskowich of the Municipal Art Society; Dewey Lintel of Dewey's Market in La Marqueta; Tom Malone of 1036 Park; David Mammen of the Institute of Public Administration; Seymour Mann of 940 Park; Vivian Meyers of Gotham Realty; Yoshiomi Nakajima of the Hotel Kitano; Michelle Oaklan of Loews Hotels; Ernest O'Brien of Bing & Bing; Patricia Raley of Metro-North; Dalibor Rehounek and John Sicetti of 1020 Park; Patricia Remer of Orsid Realty; Tim Riordan of the Doral Park Avenue Hotel; Henry and Yale Robbins of Yale Robbins, Inc.; Richard Roth and Richard Staub of Emery Roth and Sons; Judith Share of the Hotel Beekman; Oliver Trager; Jimmy Vicars of 1591 Park; Caroline Wilton of the Yale Club; Elise L. Witkin of Marilyn Evins, Ltd.; librarians of the New-York Historical Society and New York Public Library; Erika Goldman, my editor at Atheneum, and Joel Honig, the copy editor who took such pains with the manuscript. None of these people is responsible for any errors that may appear in the book, nor are the opinions expressed anyone but the author's.

Excerpts from *Fortune* magazine for July 1939. Copyright © 1939 by Time Inc. All rights reserved. Reprinted by permission. Excerpt from *Harper's* magazine copyright © 1960 by Harper's Magazine. All rights reserved. Reprinted from the

BIBLIOGRAPHY

Alpern, Andrew. *Apartments for the Affluent*. New York: McGraw-Hill, 1975.

————. "The Cost of Quality: A Contemporary View of Market Value—Past and Present." *N.Y. Habitat*, June 1986.

————. "Tuscan Tapestry—Texture and Terra Cotta at 898 Park Avenue." *N.Y. Habitat*, June 1987.

————. "Phantom Fashion: The Grand Co-operative That Never Existed." *N.Y. Habitat*, August 1987.

————. "Shrinking Space: The Evolving Apartment Floor Plan." *N.Y. Habitat*, March 1988.

————. "Multiple Mansions: Stacked Status Behind a Deceptively Modest Face at 820 Park Avenue." *N.Y. Habitat*, August 1988.

————. "Magnificent Maisonette: Proudly Palatial at 666 Park Avenue." *N.Y. Habitat*, September 1988.

Alpern, Andrew, and Seymour Durst. *Holdouts!* New York: McGraw-Hill, 1984.

Andrews, Wayne. *The Vanderbilt Legend, The Story of the Vanderbilt Family, 1794–1940*. New York: Harcourt Brace, 1941.

Auchincloss, Louis. *A Writer's Capital*. Minneapolis: University of Minnesota Press, 1974.

————. *Life, Law, and Letters: Essays and Sketches*. Boston: Houghton Mifflin, 1979.

————. Introduction to *Philip Trager: New York*. Middletown, Conn.: Wesleyan University Press, 1980.

————. *The Vanderbilt Era: Profiles of a Gilded Age*. New York: Scribners, 1989.

"Avenue of Lights Continues a Tradition." *New York Times*, December 9, 1985.

Bedingfield, Robert E. "New Haven Road Is Suing Central." *New York Times*, January 13, 1960.

Bellows, Henry W. *Historical Sketch of the Union League Club of New York: Its Origin, Organization, and Work, 1863–1879*. New York: Union League Club, 1879.

Bender, Marilyn. "If Financial Coups Are Percolating, It's Breakfast Time at the Regency." *New York Times*, July 7, 1976.

Beresky, Andrew, ed. *Fodor's New York City, 1988*. New York: Fodor's Travel Publications, 1987.

Better Than You: Social Discrimination Against Minorities in America. New York: Institute of Human Relations Press, 1971.

Birmingham, Stephen. *Real Lace: America's Irish Rich*. New York: Harper & Row, 1973.

————. *America's Secret Aristocracy*. Boston: Little, Brown, 1987.

Black, Mary. *Old New York in Early Photographs: 196 Prints, 1853–1901, from the Collection of the New-York Historical Society*. New York: Dover, 1976.

Blair, William G. "Luxuries Boundless for Some Hotels." *New York Times*, May 11, 1980.

Block, Valerie. "St. Ignatius: Serving Catholics in a Fast-Changing World." *New York Observer*, May 16, 1988.

Bradley, John A. "Changes Cited on Park Avenue." *New York Times*, October 16, 1955.

Brolin, Brent C. *The Battle of St. Bart's, A Tale of the Material and the Spiritual*. New York: Morrow, 1988.

Burnham, Alan, ed. *New York Landmarks*. Middletown, Conn.: Wesleyan University Press, 1963.

Cable, Mary. *Top Drawer: American High Society from the Gilded Age to the Roaring Twenties*. New York: Atheneum, 1984.

————. *The Blizzard of '88*. New York: Atheneum, 1988.

Callahan, John P. "Vincent Astor Plans Skyscraper on Park Avenue to Cost $75 Millions." *New York Times*, September 19, 1956.

Chapman, Lou. "In City, Who Pays $10 Million to Live Where?" *New York Observer*, June 19, 1989.

Chase, Stuart. "Park Avenue." *New Republic*, May 25, 1927.

Churchill, Allen. *The Upper Crust, An Informal History of New York's Highest Society*. Englewood Cliffs, N.J.: Prentice-Hall, 1970.

Clements, Marcelle. "A Van for All Seasons." *7 Days*, March 30, 1988.

Clines, Francis X. "Steel Men Toil from Tracks Below Park Avenue to Erect Skyscraper." *New York Times*, June 8, 1965.

"Closing a Hotel at a Profit." *Business Week*, July 23, 1966.

Cohn, Jan. *Improbable Fiction: The Life of Mary Roberts Rinehart*. Pittsburgh: University of Pittsburgh Press, 1980.

Croffut, W. A. *The Vanderbilts and the Story of Their Fortune*. Chicago: Bedford, Clarke, 1886.

Daughen, Joseph R., and Peter Binzen. *The Wreck of the Penn Central*. Boston: Little, Brown, 1971.

Diamonstein, Barbaralee. *The Landmarks of New York*. New York: Harry N. Abrams, 1988.

Diehl, Lorraine B. *The Late, Great Pennsylvania Station*. New York: American Heritage, 1985.

Duggan, Dennis. "Architects Alter Face of New York." *New York Times*, September 30, 1962.

————. "Rothscrapers." *New York Herald Tribune* Magazine, December 15, 1963.

Dullea, Georgia. "In the Realm of the Privileged." *New York Times* Magazine, November 28, 1988.

Dunlap, David W. "Grand Central at 75: Beauty and Misery." *New York Times*, February 1, 1988.

————. "Behind Grand Central's Public Areas Lies an Array of 'Secret' Chambers." *New York Times*, February 2, 1988.

————. "Seagram Landmark Move Is Backed." *New York Times*, April 21, 1988.

Engeler, Amy. "Hard Times at Hunter High." *7 Days*, September 7, 1988.

Ennis, Thomas W. "Harlem Changed by Public Housing." *New York Times*, June 23, 1957.

————. "City Lifting Face of East Harlem," *New York Times*, March 5, 1961.

Erwin, Earl Chapin May, and Joseph Hotchkiss. *A History of the Union League Club of New York City*. New York: Dodd, Mead, 1952.

Fellmeth, Robert, et. al. *The Interstate Commerce Omission, Ralph Nader's Study Group*

Report on the Interstate Commerce Commission and Transportation. New York: Grossman, 1970.

Ferber, Edna. *A Peculiar Treasure.* New York: Doubleday, 1938.

————. *A Kind of Magic.* New York: Doubleday, 1963.

Flanner, Janet. *Darlinghissima: Letters to a Friend.* Edited by Natalia Danesi Murray, New York: Random House, 1985.

Foley, Maurice. "Plan Apartment for Morgan Block." *New York Times,* June 12, 1949.

Forbes magazine, October 26, 1987; October 24, 1988. ("America's Richest People" issues)

Fortune magazine, July 1939 (entire issue dedicated to New York City for opening of World's Fair).

Fowler, Glenn. "Grand Central 'City' Is Planned; 50-story Skyscraper Slated by 1961 for Rear of Terminal." *New York Times,* May 8, 1958.

————. "Razing Building Is Intricate Job." *New York Times,* April 2, 1961.

————. "Chatham Added to List of Hotels to Be Razed for New Buildings." *New York Times,* July 30, 1965.

————. "The Old Vanderbilt to Begin a New Life as a Dual Building." *New York Times,* June 26, 1966.

Freeman, John. *Herman Melville.* London: Macmillan, 1926.

Garvey, Stephen. *Gramercy Park: An Illustrated History of a New York Neighborhood.* New York: Balsam Press, 1974.

Geist, William E. "About New York." *New York Times,* February 20, 1985.

Gilbert, Julie Goldsmith. *Ferber: A Biography.* New York: Doubleday, 1978.

Gill, Brendan. "True White From False." *New York Times Magazine,* October 19, 1975.

Goldberger, Paul. "Lever House Has a Birthday." *New York Times,* April 28, 1977.

————. *The City Observed: New York. A Guide to the Architecture of Manhattan.* New York: Vintage Books, 1979.

————. "Still Majestic, It's a Symbol of New York." *New York Times,* February 2, 1988.

Goldstone, Harmon H., and Martha Dalrymple. *History Preserved: A Guide to New York City Landmarks and Historic Districts.* New York: Simon & Schuster, 1974.

Grant, Peter. "N.Y. Penthouses: The Demand, Too, Is High." *New York Observer,* May 23, 1988.

Gray, Christopher S. "Neighborhood." *Avenue,* May 1980.

————. "Neighborhood." *Avenue,* April 1982.

————. "The Open Fields and Unkempt Streets of 1867." *Avenue,* June-August 1982.

————. "When the Railroad Tracks Led Up Through Yorkville's Farms," *Avenue,* October 1982.

————. "Institution Row," *Avenue,* November 1982.

————. "Park Avenue's Bankers, Brewers, and Bourgeoisie," *Avenue,* December 1982–January 1983.

————. "Life on a Fairy-Book Street," *Avenue,* February 1983.

————. "History of the Upper East Side." *Avenue,* September 1985.

————. "The Tunnel That Raised Park Avenue's Status." *Avenue,* September 1986.

————. "Metro-North Plans New Makeup, Not Plastic Surgery, for a Beauty." *New York Times,* September 18, 1988.

————. "A Grand Residential Boulevard or Just Monotony Lane." *New York Times,* December 18, 1988.

————. "A Grand Mystery House Up for Sale at $20 Million." *New York Times,* March 26, 1989.

Greenberg, Jonathan. "The Milsteins Go for the Jugular." *Avenue*, February 1986.

Greenhouse, Linda. "High Court Hears Challenge to New York Curb on Men's Clubs." *New York Times*, February 24, 1988.

Gross, Jane. "First Look at Homeless: A Raw Sight for Tourists." *New York Times*, November 9, 1987.

Grunwald, Lisa. "The Asia Society Finds That a New Home Fails to Put It in the Pink," *Avenue*, November 1982.

Gunther, John. *Taken at the Flood. The Story of Albert D. Lasker*. New York: Harper & Brothers, 1960.

Hammel, Faye. *Frommer's 1987–1988 Guide to New York*. New York: Prentice-Hall, 1987.

Handy, Robert T. *A History of Union Theological Seminary*. New York: Columbia University Press, 1987.

Hellman, Geoffrey T. "Mary Roberts Rinehart: For 35 Years She Has Been America's Best-Selling Lady Author." *Life*, February 25, 1946.

Horsley, Carter B. "Mystery House Revealed." *New York Post*, April 21, 1988.

Howard, Leon. *Herman Melville: A Biography*. Berkeley and Los Angeles: University of California Press, 1951.

Hoyt, Edwin B. *The Vanderbilts and Their Fortunes*. New York: Doubleday, 1962.

Huxtable, Ada Louise. "Park Avenue School of Architecture." *New York Times Magazine*, December 15, 1957.

———. *Will They Ever Finish Bruckner Boulevard?* New York: Macmillan, 1970.

———. "How Great Buildings Shape a City's Soul." *New York Times*, October 19, 1975.

———. *Kicked a Building Lately?* New York: Quandrangle, 1976.

Israel, Lee. *Kilgallen*. New York: Delacorte, 1979.

Jacobs, Jane. "Downtown Is for People," in *The Exploding Metropolis*. New York: Doubleday Anchor, 1958.

———. *The Death and Life of Great American Cities*. New York: Random House, 1961.

Josephson, Matthew. *The Robber Barons, The Great American Capitalists, 1861–1901*. New York: Harcourt, Brace & World, 1962.

Kaufman, Edgar, Jr. "Worst Luck . . . The Biggest Office Building Yet." *Harper's*, May 1960.

King, Moses. *King's Views of New York, 1896–1915*. New York: Arno, 1977.

Kleiman, Dena. "Hobo Colony Lives Molelike in Inferno of Pipes Under Park Avenue." *New York Times*, November 29, 1977.

Klein, Aaron E. *The New York Central*. New York: Bonanza Books, 1985.

Koolhaas, Rem. *Delirious New York: A Retroactive Manifesto for Manhattan*. New York: Oxford University Press, 1978.

Kozol, Jonathan. "The Homeless and Their Children." *The New Yorker*, February 1, 1988.

Leyda, Jay. *The Melville Log, A Documentary Life of Herman Melville, 1819-1891*. New York: Gordian, 1969.

Lowenstein, Roger. "After a Slight Slump, Apartment Prices in New York Have Resumed Climb." *Wall Street Journal*, August 31, 1987.

Lyons, Richard D. "Creating Penthouses From Air Rights." *New York Times*, October 2, 1988.

Margolick, David. "A Lawyer Vanishes, Leaving a Trail of Fraud Charges." *New York Times*, May 12, 1989.

Martin, Douglas. "So, What's Behind the Mess at New York's Penn Station?" *New York Times*, April 3, 1988.

Mayer, Grace M. *Once Upon a City*. New York: Macmillan, 1958.

McFadden, Robert C. "5 Killed as Copter on Pan Am Building Throws Rotor Blade." *New York Times*, May 17, 1977.

Meyers, Gustavus. *History of the Great American Fortunes*. New York: Modern Library, 1936.

Middleton, William D. *Grand Central . . . the World's Greatest Railway Terminal*. San Marino, California: Golden West Books, 1977.

Miller, Edwin Havilland. *Melville*. New York: George Braziller, 1975.

Morris, Lloyd. *Incredible New York: High Life and Low Life of the Last Hundred Years*. New York: Random House, 1951.

Moscow, Henry. *The Street Book: An Encyclopedia of Manhattan's Street Names and Their Origins*. New York: Hagstrom, 1978.

Mumford, Lewis, "The Plight of the Prosperous," "Mother Jacobs' Home Remedies." *New Yorker*, December 1, 1962.

————. *The Urban Prospects*. New York: Harcourt, Brace & World, 1968.

————. *Architecture as a Home for Man: Essays for Architectural Record*. New York: Architectural Record Books, 1975.

Nathan, Jean Elson. "Where Sinatra, Mrs. Marcos Share a Roof." *New York Observer*, November 14, 1988.

"New Viaduct Thoroughfare Relieves Park Avenue Traffic Congestion." *New York Times*, September 2, 1928.

Pearson, Marjorie, ed. *Upper East Side Historic District Designation Report*. New York: Municipal Art Society, 1981.

Peck, Richard. "Murray Hill—the Old, the New, the Blue." *New York Times*, October 19, 1975.

Peterson, Iver. "Builders Battle 'Takings' of Property." *New York Times*, February 28, 1988.

Prial, Frank J. "Pavillon Closes Doors as a Dining Era Ends." *New York Times*, September 26, 1972.

Real Estate Record and Buyer's Guide, 1902–1950.

Riis, Jacob. *How the Other Half Lives: Studies Among the Tenements of New York*. New York: Scribners, 1890.

Roberts, Sam. "Parents' Anxiety: Price of Change at Ivory Tower." *New York Times*, February 25, 1988.

Robinson, Phyllis C. *Willa, a Life of Willa Cather*. New York: Doubleday, 1983.

Ruttenbaum, Steve. *Mansions in the Clouds: The Skyscraper Palazzi of Emery Roth*. New York: Balsam Press, 1986.

Sax, Irene. "Let's Lunch: Your Place or Mine?" *Newsday*, December 30, 1987.

Shaplen, Robert. "Kreuger: Annals of Crime." *The New Yorker*, September 26, October 3, October 10, 1949.

Shepherd, William G., Jr. "On the Avenue." *Avenue*, April 1979.

Shepp, James W. and Daniel B. *Shepp's New York City Illustrated, Scene and Story of the Metropolis of the Western World*. Chicago and Philadelphia: Globe Bible Publishing Company, 1894.

Shnayerson, Michael. "The Curious Evolution of the Fishes." *Manhattan, inc.*, April 1988.

Silver, Nathan. *Lost New York*. New York: Weathervane, 1967.

Simon, Kate. *Fifth Avenue: A Very Social History*. New York: Harcourt Brace Jovanovich, 1978.

Social Register, The. New York: Social Register Association, 1987.

Stern, Robert A. M., Gregory Gilmartin, and John Massengale. *New York 1900: Metropolitan Architecture and Urbanism, 1890–1915*. New York: Rizzoli, 1983.

Stern, Robert A. M., Gregory Gilmartin, and Thomas Mellins. *New York 1930*. New York: Rizzoli, 1987.

Stokes, I. N. Phelps. *The Iconography of Manhattan Island, 1498–1909*. 6 vols. New York: Robert H. Dodd, 1915–1928.

Tarshish, Manuel B. "The 'Fourth Avenue' Book Trade." *Publishers Weekly*, October 20, October 27, November 4, 1969.

Tauranac, John, and Christopher Little. *Elegant New York: The Builders and the Buildings, 1881–1910*. New York: Abbeville Press, 1985.

Tebbel, John. *History of Book Publishing in the United States*. Vol. 3. New York: R. R. Bowker, 1978.

Townsend, Reginald T. *Mother of Clubs, Being the History of the First Hundred Years of the Union Club of the City of New York, 1836–1936*. New York: William Edwin Rudge, 1936.

Trump, Donald, with Tony Schwartz. *Trump: The Art of the Deal*. New York: Random House, 1987.

"The Union: Mother of Clubs." *Fortune* magazine, December 1932.

United States Reports. Vol. 438, *Cases Adjudged in the Supreme Court of the United States, October Term 1977, June 26 Through July 3, 1978*. Washington, D.C.: U.S. Government Printing Office, 1980.

Vanderbilt, Cornelius. *Park Avenue*. New York: Macaulay, 1930.

Virshup, Amy. "Brendan Gill, Guardian Angel." *Manhattan, inc.*, September 1988.

Wald, Matthew. "Apartments: Why Prices Are So High." *New York Times*, January 29, 1984.

Warren, Virginia Lee. "Classy Last Holdout on the Block." *New York Times*, December 15, 1977.

Wecter, Dixon. *The Saga of American Society, A Record of Social Aspirations, 1607–1937*. New York: Scribners, 1937.

Wheeler, George. *Pierpont Morgan & Friends, The Anatomy of a Myth*. Englewood Cliffs, N.J.: Prentice-Hall, 1973.

White, Norval. *New York, A Physical History*. New York: Atheneum, 1987.

White, Norval, and Elliot Willensky. *AIA Guide to New York City*. rev. ed. New York: Macmillan, 1978; 3rd ed. New York: Harcourt Brace Jovanovich, 1988.

Wilcox, Marrion. "The Yale Club's New House." *Architectural Record*, September 1915.

Wilgus, William J., "The Grand Central Terminal in Perspective," *Transactions* of the American Society of Civil Engineers, Vol. 106 (1941).

Wolf, Gerard R. *New York: A Guide to the Metropolis. Walking Tours of Architecture and History*. New York: McGraw-Hill, 1983.

Wright, William. *Lillian Hellman, the Image, the Woman*. New York: Simon & Schuster, 1986.

APPENDIX

■

Chronology of Park Avenue buildings extant in 1989
(A representative sampling. **Office buildings in boldface**)

1846	Calvary Church, 273 Park Avenue South (then Fourth Ave)	NE corner 21st Street
1869	363 Park Avenue South, Elton Hotel	5 floors
1869	629 Park	Midblock 65th-66th streets	4 floors
1878	591 Park	Midblock 63rd-64th streets	5 floors
1880	643 Park, 7th Regiment Armory	66th-67th streets
1882	94-96 Fourth Avenue Grace Church School Memorial House	
1884	709 Park	69th-70th streets	5 floors
1884	711 Park	69th-70th streets	5 floors
1885	890 Park	Midblock 78th-79th streets	5 floors
1885	MaBSTOA Bus Garage (originally trolley barn of Metropolitan Street Railway Company)	99th-100th streets, Lexington-Park avenues
1890	821 Park	NE corner 75th Street	6 floors
1891	**287 Park Avenue South (United Charities Bldg, 105 East 22nd Street)**	NE corner 22nd Street	9 floors
1894	**281 Park Avenue South (was Church Missions House)**	SE corner 22nd Street	6 floors
1895	**230 Park Avenue South Gramercy Court Building**	SW corner 19th Street	13 floors
1898	23 Park (was J. Hampden Robb house)	NE corner 35th Street	

1898	870 Park	77th-78th streets	3 floors
1899	813 Park	74th-75th streets	11 floors
1900	Church of St. Ignatius Loyola	SW corner 84th Street	
1902	92 Fourth Avenue Grace Church School Clergy House		
1904	**304 Park Avenue South Gramercy Gateway Building**	SW corner 23rd Street	12 floors/ph
1905	1240 Park (Van Cortlandt)	NW corner 96th Street	6 floors
1907	98 Fourth Avenue Grace Church School Neighborhood House		
1907	863 Park	NE corner 77th Street	12 floors
1908	**346 Park Avenue South Provident Loan Society**	NW corner 25th Street	
1909	**200 Park Avenue South**	NW corner 17th Street	17 floors
1909	**225 Park Avenue South, American Woollen Co. Bldg.**	NE corner 18th Street	19 floors
1909	**233 Park Avenue South**	SE corner 19th Street	12 floors
1909	**251 Park Avenue South**	NE corner 20th Street	16 floors
1909	535 Park	NE corner 61st Street	15 floors
1909	540 Park	NW corner 61st Street	12 floors
1909	829 Park	SE corner 76th Street	12 floors
1909	925 Park	NE corner 80th Street	14 floors
1910	American Savings Bank (was Union Square Savings Bank)	NE corner 15th Street	
1910	**222 Park Avenue South**	NW corner 18th Street	12 floors
1910	**300 Park Avenue South**	NW corner 22nd Street	15 floors
1910	**381 Park Avenue South**	SE corner 27th Street	16 floors
1910	**386 Park Avenue South**	NW corner 27th Street	18 floors
1910	**387 Park Avenue South**	NE corner 27th Street	12 floors
1910	**401 Park Avenue South**	SE corner 28th Street	12 floors/ph
1910	**460 Park Avenue South**	SW corner 31st Street	12 floors
1910	**515 Park**	SE corner 60th Street	12 floors
1910	563 Park	NE corner 62nd Street	12 floors
1910	823 Park	75th-76th streets	12 floors
1910	830 Park	SW corner 76th Street	13 floors
1911	**201 Park Avenue South Guardian Life Building**	NE corner 17th Street	20 floors

1911	250 Park Avenue South	SW corner 20th Street	12 floors
1911	315 Park Avenue South (100 East 24th Street)	SE corner 24th Street	20 floors
1911	373 Park Avenue South	Midblock 26th-27th streets	12 floors
1911	390 Park Avenue South	SW corner 27th Street	8 floors
1911	57 Park (was the Douglas house)	Midblock 37th-38th streets	
1911	521 Park Avenue	NE corner 60th Street	12 floors
1911	600 Park (was the Bulkley house)	NW corner 64th Street	
1911	680 Park, Americas Society, Council of the Americas (was the Pyne house)	NW corner 68th Street	
1911	840 Park	NW corner 76th Street	12 floors
1911	969 Park	NE corner 82nd Street	12 floors
1911	1010 Park, Park Avenue Christian Church	SW corner 85th Street	
1912	257 Park Avenue South Gramercy Park Building	SE corner 21st Street	20 floors
1912	345 Park Avenue South	25th–26th streets	12 floors
1912	352 Park Avenue South	Wraps around Provident Loan Society Bldg at 346	16 floors
1912	432 Park Avenue South	NW corner 29th Street	16 floors
1912	444 Park Avenue South	NW corner 30th Street	13 floors
1912	450–60 Park Avenue South	SW corner 31st Street	12 floors
1912	468 Park Avenue South	NW corner 31st Street	17 floors
1912	470 Park Avenue South (Schwartzenbach Bldg)	31st–32nd streets	12 (north side) and 14 (south)
1912	4 Park (was the Vanderbilt Hotel)	SW corner 33rd Street	21 floors
1912	635 Park	NE corner 66th Street	13 floors
1912	875 Park	SE corner 78th Street	12 floors
1912	903 Park	NE corner 79th Street	17 floors
1912	929 Park	80th–81st streets	12 floors
1912	960 Park	NW corner 82nd Street	13 floors
1912	969 Park	NE corner 82nd Street	12 floors
1912	970 Park	SW corner 83rd Street	12 floors
1913	260 Park Avenue South	SW corner 21st Street	8 floors
1913	331 Park Avenue South	24th–25th streets	12 floors
1913	360 Park Avenue South	SW corner 26th Street	20 floors

1913	**440 Park Avenue South**	SW corner 30th Street	12 floors
1913	Grand Central Terminal	42nd–44th streets Depew Place-Vanderbilt Avenue	8 floors
1913	1025 Park (was the de Koven house)	Midblock between 85th and 86th streets	
1914	**215 Park Avenue South**	SE corner 18th Street	20 floors
1914	**432 Park Avenue South**	NW corner 29th Street	16 floors
1914	555 Park	SE corner 62nd Street	12 floors
1914	565 Park	62nd–63rd streets	13 floors
1914	640 Park	NW corner 66th Street	13 floors
1914	755 Park	SE corner 72nd Street	13 floors
1914	850 Park	SW corner 77th Street	12 floors
1914	955 Park	near SE corner 82nd Street	12 floors
1914	983 Park	NE corner 83rd Street	9 floors
1914	100 East 85th Street (was the Morris house)	SE corner Park	
1915	Yale Club	NW corner Vanderbilt and 44th Street	20 floors
1915	**52 Vanderbilt Avenue**	SW corner Vanderbilt and 45th Street	20 floors
1915	570 Park	SW corner 63rd Street	13 floors/ph
1915	930 Park	SW corner 81st Street	13 floors
1915	941 Park	NE corner 81st Street	12 floors
1915	993 Park	SE corner 84th Street	12 floors
1915	1000 Park	NW corner 84th Street	12 floors
1915	1155 Park	SE corner 92nd Street	12 floors
1916	470 Park	SW corner 58th Street	13 floors
1916	630 Park	SW corner 66th Street	12 floors
1917	**404 Park Avenue South**	NW corner 28th Street	16 floors
1917	417 Park	SE corner 55th Street	13 floors/ph
1917	550 Park	SW corner 62nd Street	13 floors
1917	690 Park, Italian Consulate (was the Davison house)	SW corner 69th Street	
1917	550 Park	SW corner 62nd Street	13 floors
1917	715 Park	69th–70th streets	5 floors
1917	815 Park	SE corner 75th Street	14 floors
1917	876 Park	SW corner 78th Street	13 floors
1918	St. Bartholomew's Church	Eastern blockfront, 50th–51st streets	
1918	370 Park, Racquet & Tennis Club	52nd–53rd streets	

1918	686 Park, Instituto Italiano di Cultura (was the Sloane house)	Midblock, 68th–69th streets	
1918	75 East 93rd St. (was the F. F. Palmer house—see 1928)	NW corner Park	
1919	1049 Park	South of 87th Street	14 floors
1920	111 Fourth Avenue	SE corner 12th Street	12 floors
1920	**444 Park Avenue South**	NW corner 30th Street	12 floors
1920	603 Park (was the Howell house)	NE corner 64th Street	
1920	604 Park (was the Pease house)	Between 64th and 65th streets	
1920	608 Park (was the Bowron house)	Between 64th and 65th streets	
1920	Council on Foreign Relations (was the Pratt house)	58 East 68th Street SE corner Park	
1921	**270 Park Avenue South**	NW corner 21st Street	12 floors
1921	950 Park	SE corner 82nd Street	13 floors
1922	**100 East 42nd Street Pershing Square Building**	SE corner 42nd Street	26 floors
1922	485 Park	NE corner 58th Street	14 floors
1922	593 Park, Central Presbyterian Church	SE corner 64th Street	
1922	1075 Park	SE corner 88th Street	14 floors
1923	45 Park, Sheraton Park Hotel (was the Russell)	SE corner Park and 37th Street	9 floors
1923	55 Park	37th–38th streets	15 floors
1923	554 Park, Third Church of Christ, Scientist	NE corner 63rd Street	
1923	580 Park	63rd–64th streets	14 floors
1923	1045 Park	NE corner 86th Street	14 floors/ph
1923	1050 Park	SW corner 87th Street	14 floors/ph
1923	1105 Park	NE corner 89th Street	14 floors
1924	16 Park	SW corner 35th Street	16 floors
1924	Roosevelt Hotel	44th–45th streets, Vanderbilt-Madison avenues	22 floors
1924	**250 Park**	46th–47th streets	20 floors
1924	510 Park	SW corner 60th Street	13 floors/ph
1924	564 Park, Colony Club	NW corner 62nd Street	
1924	620 Park	65th–66th streets	14 floors
1924	655 Park	67th–68th streets	11 floors/ph

1924	760 Park	NW corner 72nd Street	13 floors
1924	898 Park	SW corner 79th Street	14 floors/ph
1924	910 Park	SW corner 80th Street	14 floors
1924	1009 Park	84th–85th streets	14 floors/ph
1924	1060 Park	NW corner 87th Street	14 floors/ph
1924	1133 Park	SE corner 91st Street	15 floors
1925	**1 Park**	32nd–33rd streets	20 floors
1925	15–17 Park	SE corner 35th Street	16 floors
1925	71 Park	Midblock, 38th–39th streets	16 floors
1925	77 Park, The Griffon	SE corner 39th Street	15 floors
1925	610 Park, Mayfair Regent Hotel (was Mayfair House)	SE corner 65th Street	15 floors
1925	791 Park	SE corner 74th Street	14 floors
1925	800 Park	NW corner 74th Street	14 floors
1925	860 Park	NW corner 77th Street	14 floors
1925	935 Park	SE corner 81st Street	16 floors
1925	1111 Park	SE corner 90th Street	14 floors
1925	1160 Park	NW corner 92nd Street	14 floors/ph
1926	66 Park, Kitano Hotel (was the Murray apartments)	SW corner 38th Street	18 floors
1926	Inter-Continental (Barclay) Hotel	48th–49th streets 48th Street east of Park	14 floors
1926	465 Park, Ritz Tower Hotel	NE corner 57th Street	37 floors
1926	684 Park, Spanish Institute (was the Oliver D. Filley house)	68th–69th streets	
1926	820 Park	NW corner 75th Street	14 floors
1926	940 Park	NW corner 81st Street	15 floors/ph
1926	975 Park	SE corner 83rd Street	15 floors/ph
1926	1035 Park	SE corner 86th Street	15 floors
1926	1040 Park	NW corner 86th Street	14 floors
1926	1085 Park	NE corner 88th Street	15 floors
1926	1088 Park	SE corner 89th Street	15 floors
1926	1125 Park	NE corner 90th Street	14 floors/ph
1926	1172 Park	SW corner 93rd Street	14 floors
1926	1225 Park	SE corner 95th Street	16 floors/ph
1926	1230 Park	SW corner 96th Street	17 floors/ph
1927	**386 Park Avenue South**	NW corner 27th Street	20 floors
1927	**419 Park Avenue South**	SE corner 29th Street	18 floors
1927	**425 Park Avenue South**	NE corner 29th Street	20 floors
1927	**2 Park Avenue**	NW corner 32nd Street	25 floors
1927	St. Bartholomew's Community House	Park at 50th Street	

Year	Building	Location	Floors
1927	Lombardy Hotel	111 East 56th Street	21 floors
1927	Drake Hotel	NW corner 56th Street	21 floors
1927	575 Park, Beekman Hotel	SE corner 63rd Street	16 floors
1927	660 Park	NW corner 67th Street	13 floors
1927	765–775 Park	72nd–73rd streets	13 floors
1927	812 Park	SW corner 75th Street	14 floors
1927	885 Park	NE corner 78th Street	14 floors
1927	888 Park	NW corner 78th Street	14 floors
1927	911 Park	SE corner 80th Street	14 floors
1927	983 Park	NE corner 83rd Street	14 floors
1927	1112 Park	SW corner 90th Street	14 floors/ph
1927	1165 Park	NE corner 92nd Street	14 floors/ph
1928	**New York Life Building**	26th–27th streets, Madison-Park Ave South	33 floors
1928	Synod of Bishops of Russian Orthodox Church (George F. Baker, Jr. expansion of 1918 F. F. Palmer house)	NW corner 93rd Street	
1928	1070 Park	SW corner 88th Street	15 floors/ph
1928	1235 Park	SE corner 96th Street	15 floors
1929	**100 East 17th Street (was Tammany Hall)**	SE corner Park Ave South	3 floors
1929	**230 Park**	45th–46th streets	34 floors
1929	480 Park	NW corner 58th Street	14 floors
1929	502 Park, Delmonico's Hotel	NW corner 59th Street	32 floors
1929	720 Park	NW corner 70th Street	18 floors
1929	730 Park	SW corner 71st Street	19 floors
1929	784 Park	SW corner 74th Street	19 floors
1929	944 Park	Midblock 81st–82nd streets	15 floors/ph
1929	1001 Park	NE corner 84th Street	14 floors/ph
1929	1175 Park	SE corner 93rd Street	14 floors/ph
1929	1185 Park	93rd–94th streets	15 floors/ph
1929	1192 Park	SW corner 94th Street	15 floors
1930	7 Park	NE corner 34th Street	19 floors
1930	10 Park	NW corner 34th Street	28 floors
1930	530 Park	SW corner 61st Street	18 floors
1930	740 Park	NW corner 71st Street	17 floors
1930	770 Park	SW corner 73rd Street	18 floors
1930	784 Park	SW corner 74th Street	19 floors
1930	895 Park	SE corner 79th Street	19 floors

1930	1021 Park	NE corner 85th Street	14 floors/ph
1930	1100 Park	NW corner 89th Street	17 floors
1930	1120 Park	NW corner 90th Street	19 floors
1930	1220 Park	SW corner 95th Street	19 floors
1931	Union League Club	SW corner Park and 37th Street	
1931	301 Park, Waldorf-Astoria Hotel	49th–50th streets Park-Lexington avenues	47 floors in towers
1931	625 Park	NE corner 65th Street	13 floors/ph
1931	778 Park	NW corner 73rd Street	18 floors
1931	891 Park	Midblock 78th–79th streets	15 floors/ph
1932	**Metropolitan Life North Building**	24th–25th streets Fourth-Madison avenues	29 floors
1932	520 Park, Christ Church (Methodist)	NW corner 60th Street	
1932	Union Club, 101 East 69th Street	NE corner Park	
1935	**461 Park Avenue South**	NE corner 31st Street	12 floors
1938	Brick Church	NE corner 91st Street	
1939	20–30 Park	35th–36th Streets	17 floors/ph
1940	50 Park	NW corner 37th Street	19 floors
1940	Hunter College	68th–69th streets	
1940	737 Park	NE corner 71st Street	19 floors
1940	785 Park	NE corner 73rd Street	19 floors
1940	1150 Park	SW corner 92nd Street	19 floors/ph
1941	1130 Park	SW corner 91st Street	15 floors/ph
1947	**445 Park, Universal Pictures/MCA Building**	56th–57th streets	21 floors
1948	710 Park	SW corner 70th Street	19 floors
1948	Abraham Lincoln Houses (14 buildings)	132nd–135th streets Park-Fifth avenues	6–14 floors 1,286 units
1949	**505 Park Arabian-American Oil Co. Building**	NE corner 59th Street	21 floors
1949	715 Park	SE corner 70th Street	19 floors
1949	James Weldon Johnson Houses (10 buildings)	Park-Third avenues 112th–115th streets	6, 10, 14 floors 1,310 units
1950	40 Park	NW corner 36th Street	18 floors/ph
1950	**100 Park**	40th–41st streets	36 floors
1951	750 Park	SW corner 72nd Street	17 floors/ph

1951	Lexington Houses (4	98th–99th streets	14 floors
	buildings)	Park-Third avenues	448 units
1952	**390 Park, Lever House**	53rd–54th streets	24 floors
1953	**99 Park, National**	39th–40th streets	26 floors
	Distillers Building		
1953	1095 Park	SE corner 89th Street	15 floors/ph
1954	605 Park	SE corner 65th Street	21 floors
1955	41 Park	NE corner 36th Street	18 floors/ph
1955	**300 Park**	49th–50th streets	25 floors
	Colgate-Palmolive Building		
1955	**430 Park, with automobile**	55th–56th streets	32 floors
	showroom		
1955	**460 Park, Davies Building**	NW corner 57th Street	32 floors
1956	35 Park	SE corner 36th Street	18 floors/ph
1956	80 Park	SW corner 39th Street	19 floors/ph
1956	**405 Park**	NE corner 54th Street	17 floors
1957	**400 Park, General**	NW corner 54th Street	21 floors
	Reinsurance Building		
1957	**425 Park**	55th–56th streets	32 floors
1957	1036 Park	SW corner 86th Street	19 floors
1958	475 Park	SE corner 58th Street	14 floors/ph
1958	**500 Park (originally**	SW corner 59th Street	12 floors
	Pepsi-Cola Building)		
1958	George Washington Carver	Park-Madison avenues	6–15 floors
	Houses (13 buildings)	99th–106th streets	1,246 units
1959	59 Park, Church of Our	SE corner 38th Street	
	Saviour		
1959	**375 Park, Seagram**	52nd–53rd streets	38 floors
	Building		
1959	**410 Park with Chase**	SW corner 55th Street	22 floors
	Manhattan branch		
1959	700 Park	NW corner 69th Street	19 floors
1960	**270 Park (originally Union**	47th–48th streets	52 floors
	Carbide Building)		
1960	**320 Park, ITT Building**	50th–51st streets	33 floors
1960	**350 Park, Bank of**	55th–56th streets	18 floors
	Montreal (Mfgrs Hanover)		
	Building		
1960	Lenox Hill Hospital's	SE corner 77th Street	
	Wollman Pavilion		
1961	**399 Park, Citibank Bldg**	53rd–54th streets	39 floors
1961	799 Park	NE corner 74th Street	21 floors
1961	1199 Park	NE corner 94th Street	19 floors

1961	Sen. Robert A. Taft Houses (9 buildings)	112th–115th streets Park-Fifth avenues	19 floors 1,470 units
1962	1020 Park	NW corner 85th Street	20 floors
1963	**200 Park, Pan Am Building**	44th–45th streets	56 floors
1963	**280 Park, Bankers Trust Building**	48th–49th streets	30 floors
1963	540 Park, Regency Hotel	NW corner 61st Street	21 floors
1963	650 Park	SW corner 67th Street	19 floors/ph
1963	Extension to Park Avenue Christian Church of 1911	in block between 84th and 85th streets	19 floors/ph
1963	Herbert H. Lehman Village (4 buildings)	106th–110th streets Park-Madison avenues	20 floors 622 units
1964	145 Fourth Avenue	SE corner 14th Street	20 floors
1964	70 Park, Doral Park Hotel	NE corner 38th Street	15 floors/ph
1964	**90 Park**	39th–40th streets	41 floors
1964	**277 Park, Chemical Bank New York Trust Building**	47th–48th streets	50 floors
1964	920 Park	NW corner 80th Street	20 floors/ph
1965	DeWitt Clinton Houses (6 buildings)	Park-Madison avenues 104th–106th, 108th–110th	1–9–18 floors 749 units
1966	**245 Park (originally American Tobacco Building)**	46th–47th streets	47 floors
1967	**299 Park, Westvaco Building**	48th–49th streets	42 floors
1967	1245 Park	NE corner 96th Street	18 floors/ph
1968	**280 Park, Bankers Trust Building annex**	West of 1963 building	43 floors
1969	**345 Park**	51st–52nd streets	44 floors
1969	Hunter Campus Schools (originally I.S. 29)	Park at 94th Street	
1970	**475 Park Avenue South**	SE corner 32nd Street	35 floors
1971	733 Park	SE corner 71st Street	30 floors
1971	Park Avenue E. 122nd–123rd Streets (2 buildings)	Between Park and Lex	6 floors 90 units
1972	**450 Park**	SW corner 57th Street	32 floors
1973	900 Park	NW corner 79th Street	28 floors
1974	1065 Park	NE corner 87th Street	27 floors
1975	Lenox Hill Hospital's Percy and Harold D. Uris Pavilion	NE corner 76th Street	

1976	**3 Park** and Norman Thomas High School	33rd–34th streets	42 floors
1976	870 Park (remodeling of a 1909 house)	77th–78th streets	4 floors
1979	Asia Society	NE corner 71st Street	
1980	Grand Hyatt Hotel (was Commodore Hotel)	Park at Grand Central	33 floors
1980	**499 Park**	SE corner 59th Street	27 floors
1981	**237 Park, Park Avenue Atrium**	46th Street, east of Park	21 floors
1981	**Park Avenue Plaza**	52nd–53rd streets west of Park	44 floors
1982	**101 Park**	40th–41st streets	49 floors
1983	407 Park Avenue South (Ascot apartment house)	NE corner 28th Street	26 floors
1983	**120 Park Avenue Philip Morris Building**	41st–42nd streets	26 floors
1983	500 Park Tower (mixed use building)	Just west of 500 Park	40 floors
1986	U.P.A.C.A. (site 6)	119th–122nd streets Park-Lexington avenues	10–12 floors 150 units
1987	Zeckendorf Towers (mixed-use building)	Union Square East-Irving Place, 14th–15th streets	27 floors
1987	**Park Avenue Tower** 65 East 55th Street	Just west of 430 Park	36 floors
1988	Gramercy Place	280 Park Avenue South, SE corner 22nd Street	27 floors/ph

INDEX

∎

Ace, Goodman, 137
Agnelli, Giovanni, 111, 113
Alger, Fred, 208
Allen & Collens, 66, 91
All Souls Church, 20, 21
Alpern, Andrew, 98, 101, 104, 106, 107
Ambassador Hotel, 129, 199, 260
American Bible Society, 199
A.I.A., 101, 105, 223
American Tobacco Co., 187, 199
American Woollen Co. Bldg., 39, 183
Amtrak, 228, 232, 233
Anderson, Mrs. Millbank, 98
Andrews, Wayne, 12
antique shows, 30
anti-Semitism, 167, 263, 265
apartment houses:
 998 Fifth, 82
 65 Fourth, 213
 80 Fourth, 213
 111 Fourth, 213
 115 Fourth, 213
 127 Fourth, 213
 145 Fourth, 213, 286
 7 Park, 150, 283
 10 Park, 150, 283
 15-17 Park, 96, 282
 16 Park, 96, 281
 20-30 Park, 207, 284
 35 Park, 208, 285
 40 Park, 208, 284
 41 Park, 208, 285
 50 Park, 207, 284
 55 Park, 281
 71 Park, 96, 282
 77 Park, 96, 97, 282
 80 Park, 208, 285
 417 Park, 87, 88, 256, 280
 470 Park, 87, 280
 475 Park, 209, 285
 480 Park, 80, 107, 113, 283
 485 Park, 91, 281
 500 Park Tower, 211, 287

apartment houses (continued)
 510 Park, 92, 281
 521 Park, 81, 279
 525 Park, 84, 112, 280
 530 Park, 150, 283
 535 Park, 82, 278
 540 Park, 278
 550 Park, 88, 280
 555 Park, 84, 280
 563 Park, 81, 254, 278
 565 Park, 84, 280
 570 Park, 86, 120, 176, 280
 580 Park, 91, 92, 113, 281
 605 Park, 208, 285
 620 Park, 92, 281
 625 Park, 113, 284
 630 Park, 87, 178, 180, 280
 635 Park, 82, 279
 640 Park, 84, 280
 650 Park, 143, 209, 286
 655 Park, 92, 281
 660 Park, 101, 256, 283
 700 Park, 209, 210, 285
 710 Park, 66, 208, 284
 715 Park, 65, 208, 280
 720 Park, 107, 263, 283
 730 Park, 108, 283
 733 Park, 65, 211, 212, 215, 256, 286
 737 Park, 207, 284
 740 Park, 109, 111, 150, 283
 750 Park, 72, 208, 284
 755 Park, 84, 280
 760 Park, 94, 282
 765-775 Park, 101, 105, 283
 770 Park, 111, 150, 283
 778 Park, 151, 284
 784 Park, 108, 150, 283
 785 Park, 207, 284
 791 Park, 96, 97, 177, 282
 799 Park, 209, 211, 285
 800 Park, 96, 97, 282
 812 Park, 101, 105, 253, 283
 813 Park, 80, 278

apartment houses (*continued*)
815 Park, 88, 280
820 Park, 98, 99, 282
823 Park, 82, 254, 278
829 Park, 81, 82, 278
830 Park, 82, 254, 278
840 Park, 82, 279
850 Park, 84, 254, 280
860 Park, 96, 97, 282
863 Park, 80, 254, 278
875 Park, 82, 279
876 Park, 87, 280
885 Park, 101, 105, 283
888 Park, 101, 283
891 Park, 151, 284
895 Park, 85, 112, 150, 283
898 Park, 94, 106, 282
900 Park, 71, 211, 286
903 Park, 83, 85, 279
910 Park, 94, 282
911 Park, 101, 105, 283
920 Park, 209, 286
925 Park, 81, 254, 278
929 Park, 81, 278
930 Park, 84, 280
935 Park, 96, 282
940 Park, 98, 99, 282
941 Park, 84, 280
944 Park, 108, 283
950 Park, 90, 281
955 Park, 86, 280
960 Park, 83, 279
969 Park, 83, 254, 279
970 Park, 83, 112, 279
975 Park, 98, 99, 282
983 Park, 101, 105, 283
993 Park, 86, 280
1000 Park, 86, 280
1001 Park, 107, 265, 283
1009 Park, 94, 282
1020 Park, 209, 286
1021 Park, 67, 112, 150, 284
1035 Park, 98, 99, 282
1036 Park, 209, 285
1040 Park, 98, 99, 113, 282
1045 Park, 91, 96, 281
1049 Park, 90, 281
1050 Park, 91, 96, 281
1060 Park, 91, 96, 282
1065 Park, 211, 286
1070 Park, 106, 283
1075 Park, 91, 96, 281
1085 Park, 98, 99, 282
1088 Park, 98, 99, 100, 282
1095 Park, 208, 285
1100 Park, 150, 151, 284
1105 Park, 91, 96, 281
1111 Park, 96, 97, 108, 282
1120 Park, 150, 284
1125 Park, 98, 101, 102 (doorman), 282
1130 Park, 208, 284
1133 Park, 96, 113, 282
1150 Park, 207, 284

apartment houses (*continued*)
1155 Park, 86, 87, 280
1160 Park, 96, 97, 282
1165 Park, 101, 105, 108, 283
1172 Park, 98, 101, 282
1175 Park, 108, 283
1185 Park, 108, 109, 110, 283
1192 Park, 109, 283
1199 Park, 209, 285
1220 Park, 150, 151, 284
1225 Park, 98, 101, 255, 282
1230 Park, 98, 282
1235 Park, 107, 283
1240 Park, 80, 278
1245 Park, 209, 286
254 Park Avenue South, 213
407 Park Avenue South, 213, 287
425 Park Avenue South, 213
Arabian-American Oil Co., 190
Araskog, Rand V., 111, 254
Ashland House, 37, 39
Asia Society building, 71
Astor, Brooke, 193, 195, 204
Astor, Caroline Schermerhorn, 38
Astor, John Jacob IV, 193
"Astor Plaza," 195
Astor, Vincent, 67, 84, 193
Astor, Wm. B., 37; Wm. Waldorf, 195
Atia, Elia, and Associates, 202
Auchincloss, Mrs. Hugh D., 84, 84f.
Auchincloss, Louis, 14, 97, 105, 167, 171, 181, 254
Avenue magazine, 88, 218

Backer, George, 90, 108, 129
Backer, William M., 107
Bacon, Martha, 16, 34, 118, 150, 182
Baker, George F., Jr., house, 72, 76, 108, 162, 163, 217, 283
Bankers Trust, 73, 129, 197
Bank of America Plaza, 125, 218
Bank of Montreal building, 192
Barclay Hotel, 130–132
Barnes, Edward Larrabee, 71
Beekman Hotel, 123, 139, 140, 141
Bellmore Cafeteria, 213
Belluschi, Pietro, 222, 226
Belmont Hotel, 42–44
Belvedere Hotel, 37, 39
Beyer, Blinder & Belle, 213
Bible House, 22, 174, 199
Bien, Robert L., 208, 209
Bien, Sylvan, 208
Biltmore Hotel, 61, 123–125, 217, 218
Bing & Bing, 83, 84, 86, 87, 94, 108, 137
Birmingham, Stephen, 84f., 100
Birnbaum, Philip, 211, 213
Blakeman, Ray, 72, 76
Blum, George and Edward, 82–84, 91, 97, 99, 184
Blumenthal, George, 66, 208
Board Room Club, 169
booksellers, 173–175

Boring, William A., 81
Boston Post Road, 4, 17, 20
Bowman, John McEntee, 43, 124, 126
Bowron, Clara D., house, 76, 281
Brearley School, 112, 167
Breuer, Marcel, 227
Brewster, Robert F., 65
Brick Church, 207, 261, 262
Bricken, Abraham, 108, 109
Brisbane, Arthur, 133–135
Bronfman, Samuel, 193
Buckout, Isaac, 23, 25
Bulkley, Jonathan, house, 67, 279
Bunshaft, Gordon, 190
Burnham, Daniel H., 54, 202

Calvary Church, 20, 172, 215
Campagna, A., 112, 150; & Sons, 208
Canadian Club, 146, 154
Candela, Rosario, 91, 101, 105, 107, 109,
    111, 112, 151, 267
Capasso, Carl A., 82
Carnegie Hill, 19, 64, 108; Historic District,
    216
Carnegie Terrace, 250
Carpenter, J.E.R., 82, 83, 84, 87, 88, 90–92,
    105, 113, 140, 267
Carrère & Hastings, 65, 133, 184
Caruso, Enrico, 45
Carver, Geo. Wash., Houses, 245, 285
Cassatt, Alexander, 51, 52, 54, 220
Cather, Willa, 176, 177
Cave, Edward Lee, 208
Cavendish Club, 134
Central Presbyterian Church, 91
Chase Manhattan Bank, 92, 195
Chase, Stuart, 105, 106, 133, 252, 259
Chatham Hotel, 129
Chemical Bank bldg., 197; atrium, 198
Choi, Kyu-Sung, 206
Christ Church (Methodist), 81, 150
Christie's, 139, 263
Church Missions House, 32, 215
Church of Our Saviour, 201
Cirque, Le, 140, 142
Citibank, 195, 263
City Hall, 17; subway and, 53
City Housing Auth., 241, 244–246, 249
City Planning Commission, 215
Clarendon Hotel, 37, 38, 80, 107
Clinton, Charles W., 30
Clinton, DeWitt, Houses, 245, 286
Clinton & Russell, 32, 183
Club 101, 169
Cogan, Marshall S., 113
Coleman, Val, 245, 246, 249
Colgate-Palmolive Building, 192
Collis, Lloyd, 116
Colony Club, 160–162, 171
Columbia College, 21
Commissioners' grid plan, 4, 17, 18
Commodore Hotel, 5, 116, 125–127
Connecting Railway, 61, 219–221

Connete, Albert H., 163
Conrail, 228, 232
Consolidated Edison, 51, 61
Cooper, Peter, 21
Cooper Union, 21, 173
cooperative ownership, 254, 255
Corbett, Harvey Wiley, 185
Cornell Club, 131
Council on Foreign Relations, 74
Coutan, Jules-Alexis, 56
crack, 247
Cram, Goodhue & Ferguson, 67
Cram, Ralph Adams, 150
Cross & Cross, 107, 184
Cross, Eliot, 130
Crowninshield, Frank, 136, 146
Cuddihy, Robert J., 99, 100, 175,
    202
Cuevas, Marquesa de, 73
Cummings, Nathan, 149
curtain-wall construction, 190

Dakota, 77, 82
Davies, Marion, 135, 174, 192
Davis Brody and Associates, 204
Davis, Clyde, 136
Davison, Henry P., house, 72, 73, 215
de Koven, Reginald, house, 69, 70
Delano & Aldrich, 65, 74, 76, 81, 92, 99,
    161, 164, 267
Delmonico's Hotel, 138, 139, 178
Depew, Chauncey, 11, 12–14, 47, 48, 50, 69,
    219, 239, 267
Depew Place, 11, 55, 57, 117–119, 125, 126,
    201, 224
Dewey, F. H. & Co., 92
Dewey, Thomas E., 97, 242
Diamonstein, Barbaralee, 107
Dillon, C. Douglas, 149
Doral Park Avenue Hotel, 123, 124
Drake Swissôtel, 123, 139
Drew, Daniel, 7, 9–11, 14
Drexel Burnham Lambert, 82
Dreyfuss, Henry, 197
Duke, Doris, 113, 204
Dunne, Finley Peter, 139, 177, 232
Duval, H. Gordon, 118–121, 152, 182
Dwight, Frederick, 152
Dwight School, 124

Ehret, George, 32, 108
elevators, 91, 91f.
Elliman, Douglas, 82, 159, 257
Ellsworth, Jas., Lincoln, 76
Erie Railroad, 11, 14
Everett House, 39, 42, 183

Fairbanks, Douglas, Jr., 140
Fairchild, Sherman M., 71
Farkas, Robin, 108
Ferber, Edna, 177

Field, Marshall, 73, 109
Fifth Avenue, 3, 63, 115
Fifth Avenue Association, 117–119
Filley, Oliver D., 72
Fish, Hamilton, 94
Fisk, James, 11, 14
Flagg, Ernest, 74
Flanner, Janet, 179
Florence House, 39
Forbes, 111, 114
Forbes, B. C., 146
Fortune, 4, 156, 165, 203
Four Seasons Restaurant, 193, 263
Fourth Avenue, 4, 16–18, 24, 27, 29, 182,
    206; Improvement, 25, 29
Fox, Fan, 104
Francis, Arlene, 136
Franklin National Bank, 199
Franzen, Ulrich, and Associates, 202
Fredericks, Sara, 140, 263
French, Fred F., Co., 96
Fribourg, Michel, 138, 201

Gage, Edson, 76, 87
Garbo, Greta, 136
Garvey, Stephen, 19
General Reinsurance Building, 192
Gilbert, Cass, 185
Gilbert, C. P. H., 12
Gill, Brendan, 217, 218
Goddard, Paulette, 136
Goelet, Henry, 209; Robt., 12, 192
Goelet, Robt. W., 152, 157, 190, 192
Goldberg, Bertram, 196
Goldberger, Paul, 111, 157, 190, 211,
    227
Goldin, Harrison J., 217
Goldstone, Harmon H., 223
Goldstone, Lafayette, A., 108
Goodhue, Bertram G., 67, 69, 69f.
Goodwillie, John, 4
Gorme, Eydie, 140
Gould, Jay, 11, 14, 41
Grace Church, 20, 215; School, 35f.
Gramercy Park, 18
Gramercy Place, 213
Grand Central Depot, 12, 23–26, 28, 46, 48,
    55
Grand Central Galleries, 61
Grand Central Palace, 92, 186, 197, 198
Grand Central Terminal, 1, 1f., 2, 52–62,
    124, 125, 198, 202, 215, 217, 218,
    219–234, 235–236
Grand Hyatt Hotel, 5, 123, 127, 128
Grand Union Hotel, 34, 42, 43, 184
Gray, Christopher, 12, 13, 20, 66
Green, Andrew Haswell, 34
Green, Harry F., 209, 211
Green, S. William ("Bill"), 84
Gropius, Walter, 222, 226
Guardian Life building, 176, 183
Guastavino, Rafael, 59
Guatemalan U.N. Mission, 67, 217

Haefeli, Walter, 184, 185
Hahnemann Hospital, 29, 92
Hamlisch, Marvin, 83
Hammerstein, Oscar, 239
Harlem, 236, 239–242; Board of Commerce,
    241; Opera House, 239; River, 47, 239,
    241
Harlem River Houses, 242
Harriman, Mrs. J. Borden, 160
Hearst, Wm. R., 98, 132, 133, 209
Hecksher Apartments, 92, 93, 197
Hecksher, August, 92, 122
helicopters, 195, 226, 227
Helleu, Paul, 59
Hellman, Lillian, 180, 181
Helmsley Building, 217, 222, 265, 266
    (*see* also New York Central Bldg.)
Helmsley, Harry B., 188
Hilton Hotels, 125, 147, 149
homeless, 30, 202, 234, 235–238
Hoover, Herbert C., 149
horsecars, 18, 19, 22, 23, 24, 115
Hosp. for Ruptured, Crippled, 29,
    126
Hoving, Thomas P. F., 261
Hoving, Walter, 82
Howell, Thomas A., 72, 76
Howells, John Mead, 98
Hoyt, Sherman, 71, 211
Hudson River Railroad, 5, 8, 10
Human Rights Comm., 167, 168,
    263
Hunt, Richard Morris, 66
Hunter Campus schools, 35, 35f.
Hunter College, 29, 30, 165
Huxtable, Ada Louise, 199, 226, 227
Hylan, Mayor John F., 16, 117, 125

Iacocca, Lee, 149
income tax, 10, 14
Inter-Continental Hotel, 123, 132
ILGWU, 185
ITT, 111; Bldg., 196
Italian Consulate, 73

Jacobs, Jane, 197, 246, 247
Jahn, Helmut, 200
James, Arthur Curtiss, 66, 73, 209
James, Henry, 173
Jerome, Leonard, 10, 11, 162
Jewish Agency, 81
Johnson, J. Weldon, Houses, 242, 284
Johnson, Philip, 192

Kahn & Jacobs, 190, 195, 209, 211
Kahn, Ely Jacques, 185
Kalikow, Peter, 88, 202, 213
Kaufman, Edgar, Jr., 224, 225
Kilgallen, Dorothy, 177, 178
Kitano Hotel, 123, 124
Klein, S., 203, 204
Knickerbocker Grays, 30, 171
Kobler, Albert J., 98, 99

Kohlberg Kravis Roberts, 111, 143
Kravis, Henry R., 111
Kreuger, Ivar, 97, 113, 177

La Guardia, Fiorello H., 193, 240–242
Lambert, Phyllis Bronfman, 193
Landmarks Conservancy, 217, 218
Landmarks Preservation Commission, New
    York, 216, 228
Landmarks Preservation Law, 216, 227, 229,
    230
Lasker, Mary, 259, 260
Lazar, Irving ("Swifty"), 136
Lear, Frances, 136; Norman, 136
LeBrun, Napoleon, & Sons, 183
Lehman, Herbert H., Village, 245
Lenox Hill, 17, 19, 20, 24, 27, 64, 65
Lenox Hill Hospital, 29, 285, 286
Lenox, Jas., 19, 20, 30; Robt., 17, 19
Lever House, 2, 190, 191, 197, 217, 267
Levine, Dennis, 109
Lexington Avenue, 4, 12, 19, 79, 80, 115;
    subway, 116
Lexington Houses, 245, 285
Lincoln, Abraham, Houses, 242, 284
Lipton, Martin, 88, 143
List, Albert, 209
Loews Hotels, 132
Lombardy Hotel, 132, 133
Long Island Rail Road, 53, 54, 215
Luckman, Charles, 190; Assocs., 215
Lustig, Florence, 199
Lyons, Robert T., 83, 84, 86, 150,
    184

MacArthur, Mrs. Douglas, 149, 169
Madison Avenue, 19, 22, 79, 80
Madison Square, 20, 27
Mad. Sq. Garden, 46, 185, 215, 216
Mandel, Henry, 94, 132, 185
Manufacturers Hanover Trust, 196
Marco Polo Club, 168, 169
Marcos, Imelda, 104, 149
Marguery, 89, 92, 127, 129, 196
Marqueta, La, 242, 249, 250
Marron, Donald B., Jr., 84
Martha's, 204, 205, 209, 263
Maxwell, Elsa, 146
Mayfair Regent Hotel, 123, 140
MCA Building, 189
McAllister, Ward, 39, 155
"McCoy, Sherman," 87, 251, 258
McDonnell & Co., 256
McKim, Mead & White, 71, 72, 77, 82, 84,
    88, 92, 156, 157, 159, 267
Mellon, Paul, 77, 78
Melville, Herman, 172, 173
Merrick, David, 83
Messmore, Carman H., 94
Mesta, Perle, 131
Metro-North, 219, 233, 235, 236
Metrop. Club, 146, 154, 154f., 160
Metropolitan Life, 183, 185

Metropolitan Museum of Art, 66, 216
Metropolitan Opera House, 86, 187
Mies van der Rohe, 192, 193
Milliken, Gerrish, 70
Milstein family, 217, 218
Minskoff, Sam, 107; & Sons, 207, 208
Mitsukoshi, 135
Montana apartments, 83, 189, 192
Morgan, J. P., 14, 76, 160, 208
Morris, L. G., house, 72, 74, 75, 217
Moses, Robert, 100, 242, 261
Mott, Stewart, 97
Mount Sinai Hospital, 209
Mumford, L., 115, 185, 189, 246, 247
Municipal Art Society, 217, 223
Murchison, Kenneth M., 112
Murray Hill, 16, 17, 19, 20, 26, 27, 32, 35,
    64, 67; 96, 182, 201; hotels in, 34, 37,
    124
Murray Hill Hotel, 34, 40, 41, 42

Nast, Condé, 99, 108, 113
Neville & Bagge, 80, 184
New Amsterdam Hotel, 39, 184
Newhouse, Donald, 108
Newhouse, S. I., Jr., 108
New World Foundation, 74
New York & Harlem Railroad, 8–10, 18–25,
    46, 56, 115, 117, 185, 239
New York Central & Hudson River, 12–14,
    24, 46, 55, 86, 117, 119, 120, 124, 130,
    144, 156, 189, 197, 239
New York Central Bldg., 119, 122, 187, 188,
    217, 222
New York Central, 11
New York General Bldg., 222, 224
New York Life, 88, 101, 185
New York, New Haven & Hartford, 8, 12, 46,
    56, 197, 222, 228
N.Y. State Coll. of Optometry, 184, Housing
    Finance Agency, 202
New York Steam Company, 61, 94
New York Times, 12, 13, 27, 42, 48, 49, 67,
    73, 74, 121, 122, 138, 144, 200, 206,
    215, 216, 220, 223, 226, 233, 235,
    239
New York Tribune, 38, 40
New Yorker, 108, 179, 189, 217, 221
Norman Thomas High School, 202

O'Dwyer, Paul, 127; Wm. F., 242
Onassis, Jacqueline, 217
Oyster Bar, 59, 228, 229

Palmer, Francis F., house, 72, 76, 101,
    281
Pan Am Building, 224–226
Pan American Airways, 132, 226
Park Av. Assn., 88, 118, 119, 182, 261
Park Av. Christian Church, 67, 215
Park Avenue Hotel, 39, 40
Park Avenue Methodist Church, 99
Park Avenue Plaza, 200

Park Avenue Social Review, 118
Park Avenue South, 16, 26, 182, 201, 202, 206
P.rk Avenue Synagogue, 99
Park Avenue Theatre, 204, 205
Park Avenue Tower, 200
Park Lane Hotel, 129, 130, 199
Park-Lexington Bldg., 92, 186, 197
Park Sheraton Hotel, 123, 124
Park South Tower, 213
Paterno, Michael E., 99, 101, 105
Pei, I. M. & Partners, 199
Pelham, Geo. F., 80, 97, 101, 108, 140
Pelham, Geo. Fred, Jr., 150, 207, 208
Pelton, Henry C., 91, 99
Penn Central, 126, 127, 131, 149, 218, 219, 220, 228
Penna. RR, 214, 216, 219, 220, 228
Pennsylvania Station, 52–54, 55, 214–216, 220, 221
penthouses, 84, 88, 112, 113
Pepsi-Cola Building, 195, 197, 211
Pershing Square Building, 42, 185
Pershing Square Viaduct, 217
Philip Morris Building, 44, 202
Pickering & Walker, 81, 83
Pinchot, Amos R. E., 66, 70, 74, 112
Plaza Hotel, 45, 82, 149
Polshek, James Stewart, 211
Porter, Seton, 103, 104
Post, Marjorie Merriwether, 100, 204
Postum Building, 100, 187, 256
Pound, Ezra, 173
Pratt, Harold I., house, 74, 76
Presbyterian Hospital, 29, 30, 107, 108
Price, Judith, 88
Price, Peter O., 88, 261
Princeton Club, 157, 201
prostitution, 97
Provident Loan Society, 182, 183, 184
Publishers Row, 175, 176
Putnam House, 39
Pyne, Percy R., II, house, 72, 215

Racquet & Tennis Club, 4, 103, 156, 157, 159, 160, 267
Real Estate Record, 64, 79, 81, 86, 88, 96, 97, 116
Redmond, Geraldyn, 71, 164
Reed & Stem, 54, 55, 58
Regency Hotel, 81, 123, 143, 144
Regine's, 139
Renwick, James, Jr., 20, 37, 69, 215
Revson, Charles, 113
Rich, Marc, 113
Riis, Jacob, 239
Rinehart, Mary Roberts, 178, 179
Ritz Tower Hotel, 123, 133–137, 172, 200, 209
Robb, James H., house, 63, 64, 208
Rockefeller, John D., 73, 84
Rockefeller, John D., Jr., 91, 109, 111
Roehm, Carolyne, 111

Rogers, James Gamble, 67, 156
Roosevelt Hotel, 125, 218
Root, Elihu, 64, 65, 82
Rose Hill, 16, 32, 182; Farm, 20
Ross, Harold, 221
Ross, Steven, 111
Roth, Emory, 83, 86, 87, 94, 107, 108, 133, 137, 150, 207, 267; & Sons, 190, 192, 195–197, 199, 201, 208, 222
Roundabout Theater, 185
Rouse & Goldstone, 83, 84, 87, 88, 94, 101, 124
Rubinstein, Helena, 113
Rudin family, 130, 199
Ruggles, Samuel B., 18–20
Russell Hotel (*see* Park Sheraton)
Russian Orthodox Church, 76

Sackler, Dr. Arthur M., 104
St. Bartholomew's, 67, 69, 70, 71, 200, 215, 217, 235, 237, 260
St. Ignatius Loyola, 29, 67, 215, 217
St. Sergius School, 76
Samuels, Leslie, 104
Schaeffer, F. & M. brewery, 22
schist, Manhattan, 4, 18
Schmidt, Mott B., 92, 94, 100
Schmidt, Peter B., 105
Schultze & Weaver, 130, 145, 152
Schwartz & Gross, 83, 84, 86, 87, 88, 94, 97, 101, 105, 106, 108, 189, 208
Seagram Bldg., 83, 192, 193, 197, 211, 217
7th Rgmt. Armory, 2, 30, 31, 83, 217, 235
71st Regiment Armory, 2, 32, 33, 215
Shepheard's, 138
Sheraton East (*see* Ambassador)
Sherry, Louis, 91, 192, 202
Shreve, Lamb & Harmon, 197
silk district, 175, 184
Simon, Neil, 137, 172
Skidmore, Owings & Merrill, 190, 195, 196, 200
Sky Club, 169
Sloan, John, 94, 185
Sloan & Robertson, 112
Sloane, W. & J., 43, 73
Sloane, William D., 69, 72; Mrs., 73
Social Register, 3, 15, 16, 88, 131, 160, 162, 171, 175
Spielvogel, Carl, 107
Squadron A Armory, 2, 34–36, 152
stables, 87, 117
Starrett Brothers, 92, 94, 101, 107
Stein, Andrew, 217
Steinberg, Saul P., 111, 143
Steinway Pianos, 21, 22, 83, 192
Stern, Leonard N., 77
Stern, Robert A. M., 71, 77
Stettinius, Edward R., 67
Stewart, A. T., 39, 202
Stewart House, 203
Stokes, I. N. Phelps, 71

Stone, Edward Durrell, 200
Straight, Mrs. Willard, 101
Straus, Jesse, 107
subways, 42, 52, 59, 64, 116, 240
Sulgrave Hotel, 123, 140, 143, 209
Sweden, Kingdom of, 76
Swissôtel Drake (see Drake)

Taft, Robert A., Houses, 245, 286
Tammany Hall, 185
Tauranac, John, 55
tennis courts, 61, 152
Third Church of Christ, Scientist, 92
Thompson Starrett, 125, 145
Thorne, Oakleigh, 67
Tiffany, Lewis C., 30; Studios, 130
Tisch, Jonathan, 143; Laurence, Preston
    Robert, 132, 143, 185
Tishman Brothers, 189, 201
traffic, 115–122; lights, 115, 119, 122
Tremaine, Burton, 82
Trowbridge & Livingston, 66
Trumbauer, Horace, 67
Trump, Donald, 126, 127, 149
Tucker, Carll, 70, 84
Twain, Mark, 41

Union Carbide Bldg., 196, 197
Union Club, 4, 71, 103, 154–156, 162, 164,
    165, 166, 167
Union League Club, 156, 162–164
Union Square, 1, 16, 18, 37, 203
Union Theol. Seminary, 30, 65, 66
Universal Pictures, 205; Bldg., 189
Uris Brothers, 197, 198
Uris, Harris H., 96

Valentino, 136, 204
Vanderbilt, Alfred Gwynne, 44, 45; Mrs. 45,
    67
Vanderbilt Avenue, 5, 23, 55, 57, 58, 116,
    117, 118, 156, 196, 224
Vanderbilt, Cornelius, 5, 6, 7–15, 22, 23,
    225, 267; II, 14, 69; Jr. (IV), 2, 3, 125,
    133, 175
Vanderbilt, Frederick William, 14

Vanderbilt, Geo. Washington, 14, 66
Vanderbilt, Harold Stirling, 130, 131
Vanderbilt Hotel, 5, 44, 45, 215
Vanderbilt, William Henry, 11, 14, 15, 23,
    46, 83; III, 15
Vanderbilt, William Kissam, 14, 41, 55
Vanderbilt, William K., Jr., 94
Viele, Egbert L., 29
Villars, Countess de Langier, 71

Wagner, Robert F., Jr., 244, 261
Waid, D. Everett, 83, 185
Waldorf-Astoria, 129, 143–149, 168, 169,
    198, 284
Waldorf Towers, 104, 123, 147, 149, 170
Walker & Gillette, 73, 97
Walker, James J., 129, 133, 240
Wallahora, Paul, 101
Walters, Barbara, 84
Wanamaker's, 202
Warren & Wetmore, 45, 55, 83, 89, 90, 116,
    129, 184, 187
Warren, Whitney, 55, 56
Weaver, S. Fullerton, 84, 130
Webb & Knapp, 129, 214, 222
Webb, Dr. W. Seward, 83
Westvaco Building, 199
Wharton, Edith, 127, 172, 214
White, Stanford, 30, 54, 64, 69, 160
Whitney, Harry Payne, 101; Mrs., 43
Whitney Mus., 227; Gallery, 202, 235
Wiborg, Frank, 72
widening, 119, 120
Wilgus, William L., 48, 52–55, 57, 267
Wolfe, Tom, 87, 172, 251, 259
Wolfson, Erwin S., 222, 226
Wright, Frank Lloyd, 192, 193, 224

Yale Club, 17, 103, 154, 156, 157, 158
York & Sawyer, 97, 101, 185, 207

Zeckendorf Hotels, 126, 129
Zeckendorf Towers, 203
Zeckendorf, William, 139, 203, 217, 222
Zimbalist, Alma Gluck, 105
zoning laws, 89, 90, 137, 197, 211

9-26-90